Angel Sanctuary

story and art by **Kaori Yuki**
vol.9

Angel Sanctuary

Vol. 9
Shôjo Edition

STORY AND ART BY KAORI YUKI

Translation/Alexis Kirsch
English Adaptation/Matt Segale
Touch-up & Lettering/James Hudnall
Cover, Graphics & Design/Izumi Evers
Editor/Pancha Diaz

Managing Editor/Annette Roman
Director of Production/Noboru Watanabe
Vice President of Publishing/Alvin Lu
Sr. Director of Acquisitions/Rika Inouye
VP of Sales & Marketing/Liza Coppola
Publisher/Hyoe Narita

Published by VIZ, LLC
P.O. Box 77010
San Francisco, CA 94107

Shôjo Edition
10 9 8 7 6 5 4 3 2 1
First printing, July 2005

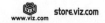

www.viz.com   store.viz.com

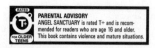

Angel Sanctuary

story and art by **Kaori Yuki**   vol.9

The Story Thus Far

High school boy Setsuna Mudo's life is hellish. He's always been a troublemaker, but his worst sin was falling incestuously in love with his beautiful sister Sara. But his troubles are preordained—Setsuna is the reincarnation of the Lady Alexiel, an angel who rebelled against Heaven and led the demons of Hell in a revolt. Her punishment was to be reborn into tragic life after tragic life. This time, her life is as Setsuna.

Setsuna's body, left behind on Earth while he searched Hell for his beloved Sara's soul, has died. When he returned from Hell along the Meidou path of reincarnation, he reemerged on Earth in the body of the Angel Alexiel. Now Setusna is determined to brave the gates of Heaven in order to retrieve his sister.

Meanwhile, Setsuna's friends have troubles of their own. Kurai has agreed to become the Demon Lord Lucifer's bride in return for the infernal resurrection elixir—the "anti-soul" that actually turns people into mindless zombies! Boyz has been mortally wonded in the fight with the Archangel Michael, and Arachne has revealed his traitorous allegiance to Hell.

In Heaven, Metatron has released the Archangel Jibril from Sevothtarte's spell, and Sara's captive soul has taken up residence in the angelic body! With Sevy hot on her heels, the newly blind Sara is desperate for safety, and instead bumps into the lecherous angel physician Raphael.

Contents

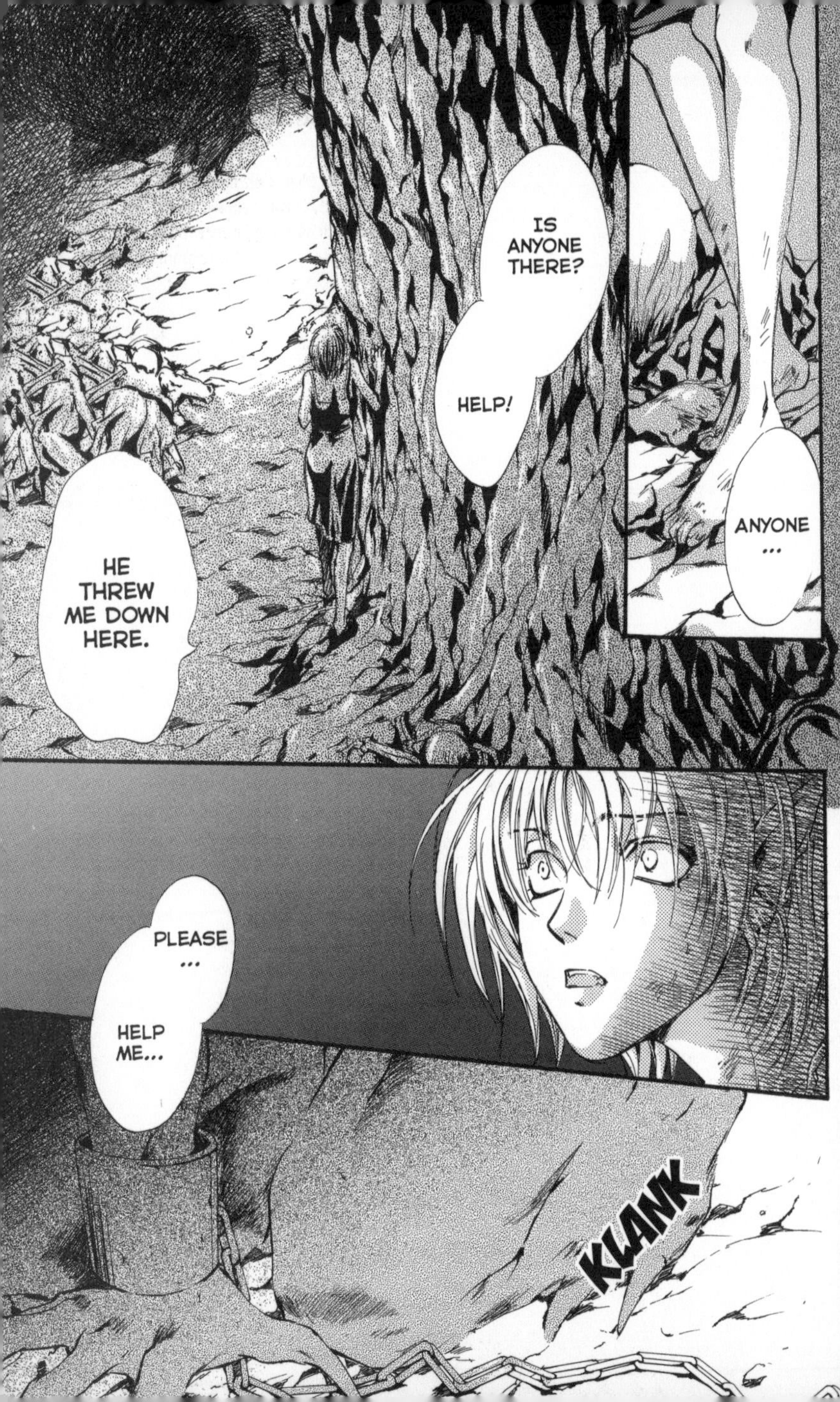
ANYONE ...
IS ANYONE THERE?
HELP!
HE THREW ME DOWN HERE.
PLEASE ...
HELP ME...
KLANK

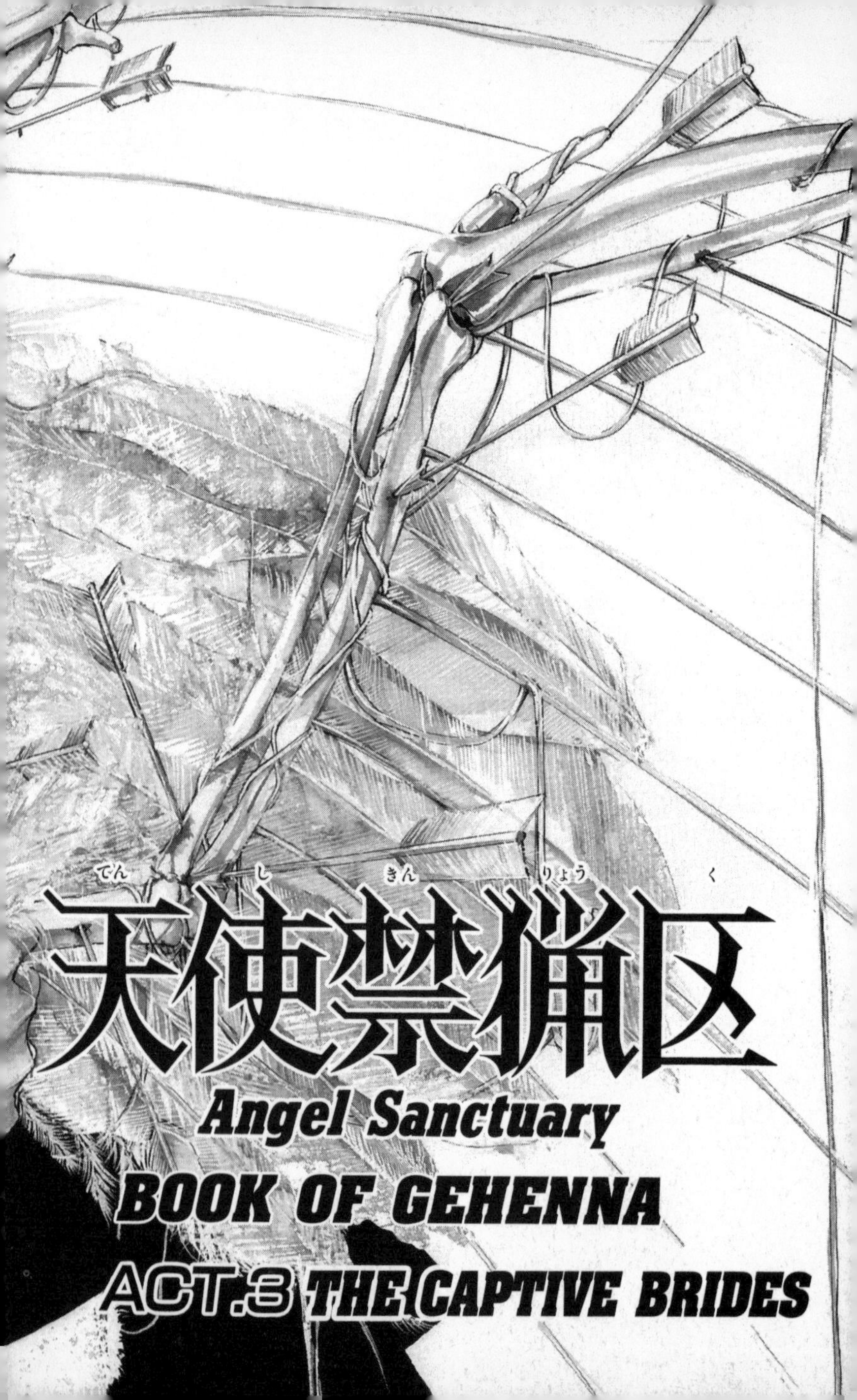
天使禁猟区
Angel Sanctuary
BOOK OF GEHENNA
ACT.3 THE CAPTIVE BRIDES

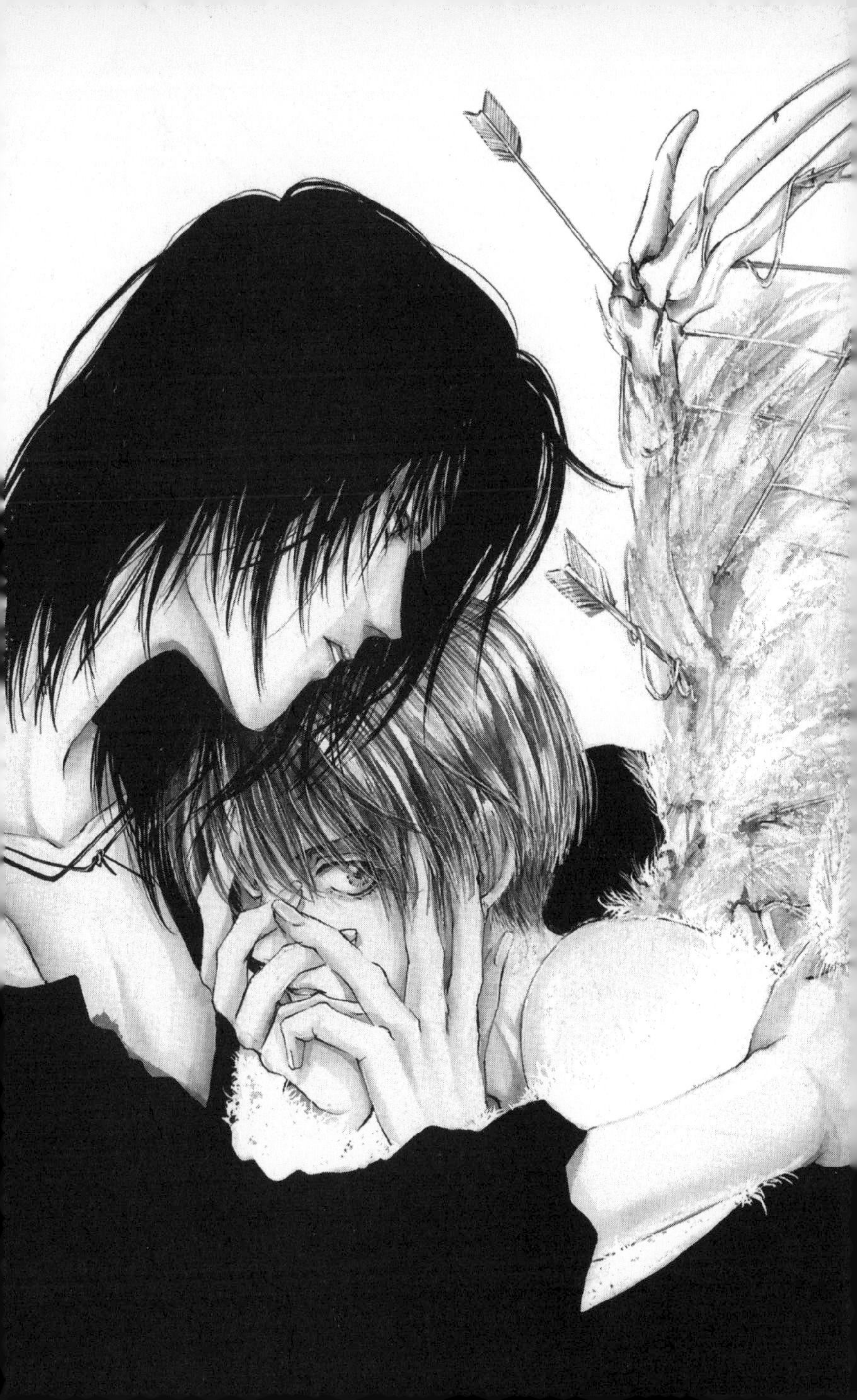

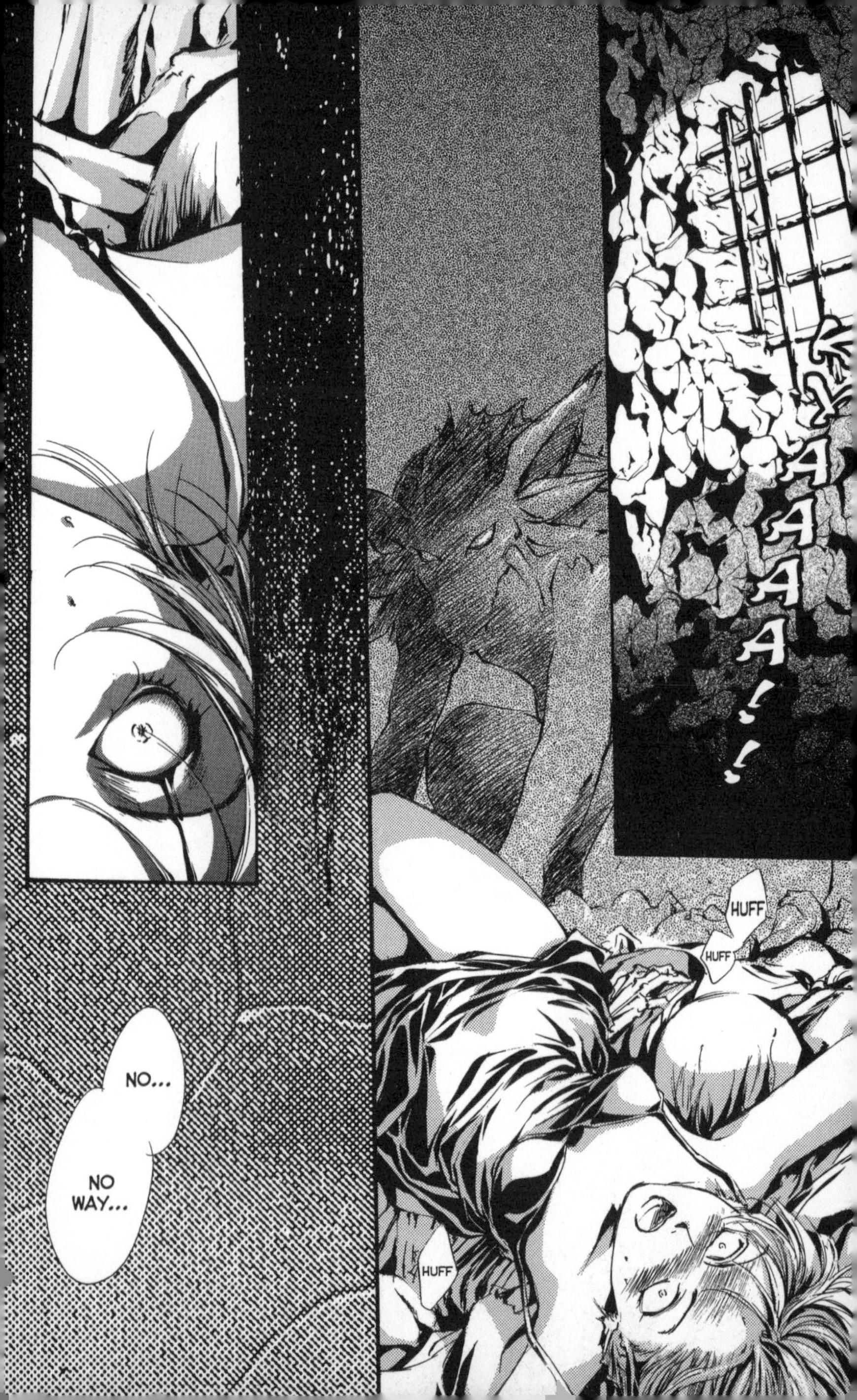
AAAA!!
HUFF
HUFF
HUFF
NO...
NO WAY...

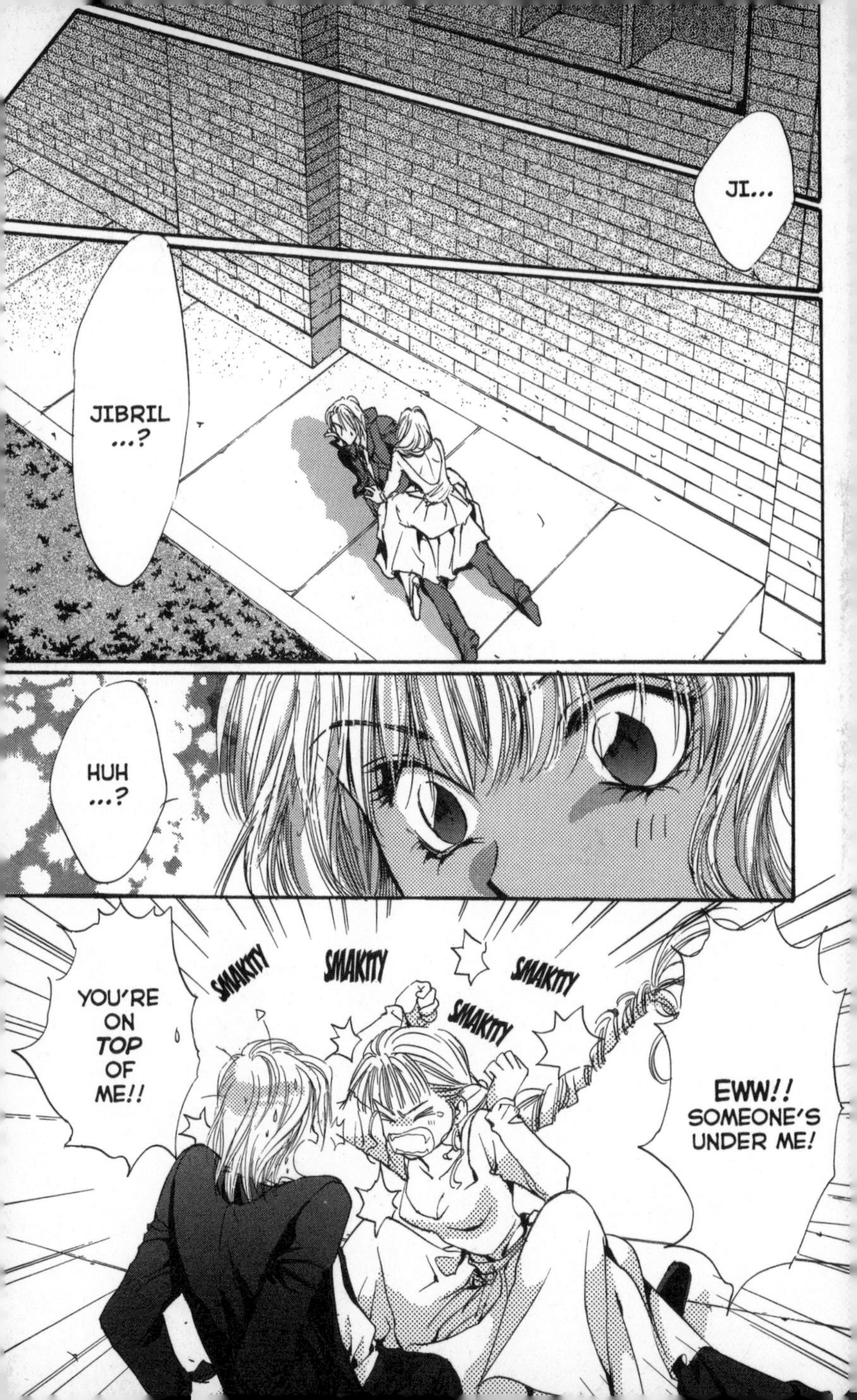
JI...
JIBRIL ...?
HUH ...?
EWW!! SOMEONE'S UNDER ME!
SMAKITTY
SMAKITTY
SMAKITTY
SMAKITTY
YOU'RE ON *TOP* OF ME!!

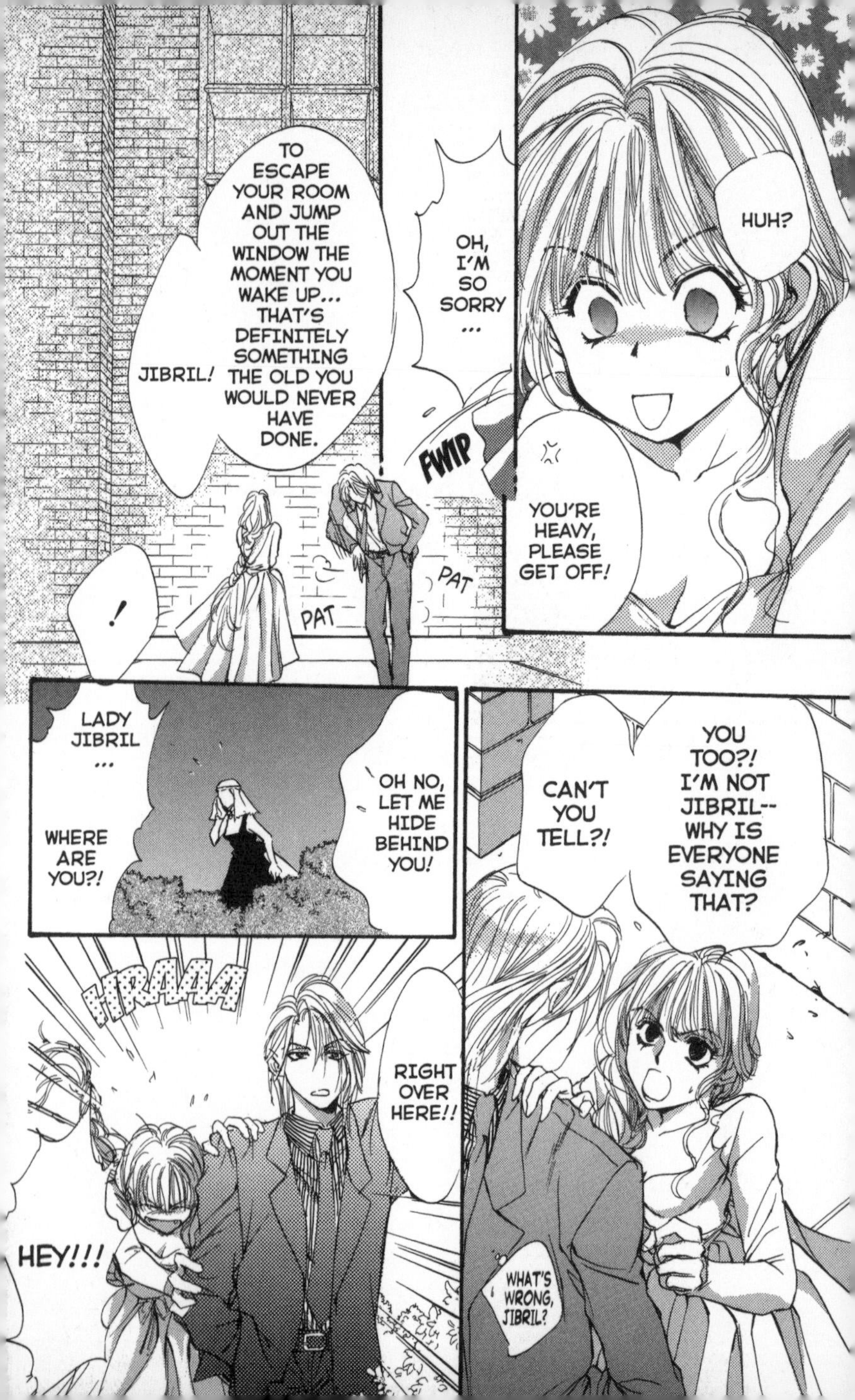
HUH?
YOU'RE HEAVY, PLEASE GET OFF!
OH, I'M SO SORRY...
FWIP
TO ESCAPE YOUR ROOM AND JUMP OUT THE WINDOW THE MOMENT YOU WAKE UP... THAT'S DEFINITELY SOMETHING THE OLD YOU WOULD NEVER HAVE DONE.
JIBRIL!
PAT
PAT
!
YOU TOO?! I'M NOT JIBRIL-- WHY IS EVERYONE SAYING THAT?
CAN'T YOU TELL?!
WHAT'S WRONG, JIBRIL?
OH NO, LET ME HIDE BEHIND YOU!
LADY JIBRIL...
WHERE ARE YOU?!
RIGHT OVER HERE!!
HIRAAA
HEY!!!

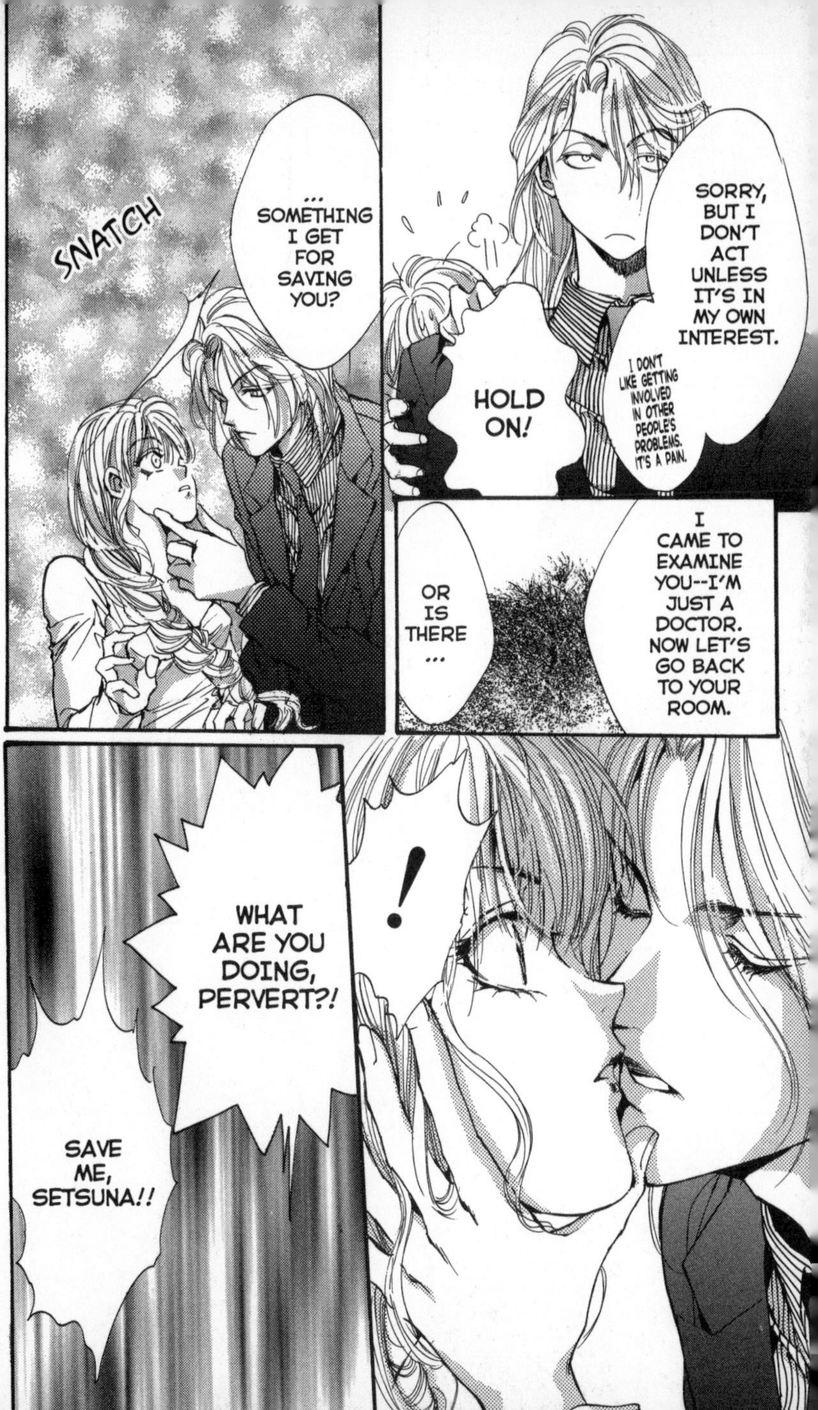
SORRY, BUT I DON'T ACT UNLESS IT'S IN MY OWN INTEREST.
I DON'T LIKE GETTING INVOLVED IN OTHER PEOPLE'S PROBLEMS. IT'S A PAIN.
HOLD ON!
I CAME TO EXAMINE YOU--I'M JUST A DOCTOR. NOW LET'S GO BACK TO YOUR ROOM.
OR IS THERE ...
... SOMETHING I GET FOR SAVING YOU?
SNATCH
!
WHAT ARE YOU DOING, PERVERT?!
SAVE ME, SETSUNA!!

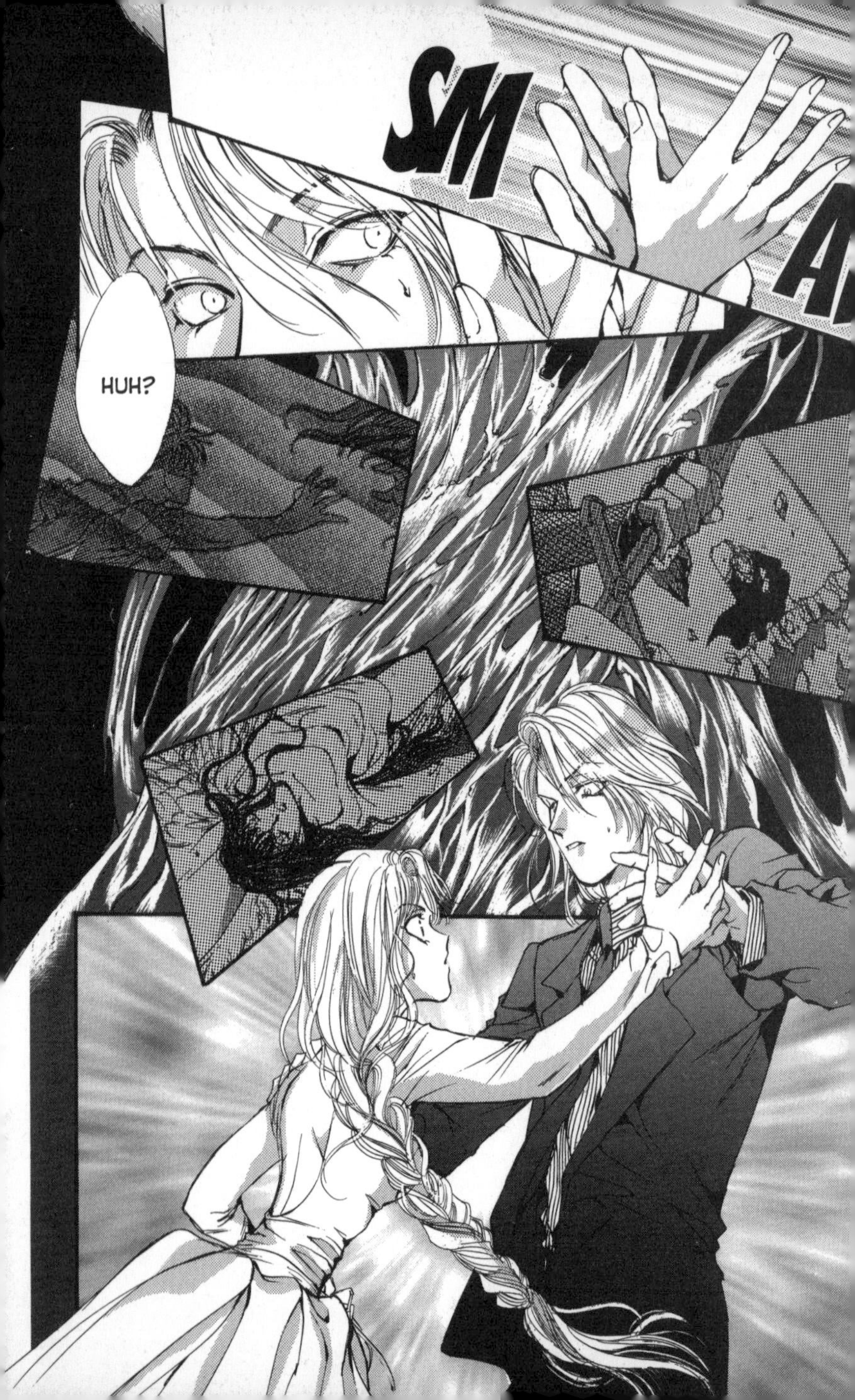
SM
A
HUH?

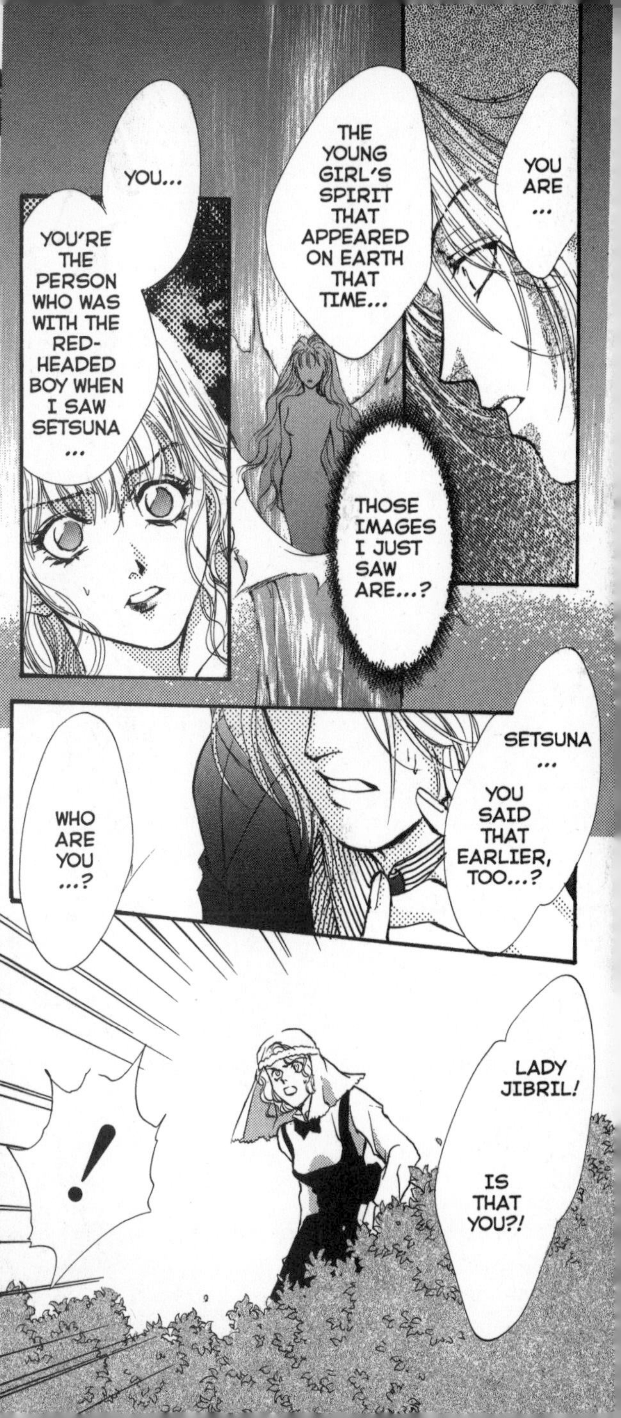
YOU ARE ...
THE YOUNG GIRL'S SPIRIT THAT APPEARED ON EARTH THAT TIME...
THOSE IMAGES I JUST SAW ARE...?
YOU...
YOU'RE THE PERSON WHO WAS WITH THE RED-HEADED BOY WHEN I SAW SETSUNA ...
SETSUNA ...
YOU SAID THAT EARLIER, TOO...?
WHO ARE YOU ...?
LADY JIBRIL!
IS THAT YOU?!
!

Book Nine came out pretty quickly, didn't it? Only one more step till double figures. For me, this has been a pretty busy year since I came out with an illustration book. The "Angel Cage" title logo was done mostly by me, and it was a lot of work, but I was really happy with how well it came out. I think it's pretty good, so please check it out. Though in the early article about Mammon, I put "appetite" when I meant "greed." Sorry about the stupid mistake!

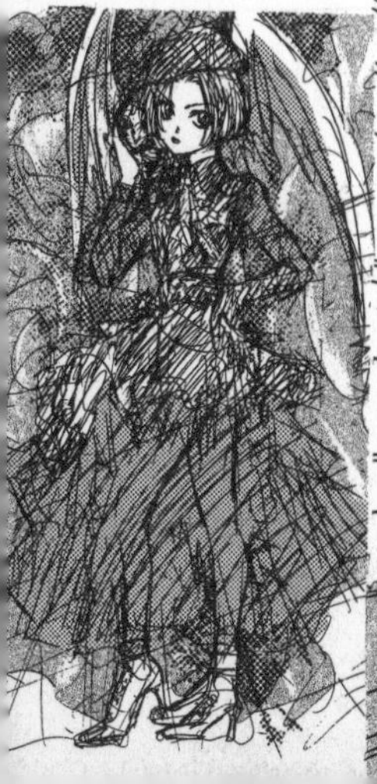

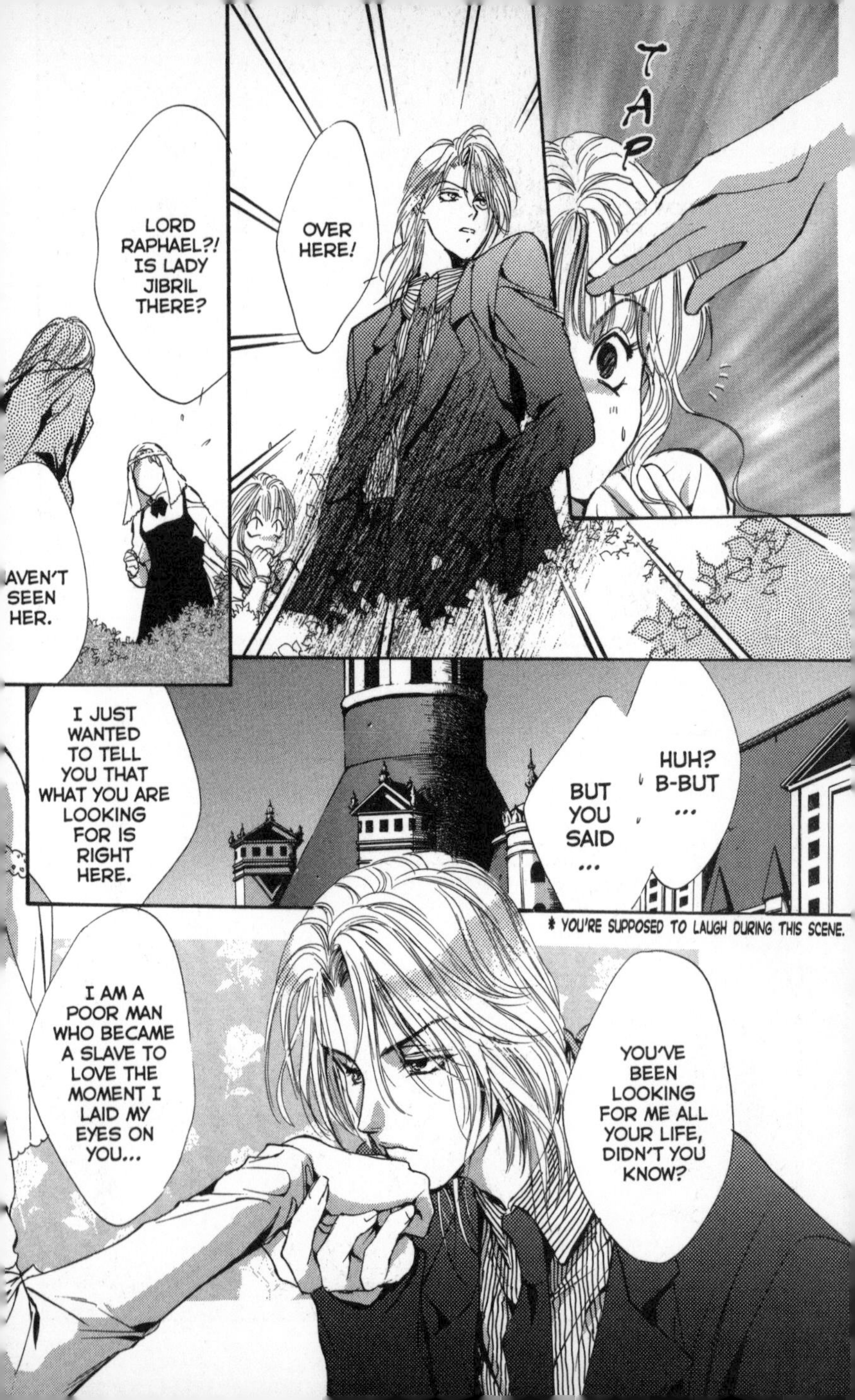
TAP
OVER HERE!
LORD RAPHAEL?! IS LADY JIBRIL THERE?
AVEN'T SEEN HER.
HUH? B-BUT ...
BUT YOU SAID ...
I JUST WANTED TO TELL YOU THAT WHAT YOU ARE LOOKING FOR IS RIGHT HERE.
* YOU'RE SUPPOSED TO LAUGH DURING THIS SCENE.
YOU'VE BEEN LOOKING FOR ME ALL YOUR LIFE, DIDN'T YOU KNOW?
I AM A POOR MAN WHO BECAME A SLAVE TO LOVE THE MOMENT I LAID MY EYES ON YOU...

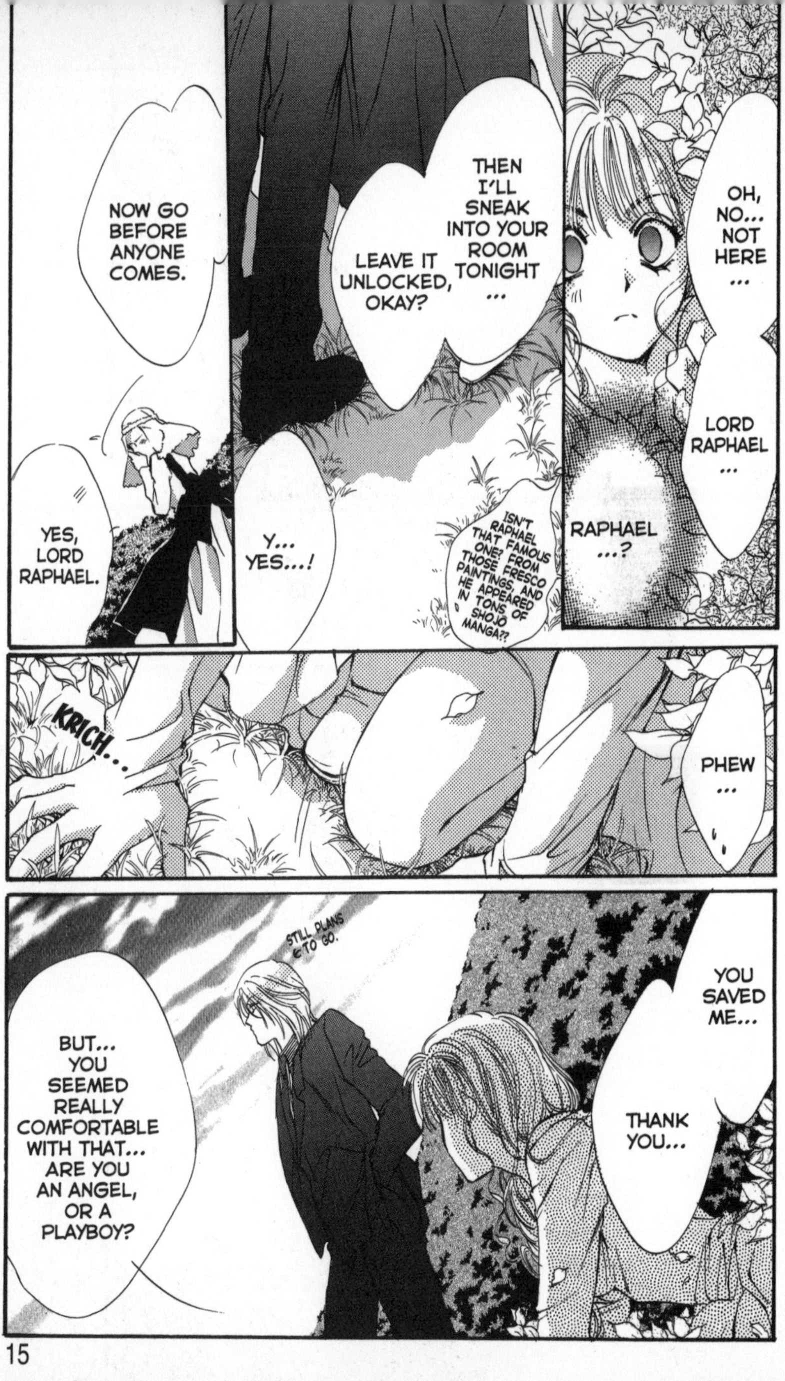
OH, NO... NOT HERE...
LORD RAPHAEL...
RAPHAEL...?
ISN'T RAPHAEL THAT FAMOUS ONE? FROM THOSE FRESCO PAINTINGS, AND HE APPEARED IN TONS OF SHOJO MANGA??
THEN I'LL SNEAK INTO YOUR ROOM TONIGHT...
LEAVE IT UNLOCKED, OKAY?
Y... YES...!
NOW GO BEFORE ANYONE COMES.
YES, LORD RAPHAEL.
PHEW...
KRICH...
YOU SAVED ME...
THANK YOU...
STILL PLANS TO GO.
BUT... YOU SEEMED REALLY COMFORTABLE WITH THAT... ARE YOU AN ANGEL, OR A PLAYBOY?

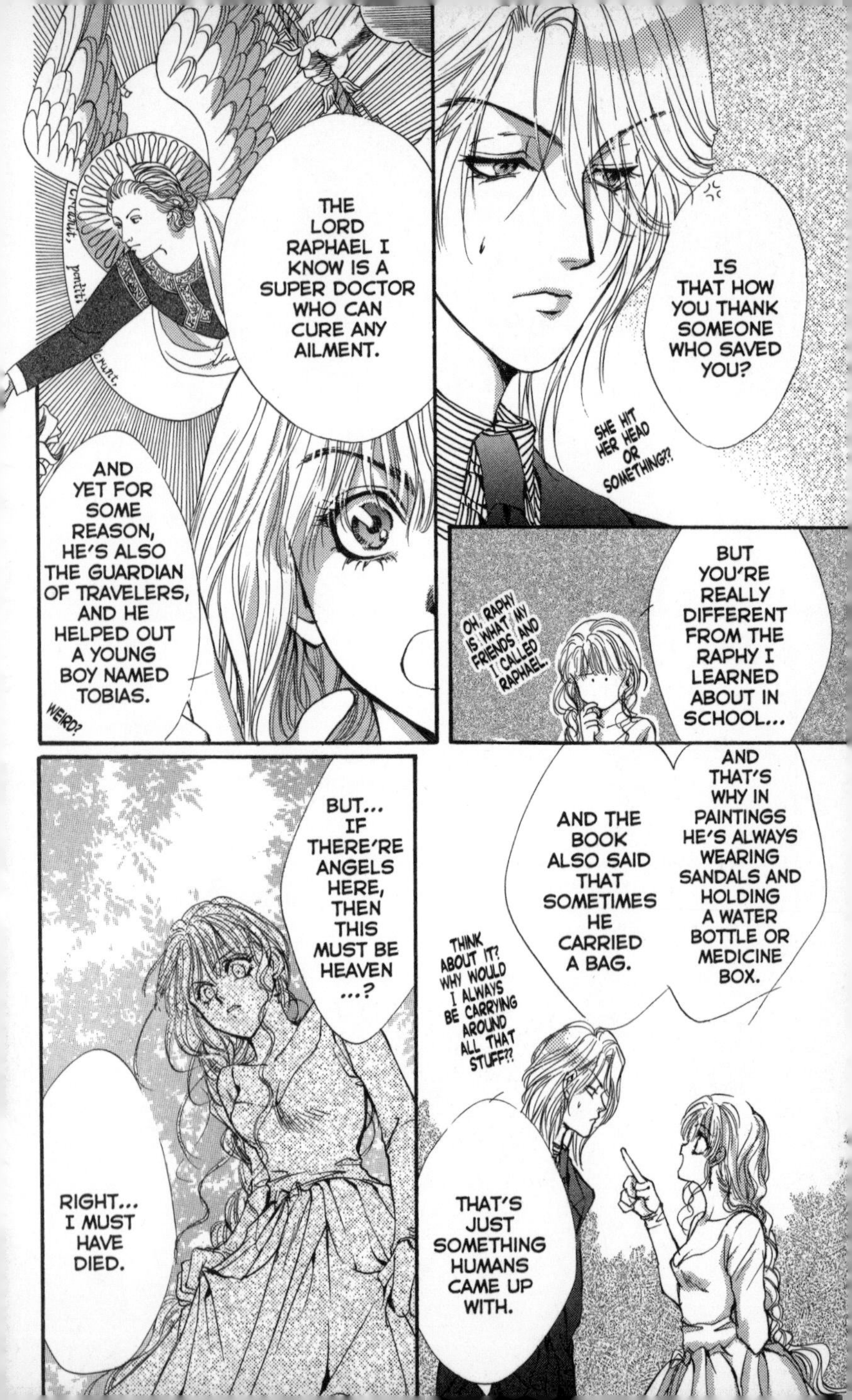
IS THAT HOW YOU THANK SOMEONE WHO SAVED YOU?
SHE HIT HER HEAD OR SOMETHING??
BUT YOU'RE REALLY DIFFERENT FROM THE RAPHY I LEARNED ABOUT IN SCHOOL...
OH, RAPHY IS WHAT MY FRIENDS AND I CALLED RAPHAEL.
THE LORD RAPHAEL I KNOW IS A SUPER DOCTOR WHO CAN CURE ANY AILMENT.
AND YET FOR SOME REASON, HE'S ALSO THE GUARDIAN OF TRAVELERS, AND HE HELPED OUT A YOUNG BOY NAMED TOBIAS.
WEIRD?
AND THAT'S WHY IN PAINTINGS HE'S ALWAYS WEARING SANDALS AND HOLDING A WATER BOTTLE OR MEDICINE BOX.
AND THE BOOK ALSO SAID THAT SOMETIMES HE CARRIED A BAG.
THINK ABOUT IT? WHY WOULD I ALWAYS BE CARRYING AROUND ALL THAT STUFF??
THAT'S JUST SOMETHING HUMANS CAME UP WITH.
BUT... IF THERE'RE ANGELS HERE, THEN THIS MUST BE HEAVEN ...?
RIGHT... I MUST HAVE DIED.

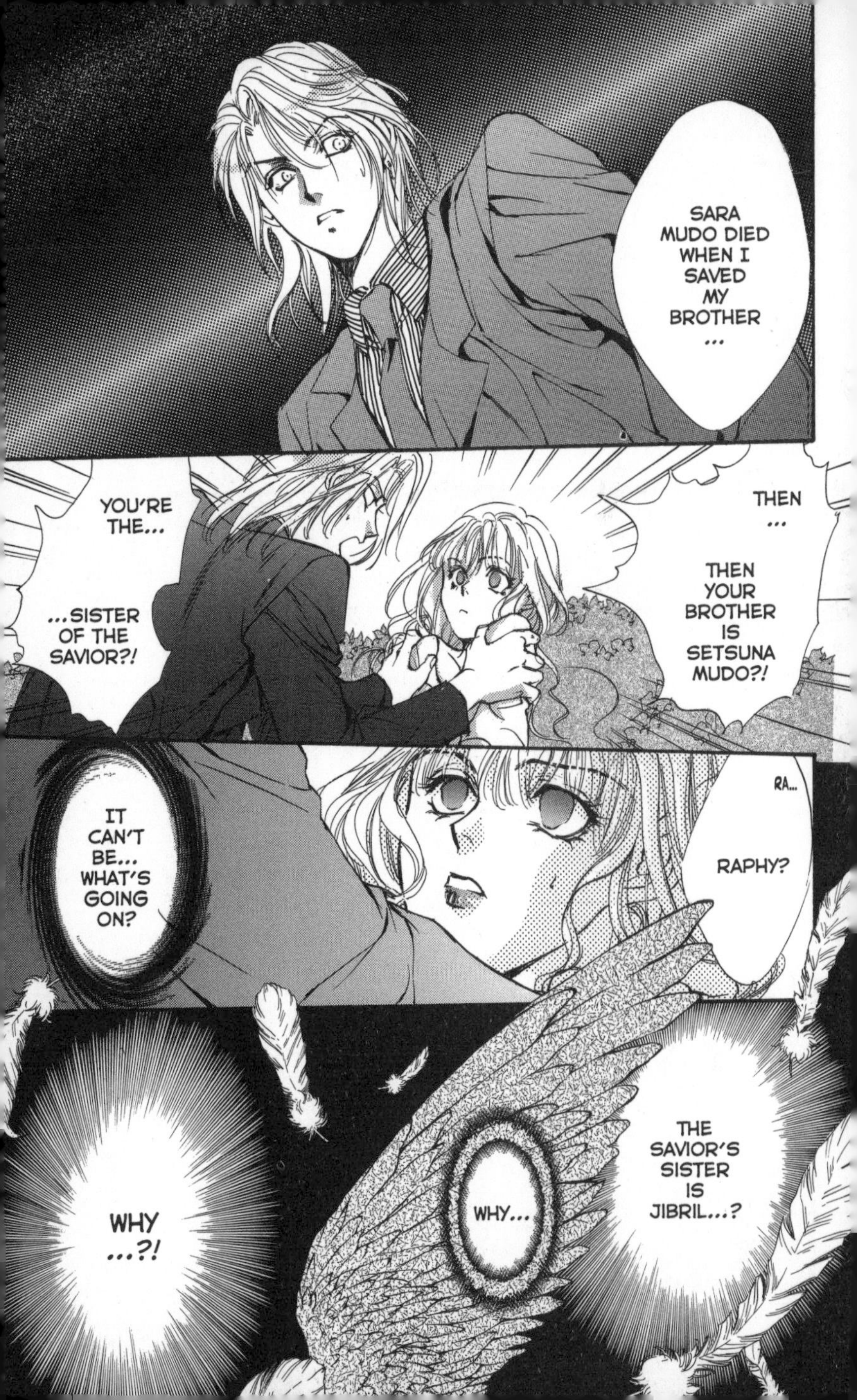
SARA MUDO DIED WHEN I SAVED MY BROTHER ...
THEN ...
THEN YOUR BROTHER IS SETSUNA MUDO?!
YOU'RE THE...
...SISTER OF THE SAVIOR?!
RA...
RAPHY?
IT CAN'T BE... WHAT'S GOING ON?
THE SAVIOR'S SISTER IS JIBRIL...?
WHY...
WHY ...?!

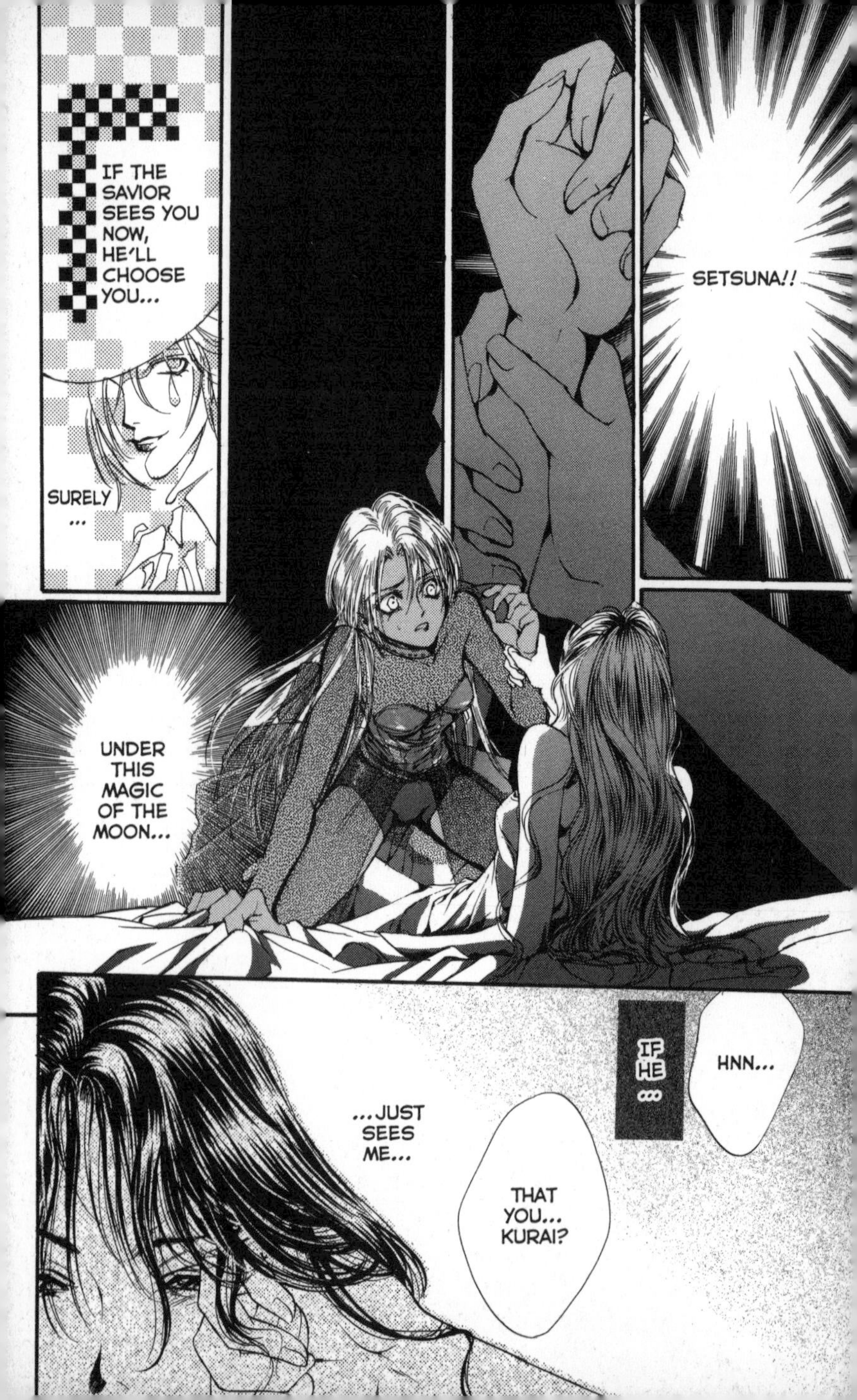
SETSUNA!!
IF THE SAVIOR SEES YOU NOW, HE'LL CHOOSE YOU...
SURELY ...
UNDER THIS MAGIC OF THE MOON...
HNN...
IF HE...
...JUST SEES ME...
THAT YOU... KURAI?

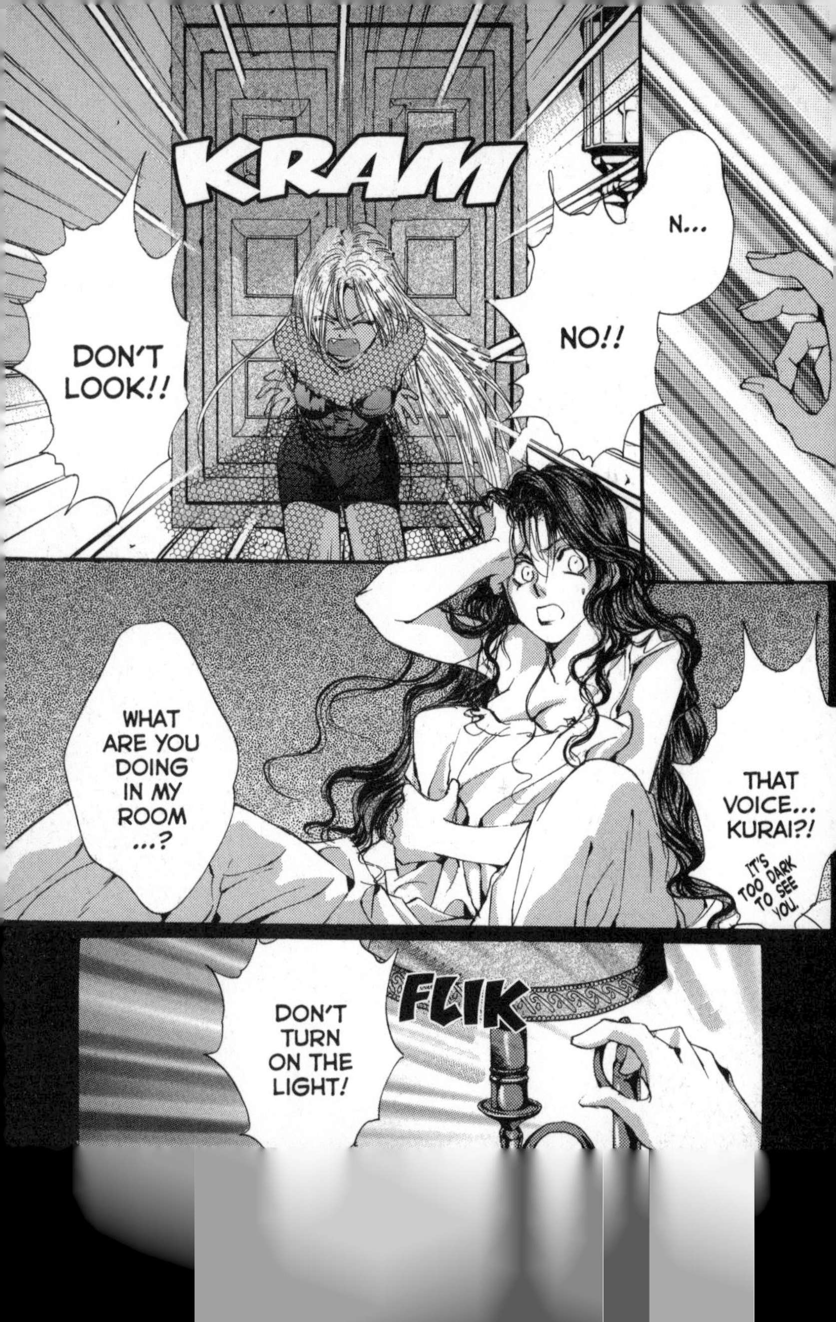
N...
KRAM
NO!!
DON'T LOOK!!
THAT VOICE... KURAI?!
IT'S TOO DARK TO SEE YOU.
WHAT ARE YOU DOING IN MY ROOM ...?
FLIK
DON'T TURN ON THE LIGHT!

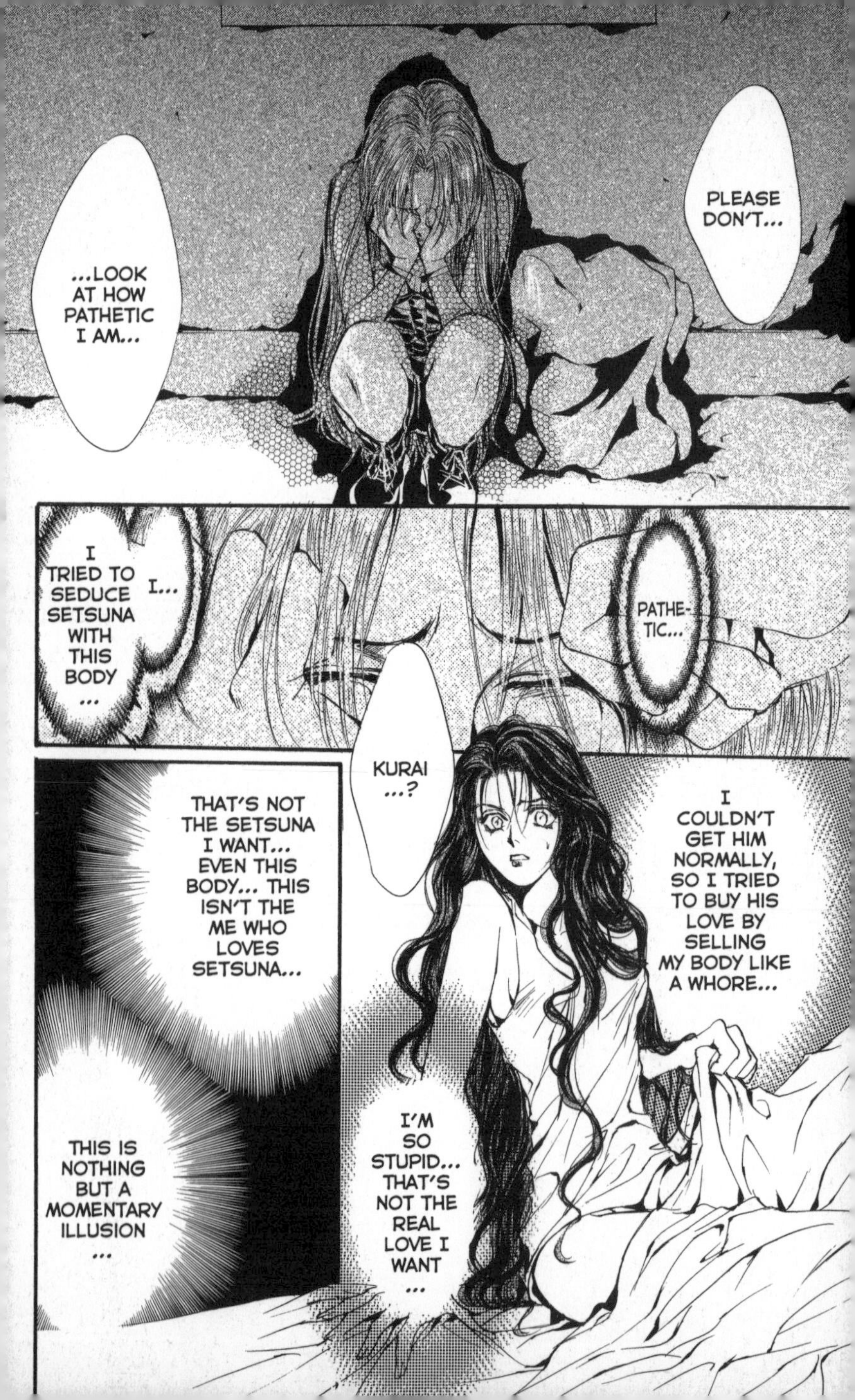
PLEASE DON'T...
...LOOK AT HOW PATHETIC I AM...
PATHE-TIC...
I...
I TRIED TO SEDUCE SETSUNA WITH THIS BODY ...
KURAI ...?
I COULDN'T GET HIM NORMALLY, SO I TRIED TO BUY HIS LOVE BY SELLING MY BODY LIKE A WHORE...
THAT'S NOT THE SETSUNA I WANT... EVEN THIS BODY... THIS ISN'T THE ME WHO LOVES SETSUNA...
I'M SO STUPID... THAT'S NOT THE REAL LOVE I WANT ...
THIS IS NOTHING BUT A MOMENTARY ILLUSION ...

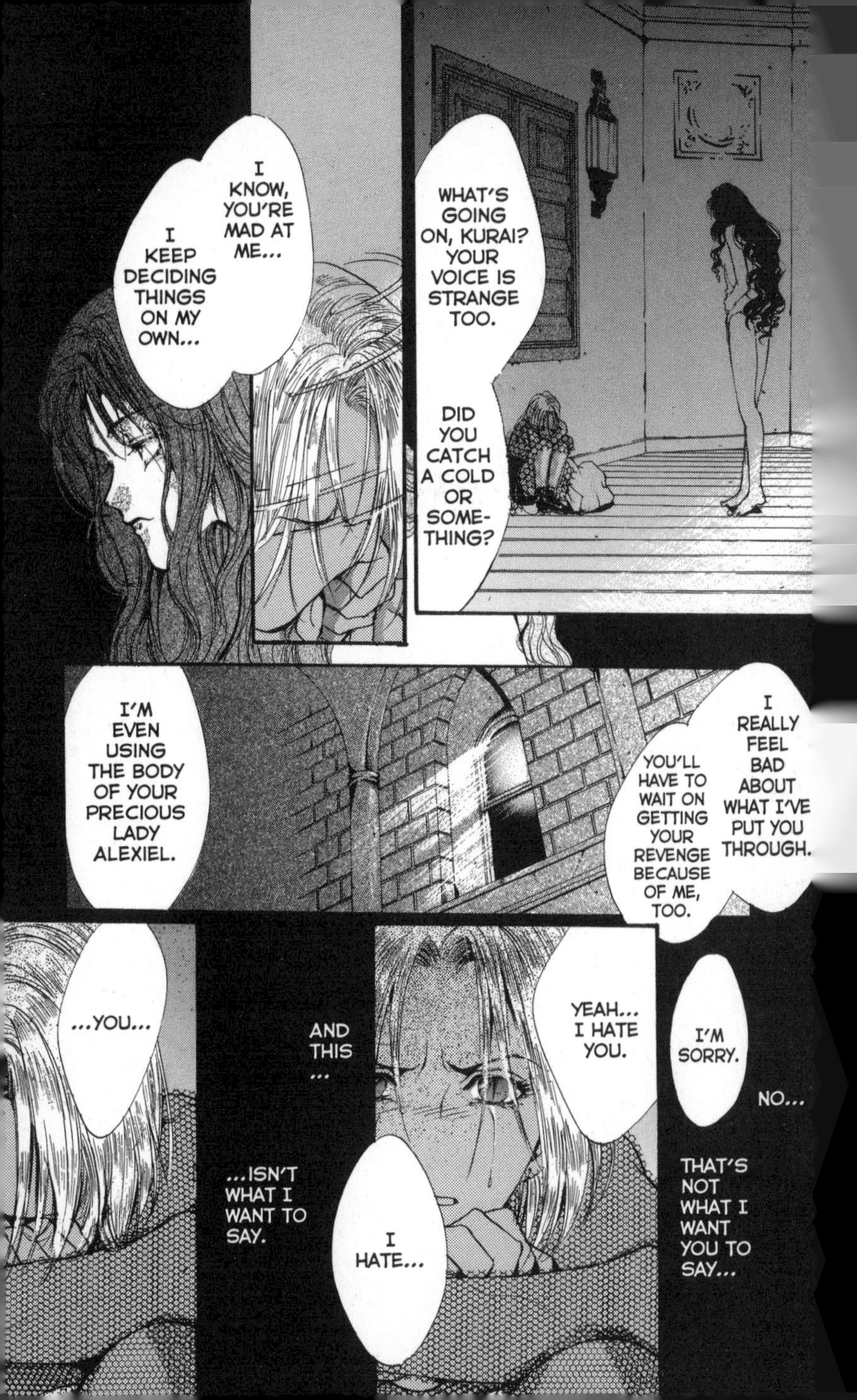
WHAT'S GOING ON, KURAI? YOUR VOICE IS STRANGE TOO.
DID YOU CATCH A COLD OR SOME-THING?
I KNOW, YOU'RE MAD AT ME...
I KEEP DECIDING THINGS ON MY OWN...
I REALLY FEEL BAD ABOUT WHAT I'VE PUT YOU THROUGH.
YOU'LL HAVE TO WAIT ON GETTING YOUR REVENGE BECAUSE OF ME, TOO.
I'M EVEN USING THE BODY OF YOUR PRECIOUS LADY ALEXIEL.
I'M SORRY.
NO...
THAT'S NOT WHAT I WANT YOU TO SAY...
YEAH... I HATE YOU.
I HATE...
...YOU...
AND THIS ...
...ISN'T WHAT I WANT TO SAY.

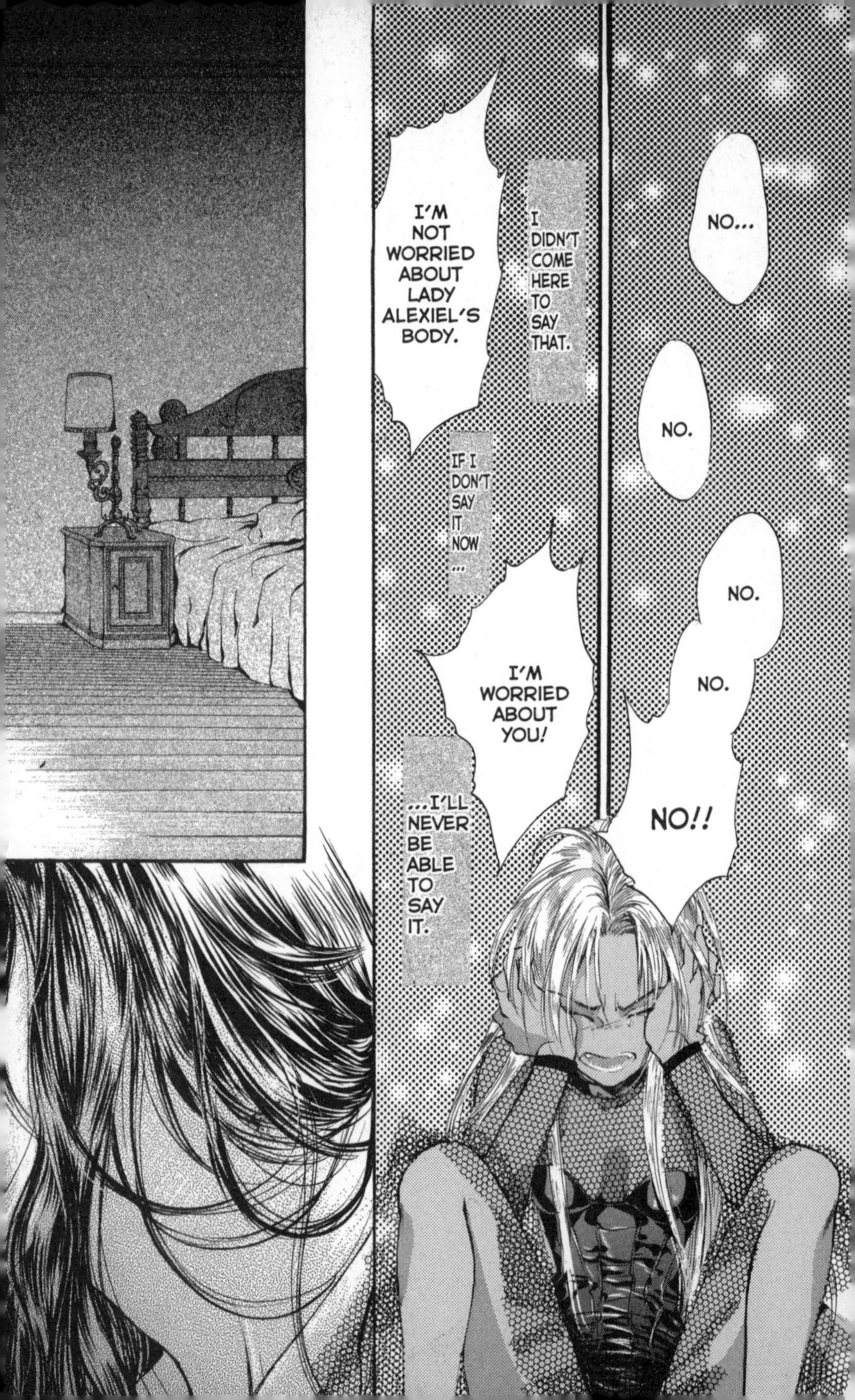

NO...
NO.
NO.
NO.
NO!!
I'M NOT WORRIED ABOUT LADY ALEXIEL'S BODY.
I DIDN'T COME HERE TO SAY THAT.
IF I DON'T SAY IT NOW...
I'M WORRIED ABOUT YOU!
...I'LL NEVER BE ABLE TO SAY IT.

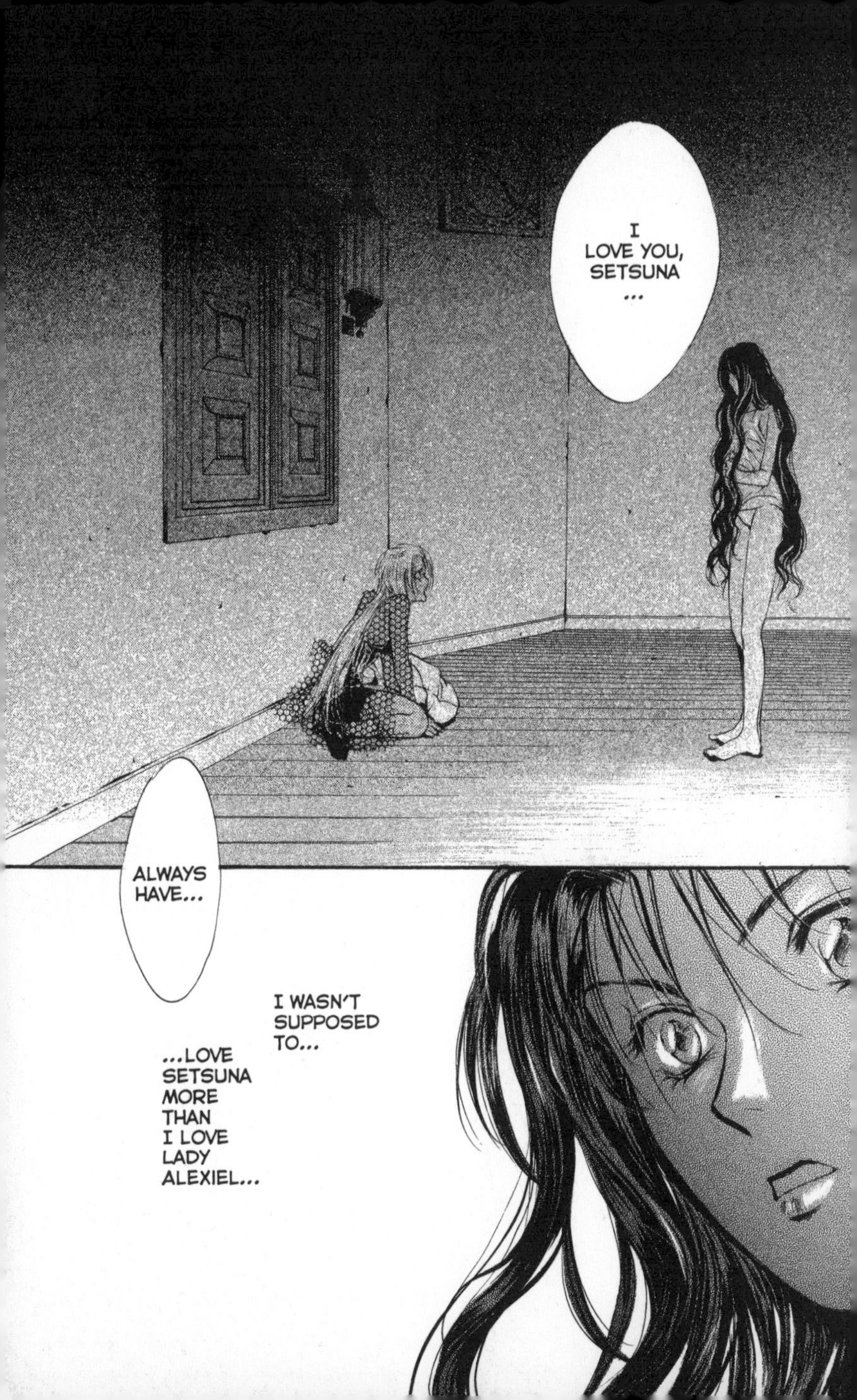
I LOVE YOU, SETSUNA ...
ALWAYS HAVE...
I WASN'T SUPPOSED TO...
...LOVE SETSUNA MORE THAN I LOVE LADY ALEXIEL...

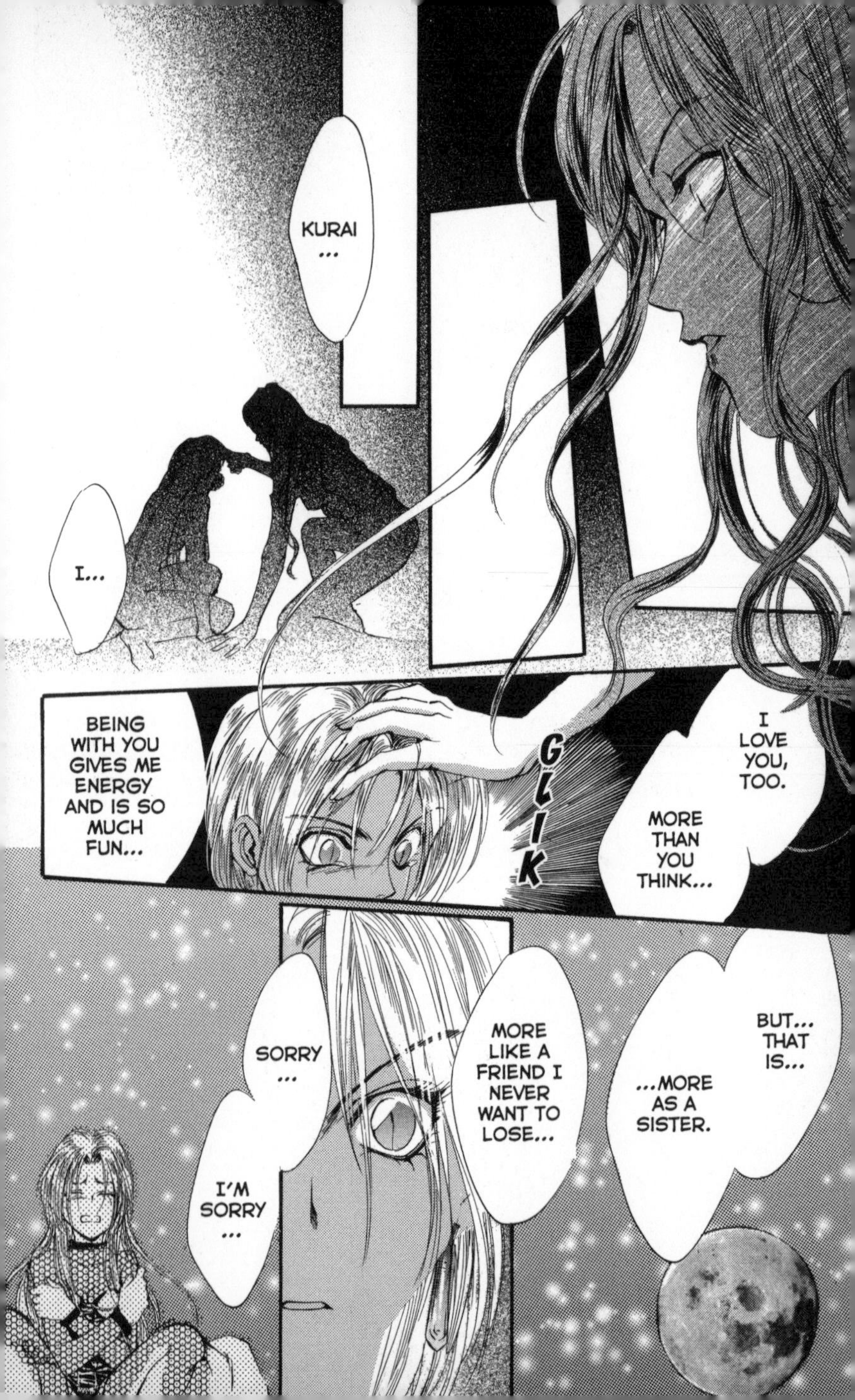
KURAI ...
I...
I LOVE YOU, TOO.
MORE THAN YOU THINK...
GLIK
BEING WITH YOU GIVES ME ENERGY AND IS SO MUCH FUN...
BUT... THAT IS...
...MORE AS A SISTER.
MORE LIKE A FRIEND I NEVER WANT TO LOSE...
SORRY ...
I'M SORRY ...

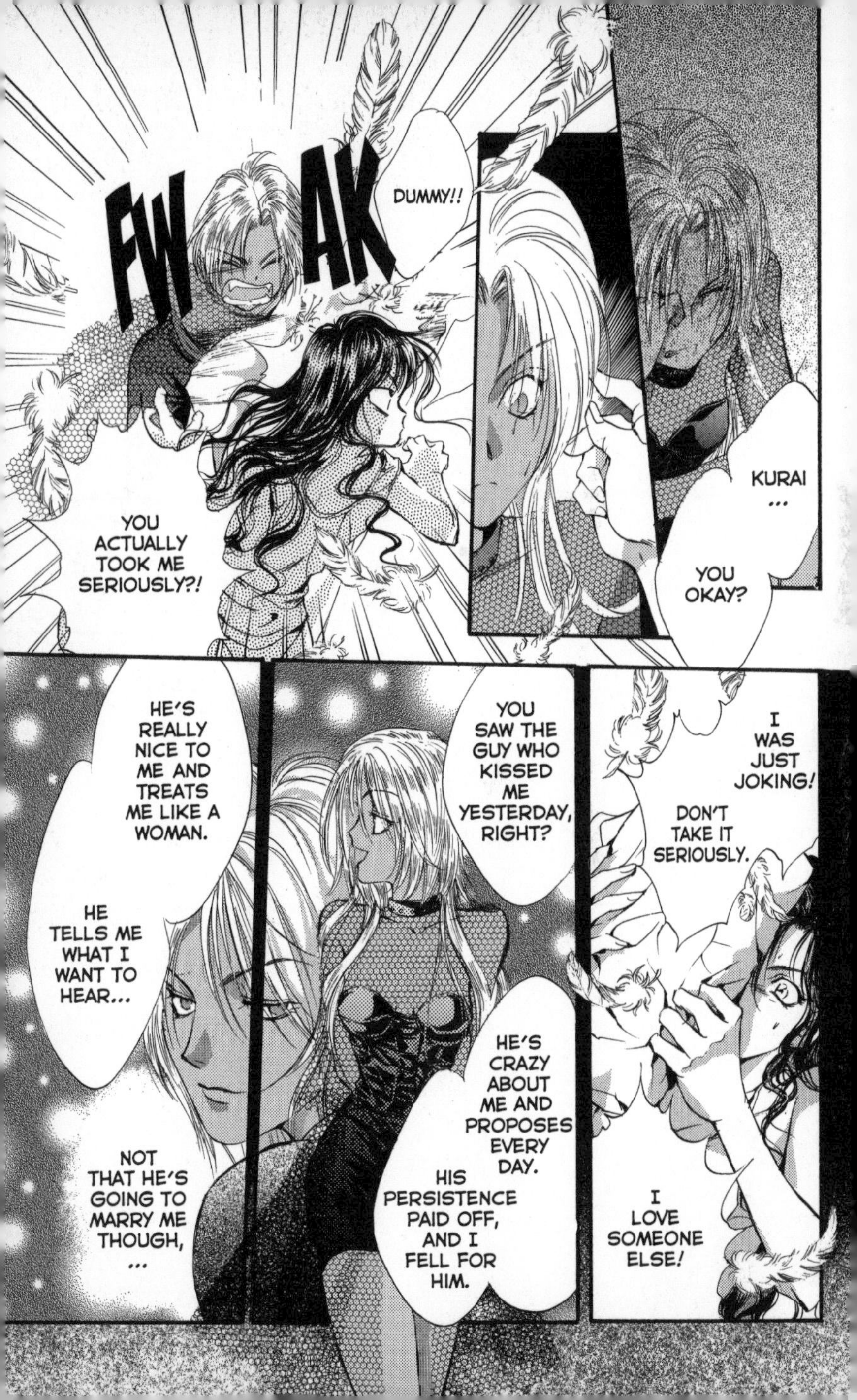
KURAI ...
YOU OKAY?
DUMMY!!
FWAK
YOU ACTUALLY TOOK ME SERIOUSLY?!
I WAS JUST JOKING!
DON'T TAKE IT SERIOUSLY.
I LOVE SOMEONE ELSE!
YOU SAW THE GUY WHO KISSED ME YESTERDAY, RIGHT?
HE'S CRAZY ABOUT ME AND PROPOSES EVERY DAY.
HIS PERSISTENCE PAID OFF, AND I FELL FOR HIM.
HE'S REALLY NICE TO ME AND TREATS ME LIKE A WOMAN.
HE TELLS ME WHAT I WANT TO HEAR...
NOT THAT HE'S GOING TO MARRY ME THOUGH, ...

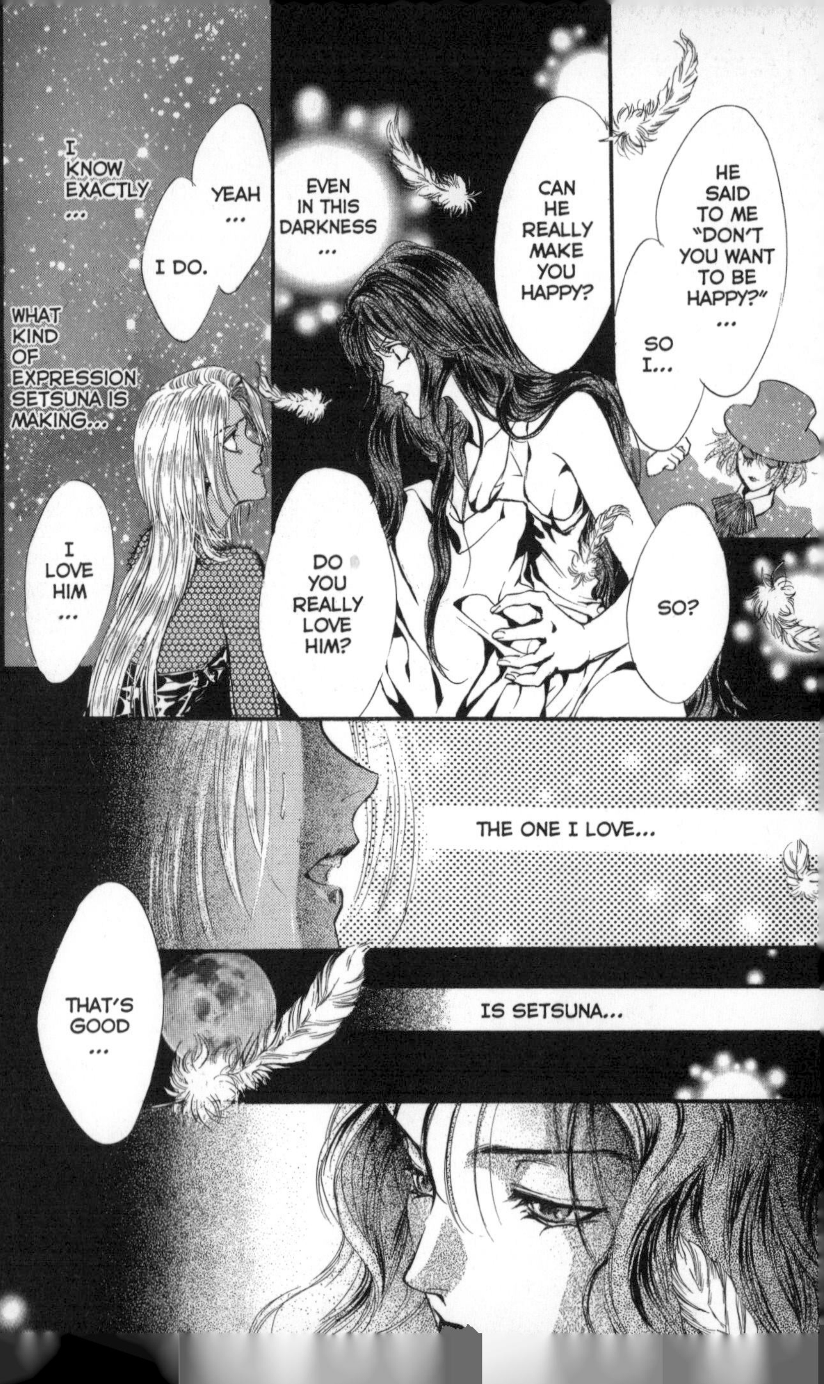
HE SAID TO ME "DON'T YOU WANT TO BE HAPPY?" ...
SO I...
CAN HE REALLY MAKE YOU HAPPY?
EVEN IN THIS DARKNESS ...
YEAH ...
I DO.
I KNOW EXACTLY ...
WHAT KIND OF EXPRESSION SETSUNA IS MAKING...
SO?
DO YOU REALLY LOVE HIM?
I LOVE HIM ...
THE ONE I LOVE...
IS SETSUNA...
THAT'S GOOD ...

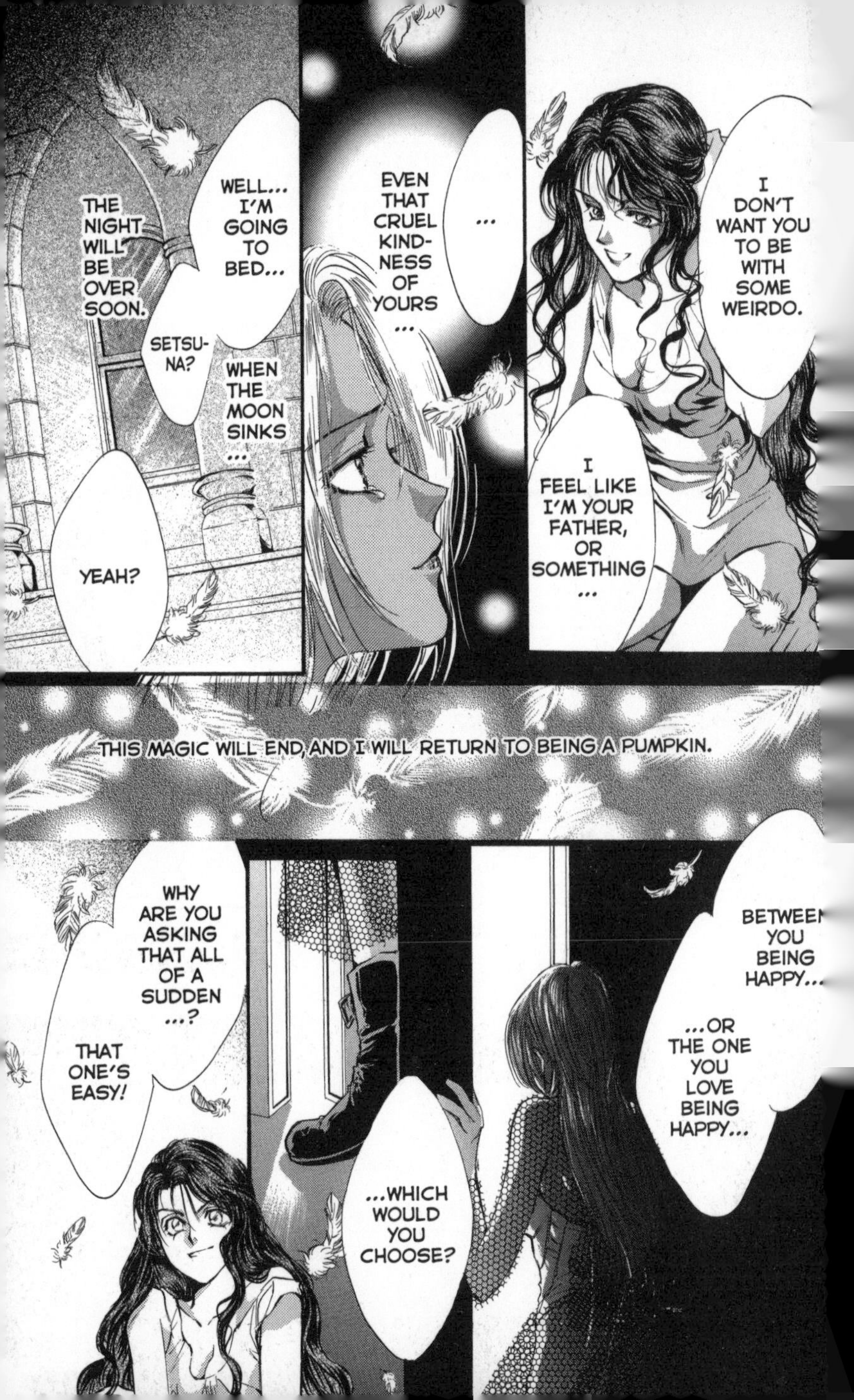
I DON'T WANT YOU TO BE WITH SOME WEIRDO.
I FEEL LIKE I'M YOUR FATHER, OR SOMETHING...
...
EVEN THAT CRUEL KINDNESS OF YOURS...
WELL... I'M GOING TO BED...
THE NIGHT WILL BE OVER SOON.
WHEN THE MOON SINKS...
SETSUNA?
YEAH?
THIS MAGIC WILL END, AND I WILL RETURN TO BEING A PUMPKIN.
BETWEEN YOU BEING HAPPY...
...OR THE ONE YOU LOVE BEING HAPPY...
...WHICH WOULD YOU CHOOSE?
WHY ARE YOU ASKING THAT ALL OF A SUDDEN...?
THAT ONE'S EASY!

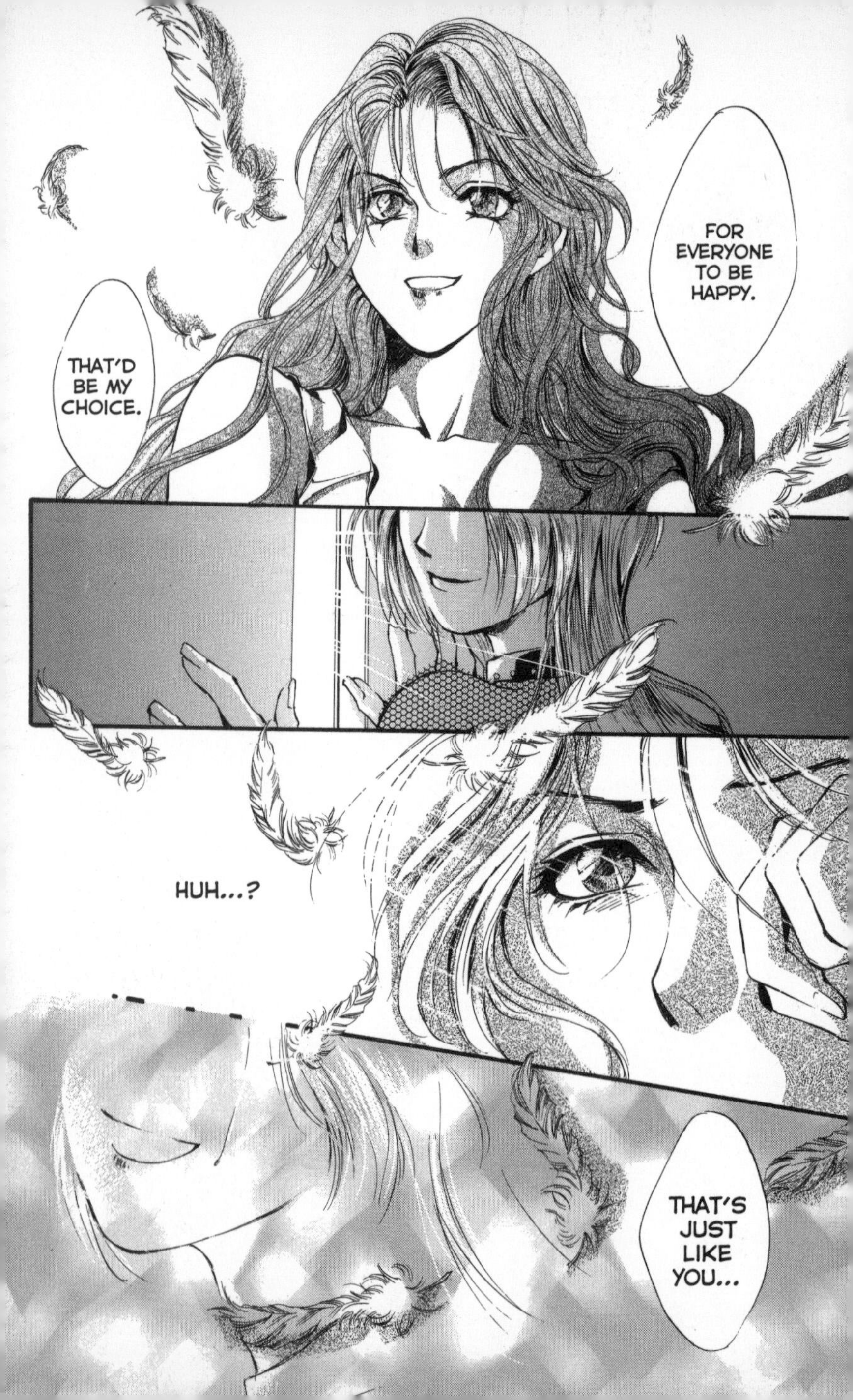
FOR EVERYONE TO BE HAPPY.
THAT'D BE MY CHOICE.
HUH...?
THAT'S JUST LIKE YOU...

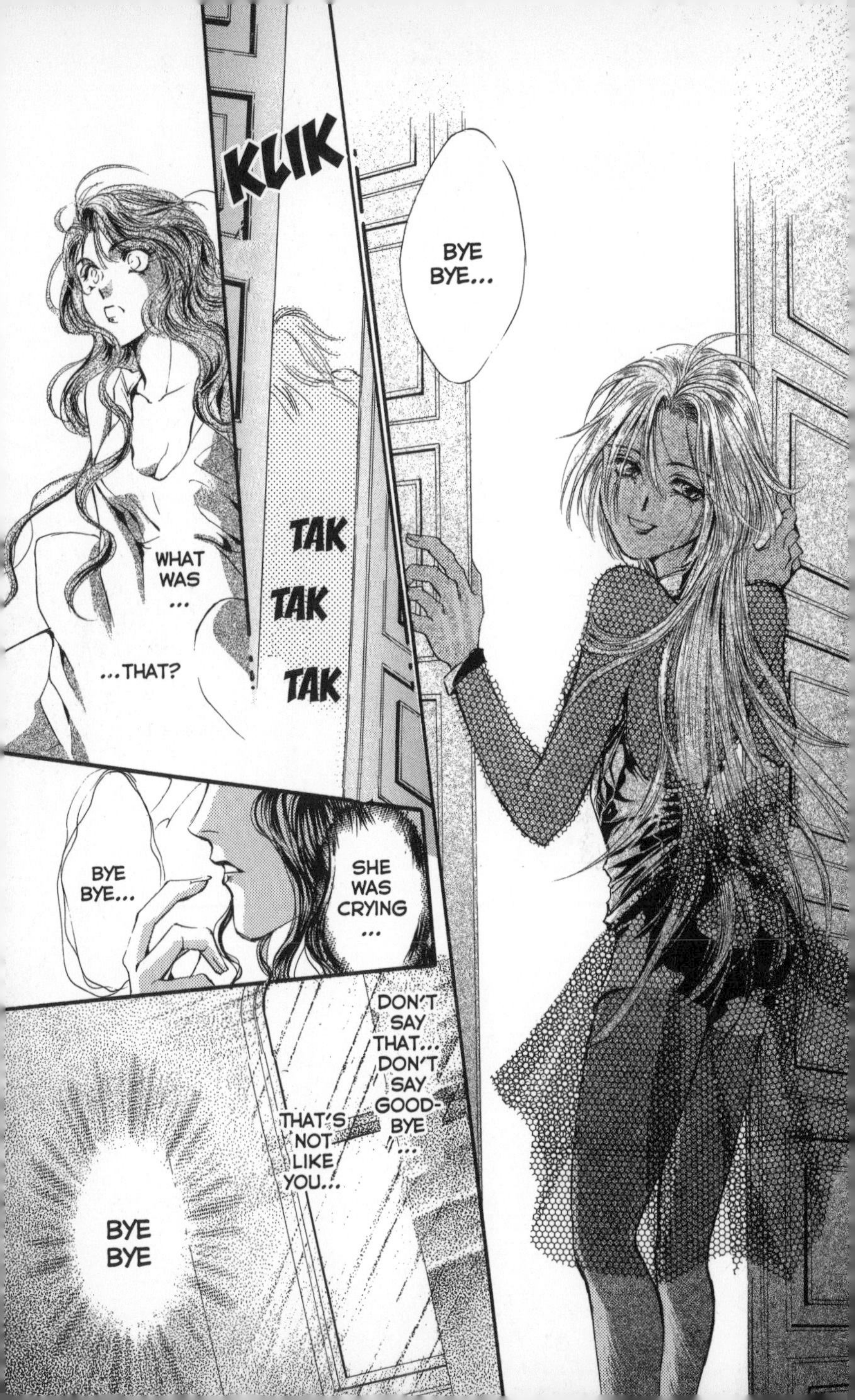
BYE BYE...
KLIK
TAK
TAK
TAK
WHAT WAS...
...THAT?
SHE WAS CRYING...
BYE BYE...
DON'T SAY THAT... DON'T SAY GOOD-BYE...
THAT'S NOT LIKE YOU...
BYE BYE

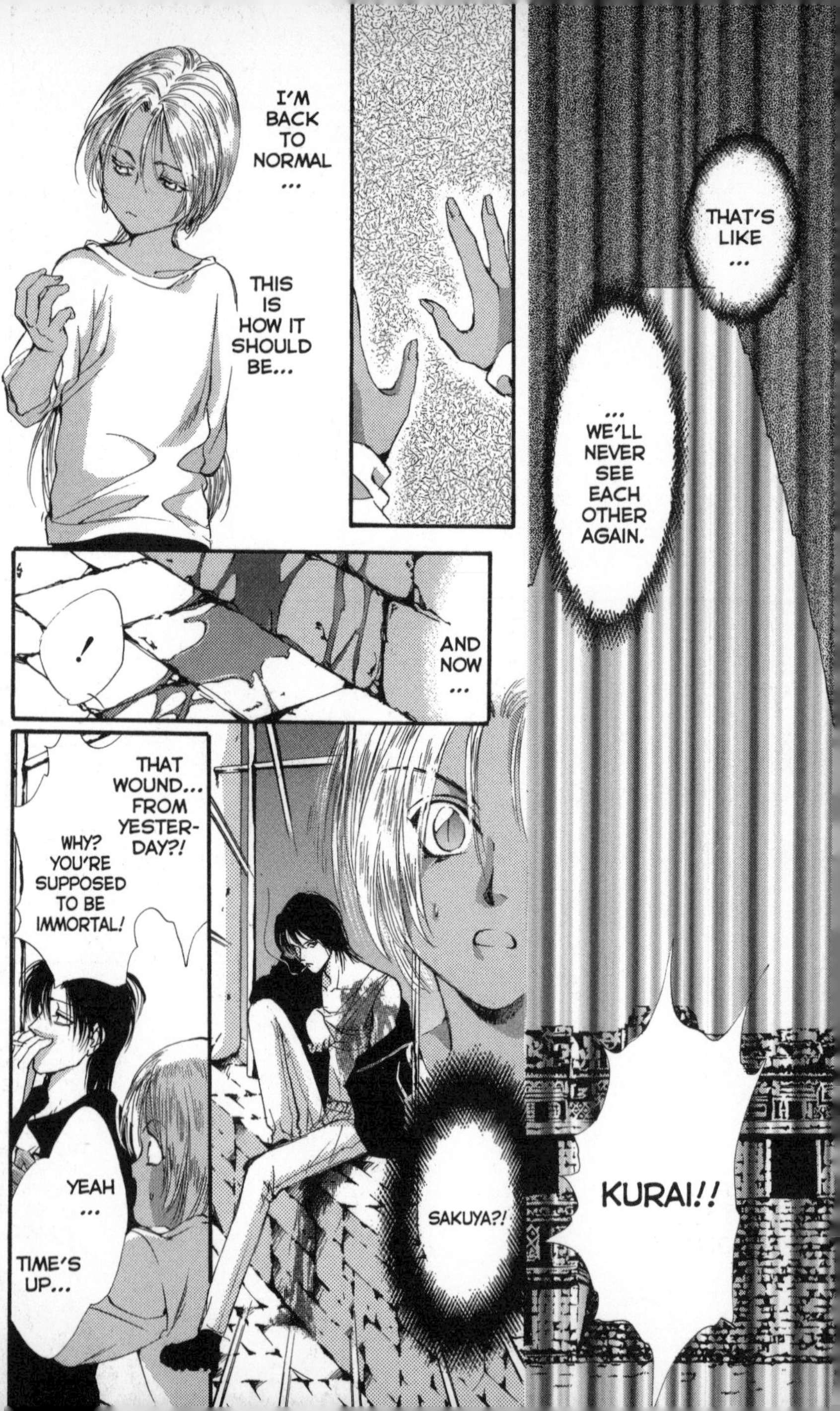
THAT'S LIKE ...
... WE'LL NEVER SEE EACH OTHER AGAIN.
KURAI!!
I'M BACK TO NORMAL ...
THIS IS HOW IT SHOULD BE...
!
AND NOW ...
SAKUYA?!
THAT WOUND... FROM YESTER-DAY?!
WHY? YOU'RE SUPPOSED TO BE IMMORTAL!
YEAH ...
TIME'S UP...

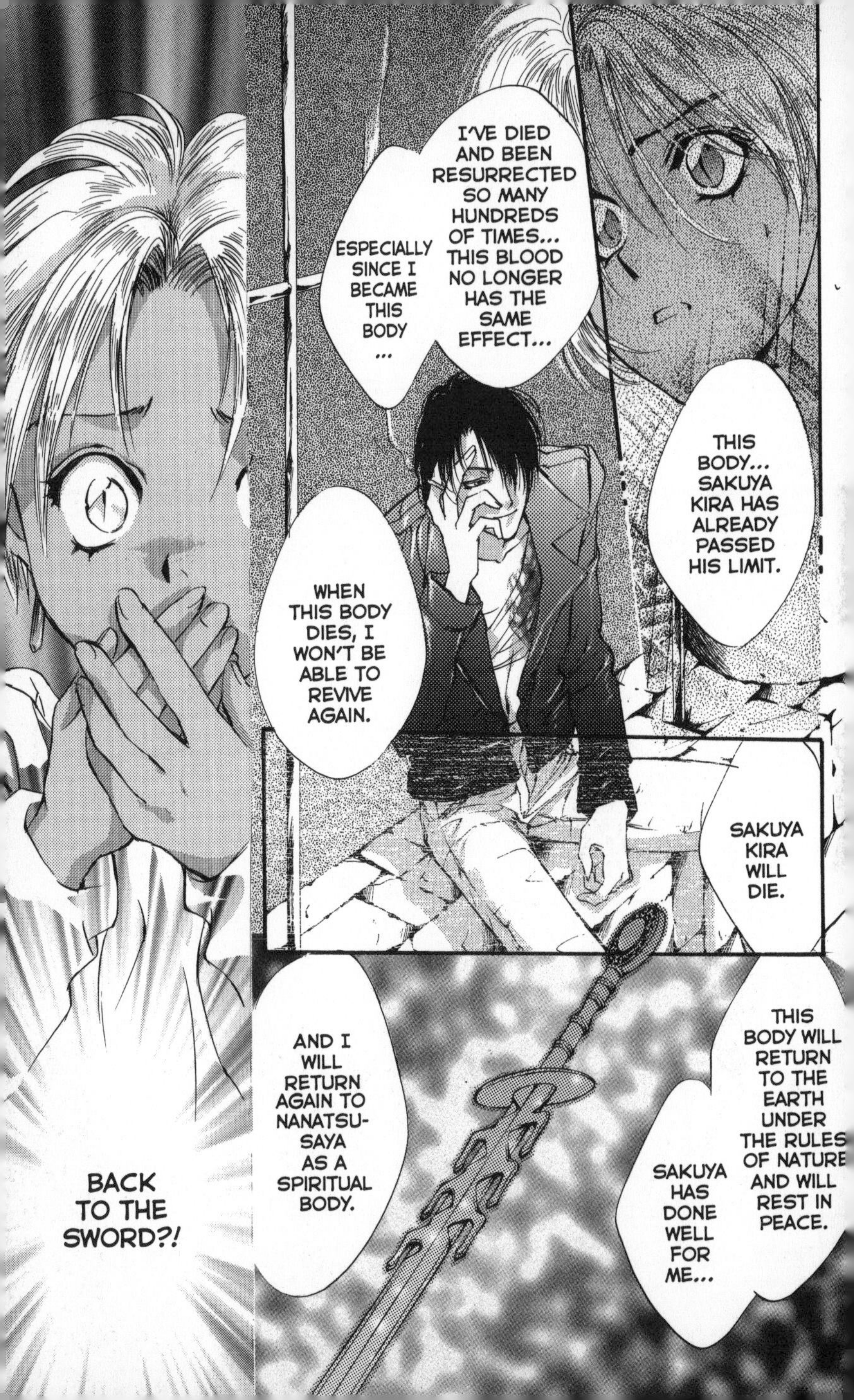
I'VE DIED AND BEEN RESURRECTED SO MANY HUNDREDS OF TIMES... THIS BLOOD NO LONGER HAS THE SAME EFFECT...
ESPECIALLY SINCE I BECAME THIS BODY ...
THIS BODY... SAKUYA KIRA HAS ALREADY PASSED HIS LIMIT.
WHEN THIS BODY DIES, I WON'T BE ABLE TO REVIVE AGAIN.
SAKUYA KIRA WILL DIE.
THIS BODY WILL RETURN TO THE EARTH UNDER THE RULES OF NATURE AND WILL REST IN PEACE.
SAKUYA HAS DONE WELL FOR ME...
AND I WILL RETURN AGAIN TO NANATSU-SAYA AS A SPIRITUAL BODY.
BACK TO THE SWORD?!

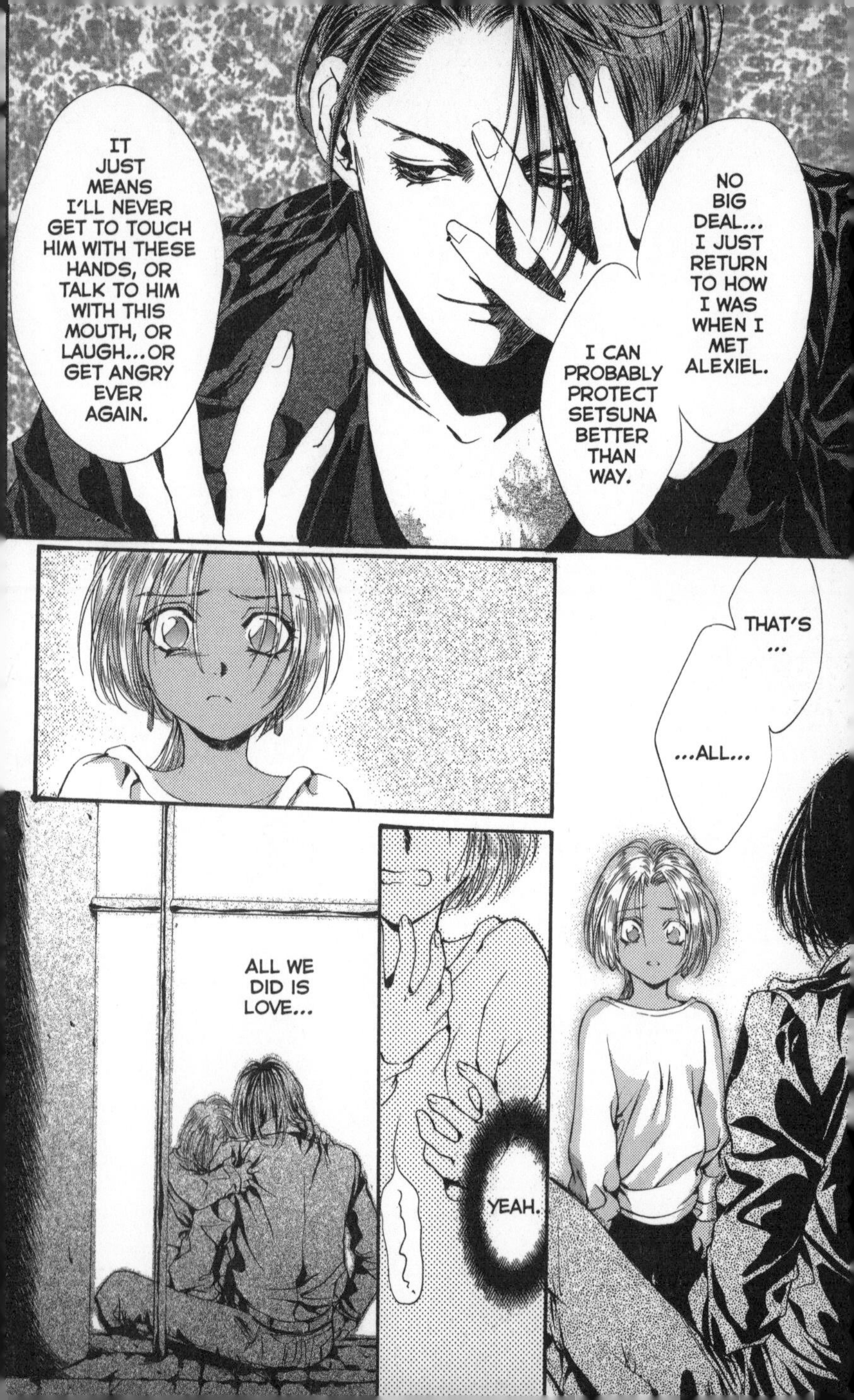
NO BIG DEAL... I JUST RETURN TO HOW I WAS WHEN I MET ALEXIEL.
I CAN PROBABLY PROTECT SETSUNA BETTER THAN WAY.
IT JUST MEANS I'LL NEVER GET TO TOUCH HIM WITH THESE HANDS, OR TALK TO HIM WITH THIS MOUTH, OR LAUGH...OR GET ANGRY EVER AGAIN.
THAT'S ... ...ALL...
YEAH.
ALL WE DID IS LOVE...

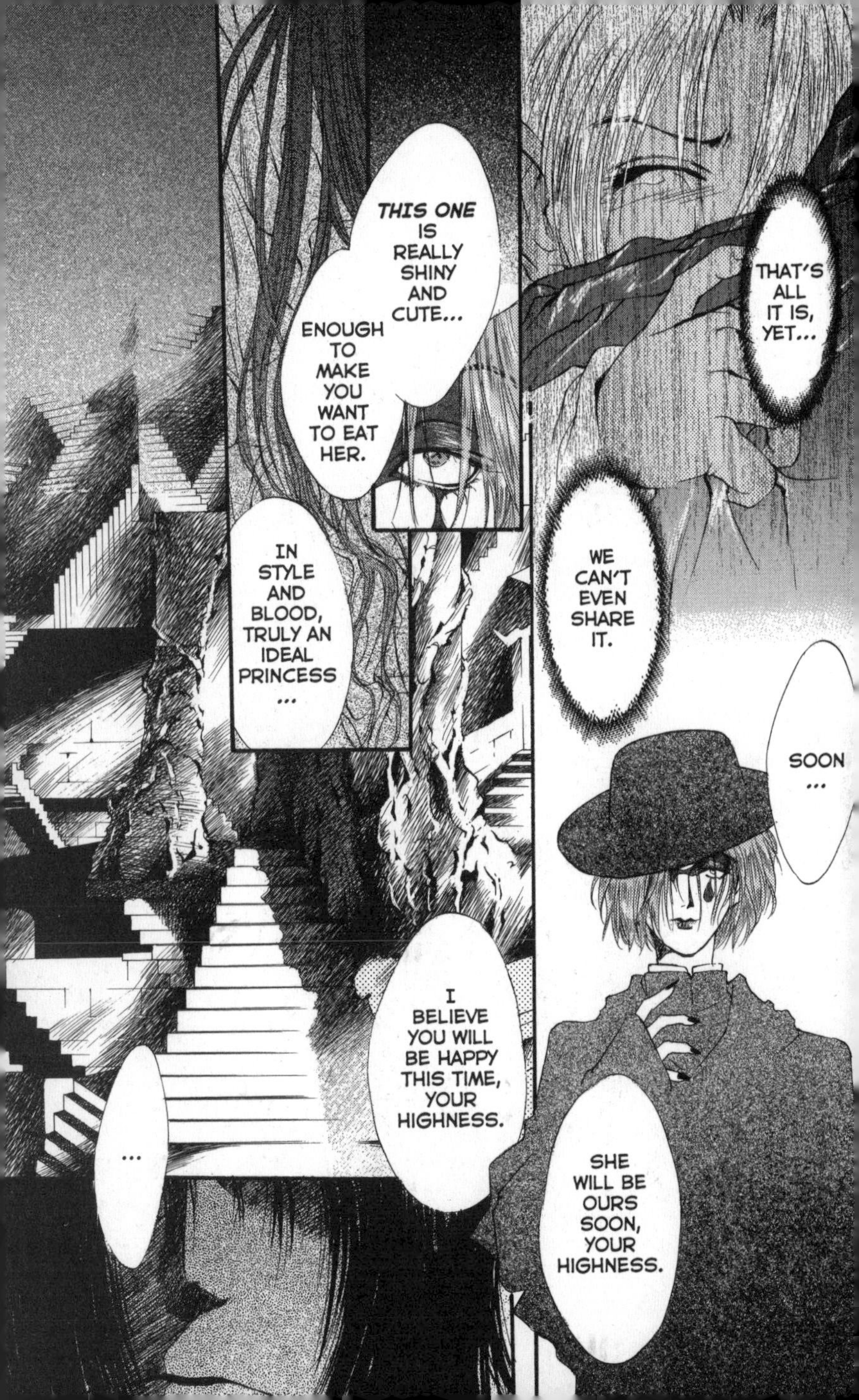
THAT'S ALL IT IS, YET...
WE CAN'T EVEN SHARE IT.
THIS ONE IS REALLY SHINY AND CUTE...
ENOUGH TO MAKE YOU WANT TO EAT HER.
IN STYLE AND BLOOD, TRULY AN IDEAL PRINCESS...
SOON...
I BELIEVE YOU WILL BE HAPPY THIS TIME, YOUR HIGHNESS.
SHE WILL BE OURS SOON, YOUR HIGHNESS.
...

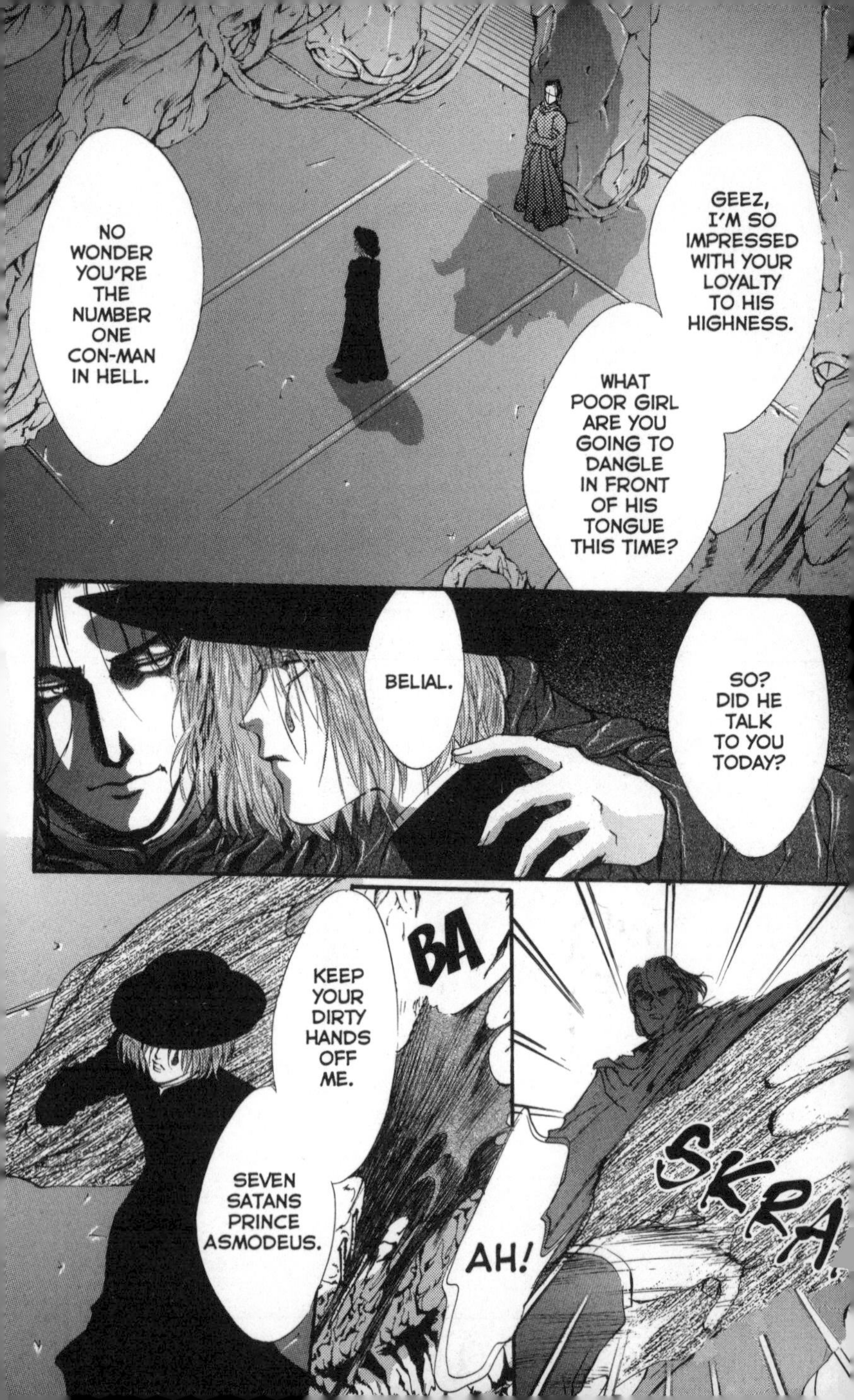
GEEZ, I'M SO IMPRESSED WITH YOUR LOYALTY TO HIS HIGHNESS.
WHAT POOR GIRL ARE YOU GOING TO DANGLE IN FRONT OF HIS TONGUE THIS TIME?
NO WONDER YOU'RE THE NUMBER ONE CON-MAN IN HELL.
SO? DID HE TALK TO YOU TODAY?
BELIAL.
SKRA.
AH!
BA
KEEP YOUR DIRTY HANDS OFF ME.
SEVEN SATANS PRINCE ASMODEUS.

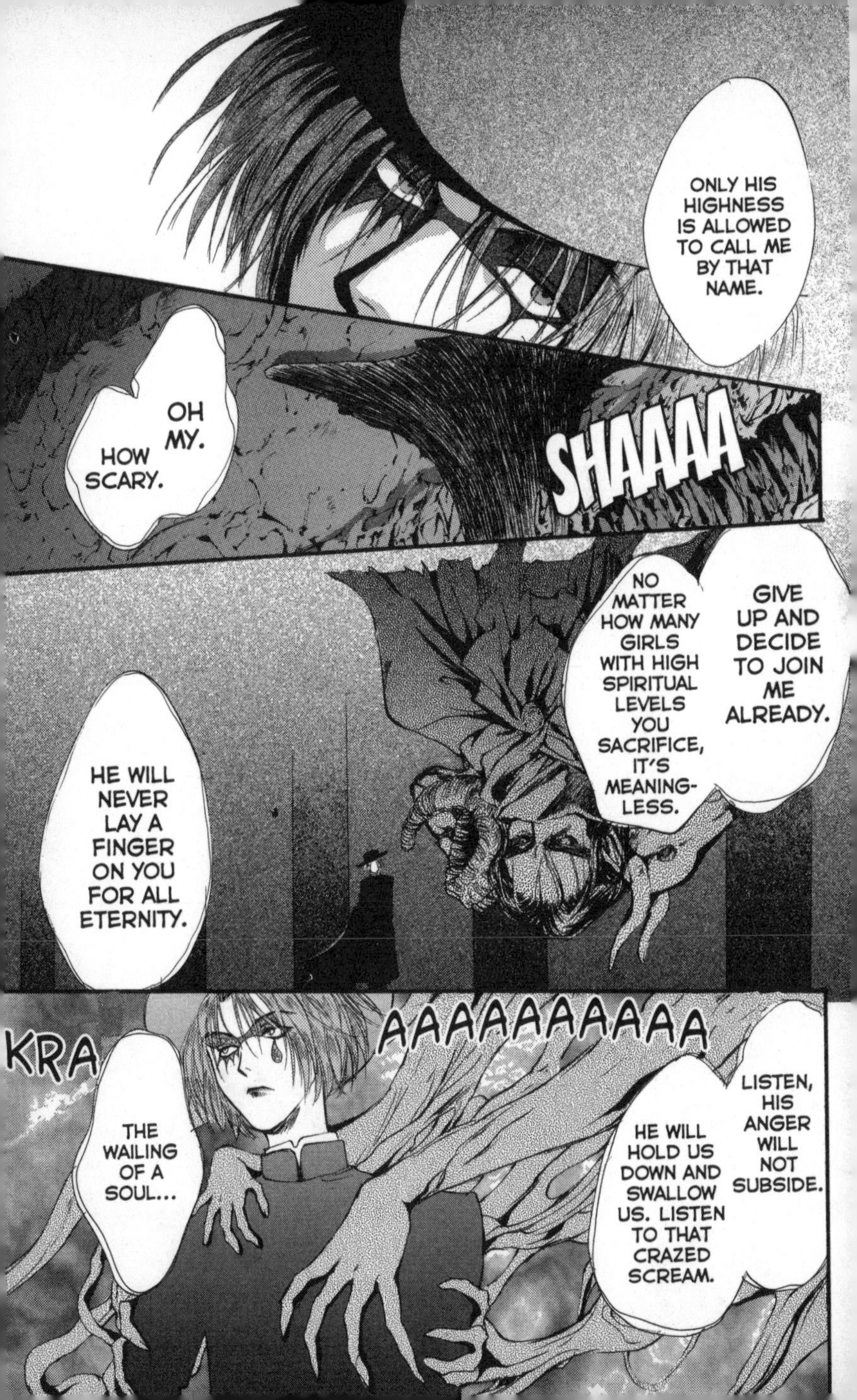

ONLY HIS HIGHNESS IS ALLOWED TO CALL ME BY THAT NAME.
SHAAAA
OH MY. HOW SCARY.
GIVE UP AND DECIDE TO JOIN ME ALREADY.
NO MATTER HOW MANY GIRLS WITH HIGH SPIRITUAL LEVELS YOU SACRIFICE, IT'S MEANING-LESS.
HE WILL NEVER LAY A FINGER ON YOU FOR ALL ETERNITY.
AAAAAAAAAA
LISTEN, HIS ANGER WILL NOT SUBSIDE.
HE WILL HOLD US DOWN AND SWALLOW US. LISTEN TO THAT CRAZED SCREAM.
THE WAILING OF A SOUL...
KRA

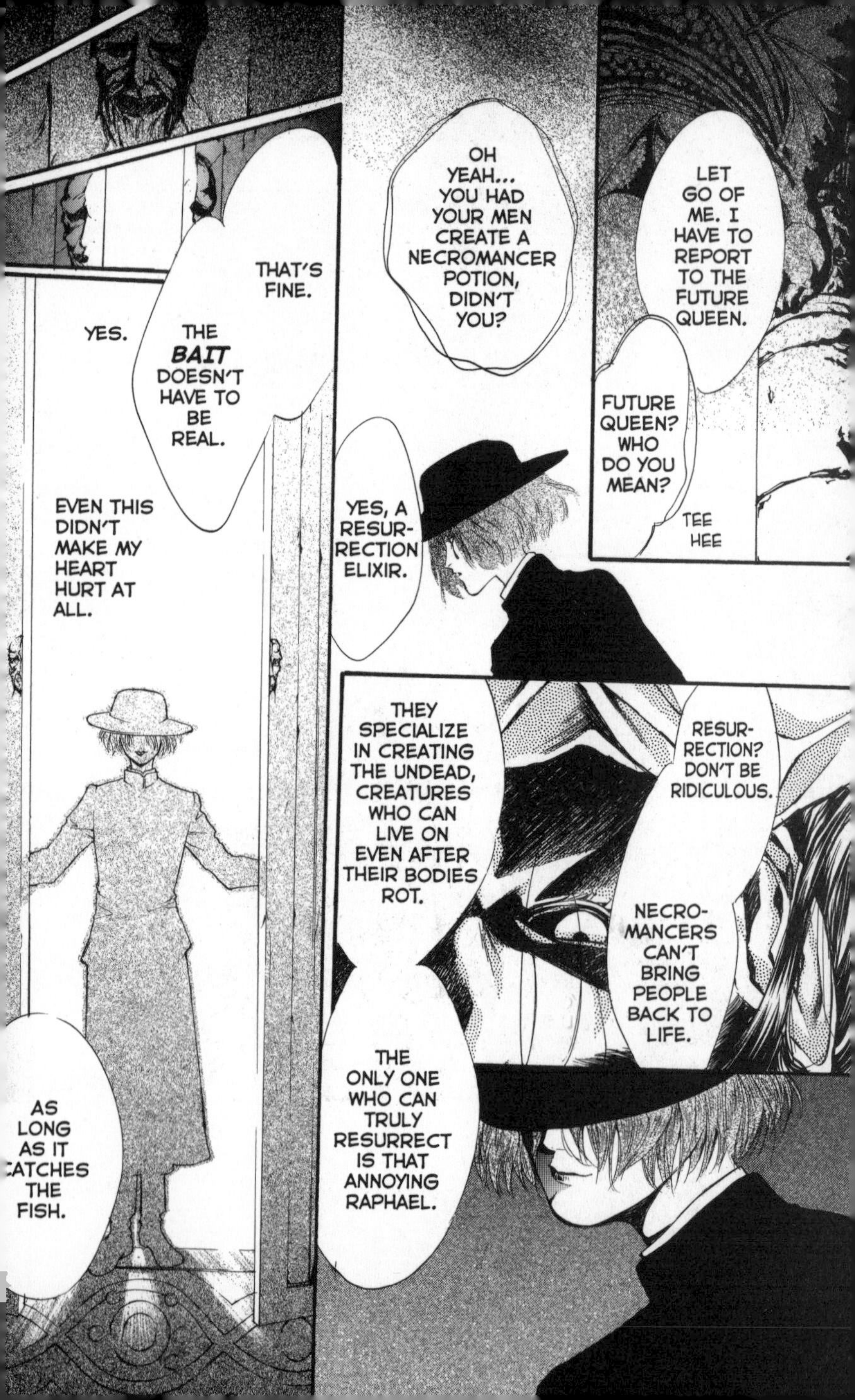
LET GO OF ME. I HAVE TO REPORT TO THE FUTURE QUEEN.
FUTURE QUEEN? WHO DO YOU MEAN?
TEE HEE
OH YEAH... YOU HAD YOUR MEN CREATE A NECROMANCER POTION, DIDN'T YOU?
YES, A RESUR-RECTION ELIXIR.
RESUR-RECTION? DON'T BE RIDICULOUS.
THEY SPECIALIZE IN CREATING THE UNDEAD, CREATURES WHO CAN LIVE ON EVEN AFTER THEIR BODIES ROT.
NECRO-MANCERS CAN'T BRING PEOPLE BACK TO LIFE.
THE ONLY ONE WHO CAN TRULY RESURRECT IS THAT ANNOYING RAPHAEL.
THAT'S FINE. THE BAIT DOESN'T HAVE TO BE REAL.
YES.
EVEN THIS DIDN'T MAKE MY HEART HURT AT ALL.
AS LONG AS IT CATCHES THE FISH.

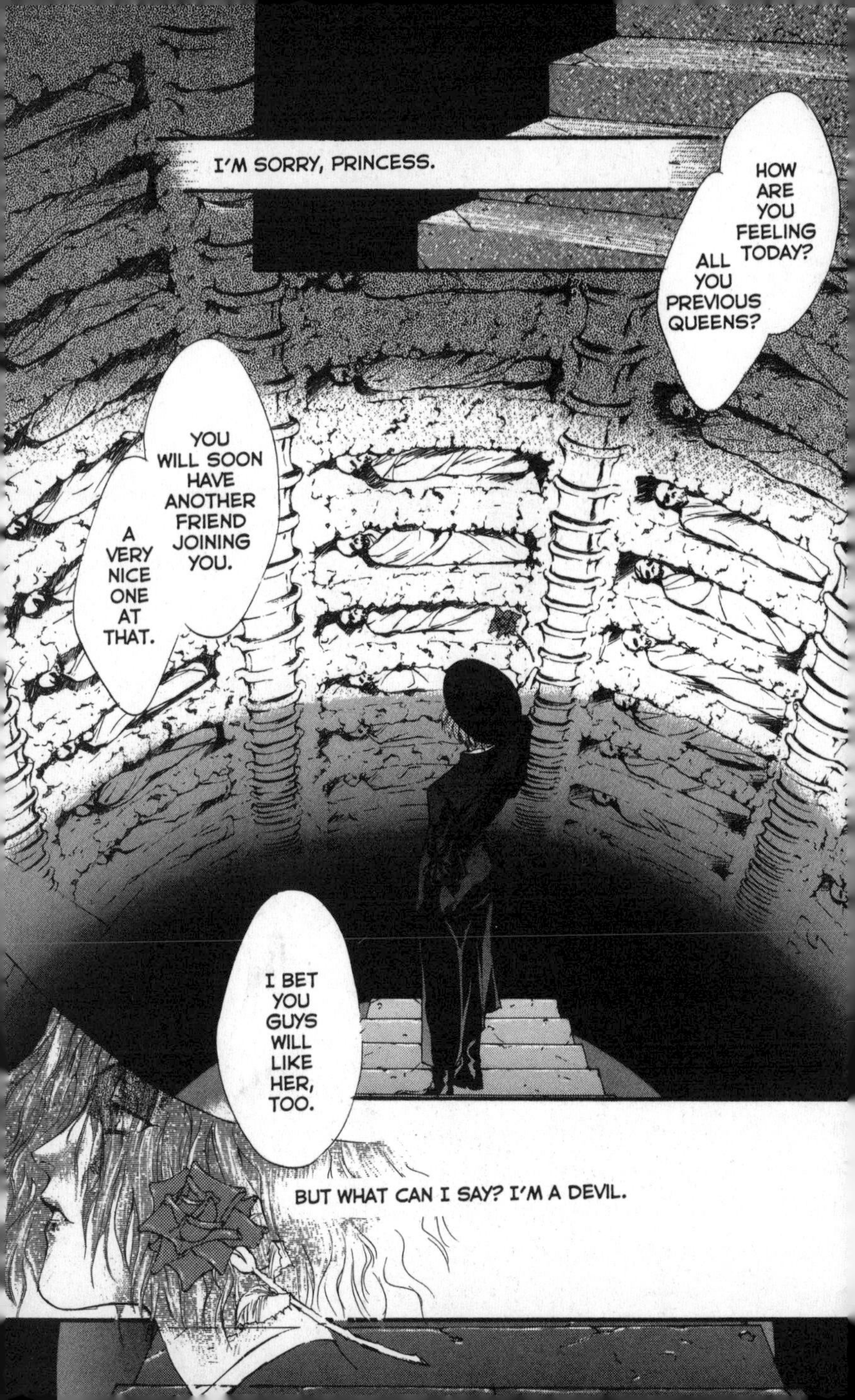
I'M SORRY, PRINCESS.
HOW ARE YOU FEELING TODAY? ALL YOU PREVIOUS QUEENS?
YOU WILL SOON HAVE ANOTHER FRIEND JOINING YOU. A VERY NICE ONE AT THAT.
I BET YOU GUYS WILL LIKE HER, TOO.
BUT WHAT CAN I SAY? I'M A DEVIL.

THE SEVEN VICES I LOVE.

ENVY, DESTRUCTION, AFFLICTION,
CAPTIVITY, FAMINE, CHAOS, RUIN.

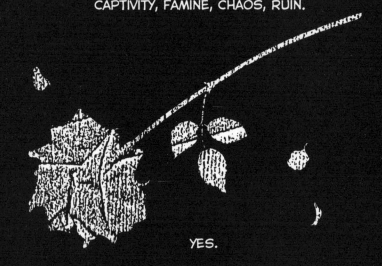

YES.

THEY ARE ALL SWEET POISON.

BORN FROM MY MOUTH.

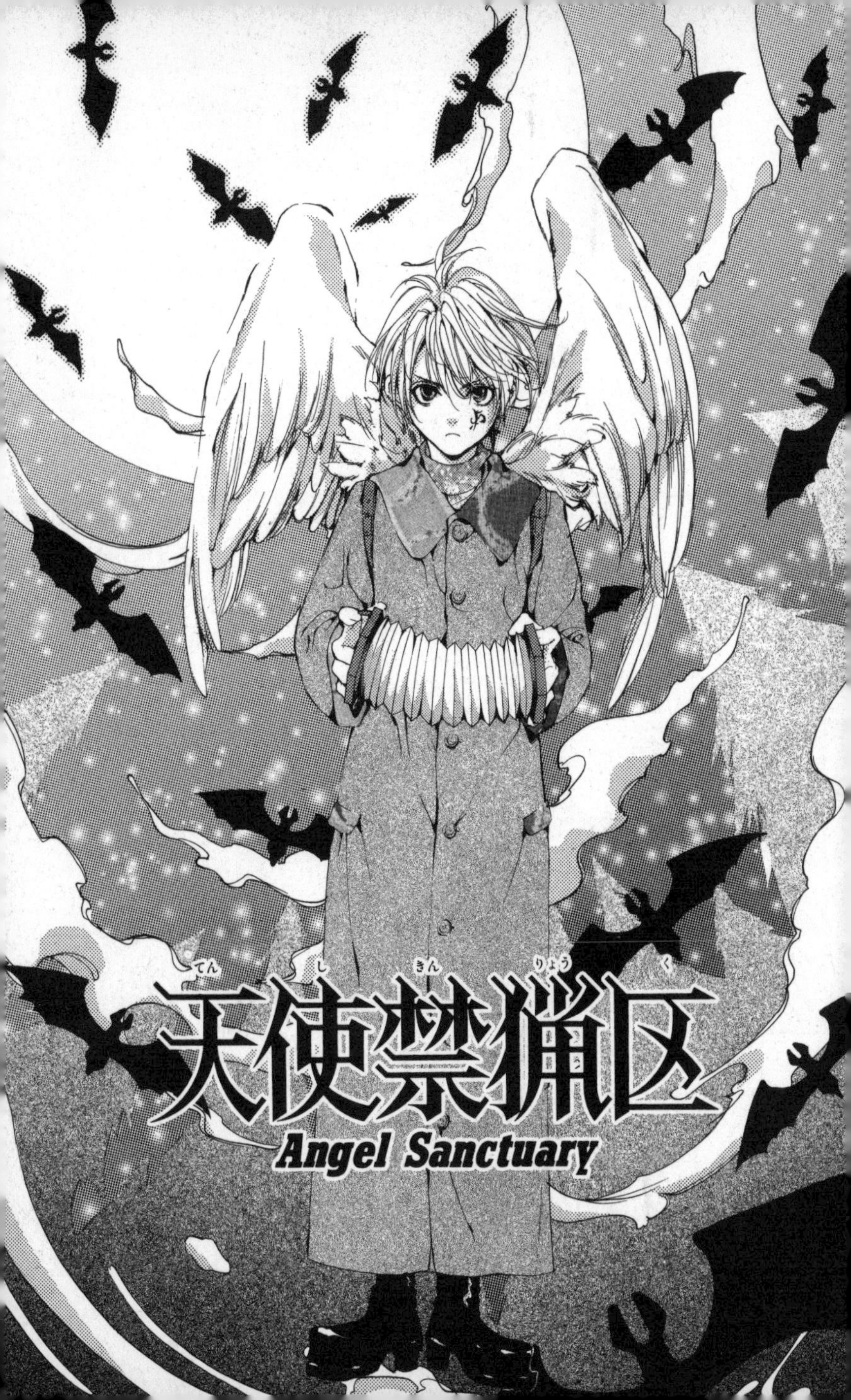
天使禁猟区
Angel Sanctuary

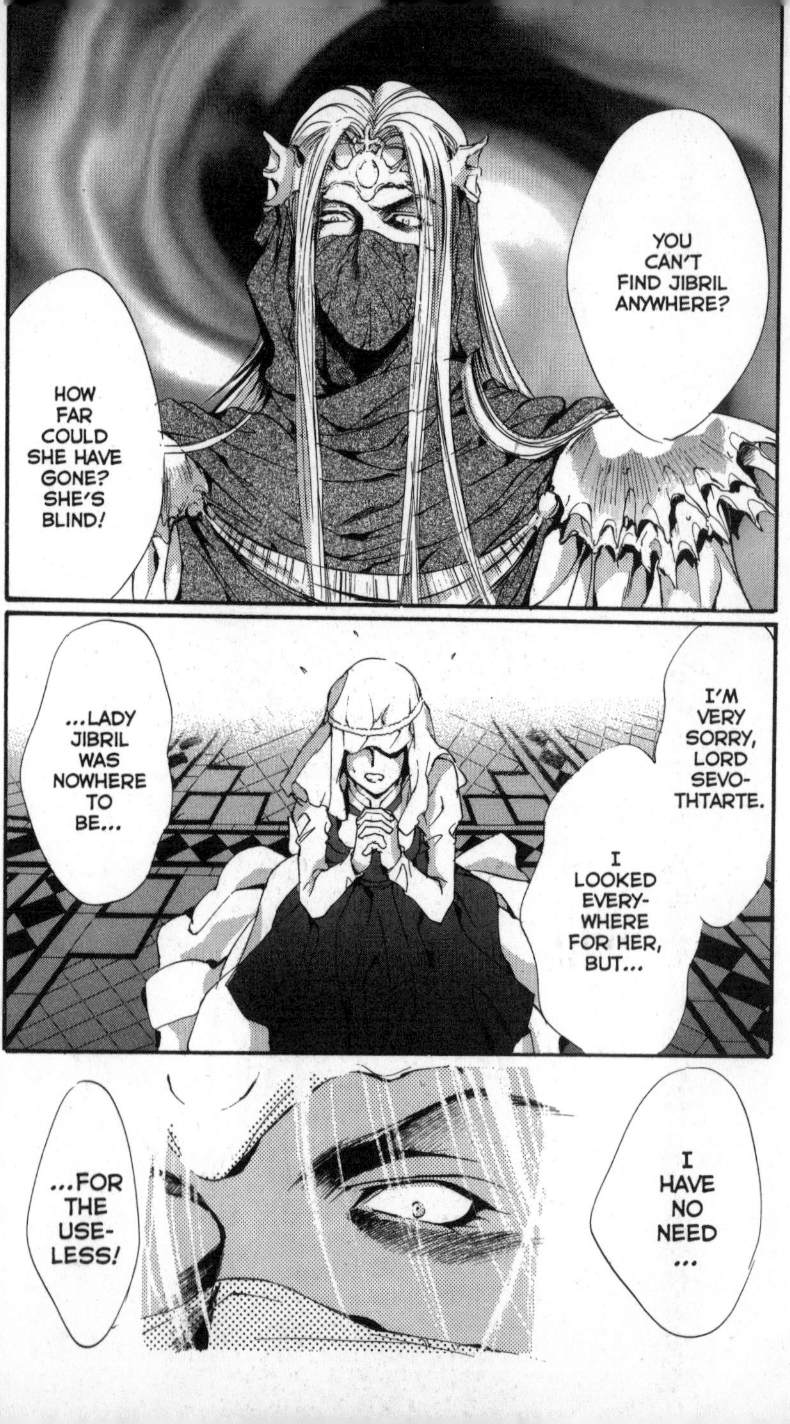
YOU CAN'T FIND JIBRIL ANYWHERE?
HOW FAR COULD SHE HAVE GONE? SHE'S BLIND!
I'M VERY SORRY, LORD SEVO-THTARTE.
I LOOKED EVERY-WHERE FOR HER, BUT...
...LADY JIBRIL WAS NOWHERE TO BE...
I HAVE NO NEED ...
...FOR THE USE-LESS!

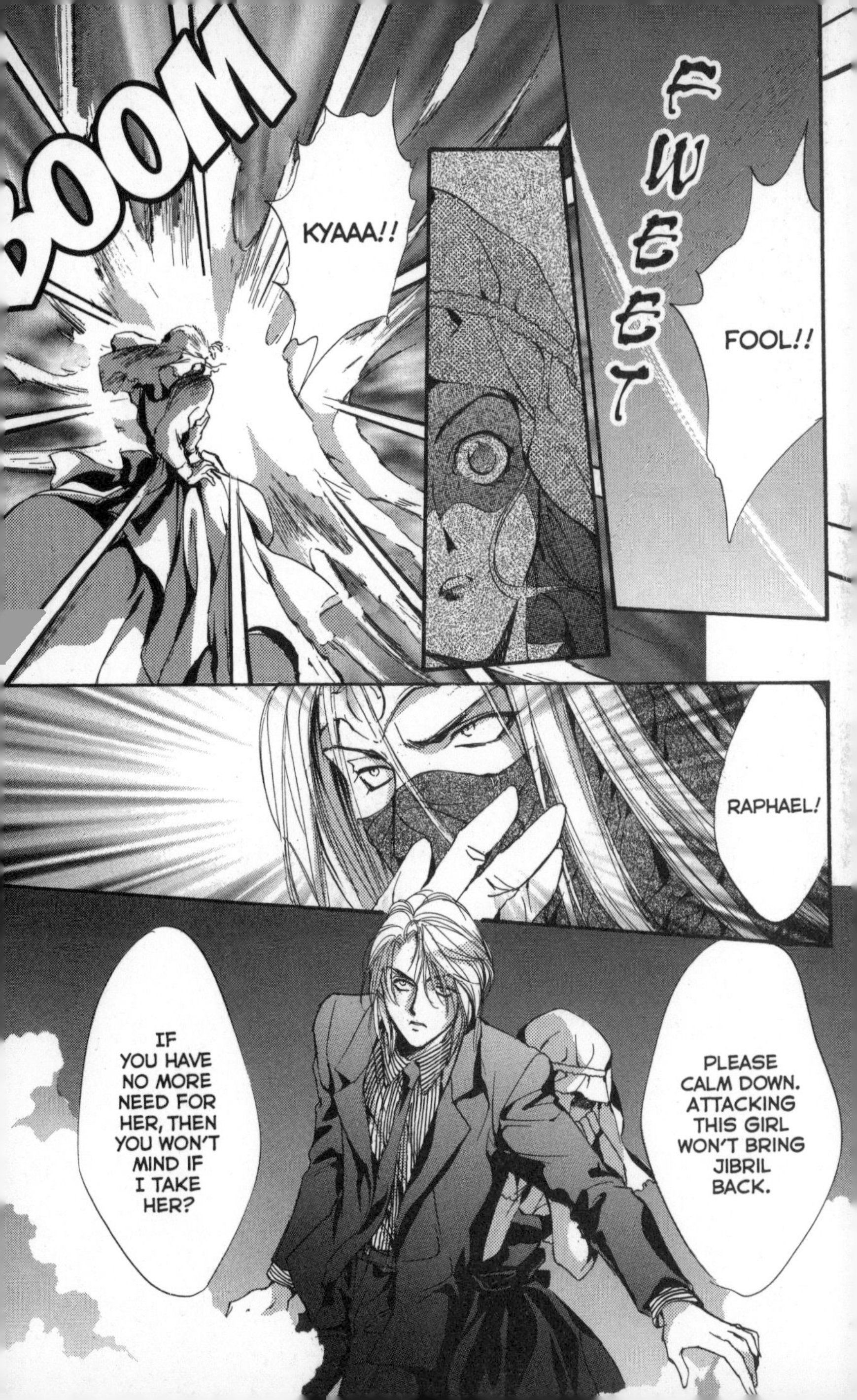

FOOL!!
FWEET
BOOM
KYAAA!!
RAPHAEL!
PLEASE CALM DOWN. ATTACKING THIS GIRL WON'T BRING JIBRIL BACK.
IF YOU HAVE NO MORE NEED FOR HER, THEN YOU WON'T MIND IF I TAKE HER?

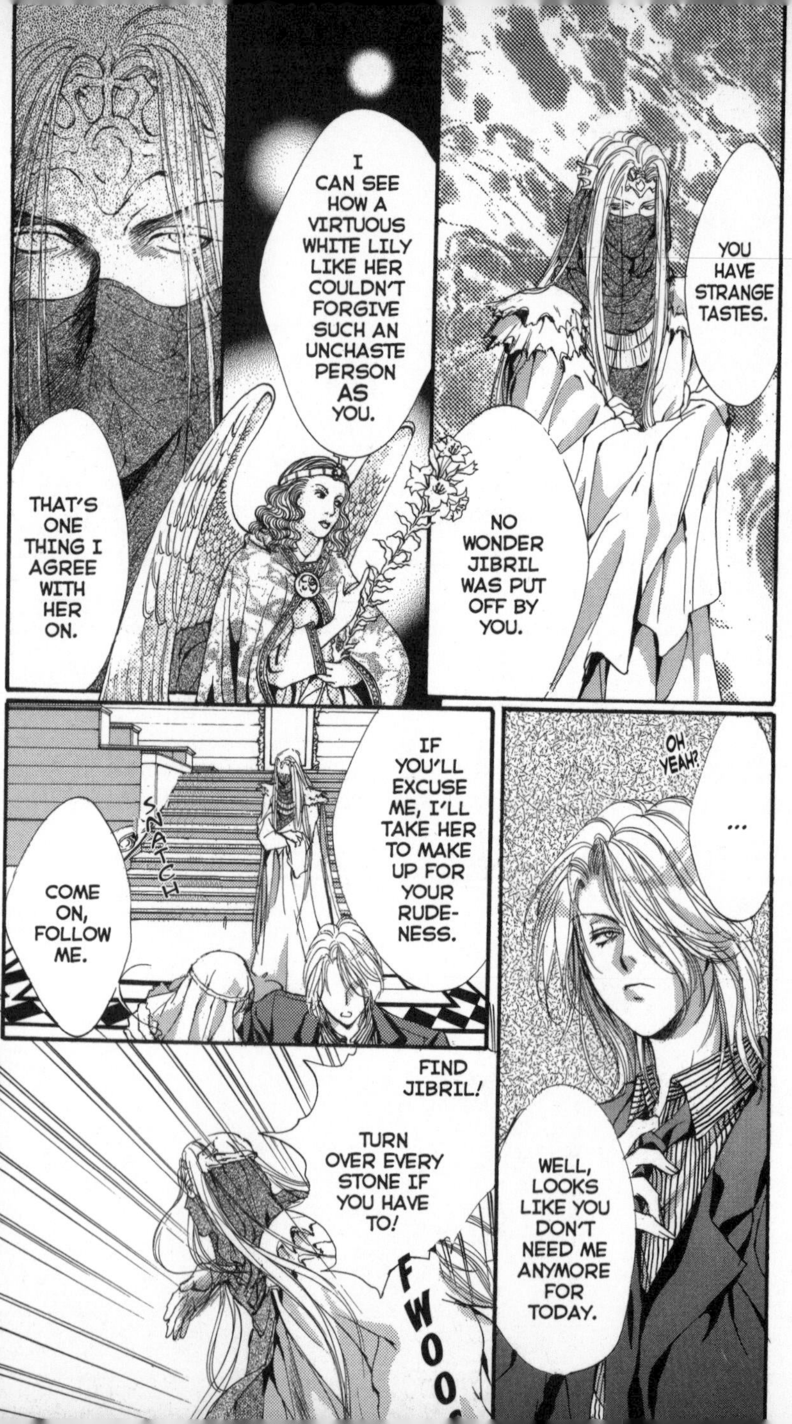
YOU HAVE STRANGE TASTES.
NO WONDER JIBRIL WAS PUT OFF BY YOU.
I CAN SEE HOW A VIRTUOUS WHITE LILY LIKE HER COULDN'T FORGIVE SUCH AN UNCHASTE PERSON AS YOU.
THAT'S ONE THING I AGREE WITH HER ON.
OH YEAH?
...
WELL, LOOKS LIKE YOU DON'T NEED ME ANYMORE FOR TODAY.
IF YOU'LL EXCUSE ME, I'LL TAKE HER TO MAKE UP FOR YOUR RUDE-NESS.
SNATCH
COME ON, FOLLOW ME.
FIND JIBRIL!
TURN OVER EVERY STONE IF YOU HAVE TO!
FWOO

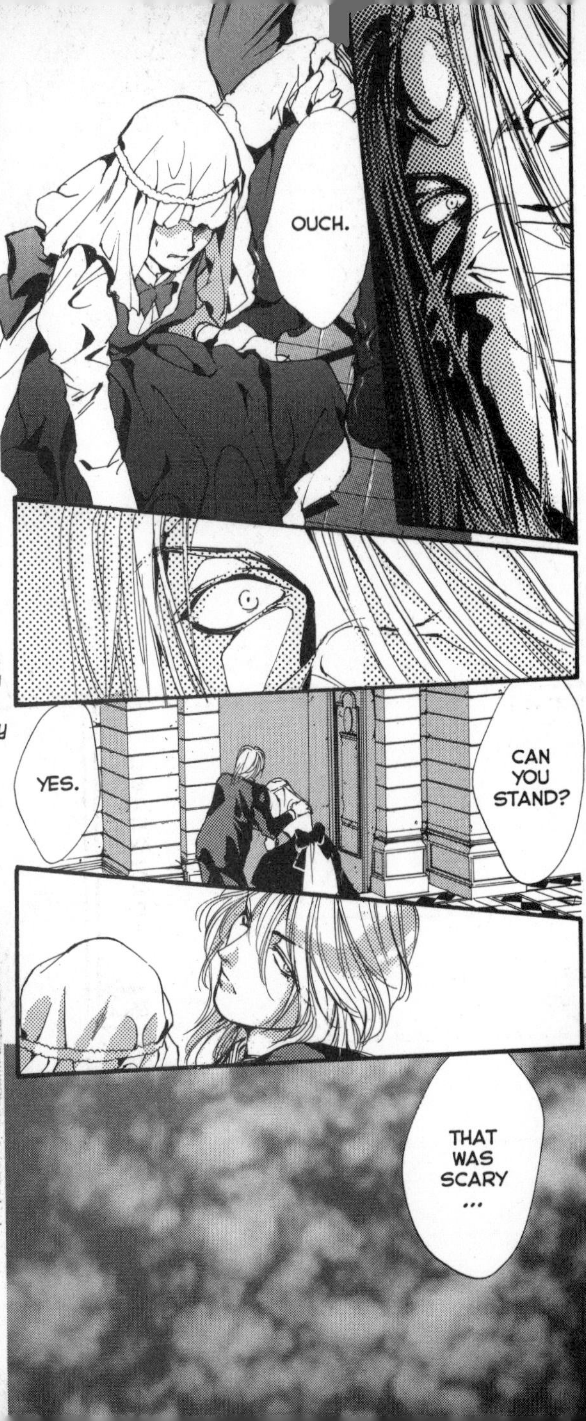
OUCH.
CAN YOU STAND?
YES.
THAT WAS SCARY ...

It's been a long time since I drew it, but the cover to this chapter and Hatter's costume is kind of ***Guniw Tool***-ish... This was the fiftieth chapter. Fifty chapters... It's the first time I've done a manga for so long. How many more chapters until it ***ends?*** I based the Demon Lord's room after the movie ***Labyrinth***, the one with Jennifer Connelly and David Bowie. I really like Jennifer. I watched the extended version of ***Phenomena***, but couldn't tell what they extended. Jennifer was really beautiful as always. I like the theme song in ***Phenomena***.

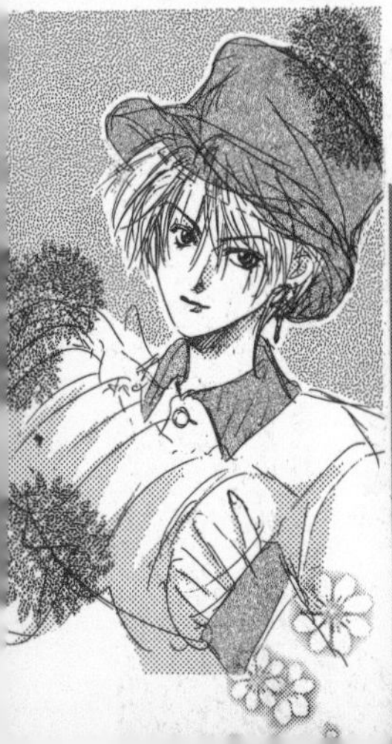

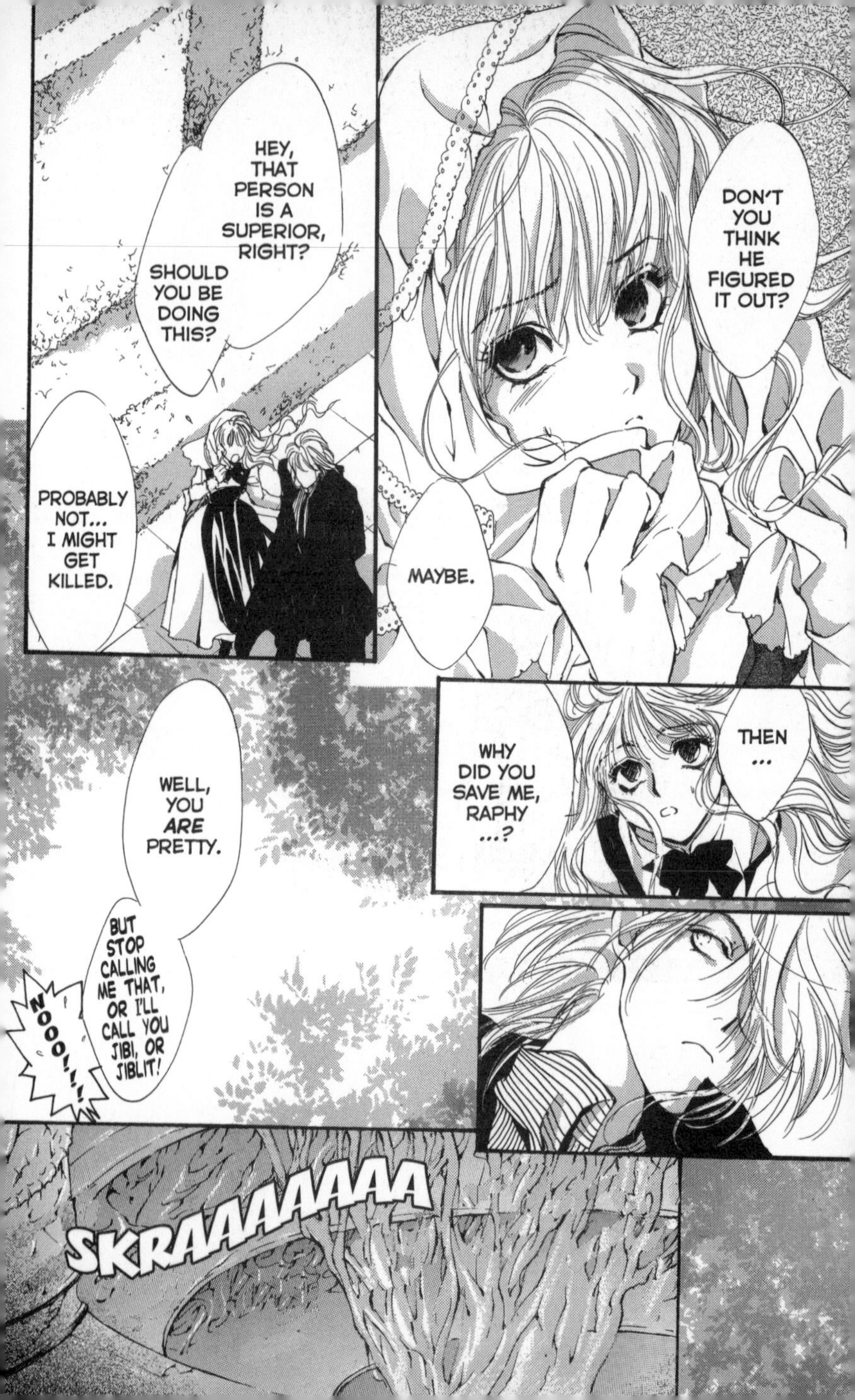
DON'T YOU THINK HE FIGURED IT OUT?
MAYBE.
HEY, THAT PERSON IS A SUPERIOR, RIGHT?
SHOULD YOU BE DOING THIS?
PROBABLY NOT... I MIGHT GET KILLED.
THEN ...
WHY DID YOU SAVE ME, RAPHY ...?
WELL, YOU *ARE* PRETTY.
BUT STOP CALLING ME THAT, OR I'LL CALL YOU JIBI, OR JIBLIT!
NOOO!!!!
SKRAAAAAAAA

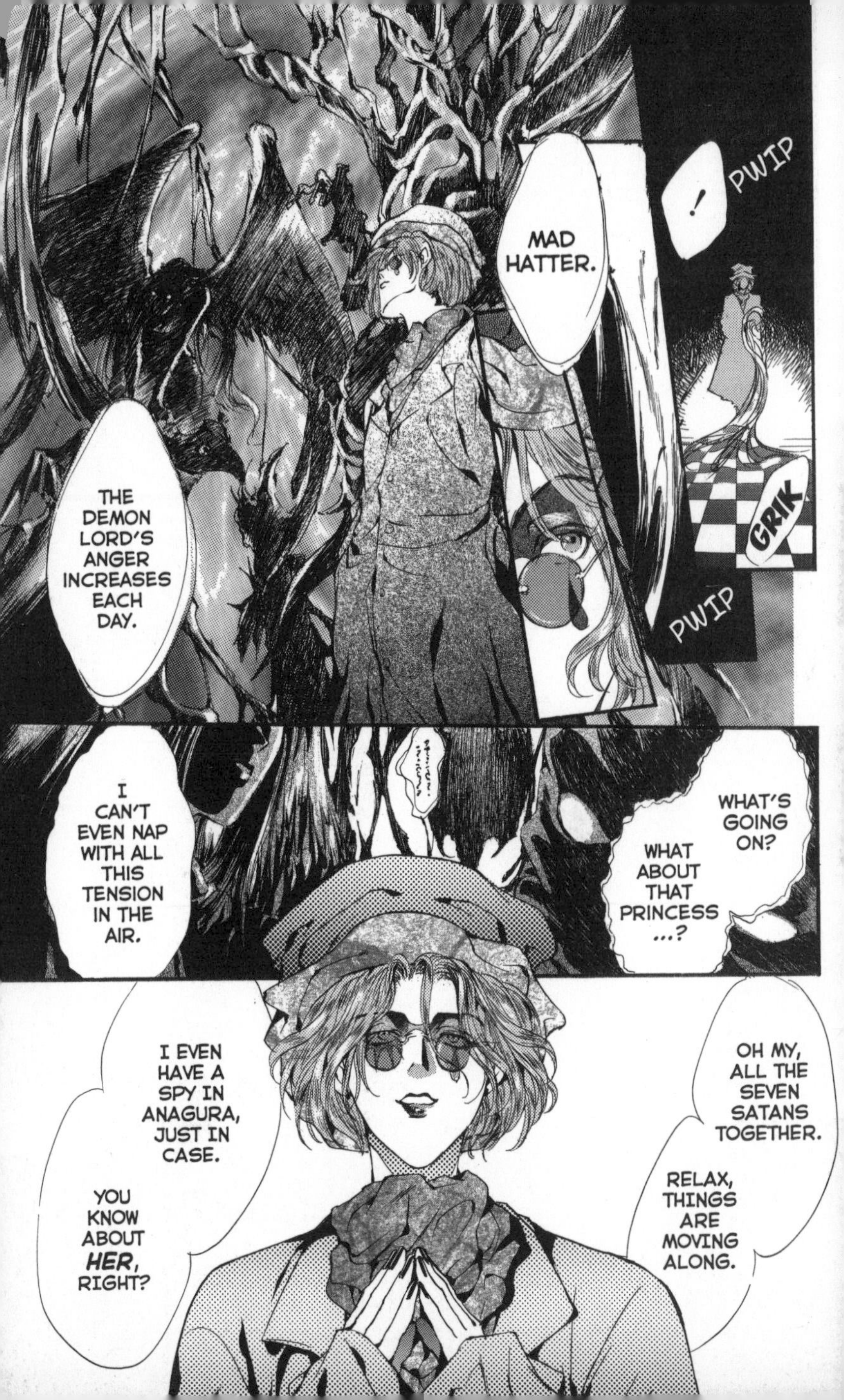
!
PWIP
GRIK
PWIP
MAD HATTER.
THE DEMON LORD'S ANGER INCREASES EACH DAY.
WHAT'S GOING ON?
WHAT ABOUT THAT PRINCESS ...?
I CAN'T EVEN NAP WITH ALL THIS TENSION IN THE AIR.
OH MY, ALL THE SEVEN SATANS TOGETHER.
RELAX, THINGS ARE MOVING ALONG.
I EVEN HAVE A SPY IN ANAGURA, JUST IN CASE.
YOU KNOW ABOUT **HER**, RIGHT?

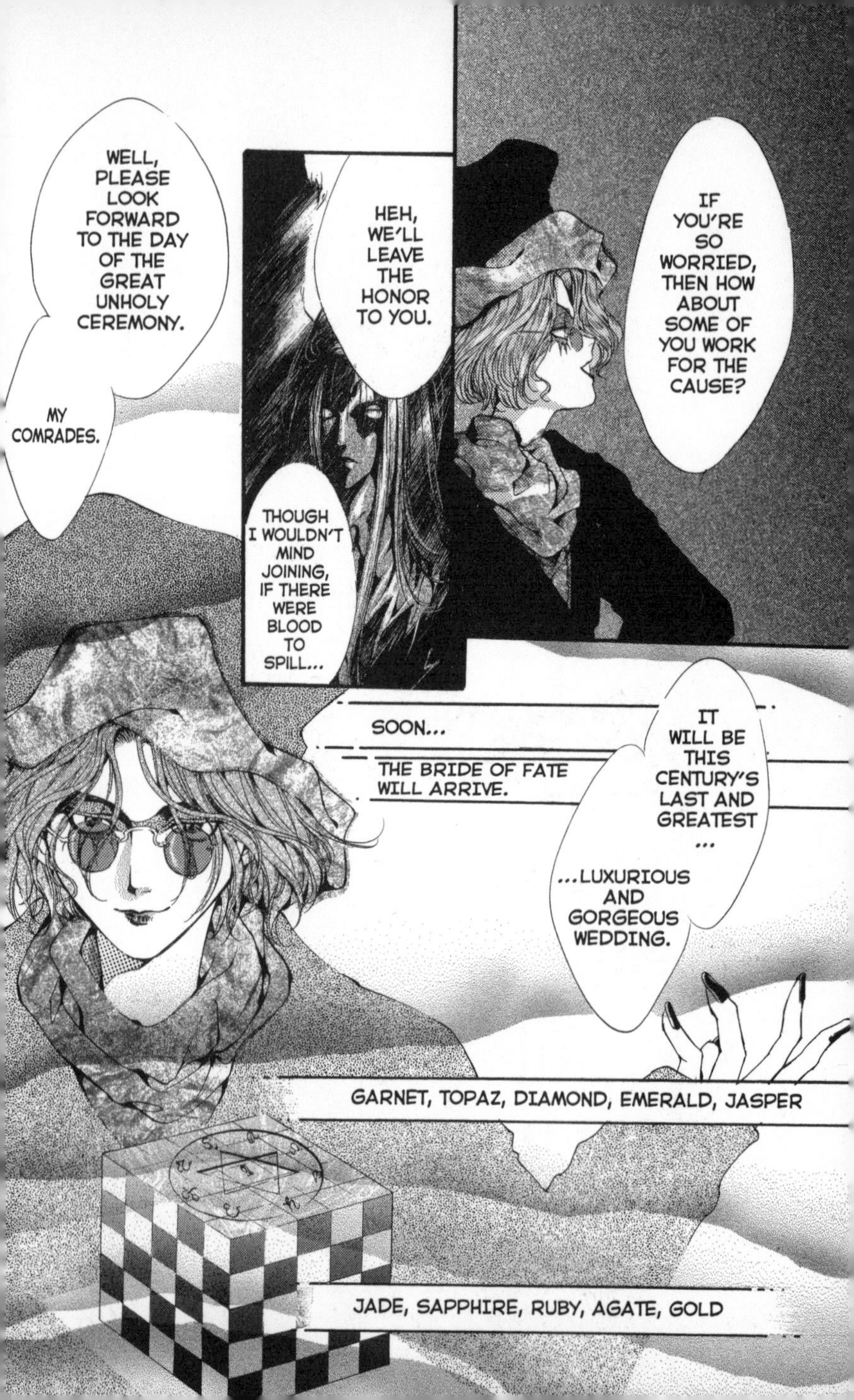
IF YOU'RE SO WORRIED, THEN HOW ABOUT SOME OF YOU WORK FOR THE CAUSE?
HEH, WE'LL LEAVE THE HONOR TO YOU.
THOUGH I WOULDN'T MIND JOINING, IF THERE WERE BLOOD TO SPILL...
WELL, PLEASE LOOK FORWARD TO THE DAY OF THE GREAT UNHOLY CEREMONY.
MY COMRADES.
IT WILL BE THIS CENTURY'S LAST AND GREATEST ...
...LUXURIOUS AND GORGEOUS WEDDING.
SOON...
THE BRIDE OF FATE WILL ARRIVE.
GARNET, TOPAZ, DIAMOND, EMERALD, JASPER
JADE, SAPPHIRE, RUBY, AGATE, GOLD

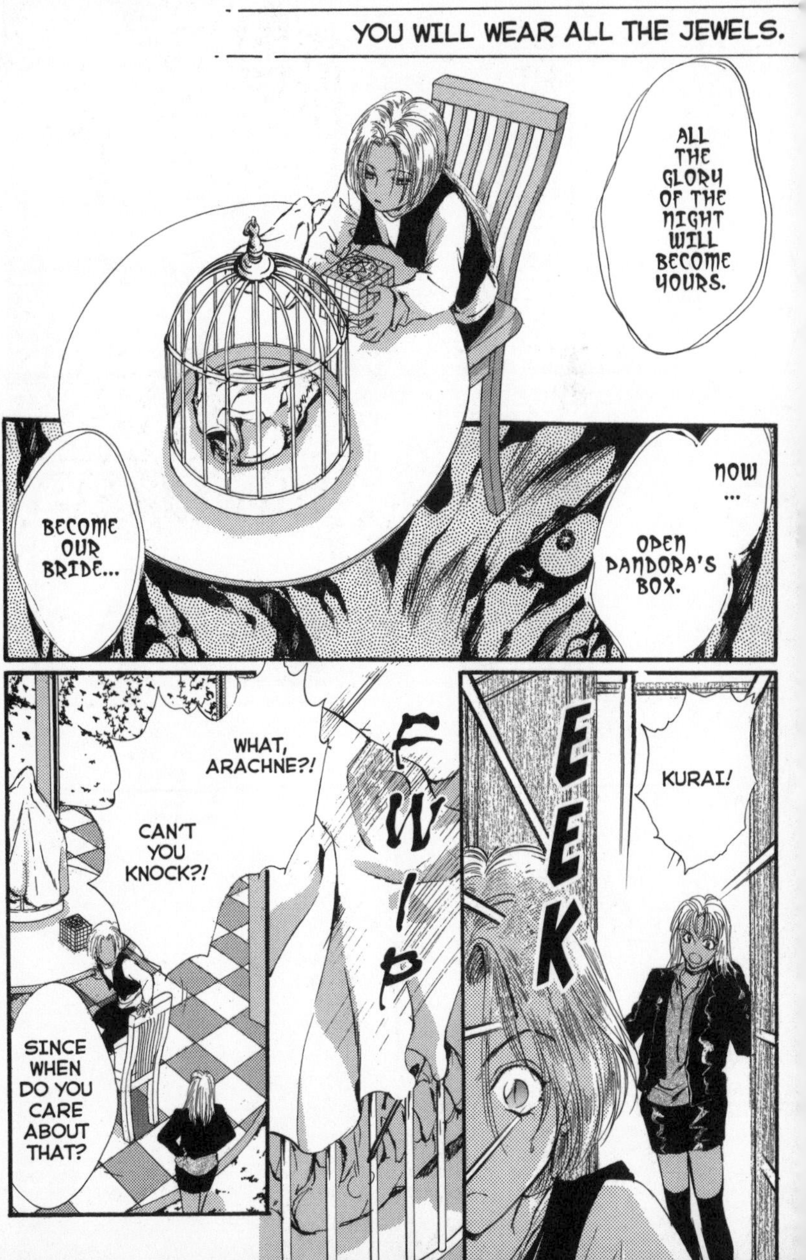
YOU WILL WEAR ALL THE JEWELS.
ALL THE GLORY OF THE NIGHT WILL BECOME YOURS.
NOW... OPEN PANDORA'S BOX.
BECOME OUR BRIDE...
EEK
KURAI!
FWIP
WHAT, ARACHNE?!
CAN'T YOU KNOCK?!
SINCE WHEN DO YOU CARE ABOUT THAT?

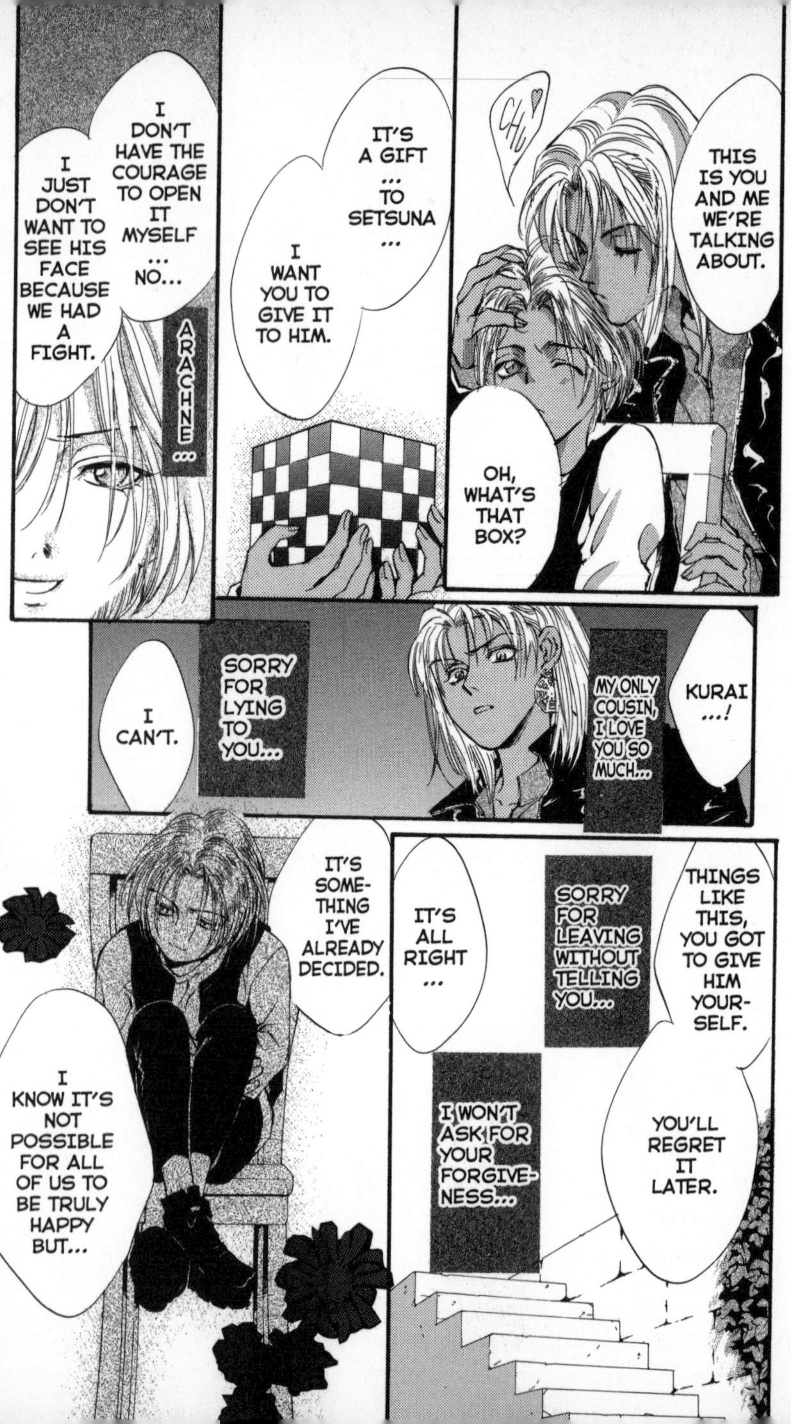
CHU ♡
THIS IS YOU AND ME WE'RE TALKING ABOUT.
OH, WHAT'S THAT BOX?
IT'S A GIFT ... TO SETSUNA ...
I WANT YOU TO GIVE IT TO HIM.
I DON'T HAVE THE COURAGE TO OPEN IT MYSELF ... NO...
I JUST DON'T WANT TO SEE HIS FACE BECAUSE WE HAD A FIGHT.
ARACHNE...
KURAI ...!
MY ONLY COUSIN, I LOVE YOU SO MUCH...
SORRY FOR LYING TO YOU...
I CAN'T.
THINGS LIKE THIS, YOU GOT TO GIVE HIM YOUR-SELF.
YOU'LL REGRET IT LATER.
SORRY FOR LEAVING WITHOUT TELLING YOU...
IT'S ALL RIGHT ...
I WON'T ASK FOR YOUR FORGIVE-NESS...
IT'S SOME-THING I'VE ALREADY DECIDED.
I KNOW IT'S NOT POSSIBLE FOR ALL OF US TO BE TRULY HAPPY BUT...

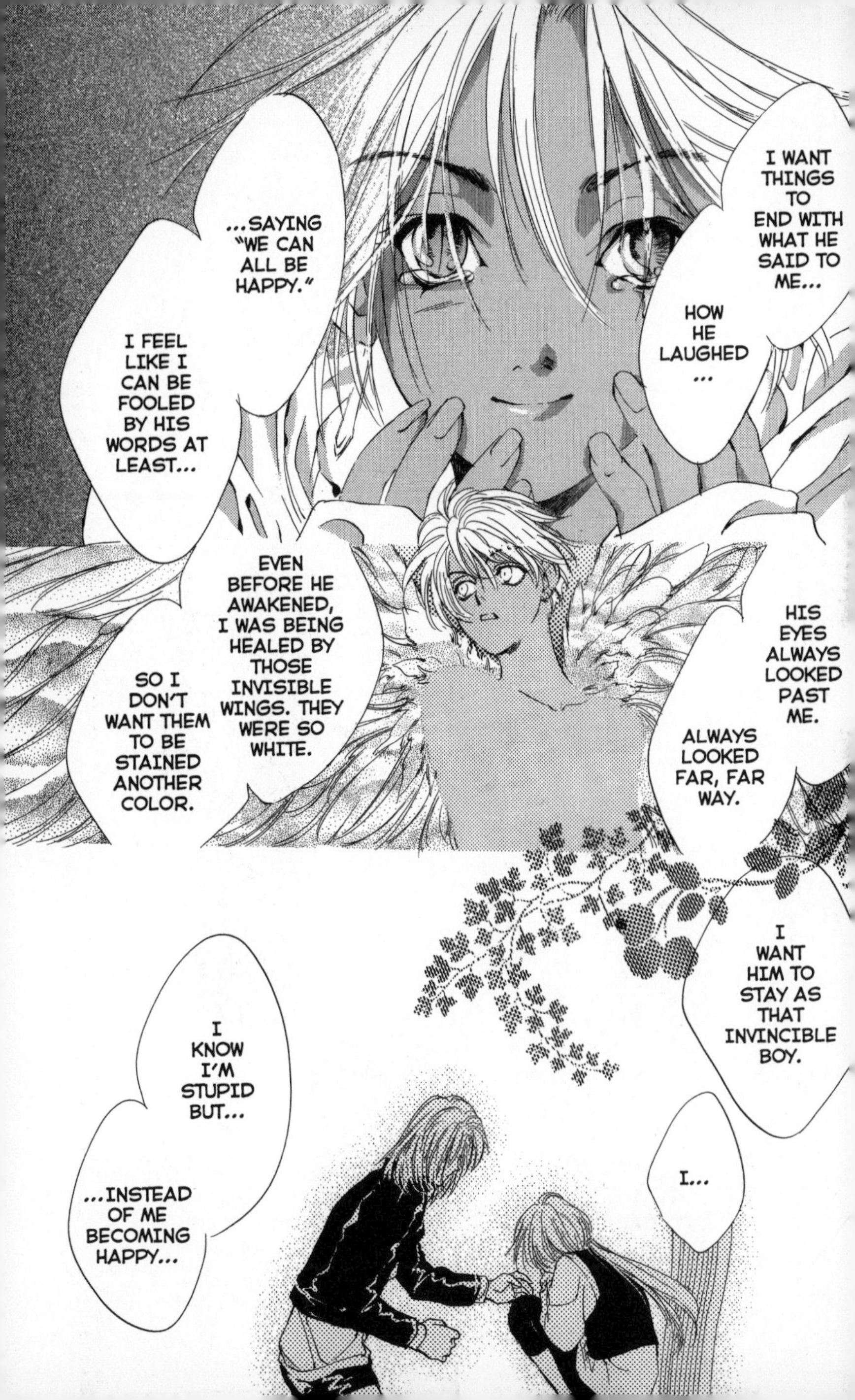
I WANT THINGS TO END WITH WHAT HE SAID TO ME...
HOW HE LAUGHED...
...SAYING "WE CAN ALL BE HAPPY."
I FEEL LIKE I CAN BE FOOLED BY HIS WORDS AT LEAST...
HIS EYES ALWAYS LOOKED PAST ME.
ALWAYS LOOKED FAR, FAR WAY.
EVEN BEFORE HE AWAKENED, I WAS BEING HEALED BY THOSE INVISIBLE WINGS. THEY WERE SO WHITE.
SO I DON'T WANT THEM TO BE STAINED ANOTHER COLOR.
I WANT HIM TO STAY AS THAT INVINCIBLE BOY.
I...
I KNOW I'M STUPID BUT...
...INSTEAD OF ME BECOMING HAPPY...

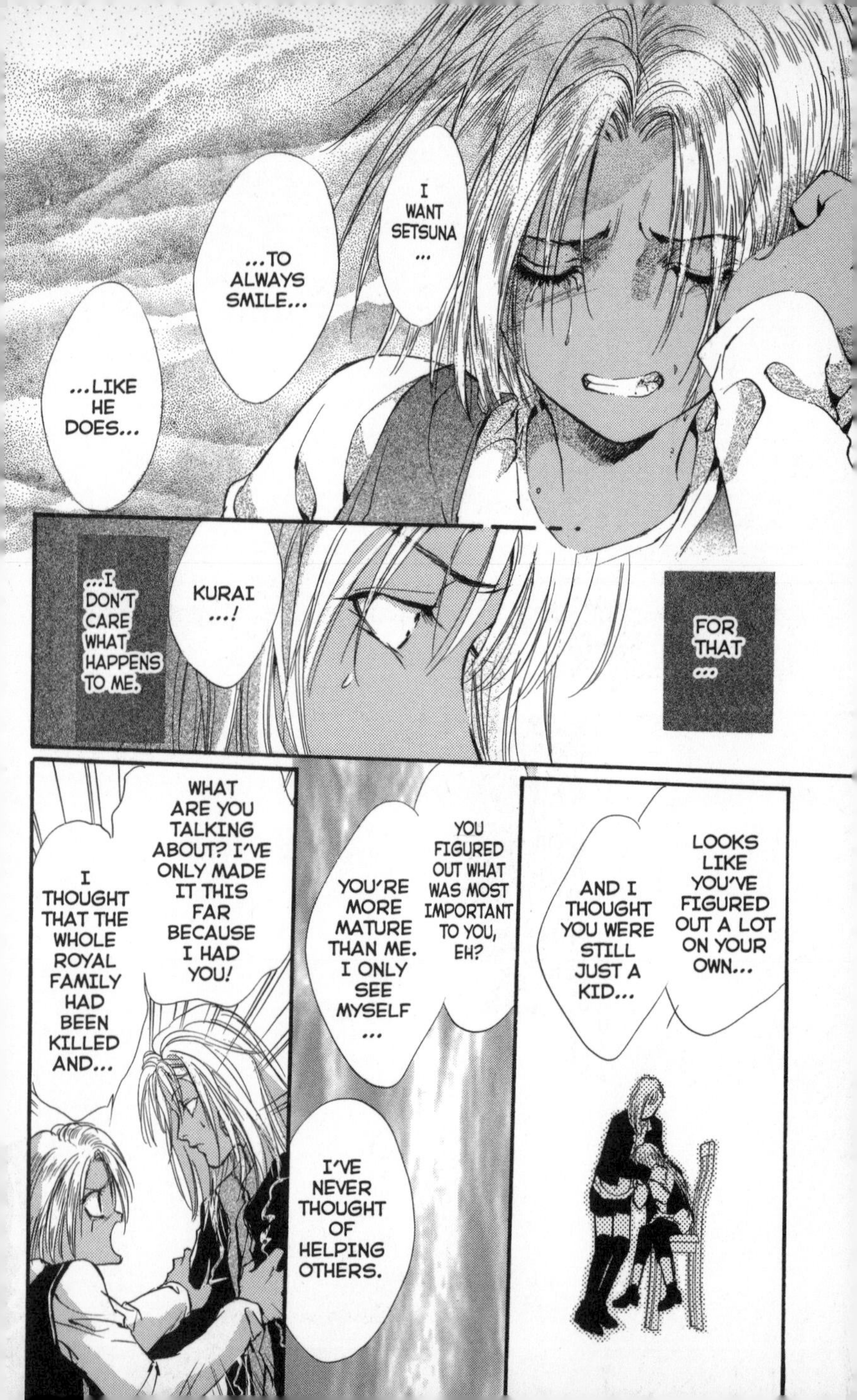
I WANT SETSUNA ...
...TO ALWAYS SMILE...
...LIKE HE DOES...
FOR THAT ...
KURAI ...!
...I DON'T CARE WHAT HAPPENS TO ME.
LOOKS LIKE YOU'VE FIGURED OUT A LOT ON YOUR OWN...
AND I THOUGHT YOU WERE STILL JUST A KID...
YOU FIGURED OUT WHAT WAS MOST IMPORTANT TO YOU, EH?
YOU'RE MORE MATURE THAN ME. I ONLY SEE MYSELF ...
I'VE NEVER THOUGHT OF HELPING OTHERS.
WHAT ARE YOU TALKING ABOUT? I'VE ONLY MADE IT THIS FAR BECAUSE I HAD YOU!
I THOUGHT THAT THE WHOLE ROYAL FAMILY HAD BEEN KILLED AND...

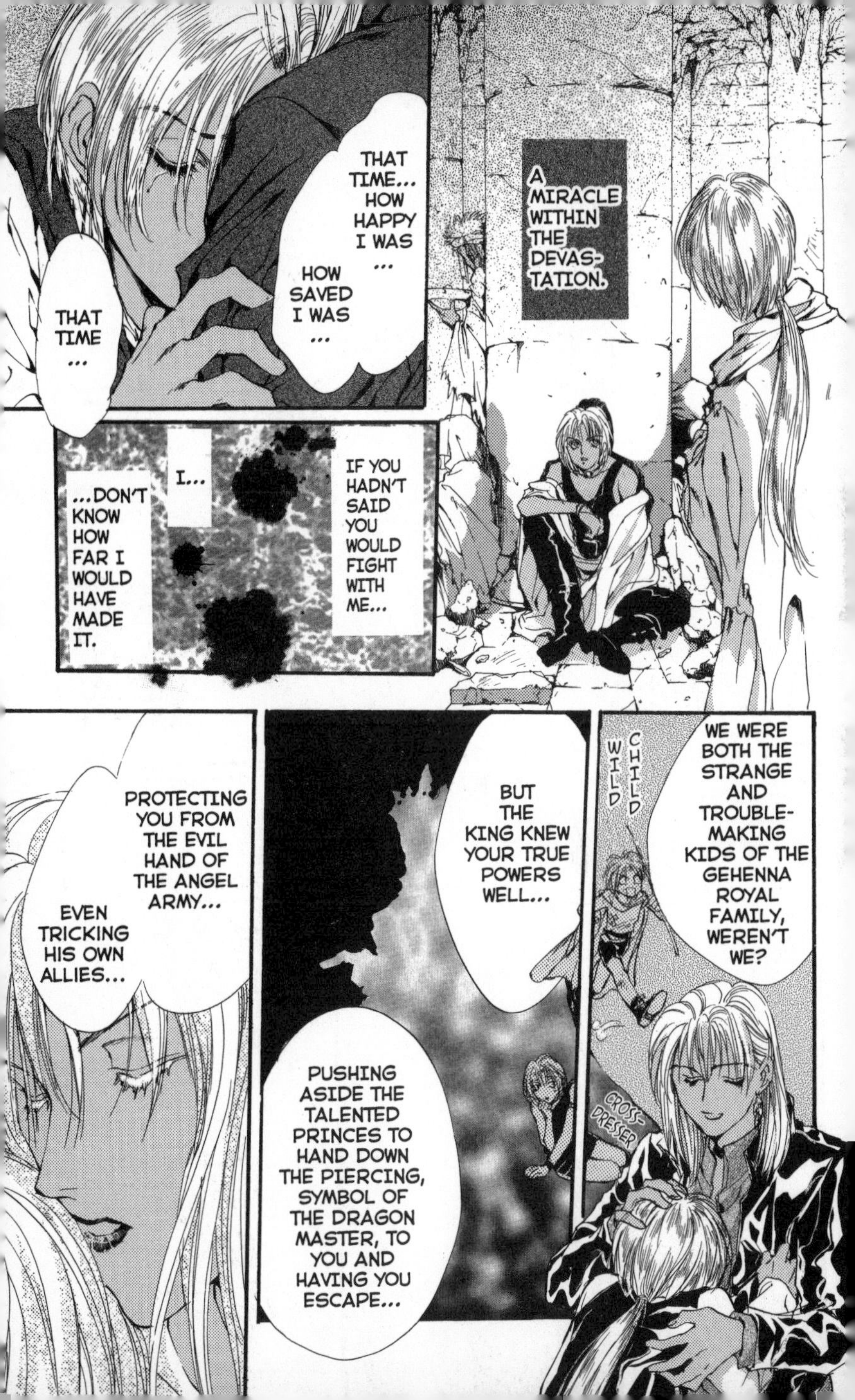
A MIRACLE WITHIN THE DEVASTATION.
THAT TIME... HOW HAPPY I WAS...
HOW SAVED I WAS...
THAT TIME...
IF YOU HADN'T SAID YOU WOULD FIGHT WITH ME...
I...
...DON'T KNOW HOW FAR I WOULD HAVE MADE IT.
WE WERE BOTH THE STRANGE AND TROUBLE-MAKING KIDS OF THE GEHENNA ROYAL FAMILY, WEREN'T WE?
WILD CHILD
CROSS-DRESSER
BUT THE KING KNEW YOUR TRUE POWERS WELL...
PUSHING ASIDE THE TALENTED PRINCES TO HAND DOWN THE PIERCING, SYMBOL OF THE DRAGON MASTER, TO YOU AND HAVING YOU ESCAPE...
PROTECTING YOU FROM THE EVIL HAND OF THE ANGEL ARMY...
EVEN TRICKING HIS OWN ALLIES...

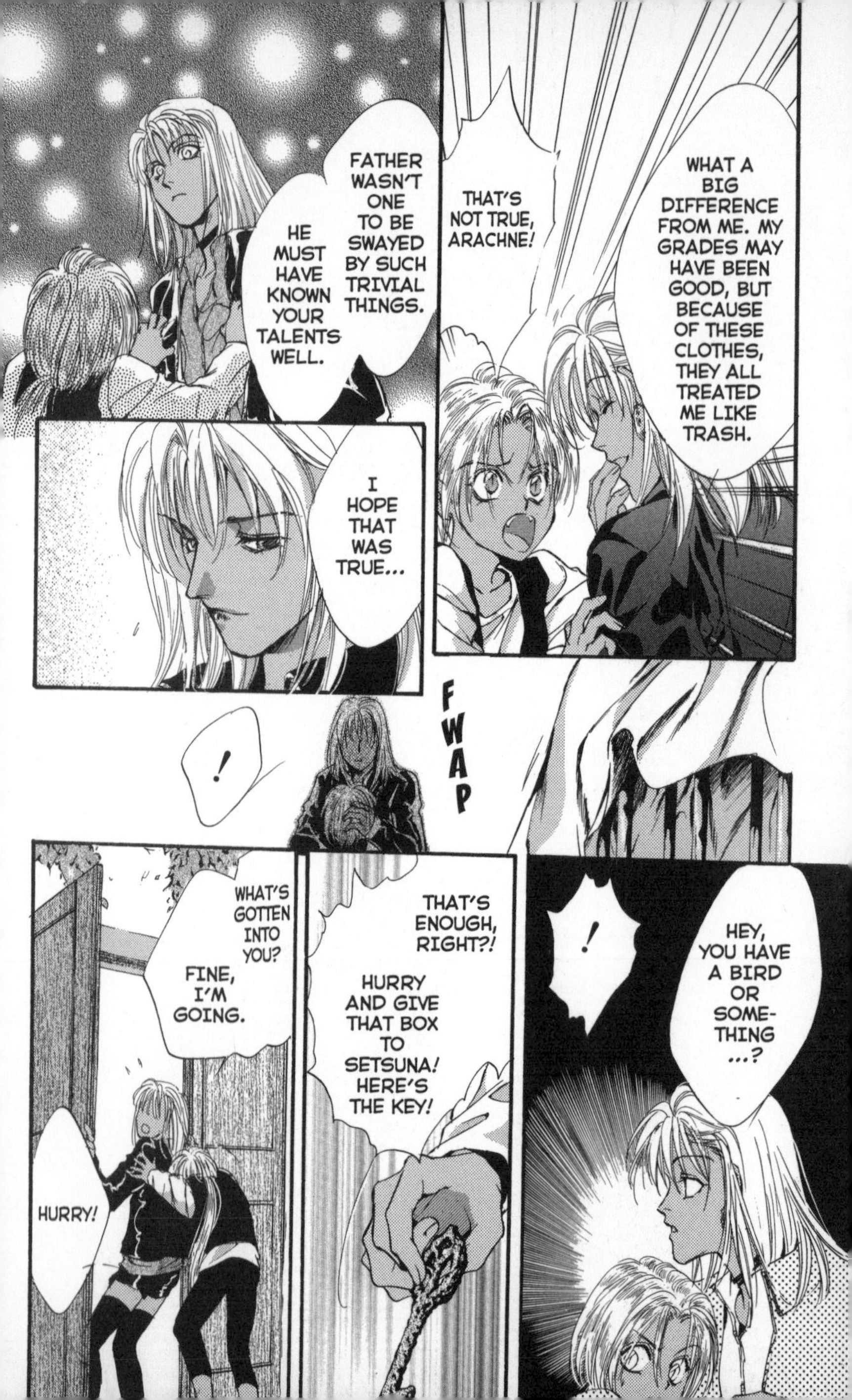
WHAT A BIG DIFFERENCE FROM ME. MY GRADES MAY HAVE BEEN GOOD, BUT BECAUSE OF THESE CLOTHES, THEY ALL TREATED ME LIKE TRASH.
THAT'S NOT TRUE, ARACHNE!
FATHER WASN'T ONE TO BE SWAYED BY SUCH TRIVIAL THINGS.
HE MUST HAVE KNOWN YOUR TALENTS WELL.
I HOPE THAT WAS TRUE...
FWAP
!
!
HEY, YOU HAVE A BIRD OR SOME-THING ...?
THAT'S ENOUGH, RIGHT?!
HURRY AND GIVE THAT BOX TO SETSUNA! HERE'S THE KEY!
WHAT'S GOTTEN INTO YOU?
FINE, I'M GOING.
HURRY!

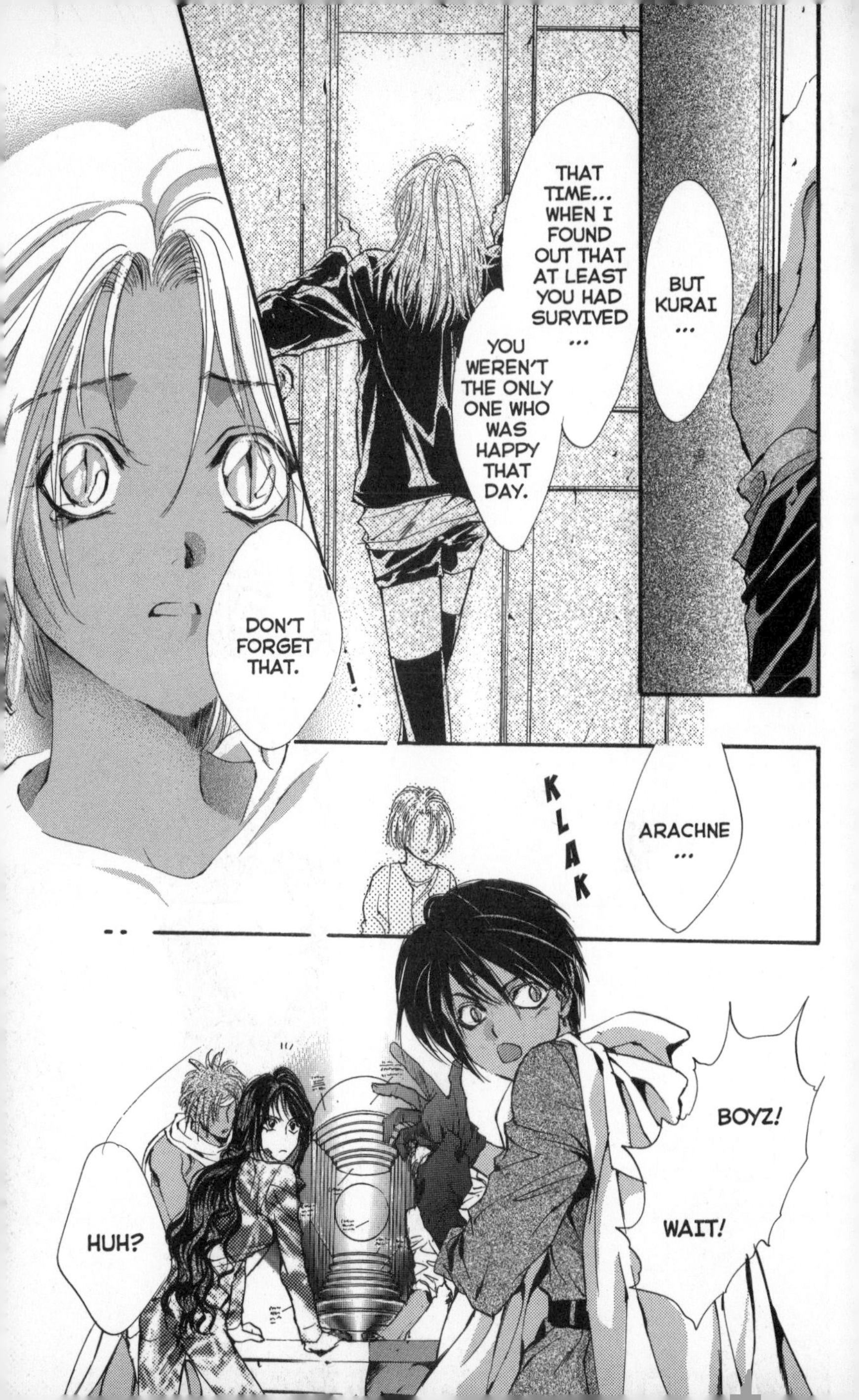
BUT KURAI ...
THAT TIME... WHEN I FOUND OUT THAT AT LEAST YOU HAD SURVIVED ...
YOU WEREN'T THE ONLY ONE WHO WAS HAPPY THAT DAY.
DON'T FORGET THAT.
!
ARACHNE ...
KLAK
BOYZ!
WAIT!
HUH?

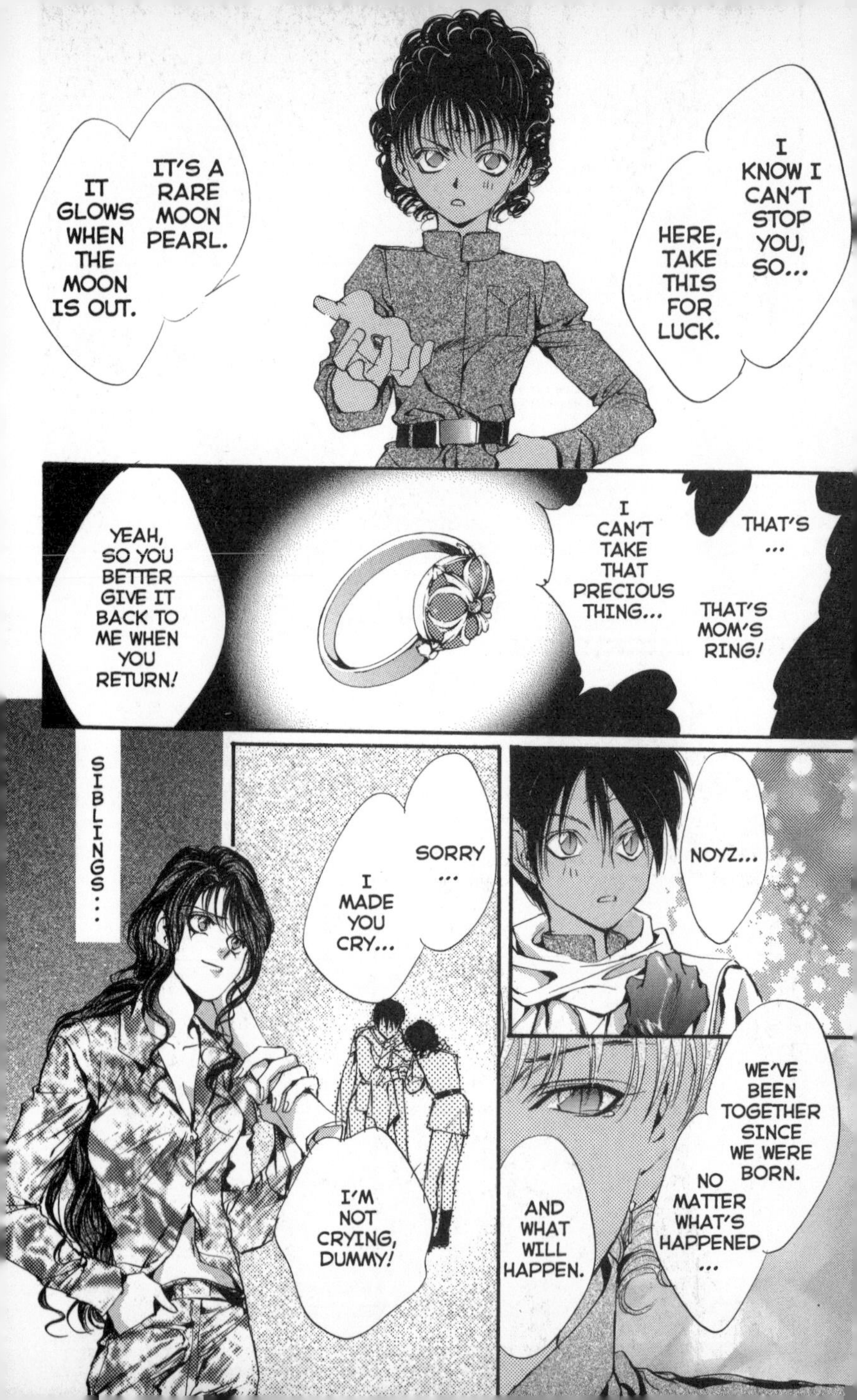
I KNOW I CAN'T STOP YOU, SO...
HERE, TAKE THIS FOR LUCK.
IT'S A RARE MOON PEARL.
IT GLOWS WHEN THE MOON IS OUT.
THAT'S...
THAT'S MOM'S RING!
I CAN'T TAKE THAT PRECIOUS THING...
YEAH, SO YOU BETTER GIVE IT BACK TO ME WHEN YOU RETURN!
NOYZ...
WE'VE BEEN TOGETHER SINCE WE WERE BORN.
NO MATTER WHAT'S HAPPENED...
AND WHAT WILL HAPPEN.
SORRY...
I MADE YOU CRY...
I'M NOT CRYING, DUMMY!
SIBLINGS...

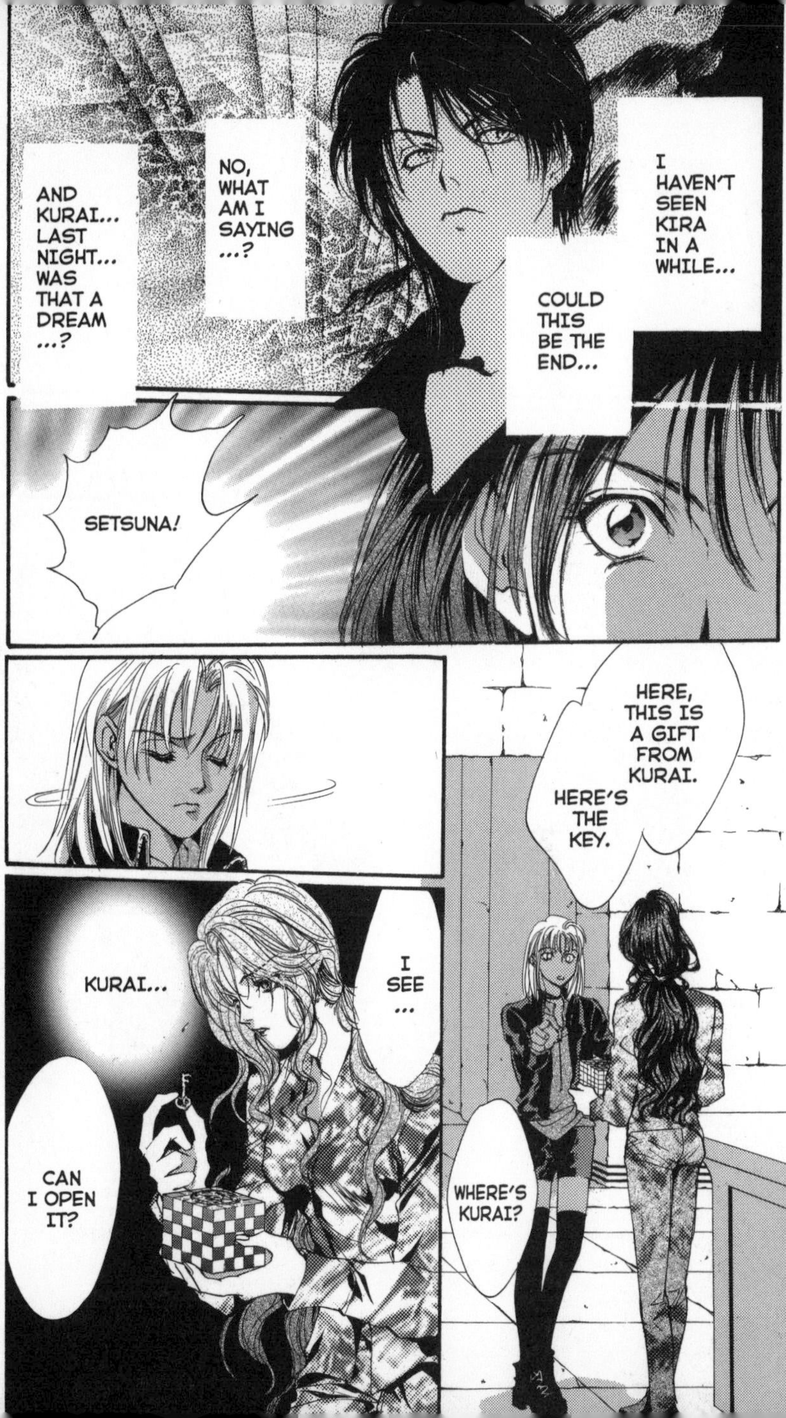
I HAVEN'T SEEN KIRA IN A WHILE...
COULD THIS BE THE END...
NO, WHAT AM I SAYING ...?
AND KURAI... LAST NIGHT... WAS THAT A DREAM ...?
SETSUNA!
HERE, THIS IS A GIFT FROM KURAI.
HERE'S THE KEY.
WHERE'S KURAI?
I SEE ...
KURAI...
CAN I OPEN IT?

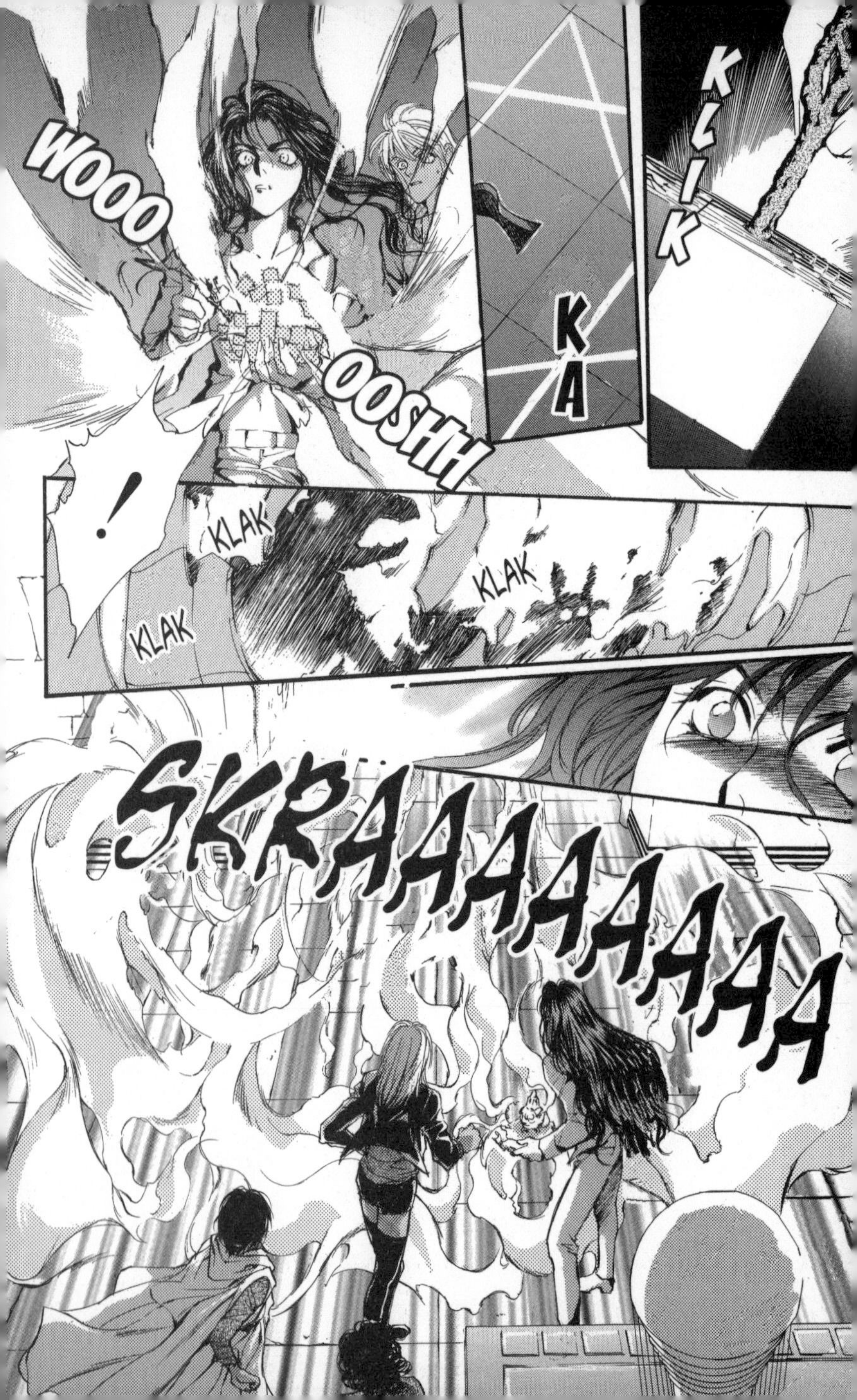
KLIK
KA
WOOO
OOSHH
!
KLAK
KLAK
KLAK
SKRAAAAAAAAAA

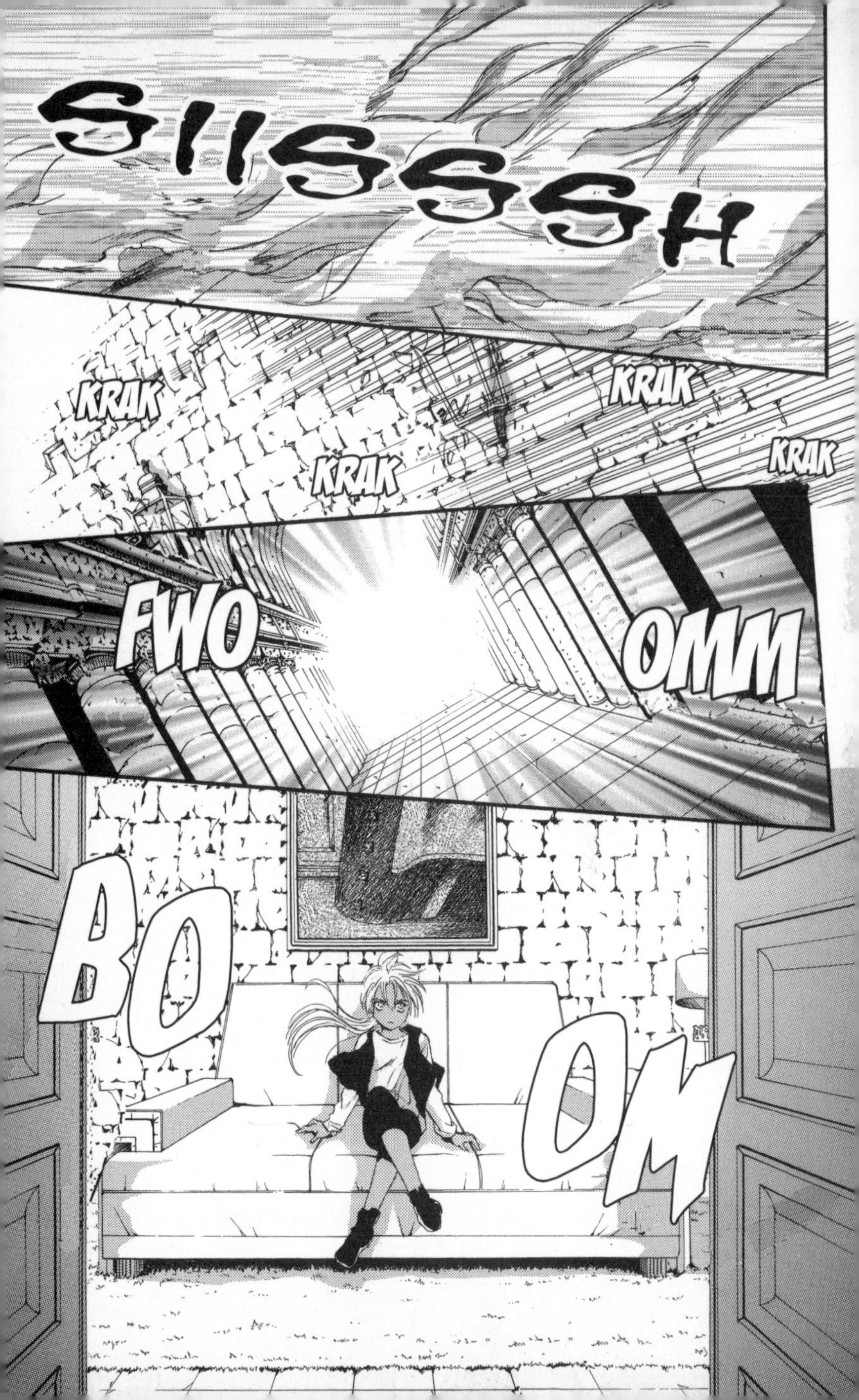
SIISSSH
KRAK
KRAK
KRAK
KRAK
FWOOMM
BOOM

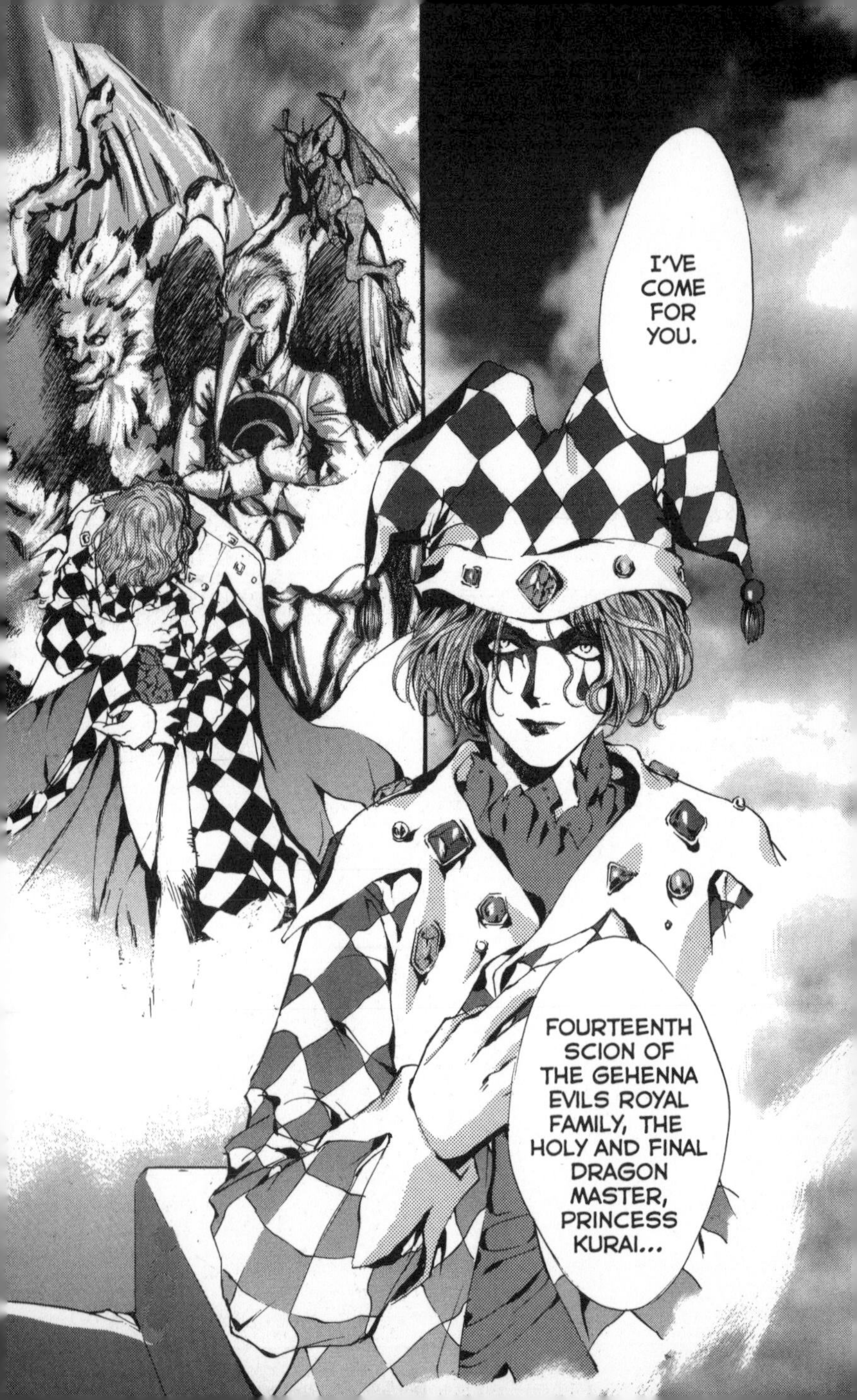
I'VE COME FOR YOU.
FOURTEENTH SCION OF THE GEHENNA EVILS ROYAL FAMILY, THE HOLY AND FINAL DRAGON MASTER, PRINCESS KURAI...

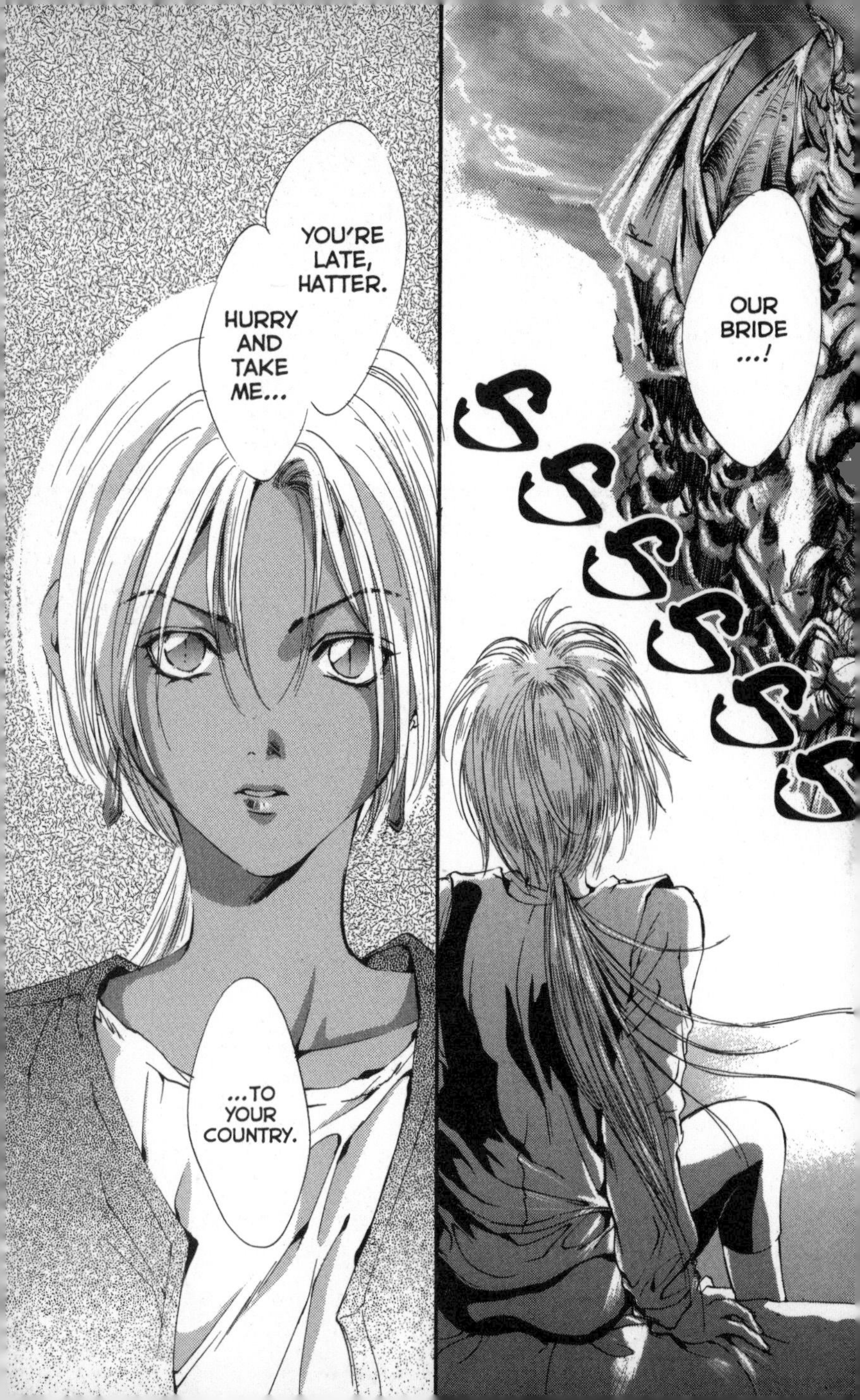
OUR BRIDE ...!
YOU'RE LATE, HATTER.
HURRY AND TAKE ME...
...TO YOUR COUNTRY.

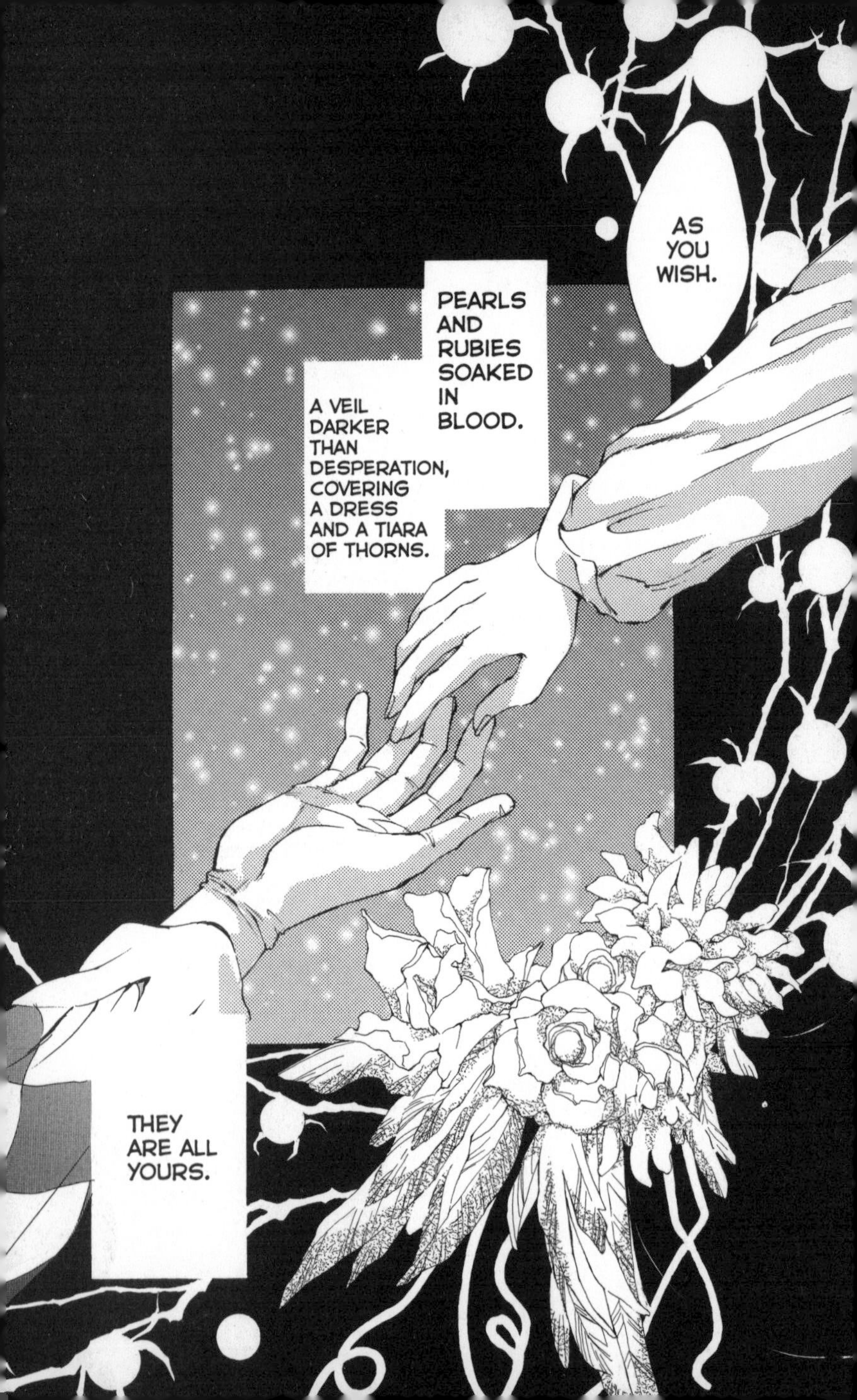
AS YOU WISH.
PEARLS AND RUBIES SOAKED IN BLOOD.
A VEIL DARKER THAN DESPERATION, COVERING A DRESS AND A TIARA OF THORNS.
THEY ARE ALL YOURS.

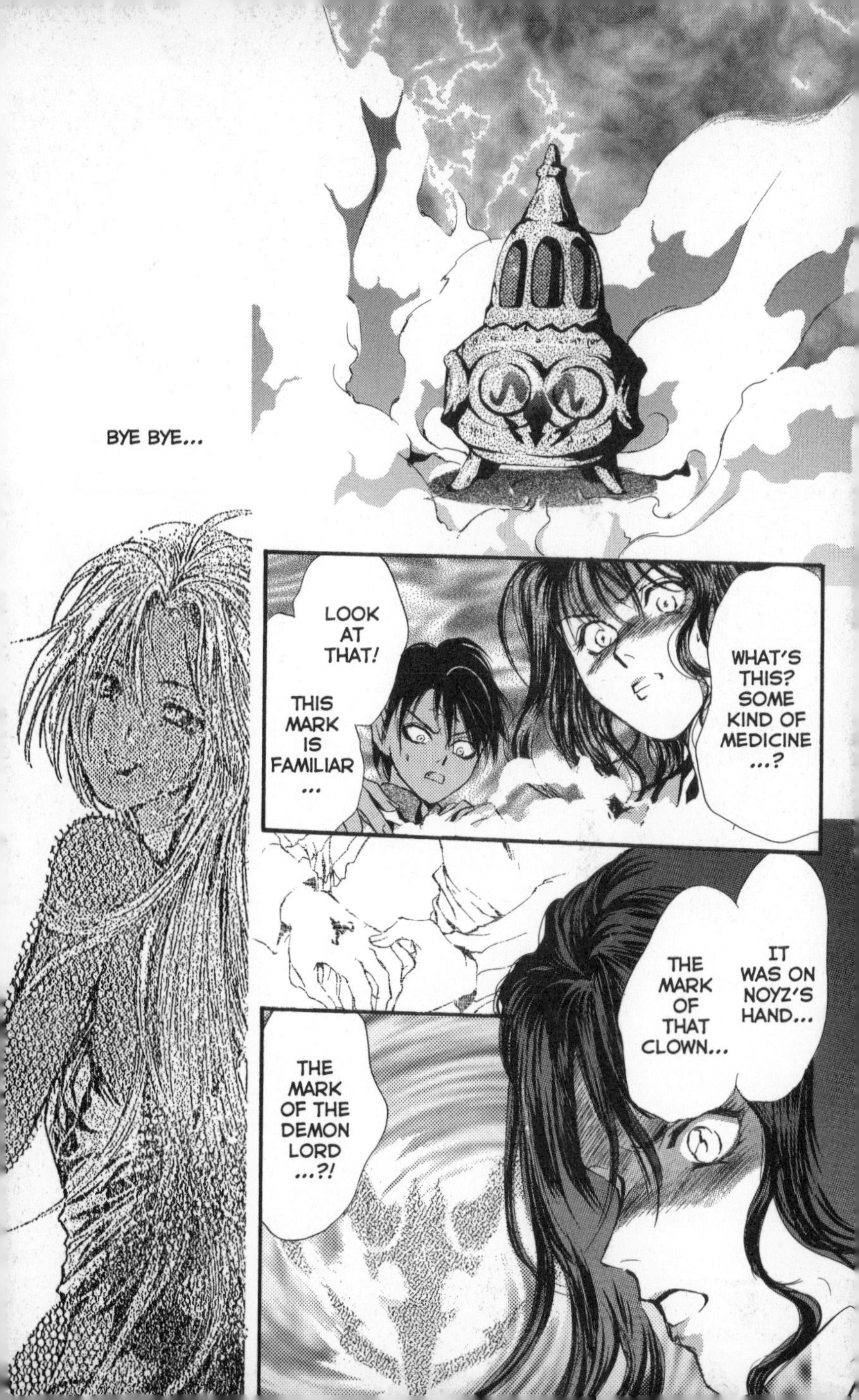
WHAT'S THIS? SOME KIND OF MEDICINE ...?
LOOK AT THAT!
THIS MARK IS FAMILIAR ...
IT WAS ON NOYZ'S HAND...
THE MARK OF THAT CLOWN...
THE MARK OF THE DEMON LORD ...?!
BYE BYE...

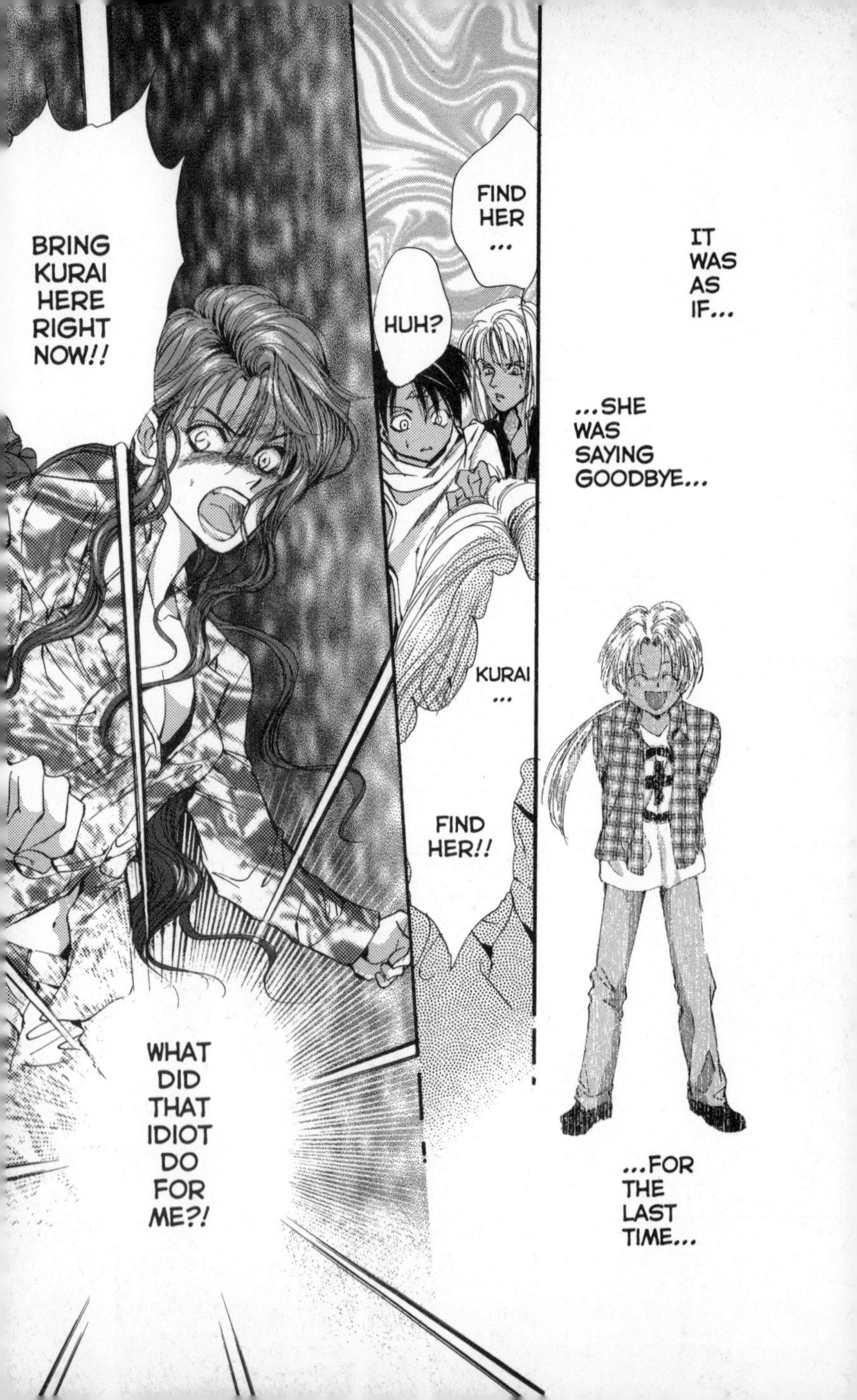
IT WAS AS IF...
...SHE WAS SAYING GOODBYE...
...FOR THE LAST TIME...
FIND HER...
HUH?
KURAI...
FIND HER!!
BRING KURAI HERE RIGHT NOW!!
WHAT DID THAT IDIOT DO FOR ME?!

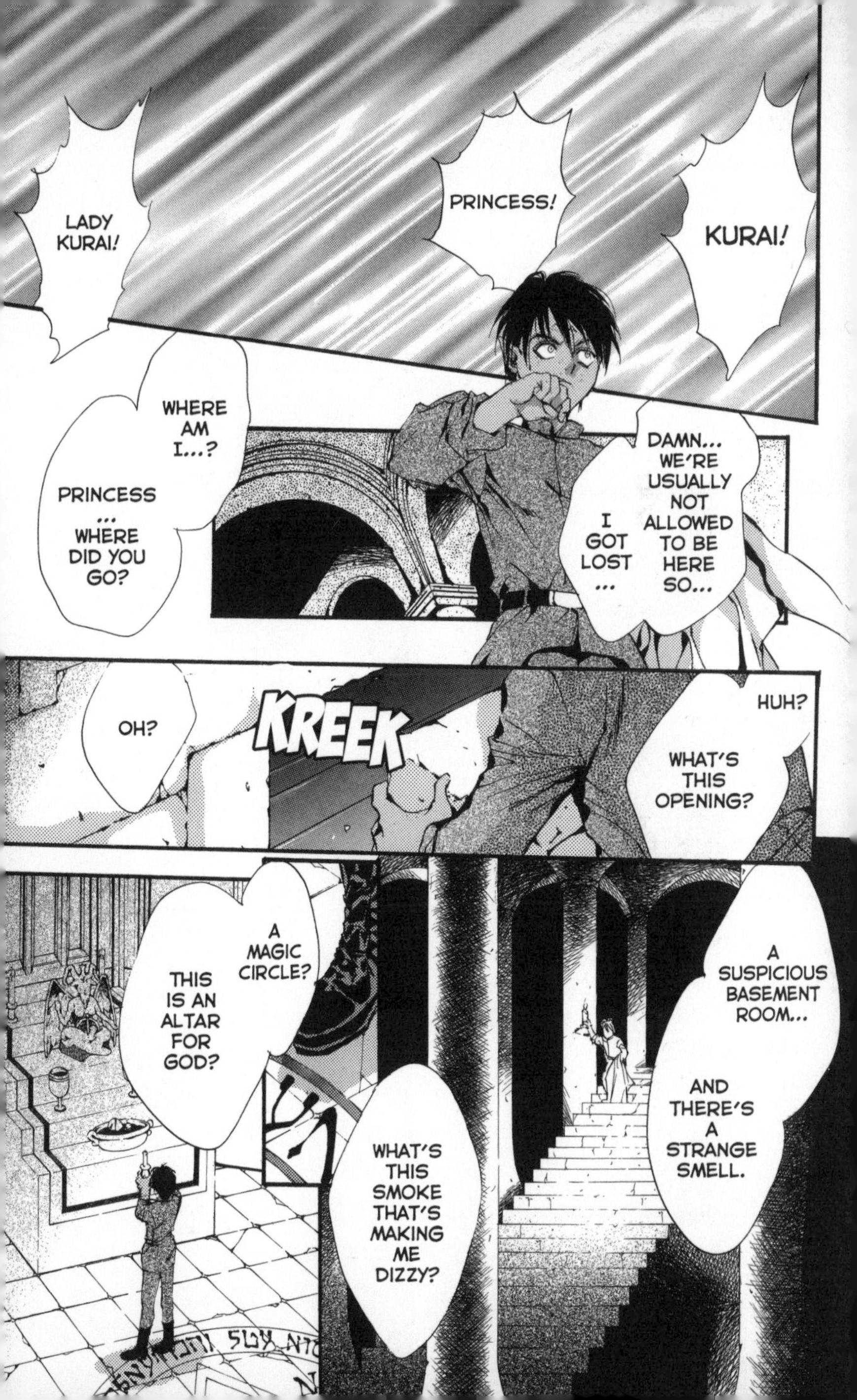
KURAI!
PRINCESS!
LADY KURAI!
DAMN... WE'RE USUALLY NOT ALLOWED TO BE HERE SO...
I GOT LOST ...
WHERE AM I...?
PRINCESS ... WHERE DID YOU GO?
HUH?
WHAT'S THIS OPENING?
KREEK
OH?
A SUSPICIOUS BASEMENT ROOM...
AND THERE'S A STRANGE SMELL.
A MAGIC CIRCLE?
THIS IS AN ALTAR FOR GOD?
WHAT'S THIS SMOKE THAT'S MAKING ME DIZZY?

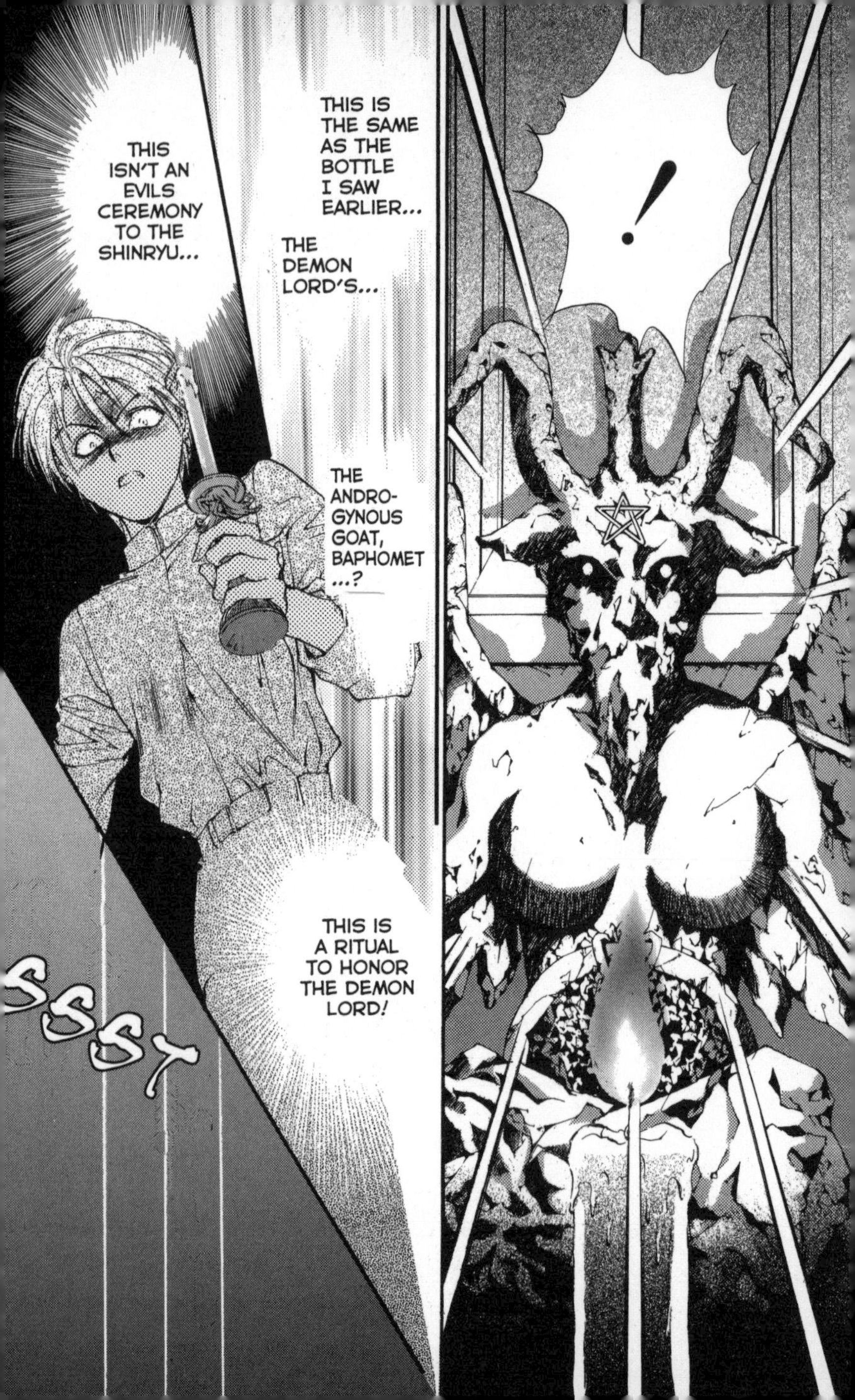
!
THIS IS THE SAME AS THE BOTTLE I SAW EARLIER...
THIS ISN'T AN EVILS CEREMONY TO THE SHINRYU...
THE DEMON LORD'S...
THE ANDRO-GYNOUS GOAT, BAPHOMET ...?
THIS IS A RITUAL TO HONOR THE DEMON LORD!
SSST

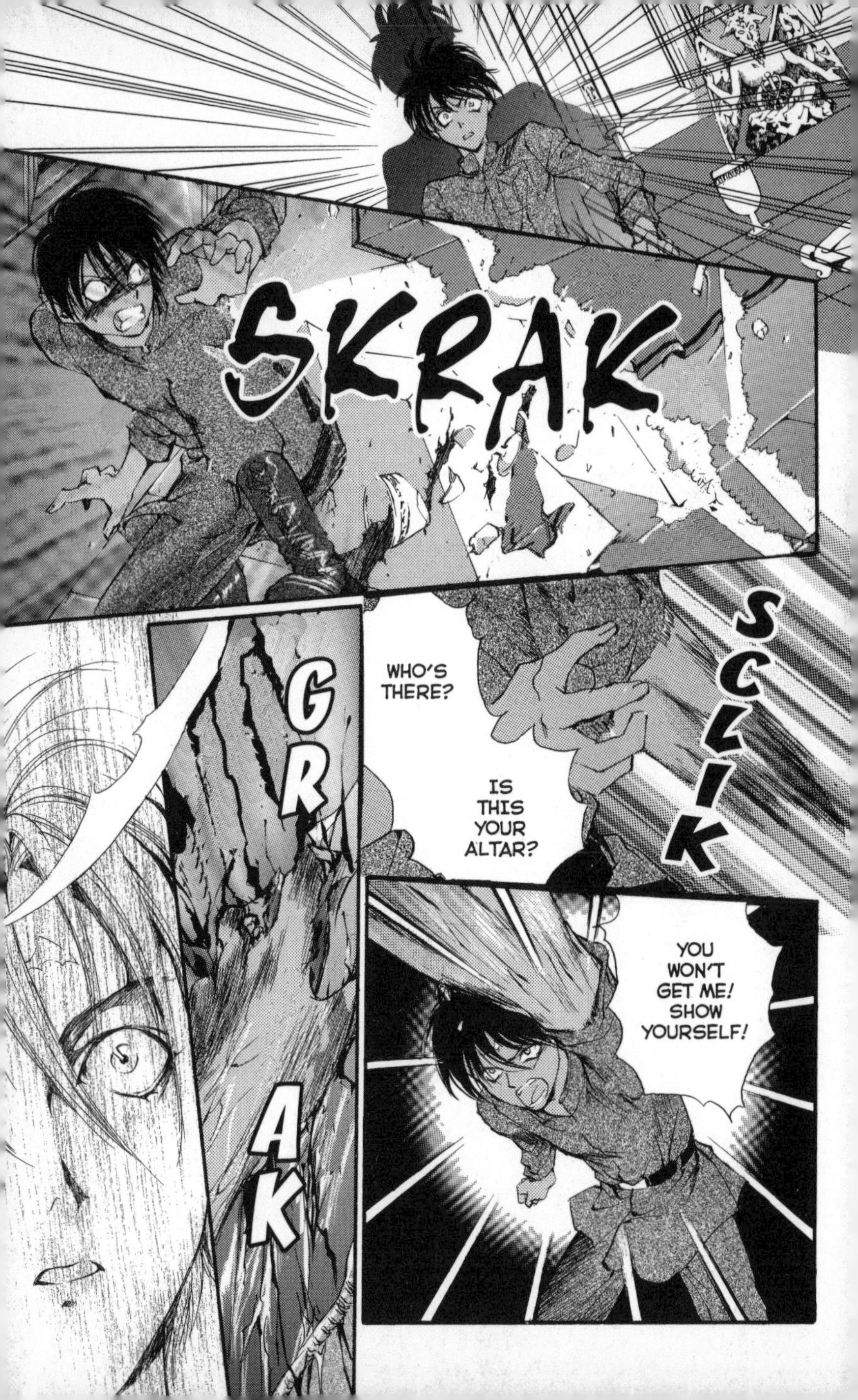
SKRAK
SCLIK
WHO'S THERE?
IS THIS YOUR ALTAR?
YOU WON'T GET ME! SHOW YOURSELF!
GRAK

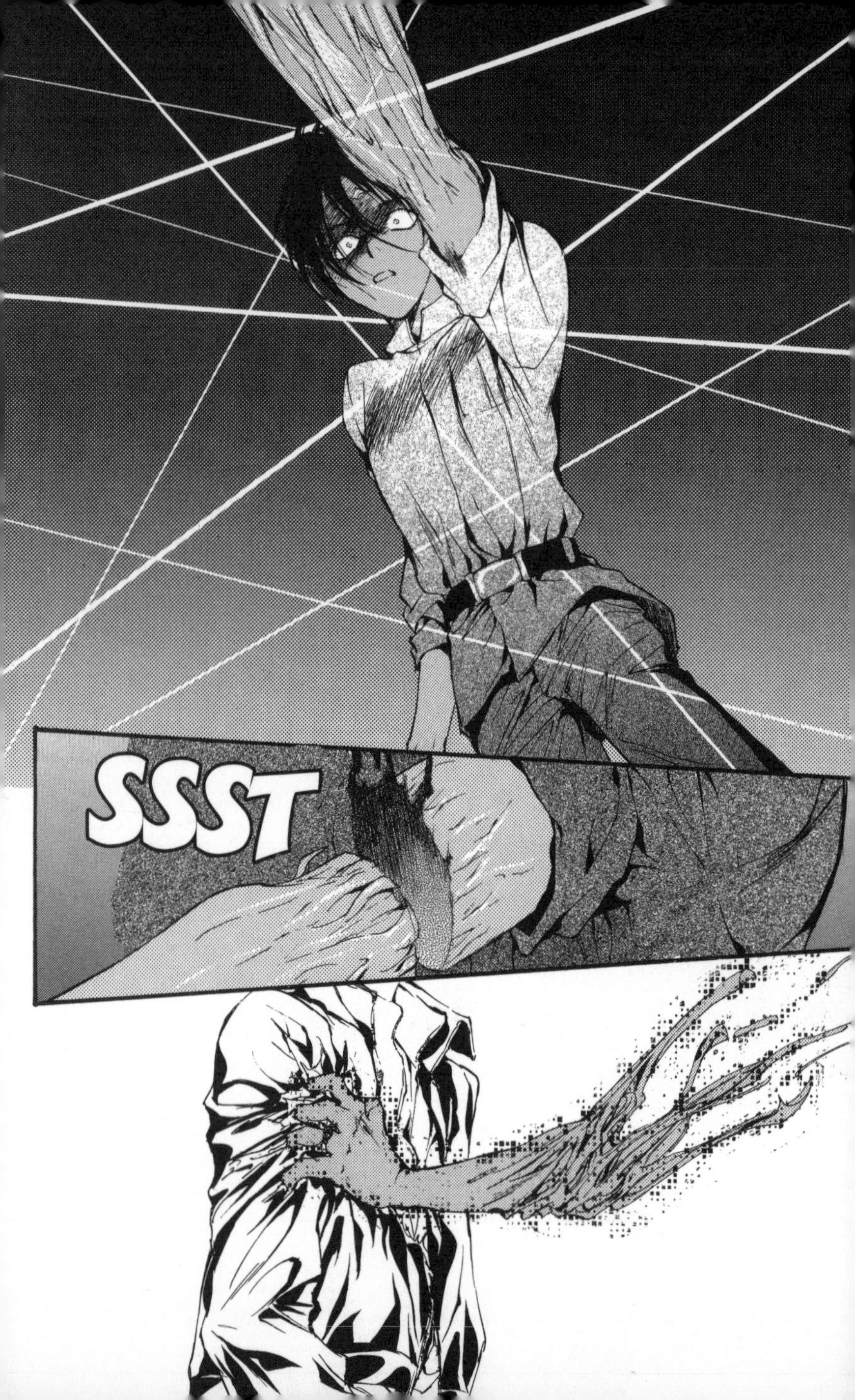
SSST

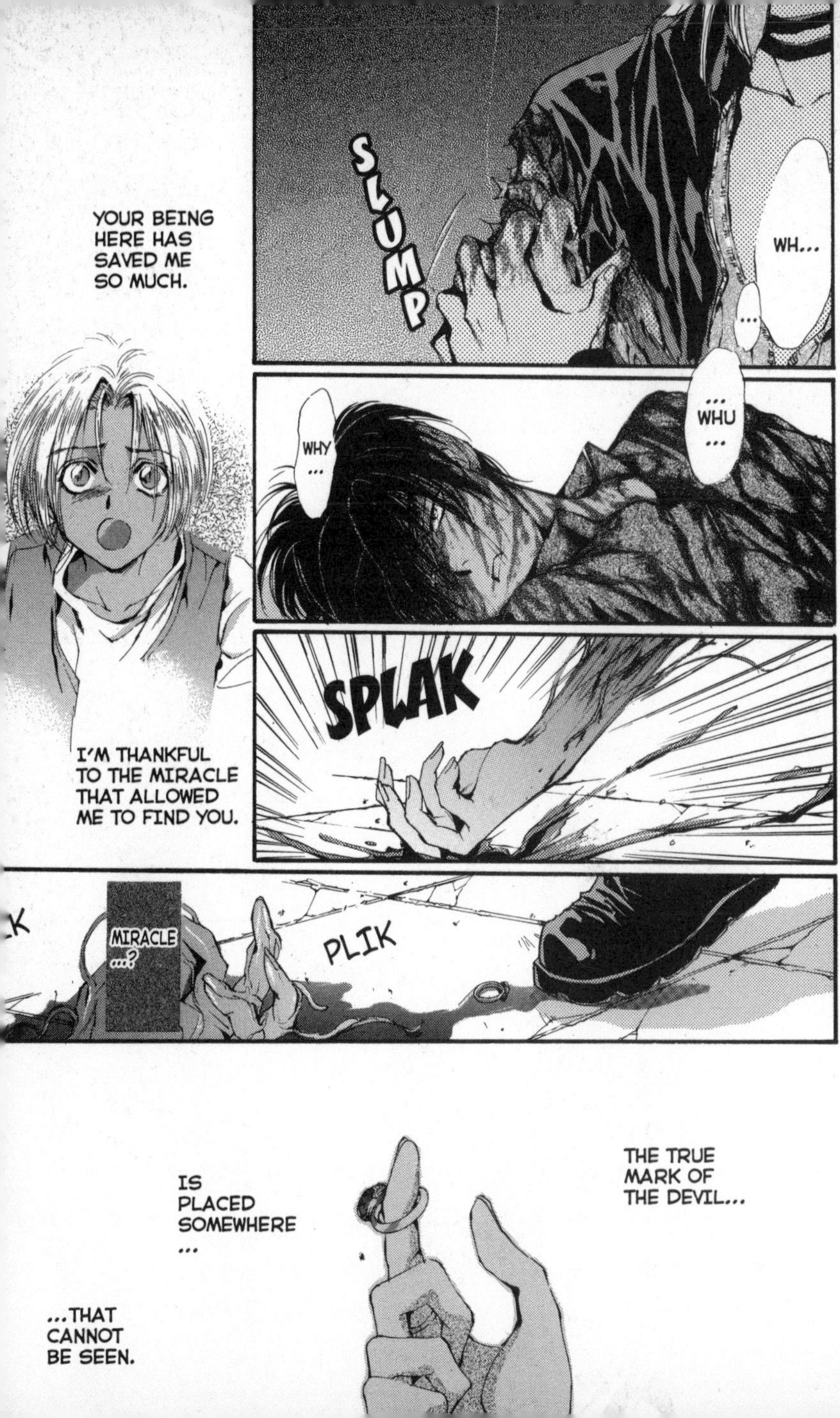
SLUMP
WH...
...
... WHU ...
WHY ...
SPLAK
YOUR BEING HERE HAS SAVED ME SO MUCH.
I'M THANKFUL TO THE MIRACLE THAT ALLOWED ME TO FIND YOU.
PLIK
MIRACLE ...?
THE TRUE MARK OF THE DEVIL...
IS PLACED SOMEWHERE ...
...THAT CANNOT BE SEEN.

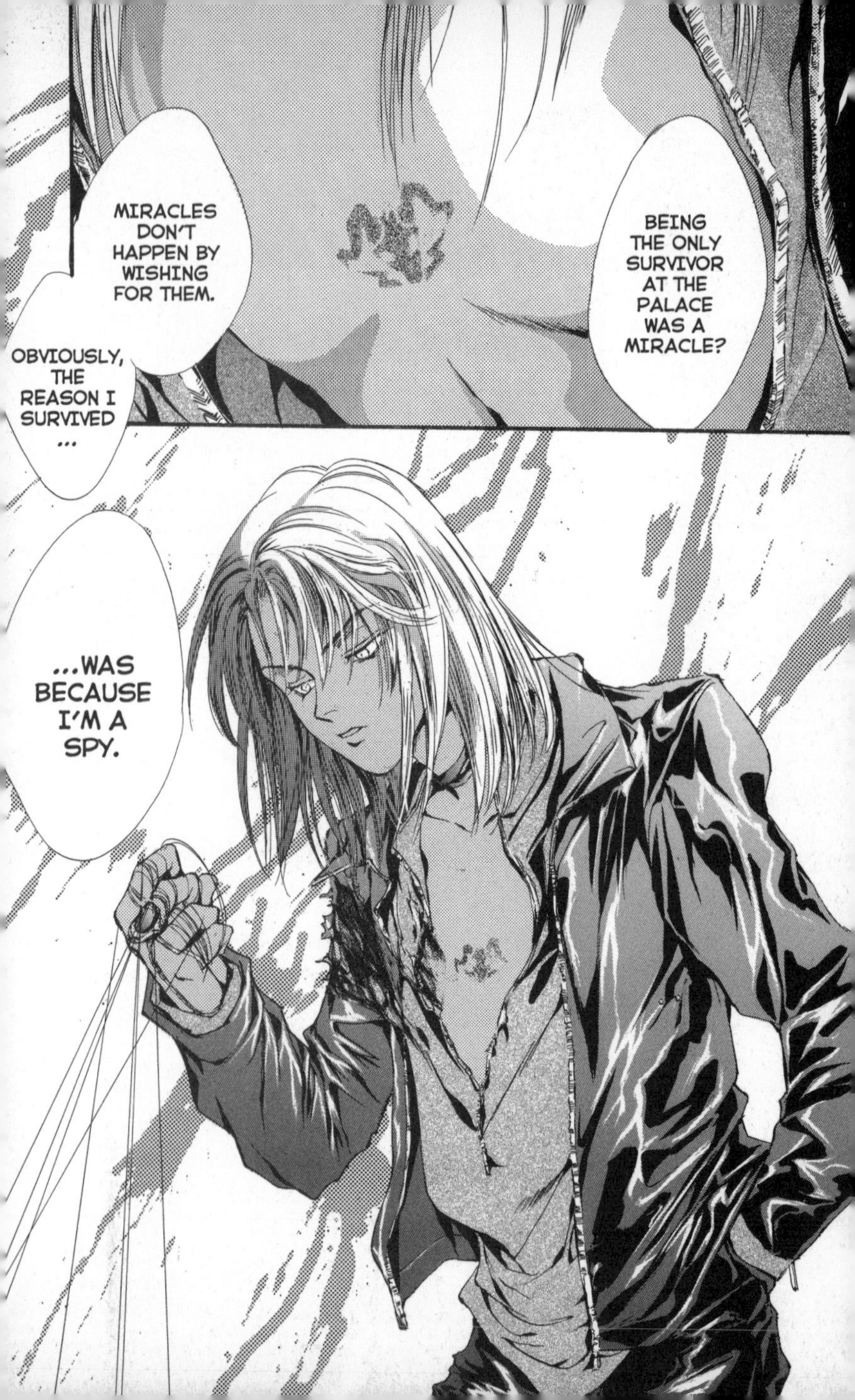
BEING THE ONLY SURVIVOR AT THE PALACE WAS A MIRACLE?
MIRACLES DON'T HAPPEN BY WISHING FOR THEM.
OBVIOUSLY, THE REASON I SURVIVED ...
...WAS BECAUSE I'M A SPY.

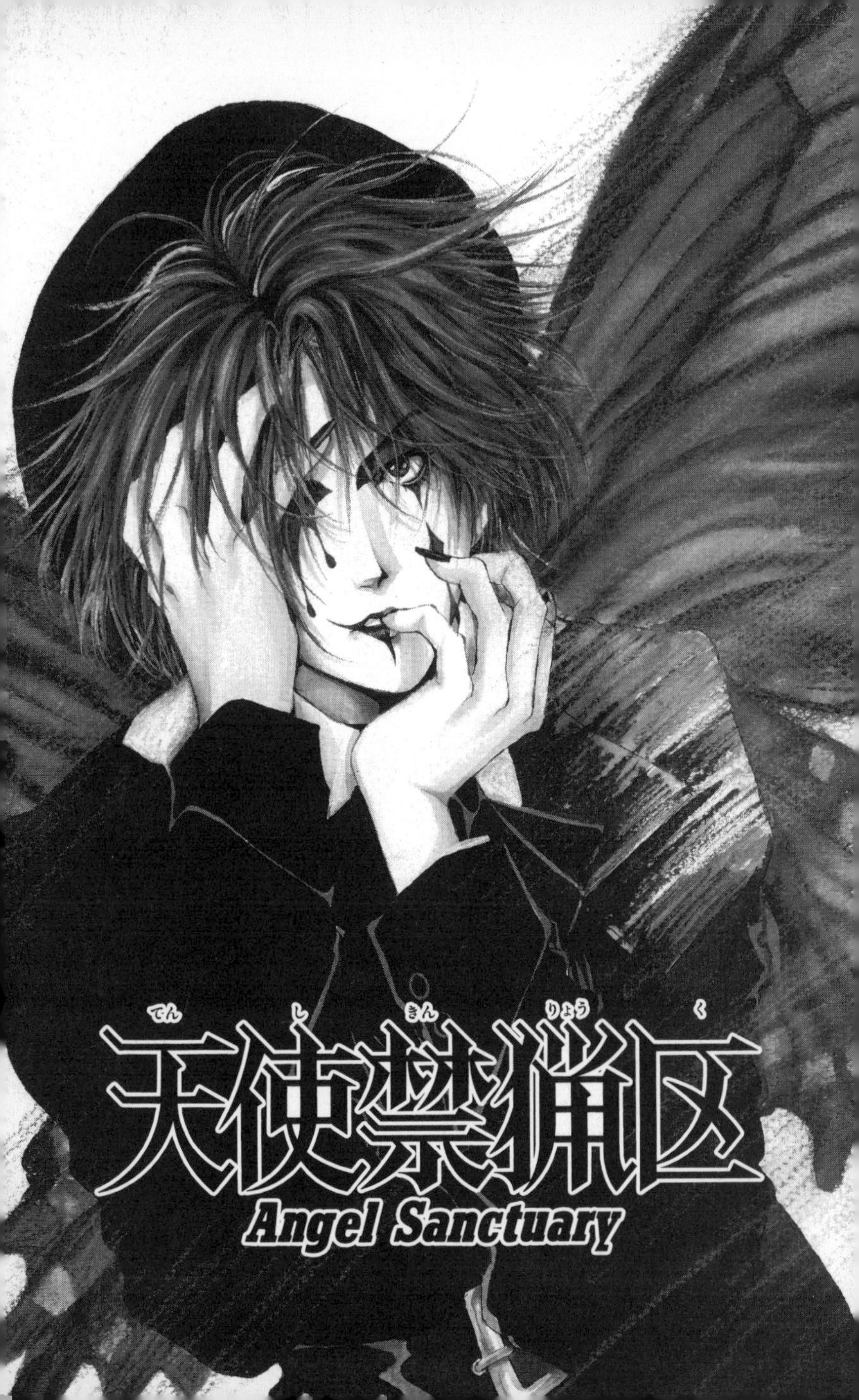
天使禁猟区
Angel Sanctuary

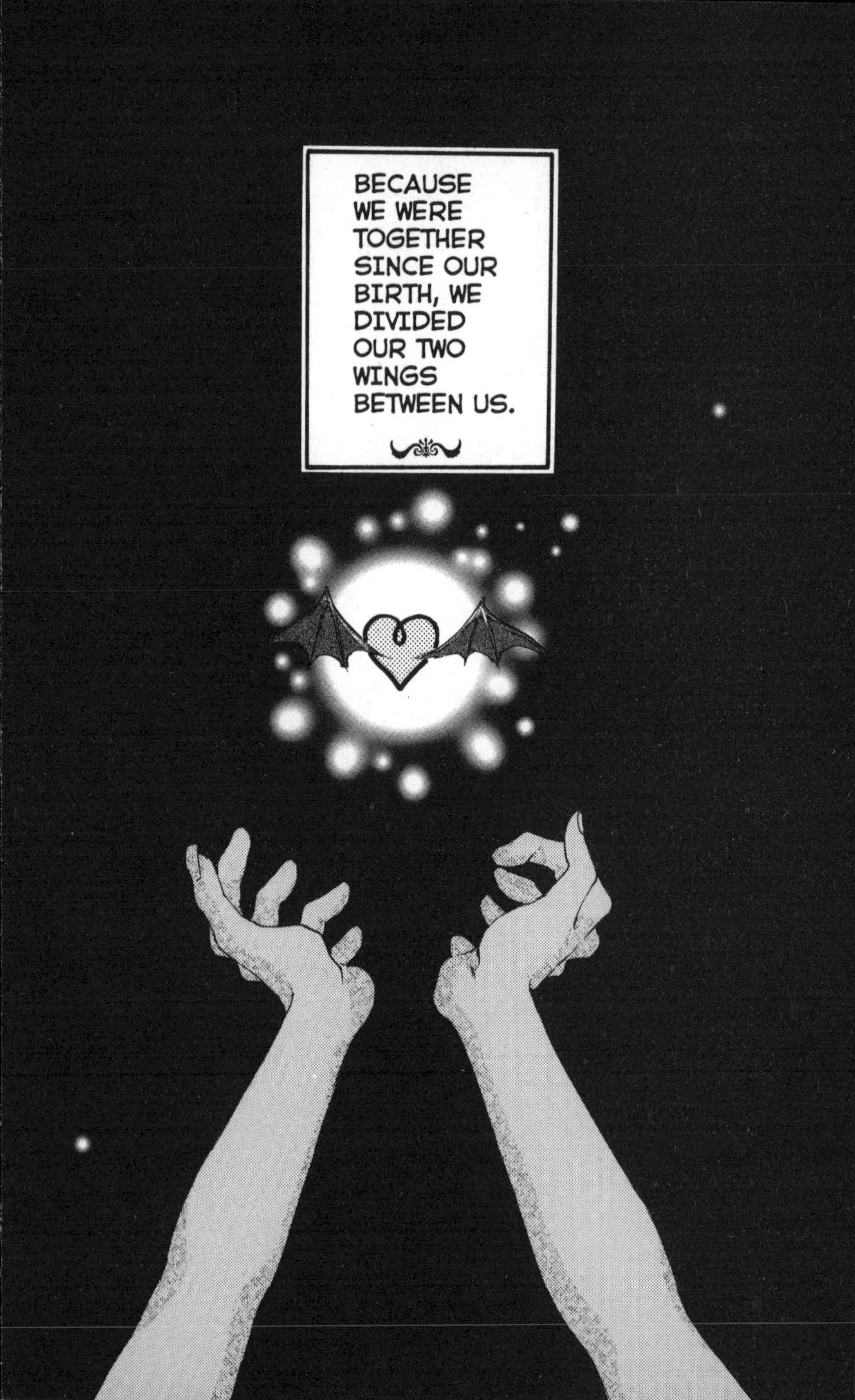
BECAUSE WE WERE TOGETHER SINCE OUR BIRTH, WE DIVIDED OUR TWO WINGS BETWEEN US.

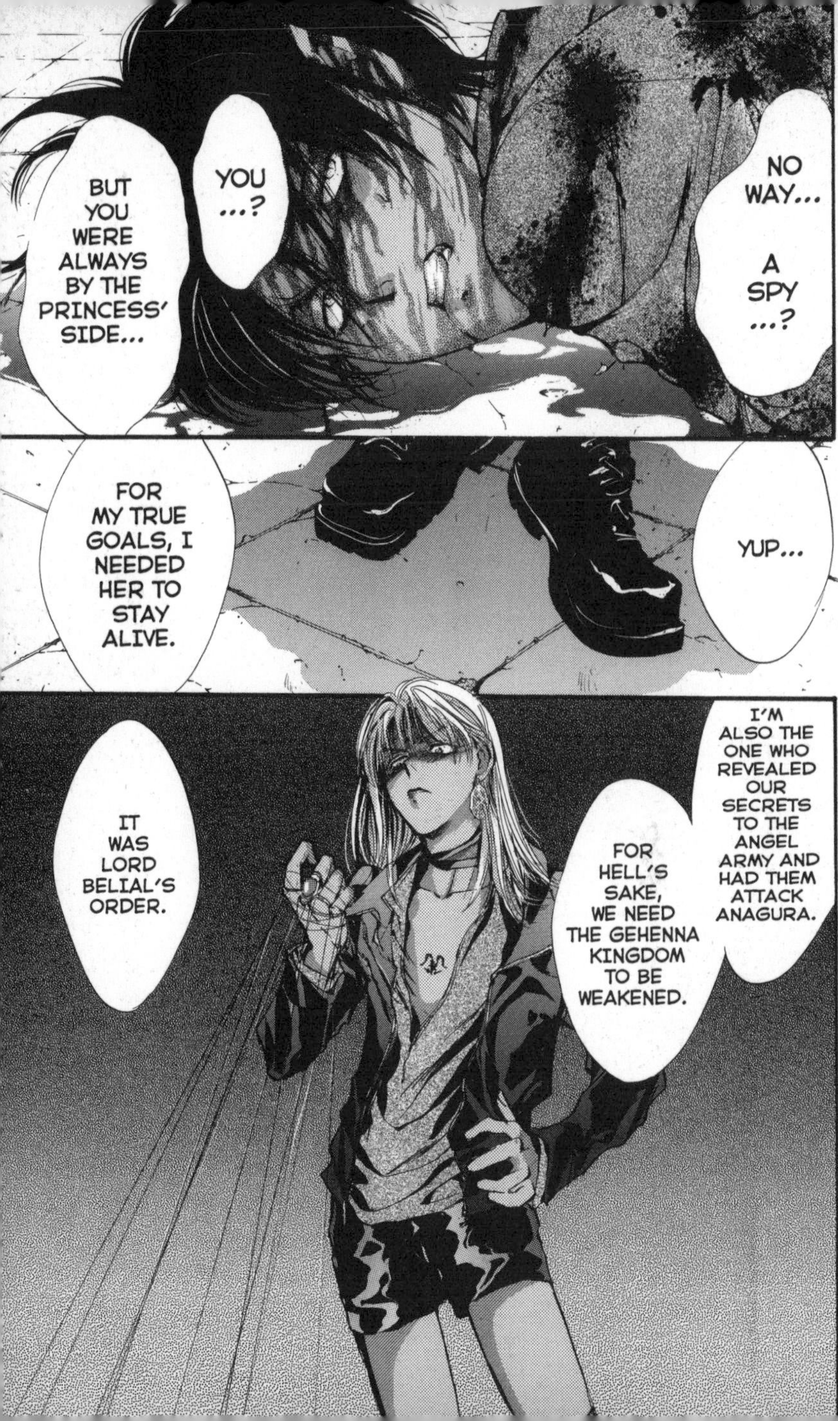
NO WAY... A SPY ...?
YOU ...?
BUT YOU WERE ALWAYS BY THE PRINCESS' SIDE...
YUP...
FOR MY TRUE GOALS, I NEEDED HER TO STAY ALIVE.
I'M ALSO THE ONE WHO REVEALED OUR SECRETS TO THE ANGEL ARMY AND HAD THEM ATTACK ANAGURA.
FOR HELL'S SAKE, WE NEED THE GEHENNA KINGDOM TO BE WEAKENED.
IT WAS LORD BELIAL'S ORDER.

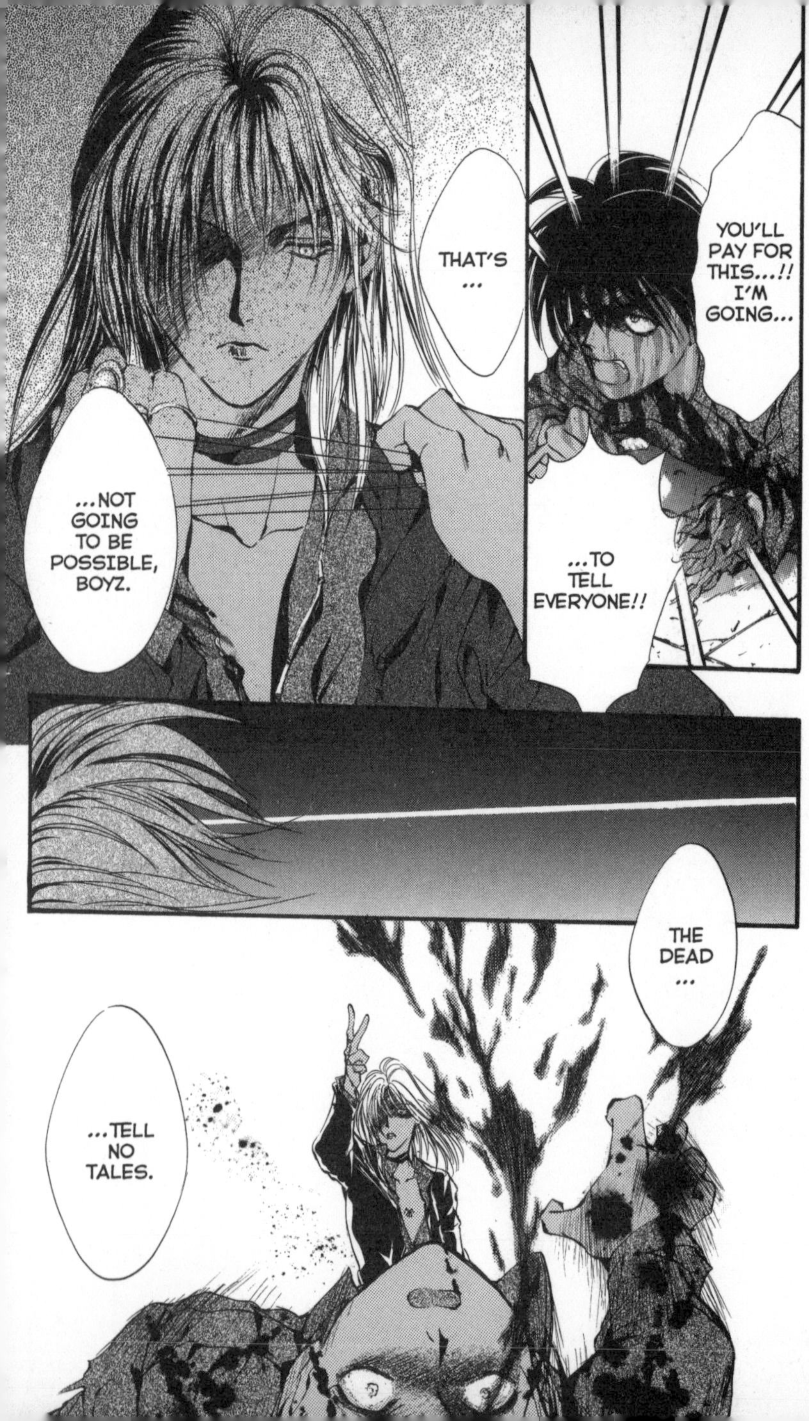
YOU'LL PAY FOR THIS...!! I'M GOING...
...TO TELL EVERYONE!!
THAT'S ...
...NOT GOING TO BE POSSIBLE, BOYZ.
THE DEAD ...
...TELL NO TALES.

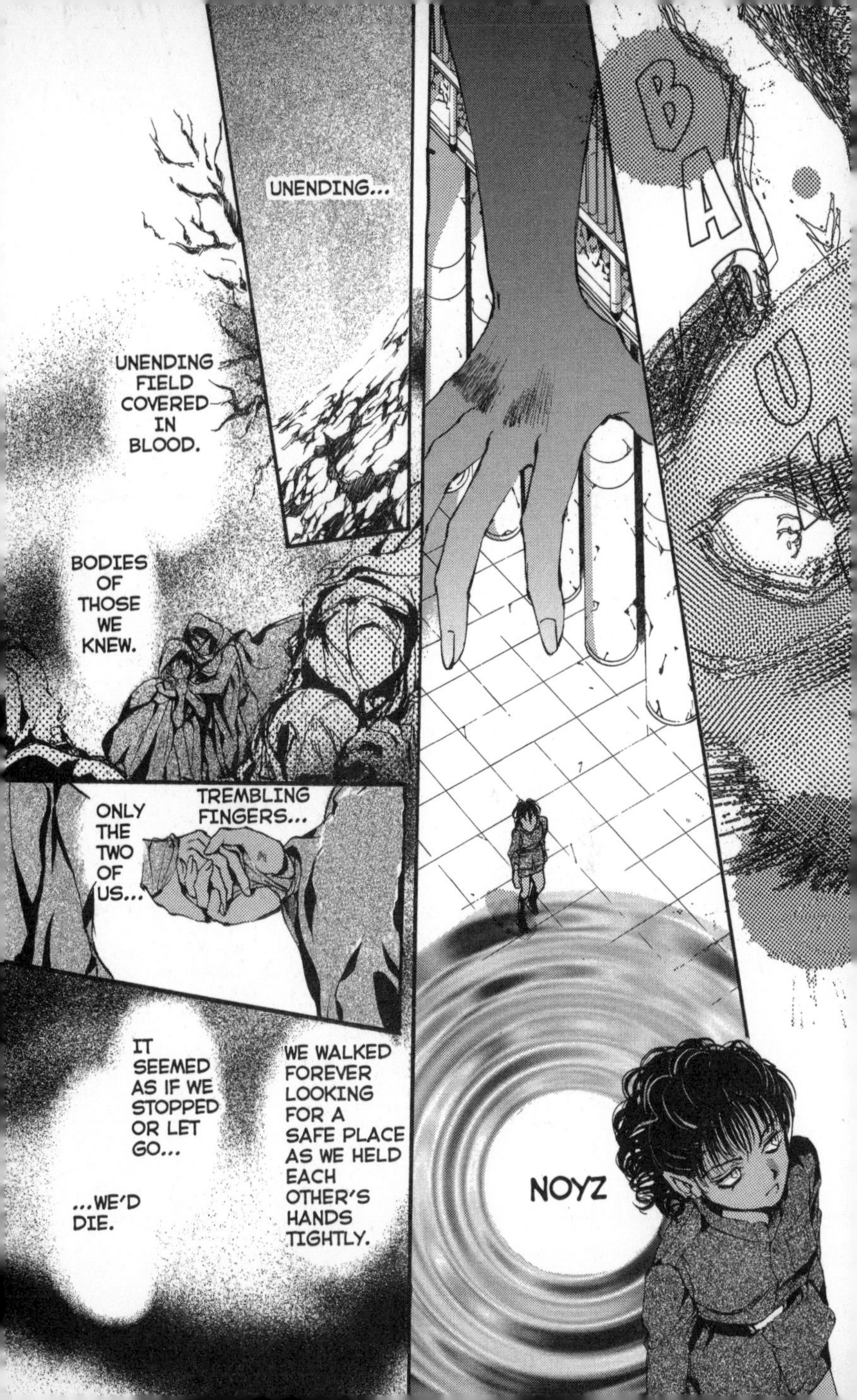
BAU
NOYZ
UNENDING...
UNENDING FIELD COVERED IN BLOOD.
BODIES OF THOSE WE KNEW.
TREMBLING FINGERS...
ONLY THE TWO OF US...
WE WALKED FOREVER LOOKING FOR A SAFE PLACE AS WE HELD EACH OTHER'S HANDS TIGHTLY.
IT SEEMED AS IF WE STOPPED OR LET GO...
...WE'D DIE.

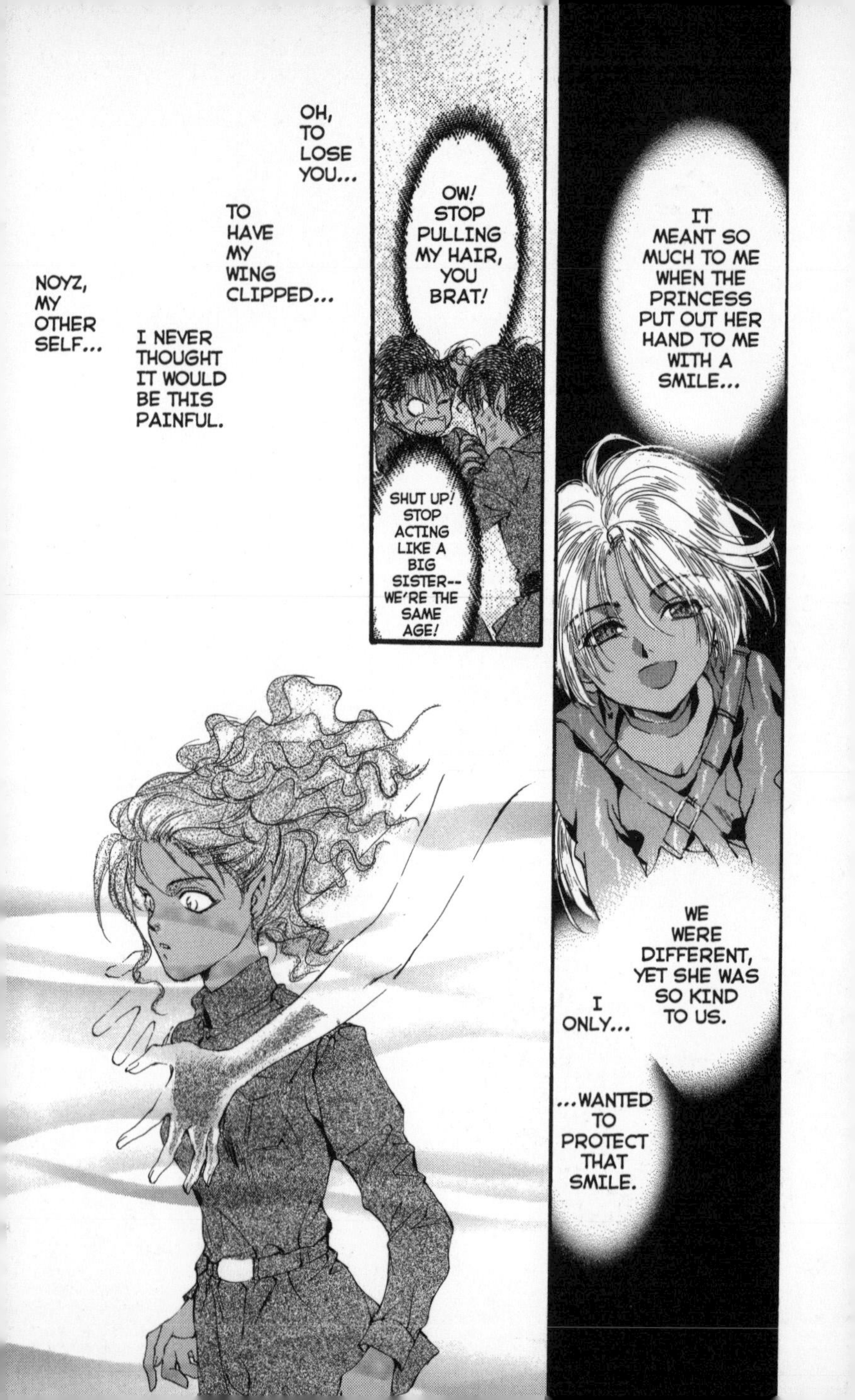
IT MEANT SO MUCH TO ME WHEN THE PRINCESS PUT OUT HER HAND TO ME WITH A SMILE...
WE WERE DIFFERENT, YET SHE WAS SO KIND TO US.
I ONLY...
...WANTED TO PROTECT THAT SMILE.
OW! STOP PULLING MY HAIR, YOU BRAT!
SHUT UP! STOP ACTING LIKE A BIG SISTER-- WE'RE THE SAME AGE!
OH, TO LOSE YOU...
TO HAVE MY WING CLIPPED...
I NEVER THOUGHT IT WOULD BE THIS PAINFUL.
NOYZ, MY OTHER SELF...

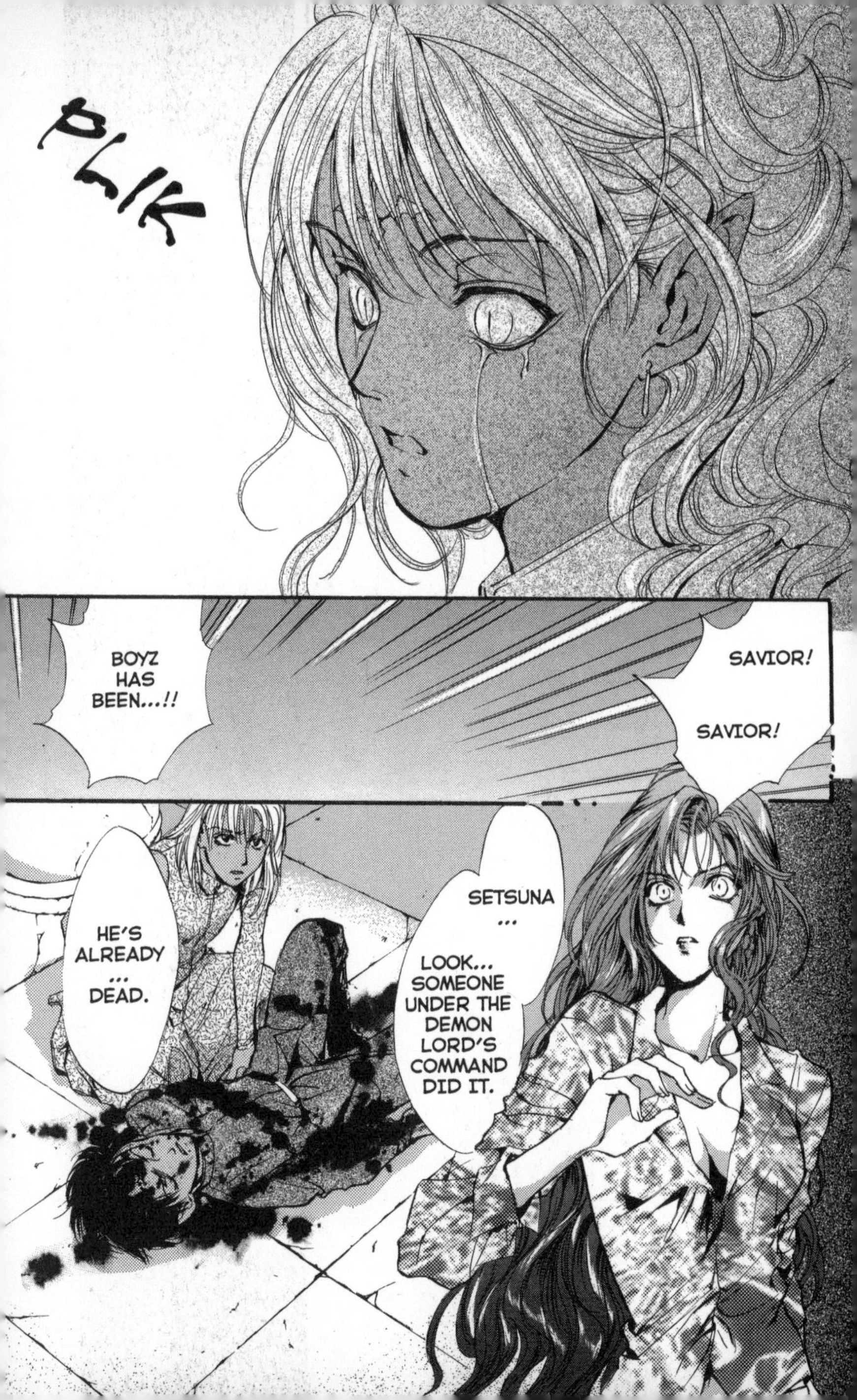
PLIK
SAVIOR!
SAVIOR!
BOYZ HAS BEEN...!!
SETSUNA ...
LOOK... SOMEONE UNDER THE DEMON LORD'S COMMAND DID IT.
HE'S ALREADY ... DEAD.

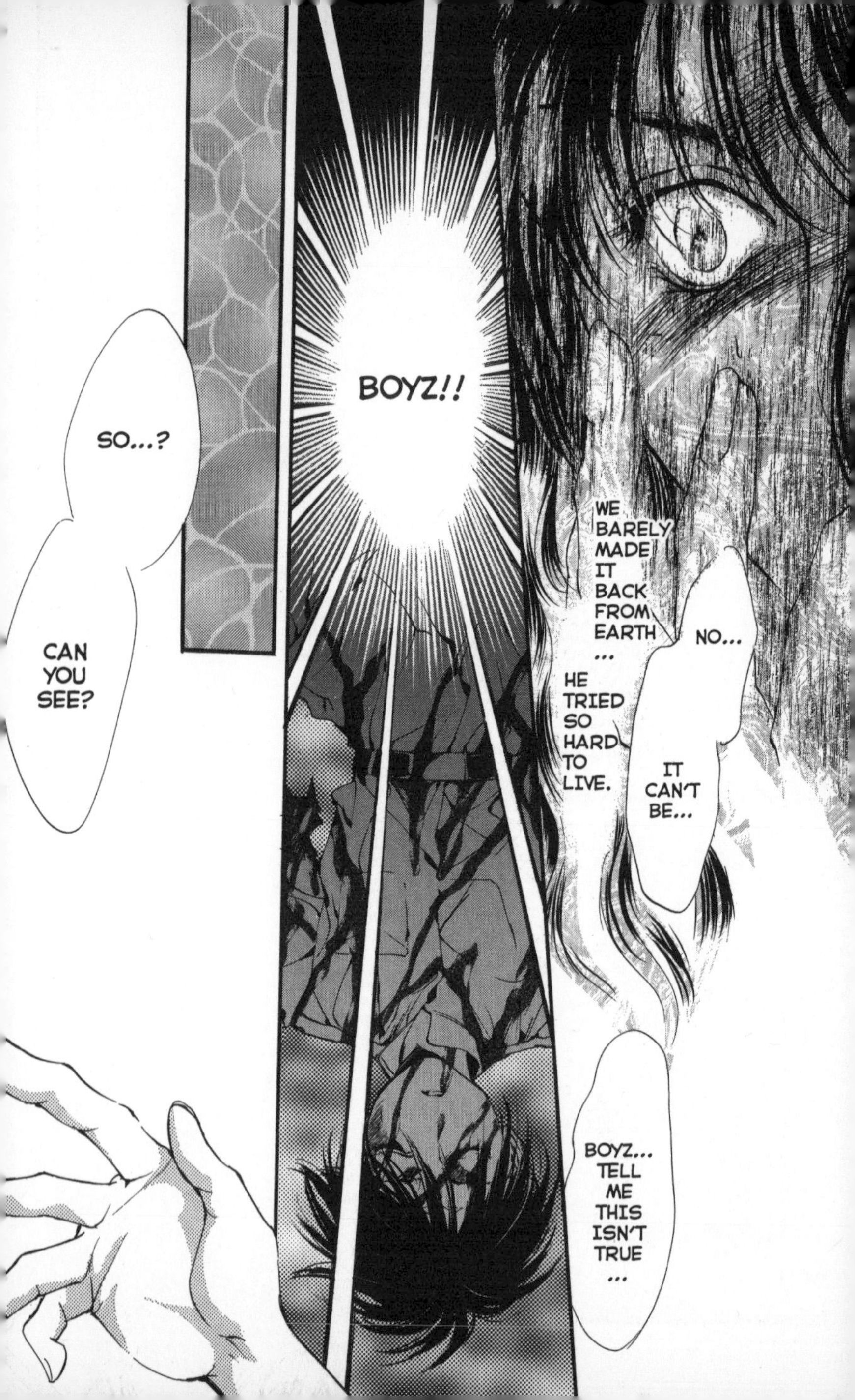
NO...
IT CAN'T BE...
WE BARELY MADE IT BACK FROM EARTH...
HE TRIED SO HARD TO LIVE.
BOYZ!!
BOYZ... TELL ME THIS ISN'T TRUE...
SO...?
CAN YOU SEE?

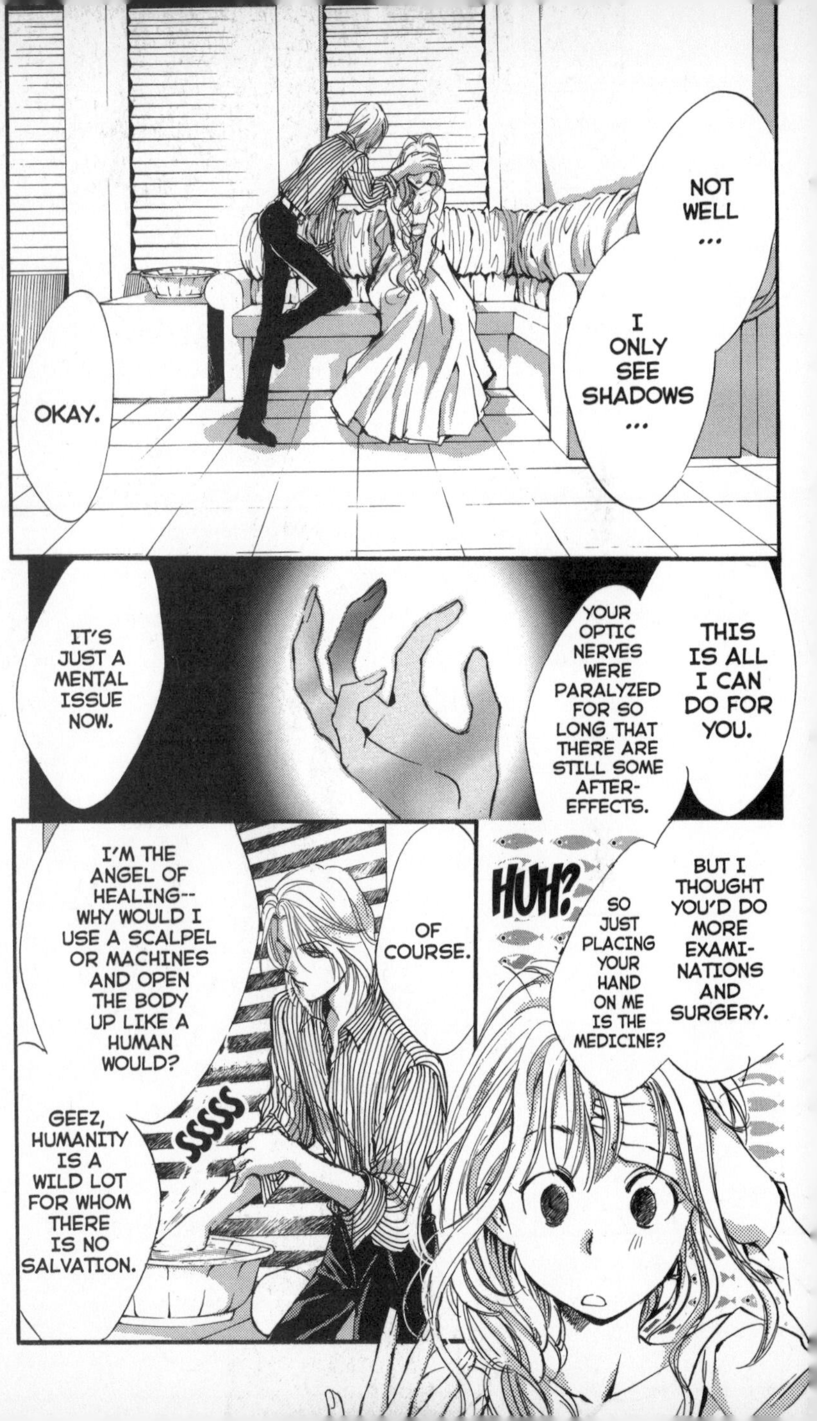
NOT WELL ...
I ONLY SEE SHADOWS ...
OKAY.
THIS IS ALL I CAN DO FOR YOU.
YOUR OPTIC NERVES WERE PARALYZED FOR SO LONG THAT THERE ARE STILL SOME AFTER-EFFECTS.
IT'S JUST A MENTAL ISSUE NOW.
HUH?
BUT I THOUGHT YOU'D DO MORE EXAMI-NATIONS AND SURGERY.
SO JUST PLACING YOUR HAND ON ME IS THE MEDICINE?
OF COURSE.
I'M THE ANGEL OF HEALING--WHY WOULD I USE A SCALPEL OR MACHINES AND OPEN THE BODY UP LIKE A HUMAN WOULD?
SSSSS
GEEZ, HUMANITY IS A WILD LOT FOR WHOM THERE IS NO SALVATION.

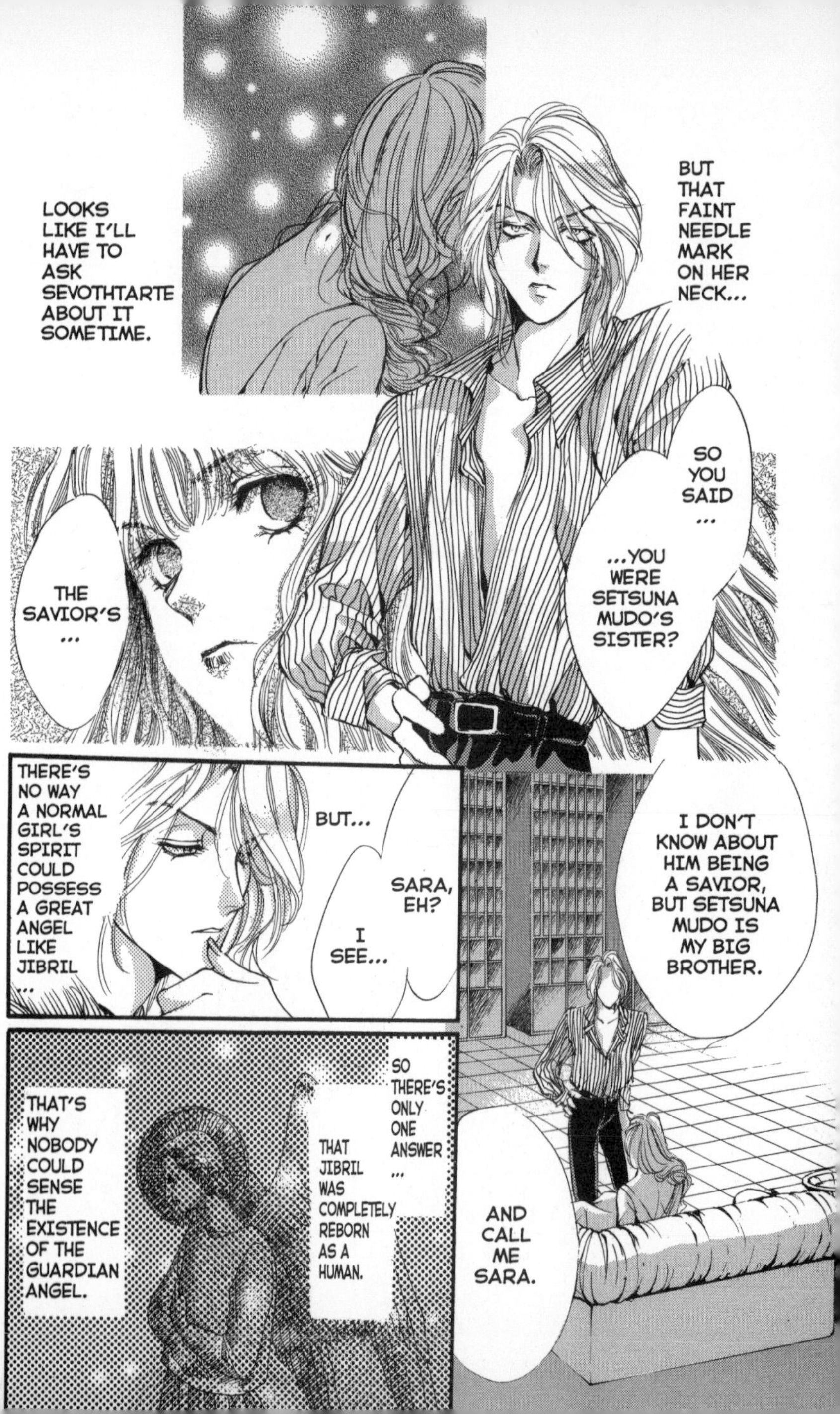
BUT THAT FAINT NEEDLE MARK ON HER NECK...
LOOKS LIKE I'LL HAVE TO ASK SEVOTHTARTE ABOUT IT SOMETIME.
SO YOU SAID ...
...YOU WERE SETSUNA MUDO'S SISTER?
THE SAVIOR'S ...
I DON'T KNOW ABOUT HIM BEING A SAVIOR, BUT SETSUNA MUDO IS MY BIG BROTHER.
AND CALL ME SARA.
SARA, EH?
I SEE...
BUT...
THERE'S NO WAY A NORMAL GIRL'S SPIRIT COULD POSSESS A GREAT ANGEL LIKE JIBRIL ...
SO THERE'S ONLY ONE ANSWER ...
THAT JIBRIL WAS COMPLETELY REBORN AS A HUMAN.
THAT'S WHY NOBODY COULD SENSE THE EXISTENCE OF THE GUARDIAN ANGEL.

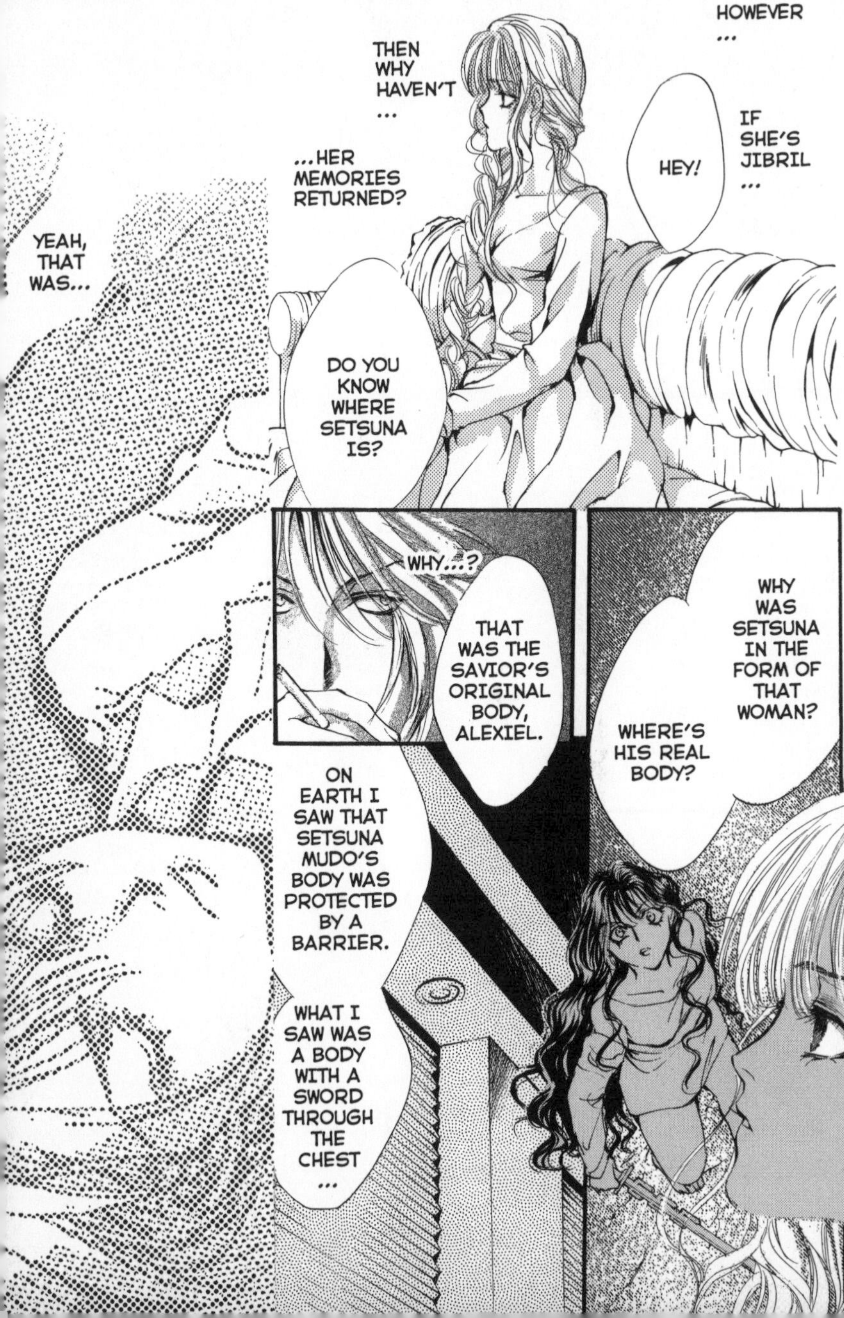
HOWEVER...
IF SHE'S JIBRIL...
HEY!
THEN WHY HAVEN'T...
...HER MEMORIES RETURNED?
DO YOU KNOW WHERE SETSUNA IS?
WHY WAS SETSUNA IN THE FORM OF THAT WOMAN?
WHERE'S HIS REAL BODY?
WHY...?
THAT WAS THE SAVIOR'S ORIGINAL BODY, ALEXIEL.
ON EARTH I SAW THAT SETSUNA MUDO'S BODY WAS PROTECTED BY A BARRIER.
WHAT I SAW WAS A BODY WITH A SWORD THROUGH THE CHEST...
YEAH, THAT WAS...

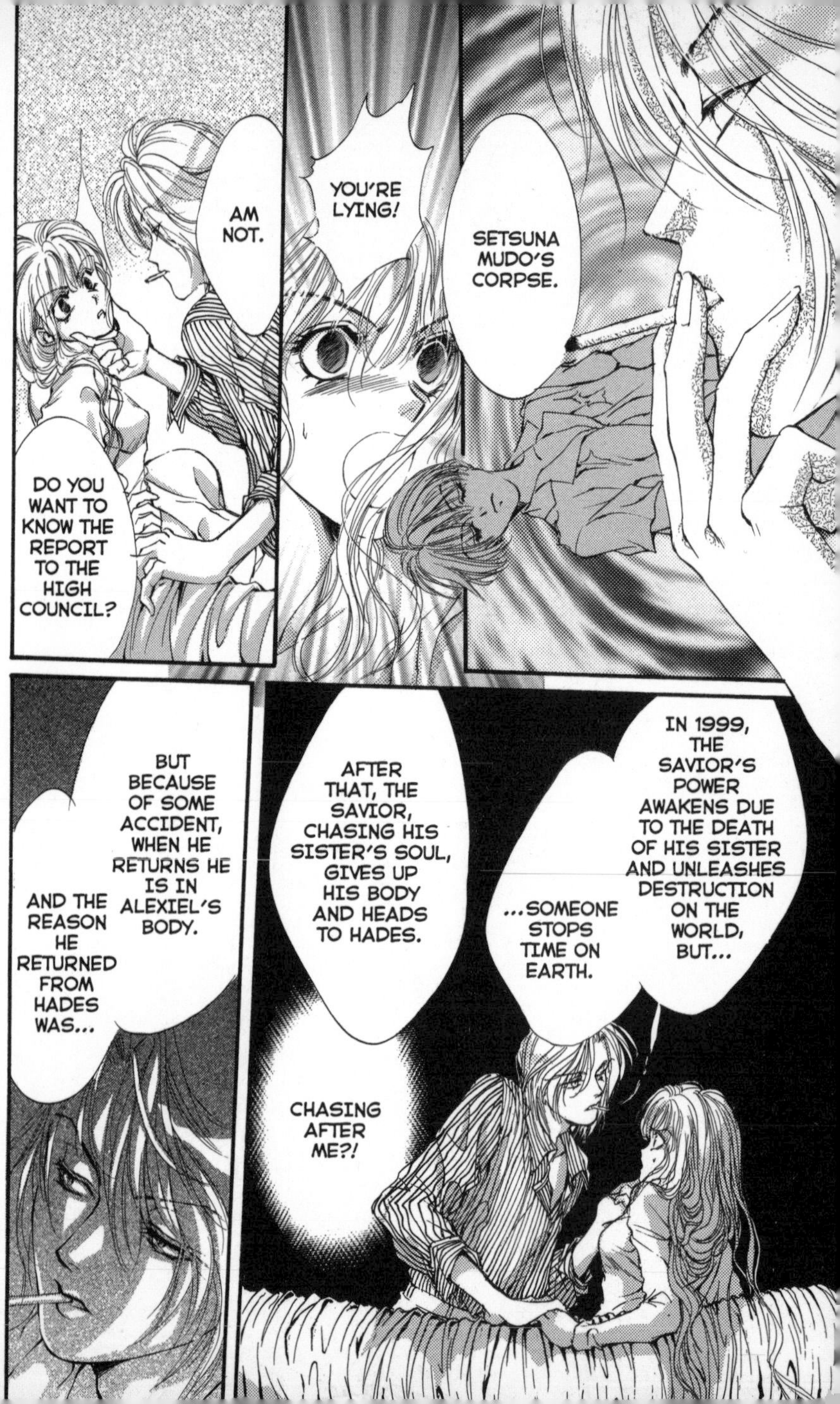
SETSUNA MUDO'S CORPSE.
YOU'RE LYING!
AM NOT.
DO YOU WANT TO KNOW THE REPORT TO THE HIGH COUNCIL?
IN 1999, THE SAVIOR'S POWER AWAKENS DUE TO THE DEATH OF HIS SISTER AND UNLEASHES DESTRUCTION ON THE WORLD, BUT...
...SOMEONE STOPS TIME ON EARTH.
AFTER THAT, THE SAVIOR, CHASING HIS SISTER'S SOUL, GIVES UP HIS BODY AND HEADS TO HADES.
CHASING AFTER ME?!
BUT BECAUSE OF SOME ACCIDENT, WHEN HE RETURNS HE IS IN ALEXIEL'S BODY.
AND THE REASON HE RETURNED FROM HADES WAS...

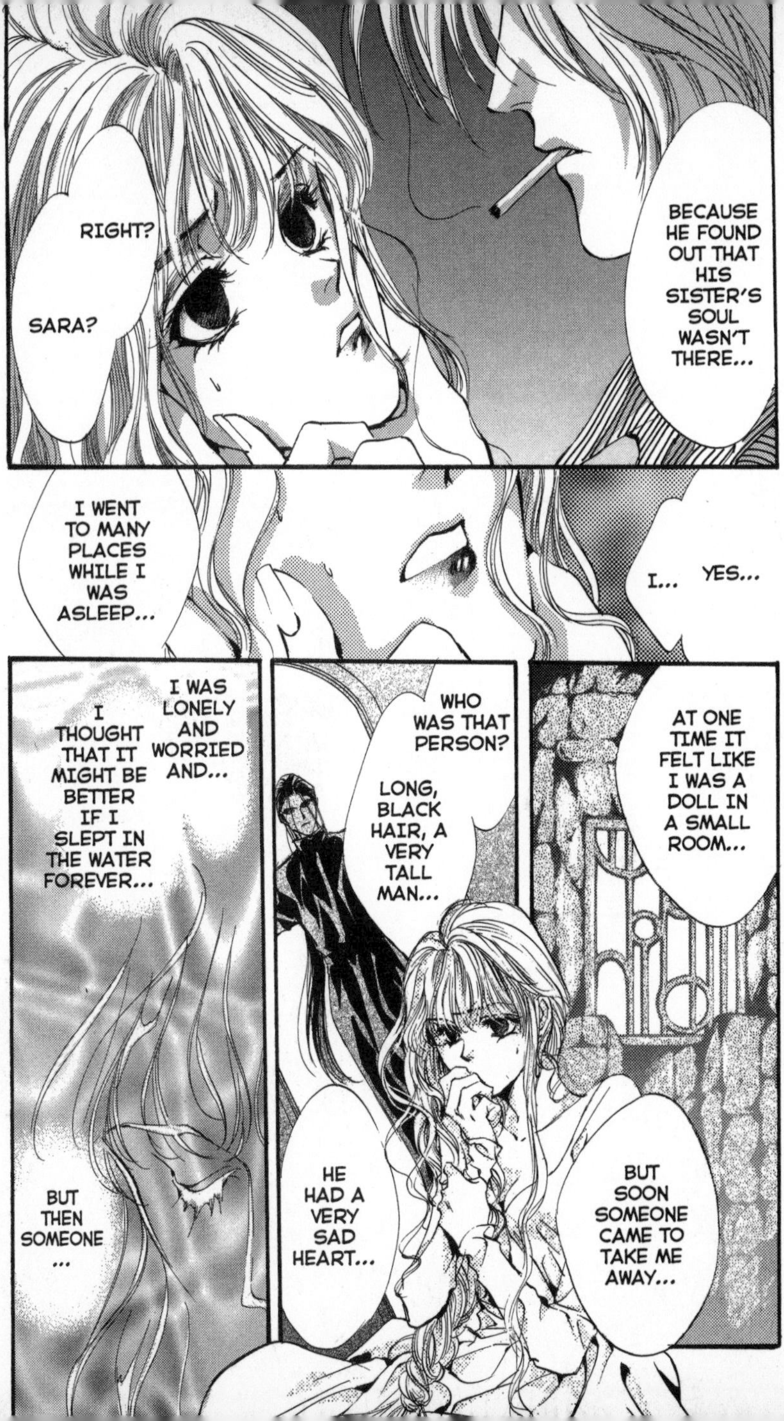
BECAUSE HE FOUND OUT THAT HIS SISTER'S SOUL WASN'T THERE...
RIGHT?
SARA?
I... YES...
I WENT TO MANY PLACES WHILE I WAS ASLEEP...
AT ONE TIME IT FELT LIKE I WAS A DOLL IN A SMALL ROOM...
BUT SOON SOMEONE CAME TO TAKE ME AWAY...
WHO WAS THAT PERSON?
LONG, BLACK HAIR, A VERY TALL MAN...
HE HAD A VERY SAD HEART...
I WAS LONELY AND WORRIED AND...
I THOUGHT THAT IT MIGHT BE BETTER IF I SLEPT IN THE WATER FOREVER...
BUT THEN SOMEONE ...

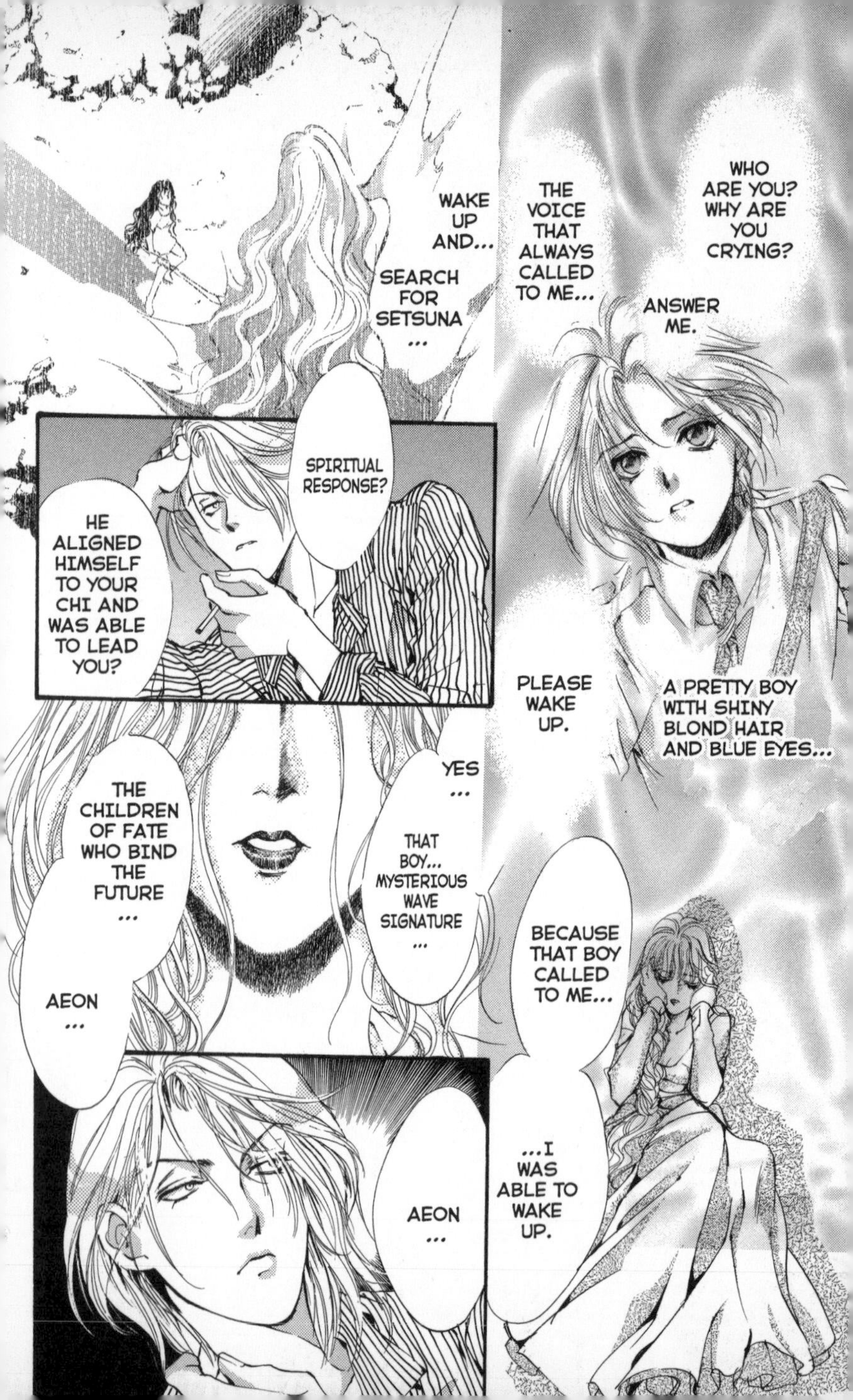
WHO ARE YOU? WHY ARE YOU CRYING?
ANSWER ME.
THE VOICE THAT ALWAYS CALLED TO ME...
A PRETTY BOY WITH SHINY BLOND HAIR AND BLUE EYES...
PLEASE WAKE UP.
BECAUSE THAT BOY CALLED TO ME...
...I WAS ABLE TO WAKE UP.
WAKE UP AND...
SEARCH FOR SETSUNA ...
SPIRITUAL RESPONSE?
HE ALIGNED HIMSELF TO YOUR CHI AND WAS ABLE TO LEAD YOU?
YES ...
THAT BOY... MYSTERIOUS WAVE SIGNATURE ...
THE CHILDREN OF FATE WHO BIND THE FUTURE ...
AEON ...
AEON ...

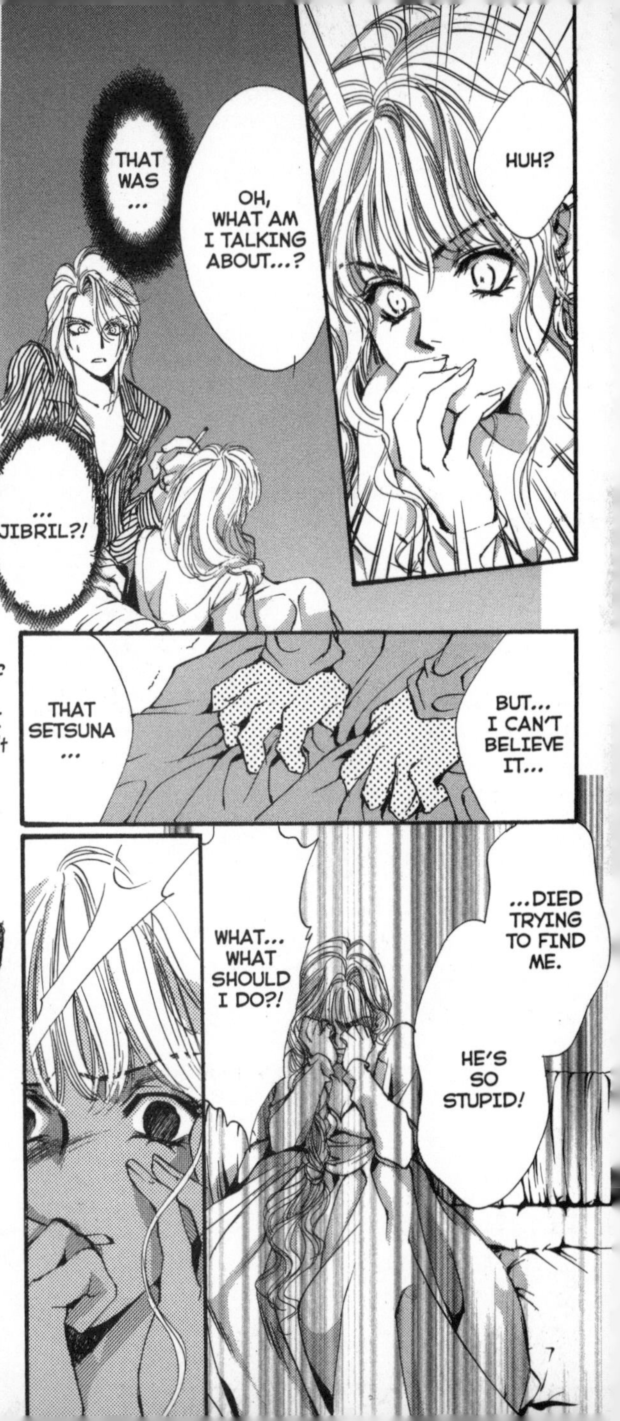
HUH?
OH, WHAT AM I TALKING ABOUT...?
THAT WAS ...
... JIBRIL?!
BUT... I CAN'T BELIEVE IT...
THAT SETSUNA ...
...DIED TRYING TO FIND ME.
HE'S SO STUPID!
WHAT... WHAT SHOULD I DO?!

I wanted to draw Hatter in color, so I came up with a lot of rough sketches, but the ones I like the best are the one I used and the one below. But then he doesn't even appear in this chapter! WAH! Arachne being bad was something I intended to do from the beginning, but I planned on it taking place near the end of the story. But I figured I'd get in trouble unless I revealed it soon so... I did it! I got a lot of letters from shocked readers. Sorry. But I couldn't help it. I can't reveal how things will end up with her yet, though.

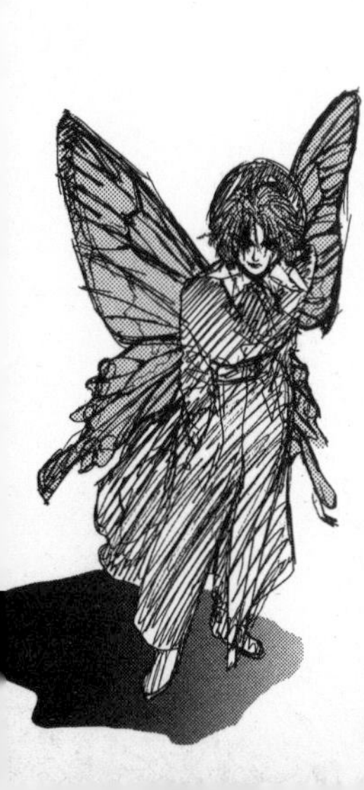

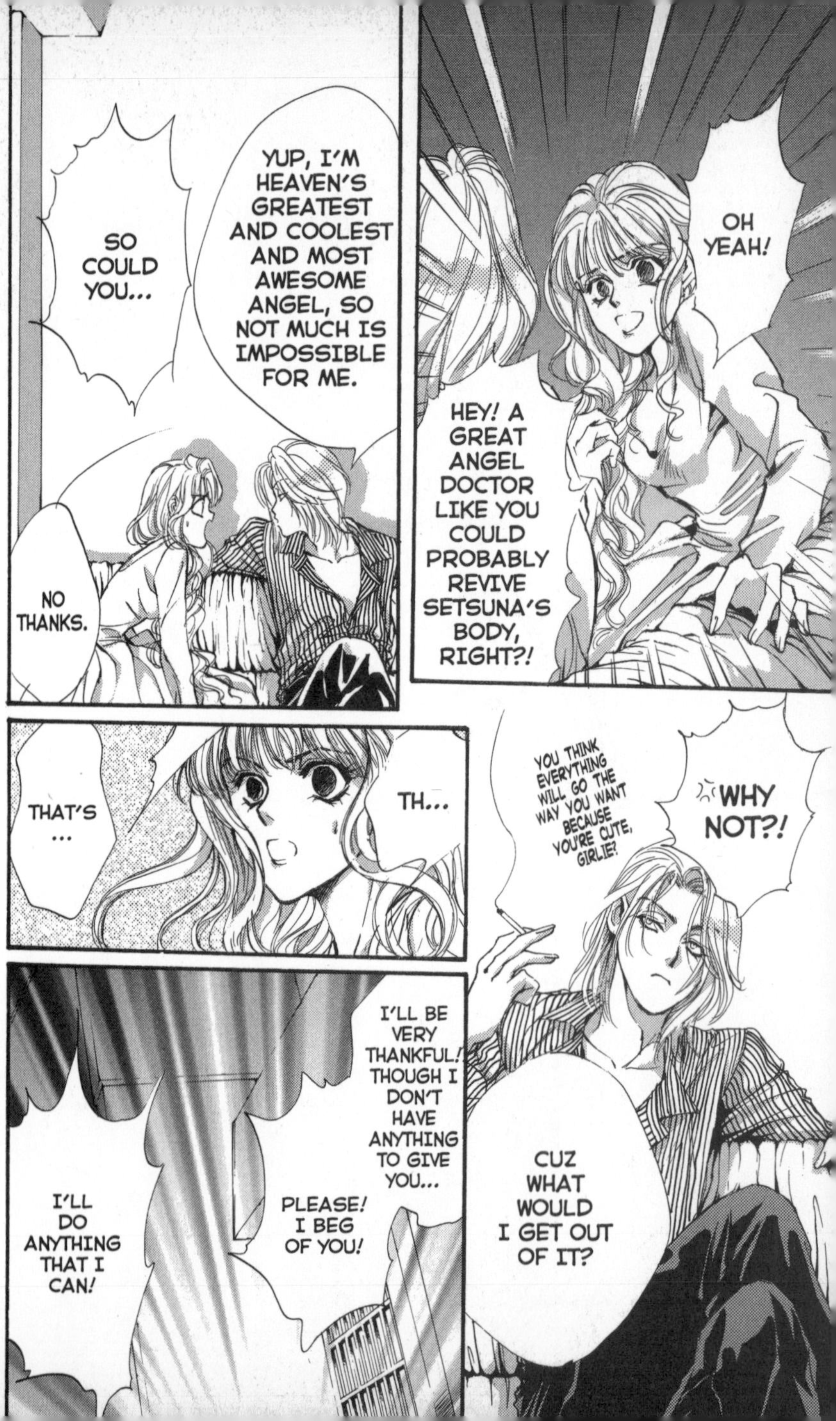
OH YEAH!
HEY! A GREAT ANGEL DOCTOR LIKE YOU COULD PROBABLY REVIVE SETSUNA'S BODY, RIGHT?!
YUP, I'M HEAVEN'S GREATEST AND COOLEST AND MOST AWESOME ANGEL, SO NOT MUCH IS IMPOSSIBLE FOR ME.
SO COULD YOU...
NO THANKS.
WHY NOT?!
YOU THINK EVERYTHING WILL GO THE WAY YOU WANT BECAUSE YOU'RE CUTE, GIRLIE?
CUZ WHAT WOULD I GET OUT OF IT?
TH...
THAT'S ...
I'LL BE VERY THANKFUL! THOUGH I DON'T HAVE ANYTHING TO GIVE YOU...
PLEASE! I BEG OF YOU!
I'LL DO ANYTHING THAT I CAN!

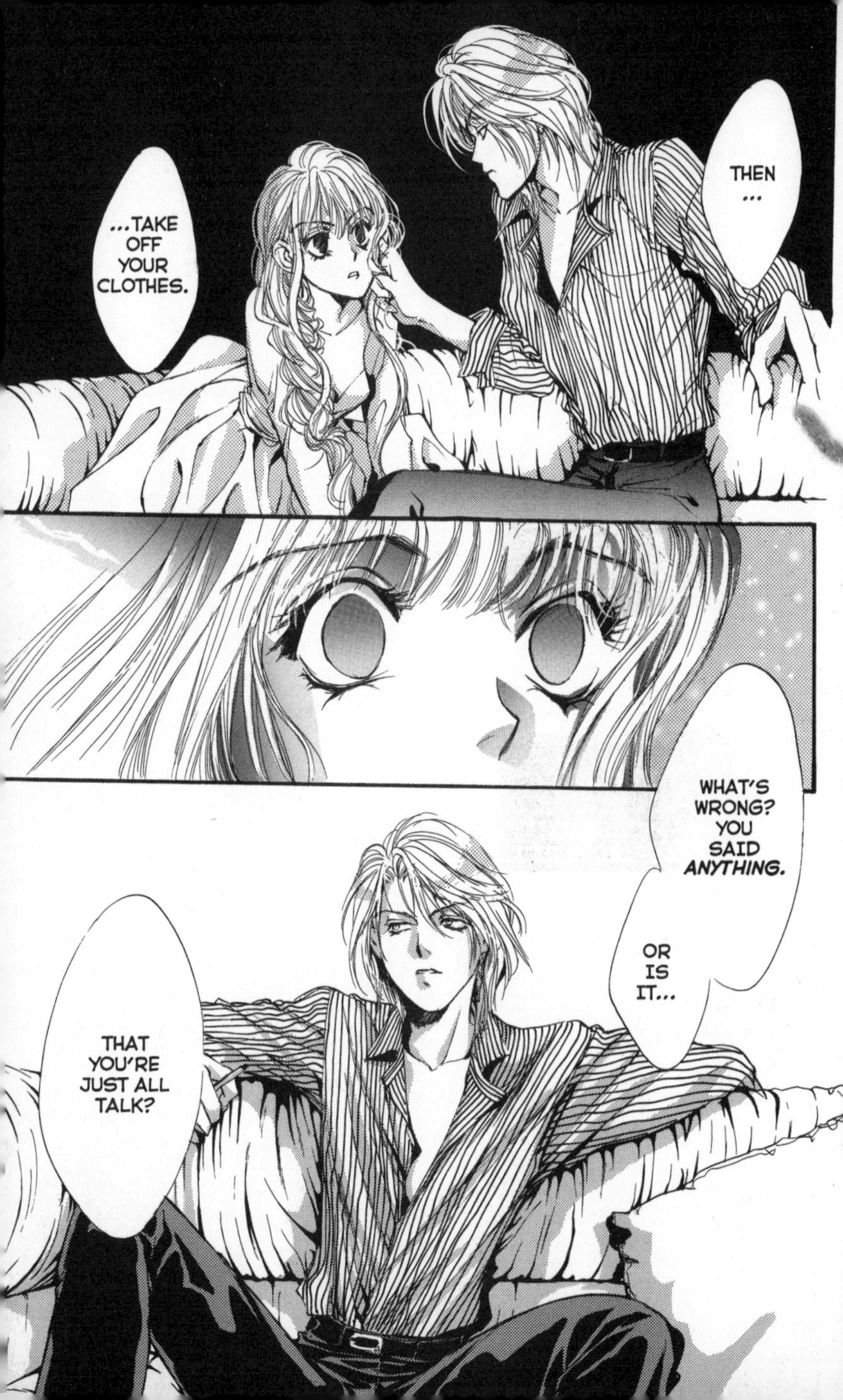
THEN ...
...TAKE OFF YOUR CLOTHES.
WHAT'S WRONG? YOU SAID *ANYTHING.*
OR IS IT...
THAT YOU'RE JUST ALL TALK?

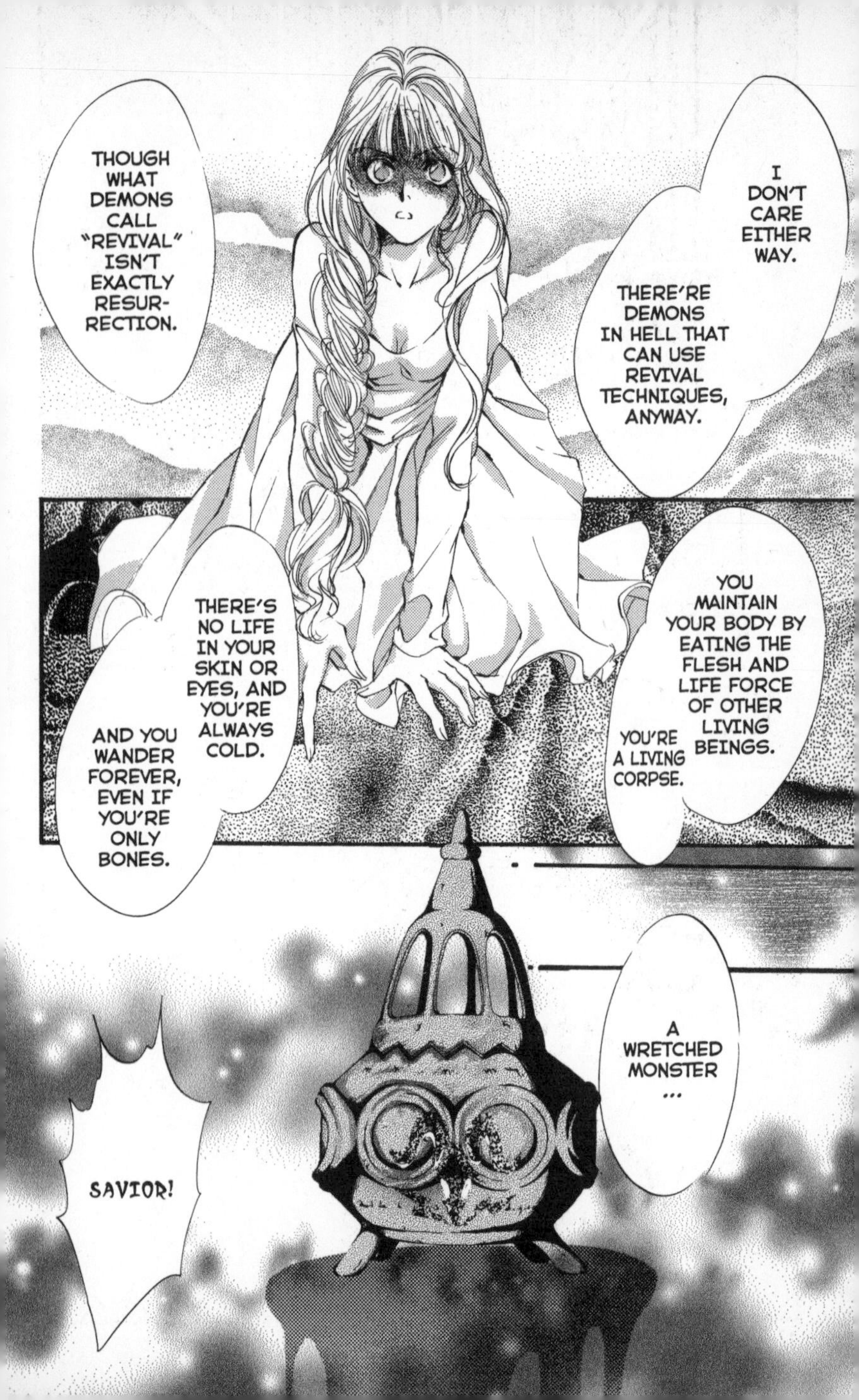
I DON'T CARE EITHER WAY.
THERE'RE DEMONS IN HELL THAT CAN USE REVIVAL TECHNIQUES, ANYWAY.
THOUGH WHAT DEMONS CALL "REVIVAL" ISN'T EXACTLY RESUR-RECTION.
YOU MAINTAIN YOUR BODY BY EATING THE FLESH AND LIFE FORCE OF OTHER LIVING BEINGS.
YOU'RE A LIVING CORPSE.
THERE'S NO LIFE IN YOUR SKIN OR EYES, AND YOU'RE ALWAYS COLD.
AND YOU WANDER FOREVER, EVEN IF YOU'RE ONLY BONES.
A WRETCHED MONSTER ...
SAVIOR!

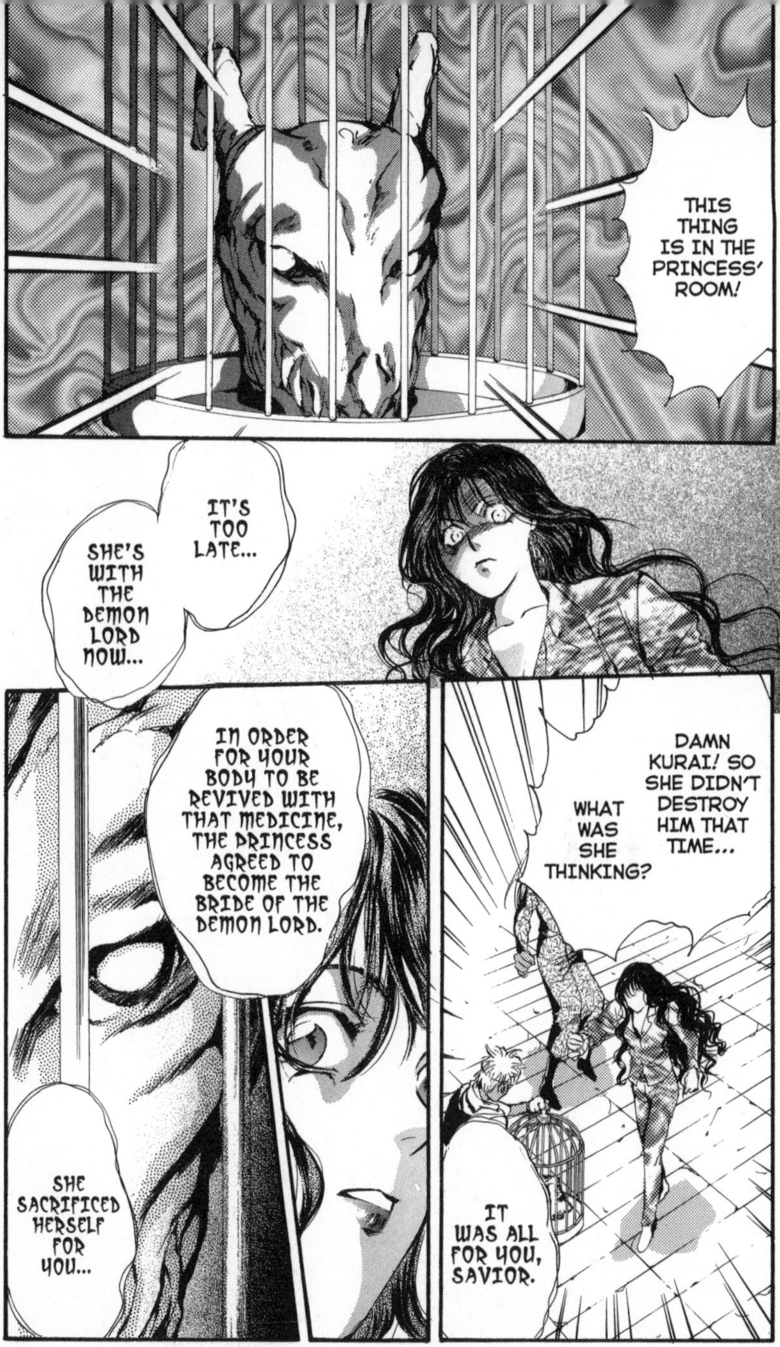
THIS THING IS IN THE PRINCESS' ROOM!
IT'S TOO LATE...
SHE'S WITH THE DEMON LORD NOW...
DAMN KURAI! SO SHE DIDN'T DESTROY HIM THAT TIME...
WHAT WAS SHE THINKING?
IT WAS ALL FOR YOU, SAVIOR.
IN ORDER FOR YOUR BODY TO BE REVIVED WITH THAT MEDICINE, THE PRINCESS AGREED TO BECOME THE BRIDE OF THE DEMON LORD.
SHE SACRIFICED HERSELF FOR YOU...

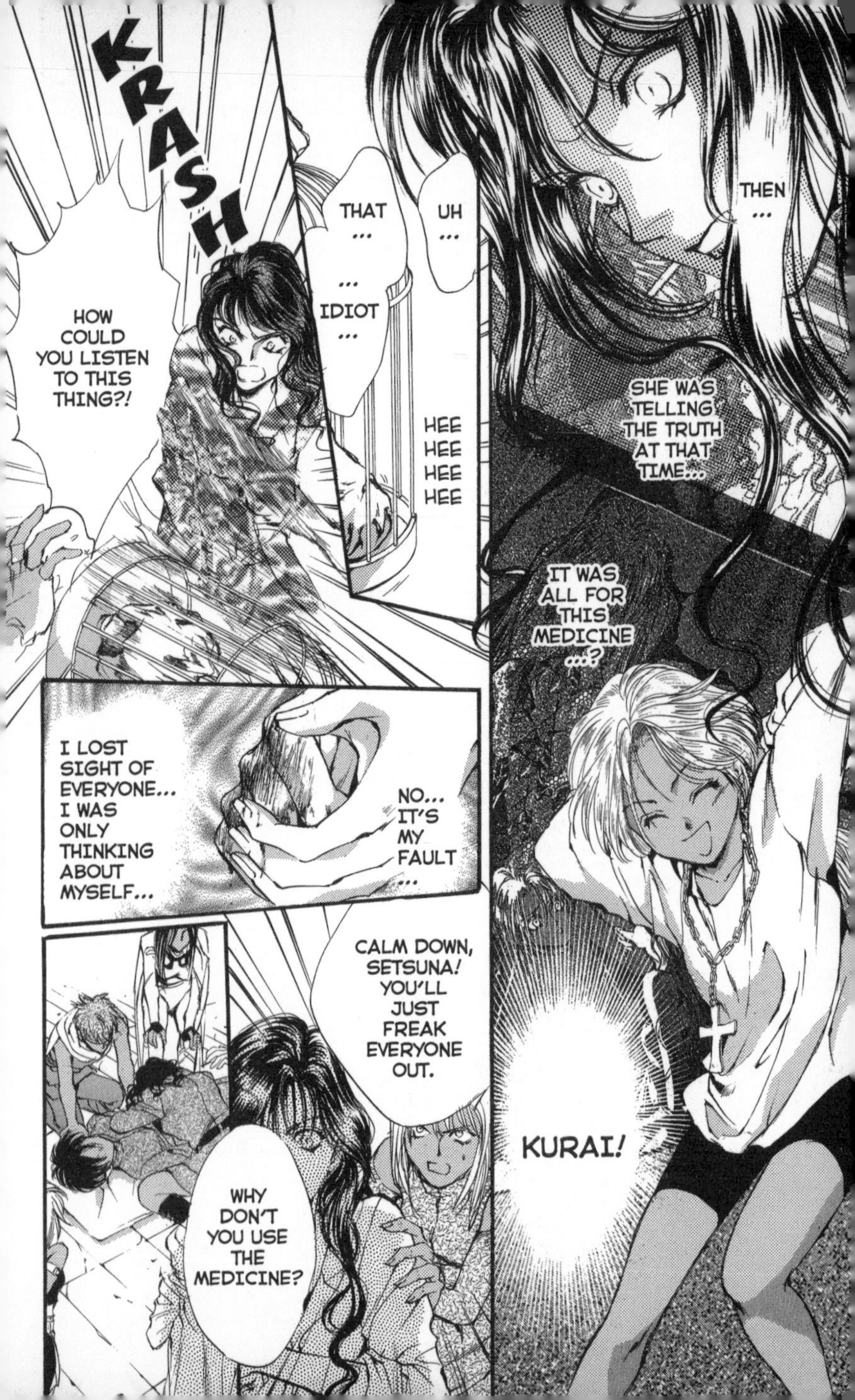
THEN ...
SHE WAS TELLING THE TRUTH AT THAT TIME...
IT WAS ALL FOR THIS MEDICINE ...?
KURAI!
UH ...
THAT ...
... IDIOT ...
HEE HEE HEE HEE
KRASH
HOW COULD YOU LISTEN TO THIS THING?!
NO... IT'S MY FAULT ...
I LOST SIGHT OF EVERYONE... I WAS ONLY THINKING ABOUT MYSELF...
CALM DOWN, SETSUNA! YOU'LL JUST FREAK EVERYONE OUT.
WHY DON'T YOU USE THE MEDICINE?

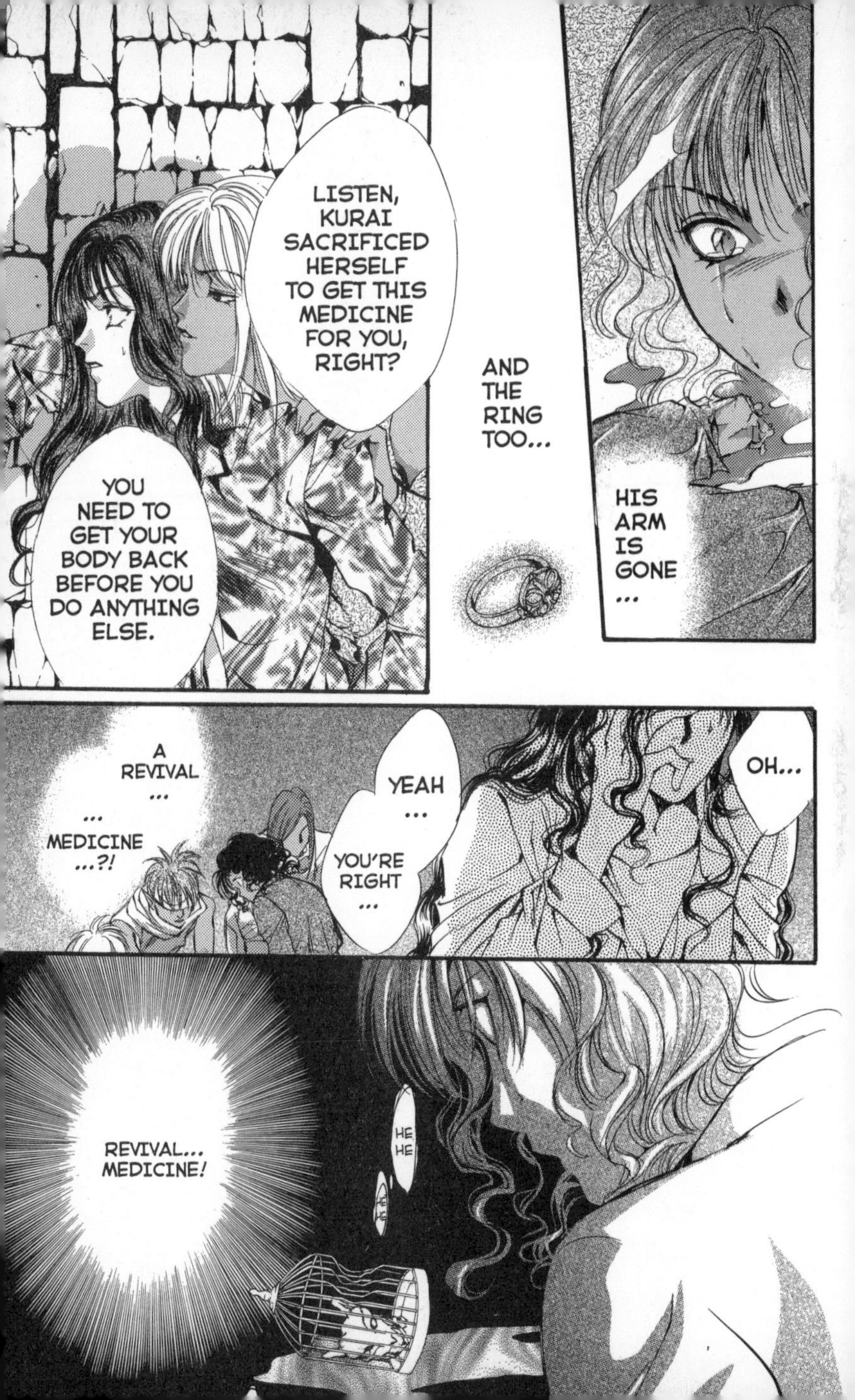
HIS ARM IS GONE ...
AND THE RING TOO...
LISTEN, KURAI SACRIFICED HERSELF TO GET THIS MEDICINE FOR YOU, RIGHT?
YOU NEED TO GET YOUR BODY BACK BEFORE YOU DO ANYTHING ELSE.
OH...
YEAH ... YOU'RE RIGHT ...
A REVIVAL ... ... MEDICINE ...?!
HE HE
HE HE
REVIVAL... MEDICINE!

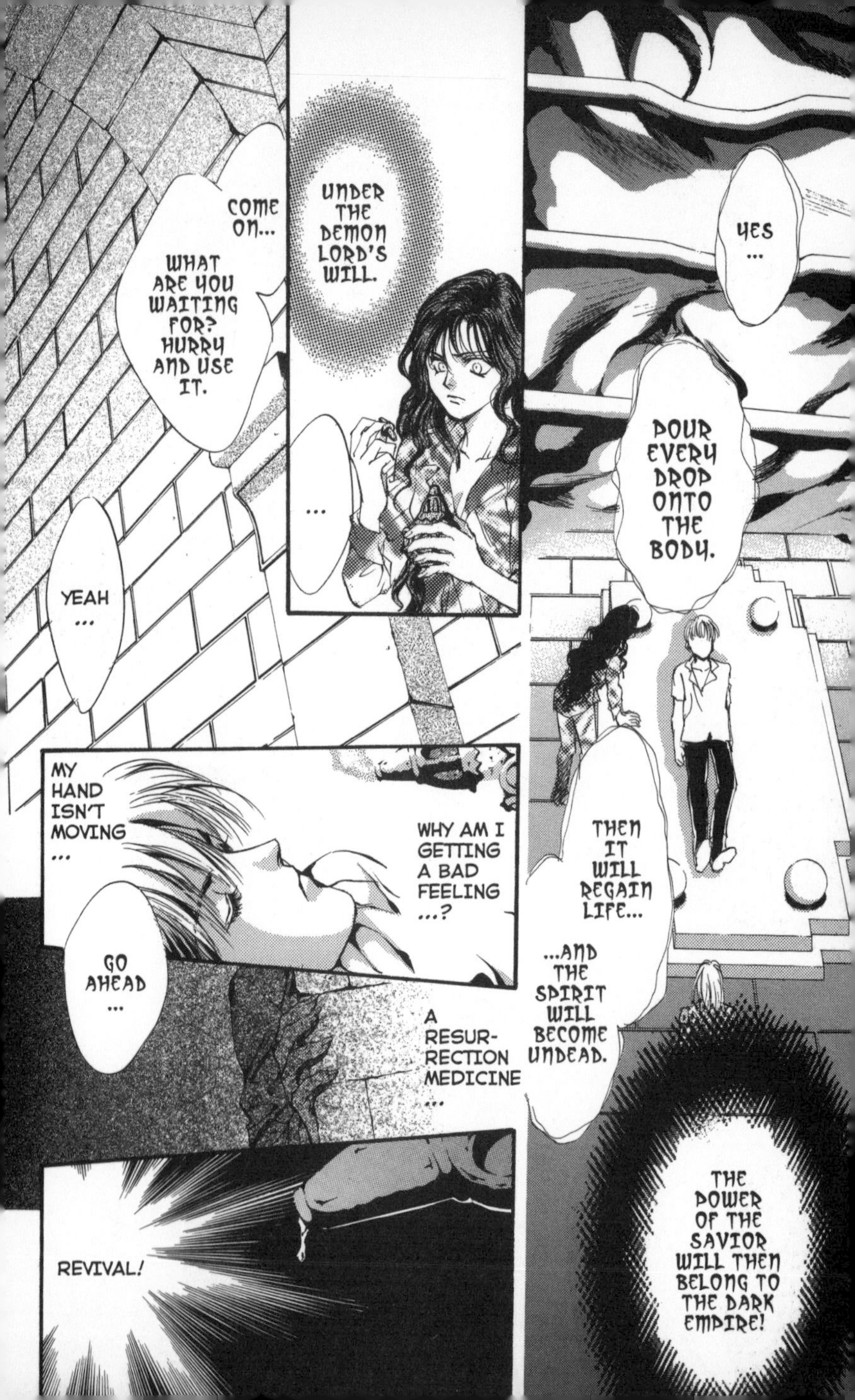
YES ...
POUR EVERY DROP ONTO THE BODY.
THEN IT WILL REGAIN LIFE...
...AND THE SPIRIT WILL BECOME UNDEAD.
THE POWER OF THE SAVIOR WILL THEN BELONG TO THE DARK EMPIRE!
UNDER THE DEMON LORD'S WILL.
...
COME ON...
WHAT ARE YOU WAITING FOR? HURRY AND USE IT.
YEAH ...
WHY AM I GETTING A BAD FEELING ...?
MY HAND ISN'T MOVING ...
GO AHEAD ...
A RESUR-RECTION MEDICINE ...
REVIVAL!

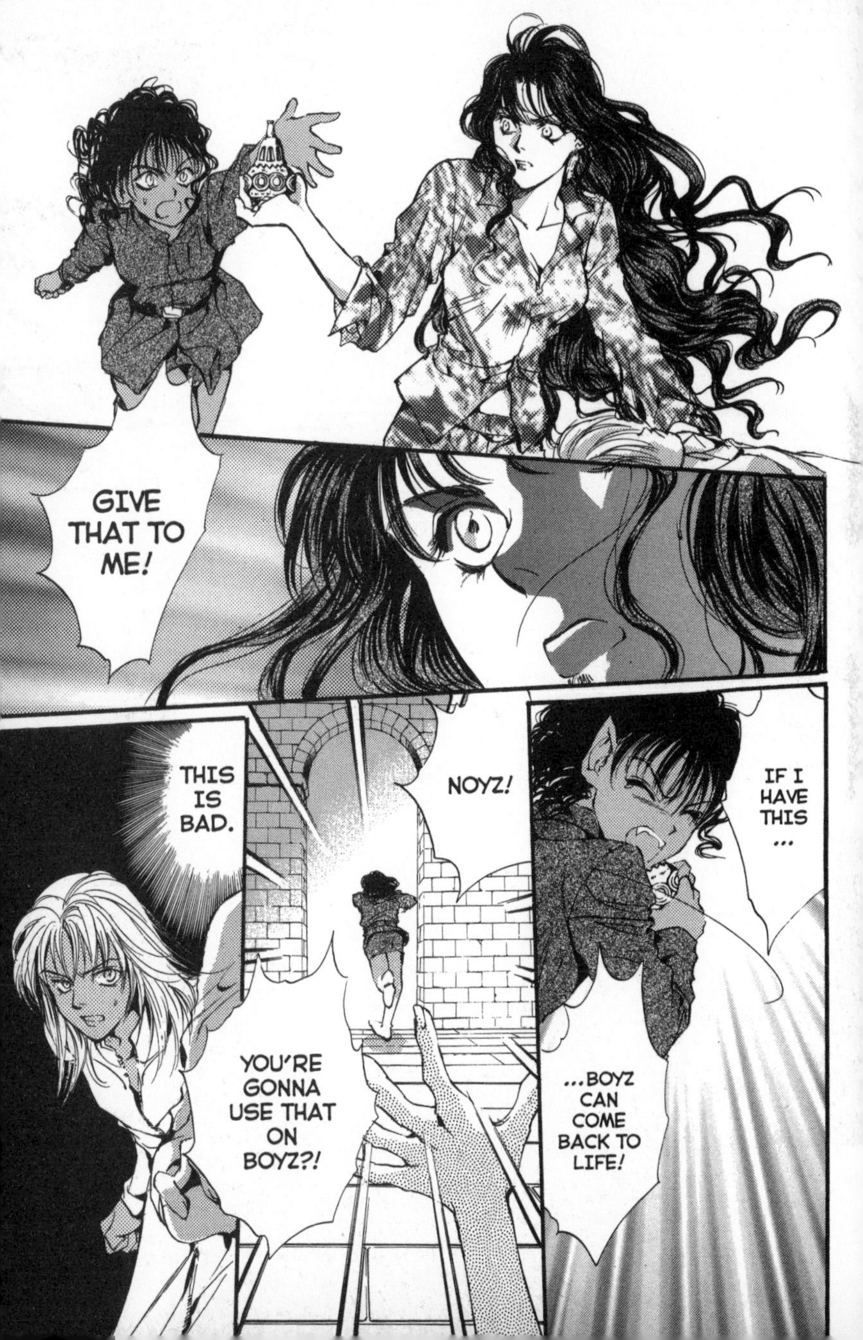
GIVE THAT TO ME!
IF I HAVE THIS ...
...BOYZ CAN COME BACK TO LIFE!
NOYZ!
YOU'RE GONNA USE THAT ON BOYZ?!
THIS IS BAD.

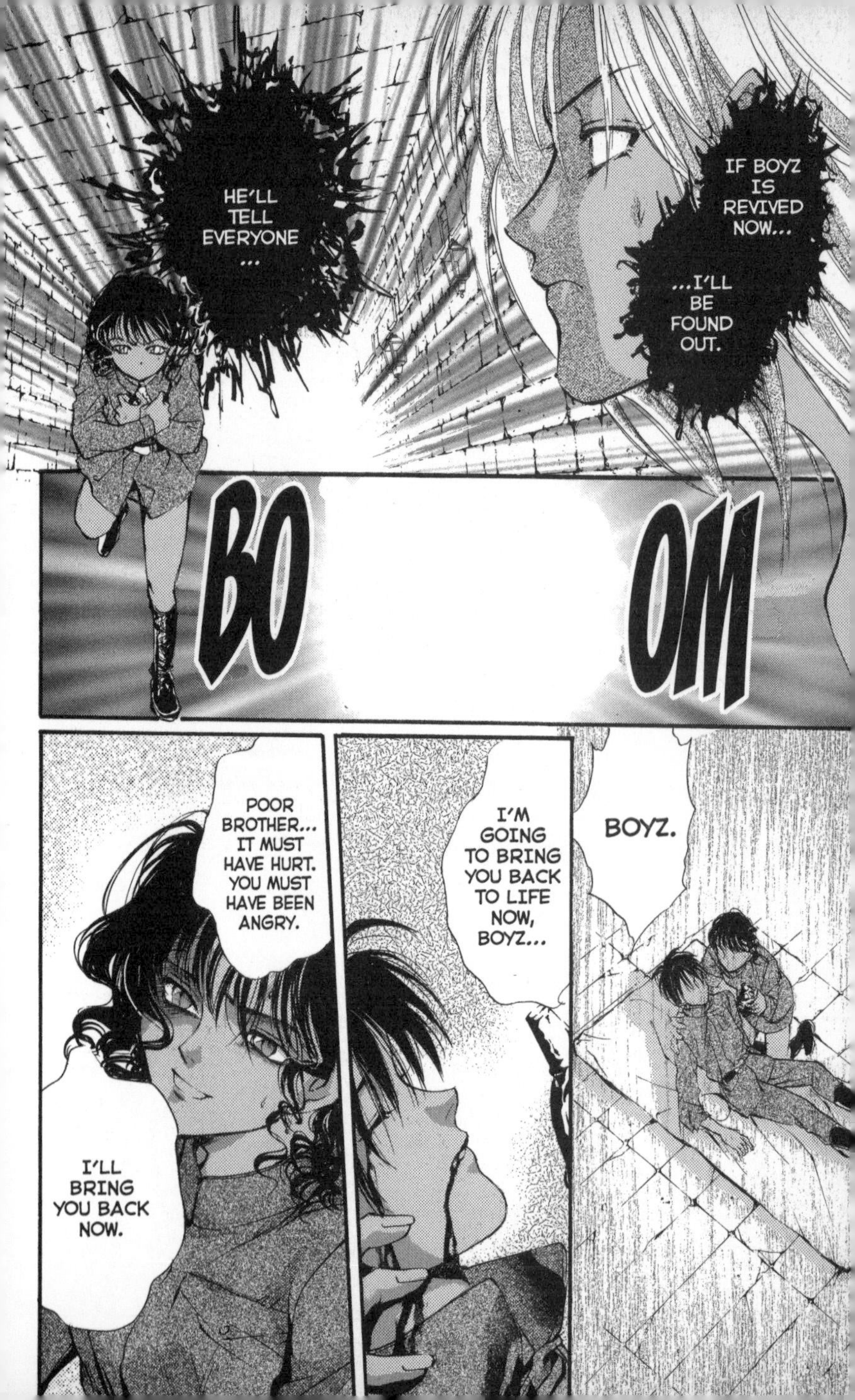
IF BOYZ IS REVIVED NOW...
...I'LL BE FOUND OUT.
HE'LL TELL EVERYONE ...
BO OM
BOYZ.
I'M GOING TO BRING YOU BACK TO LIFE NOW, BOYZ...
POOR BROTHER... IT MUST HAVE HURT. YOU MUST HAVE BEEN ANGRY.
I'LL BRING YOU BACK NOW.

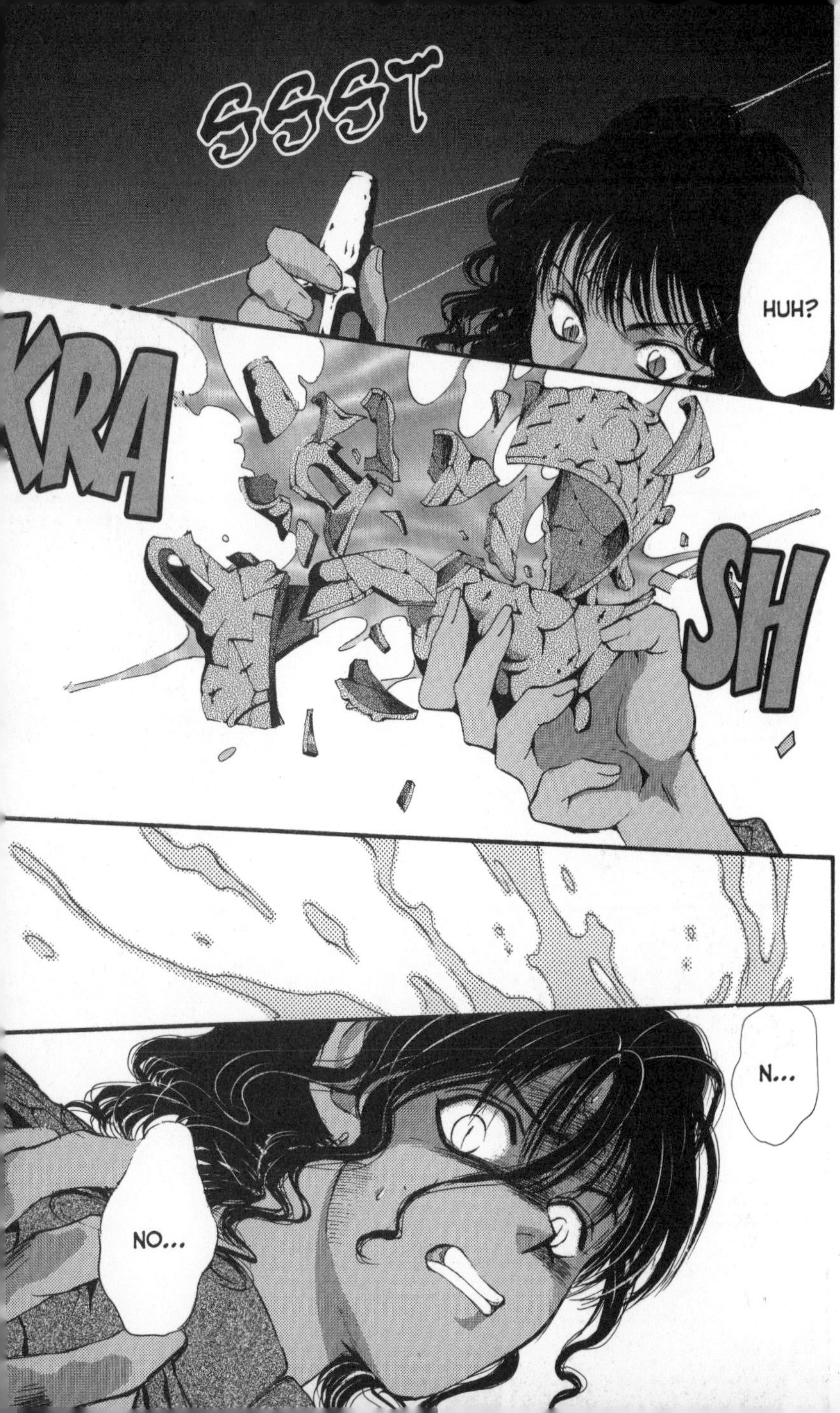
SSST
HUH?
KRASH
N...
NO...

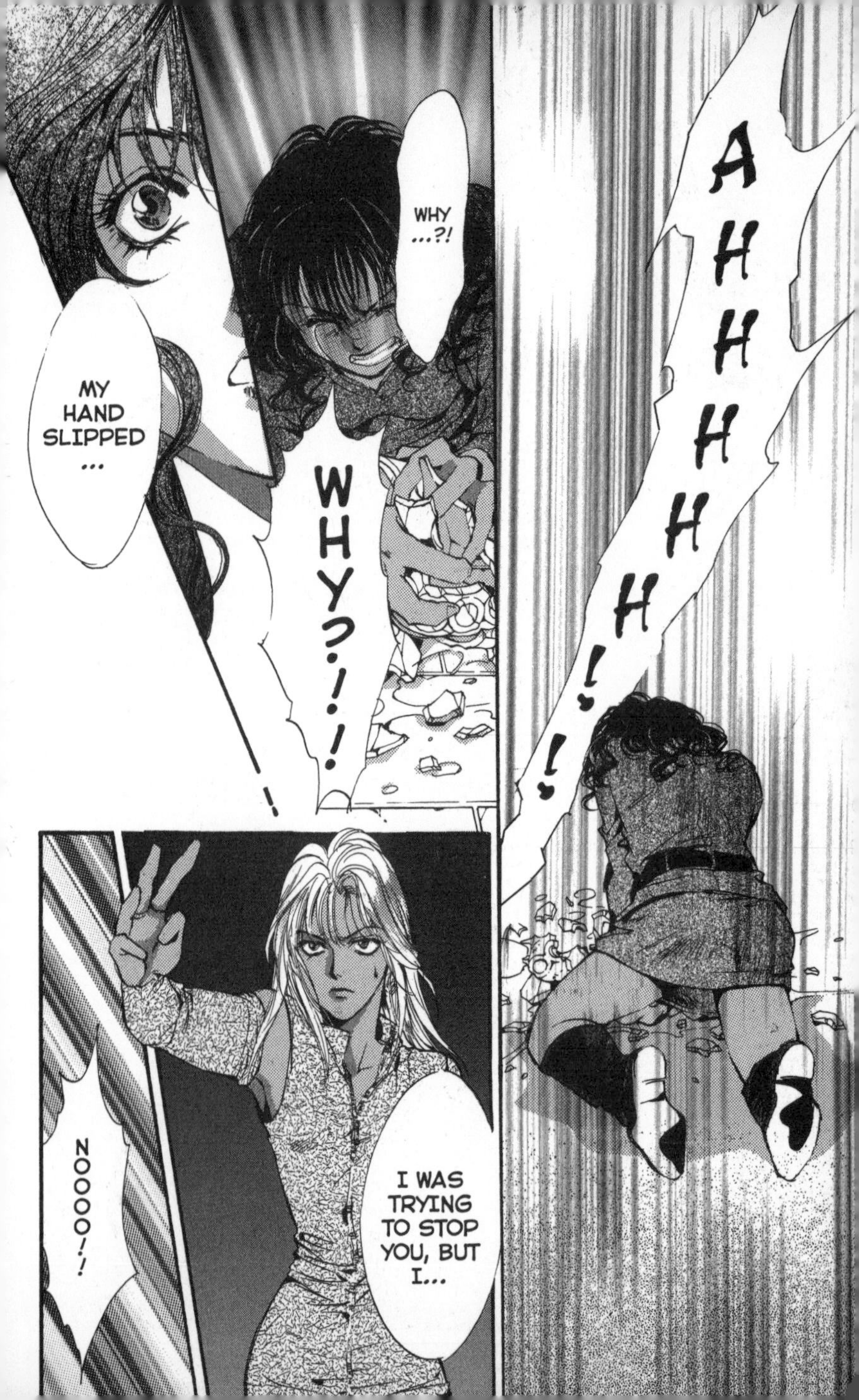
AHHHHHH!!
WHY ...?!
MY HAND SLIPPED ...
WHY?!!
I WAS TRYING TO STOP YOU, BUT I...
NOOOO!!

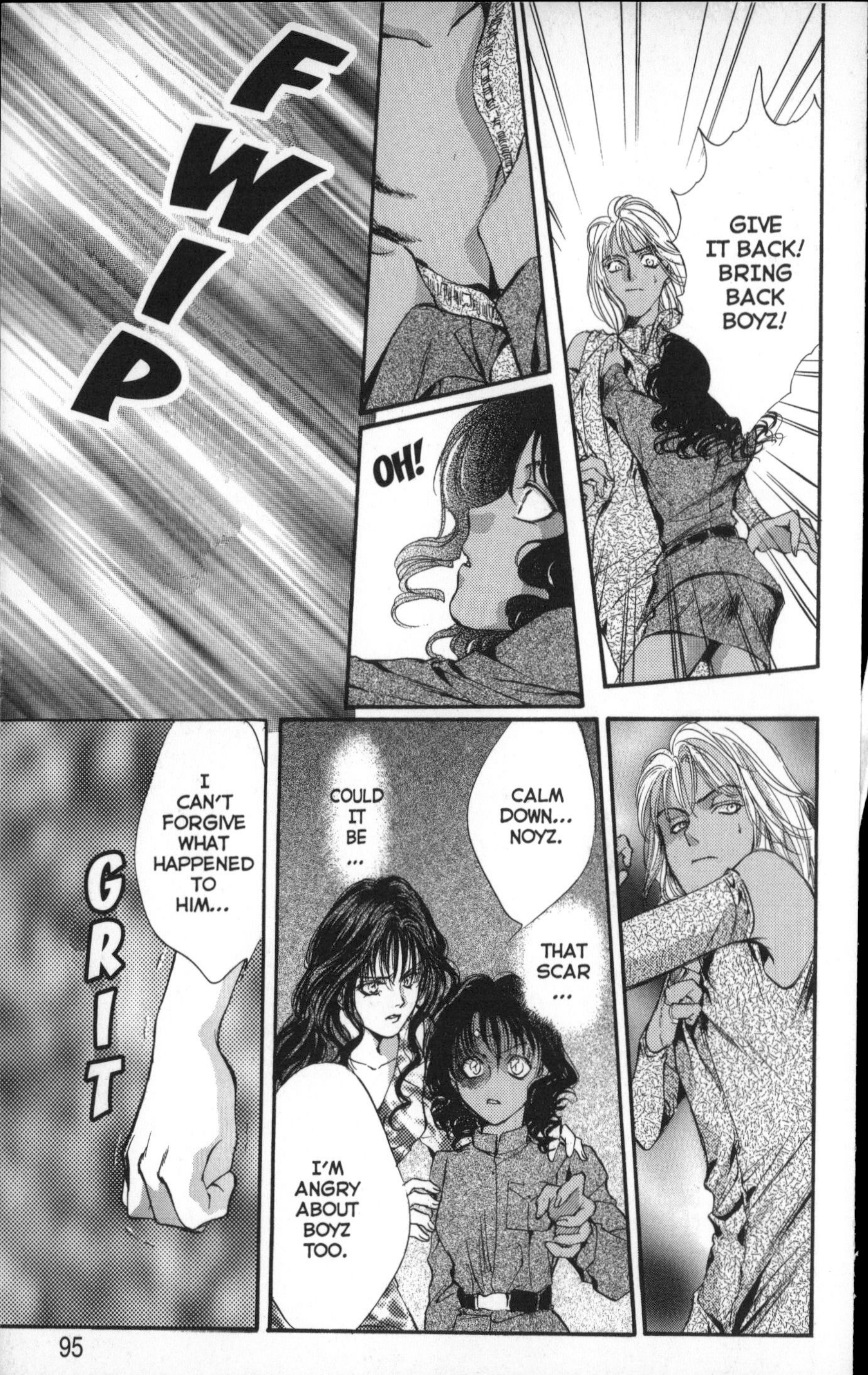
GIVE IT BACK! BRING BACK BOYZ!
OH!
FWIP
CALM DOWN... NOYZ.
COULD IT BE ...
THAT SCAR ...
I'M ANGRY ABOUT BOYZ TOO.
I CAN'T FORGIVE WHAT HAPPENED TO HIM...
GRIT

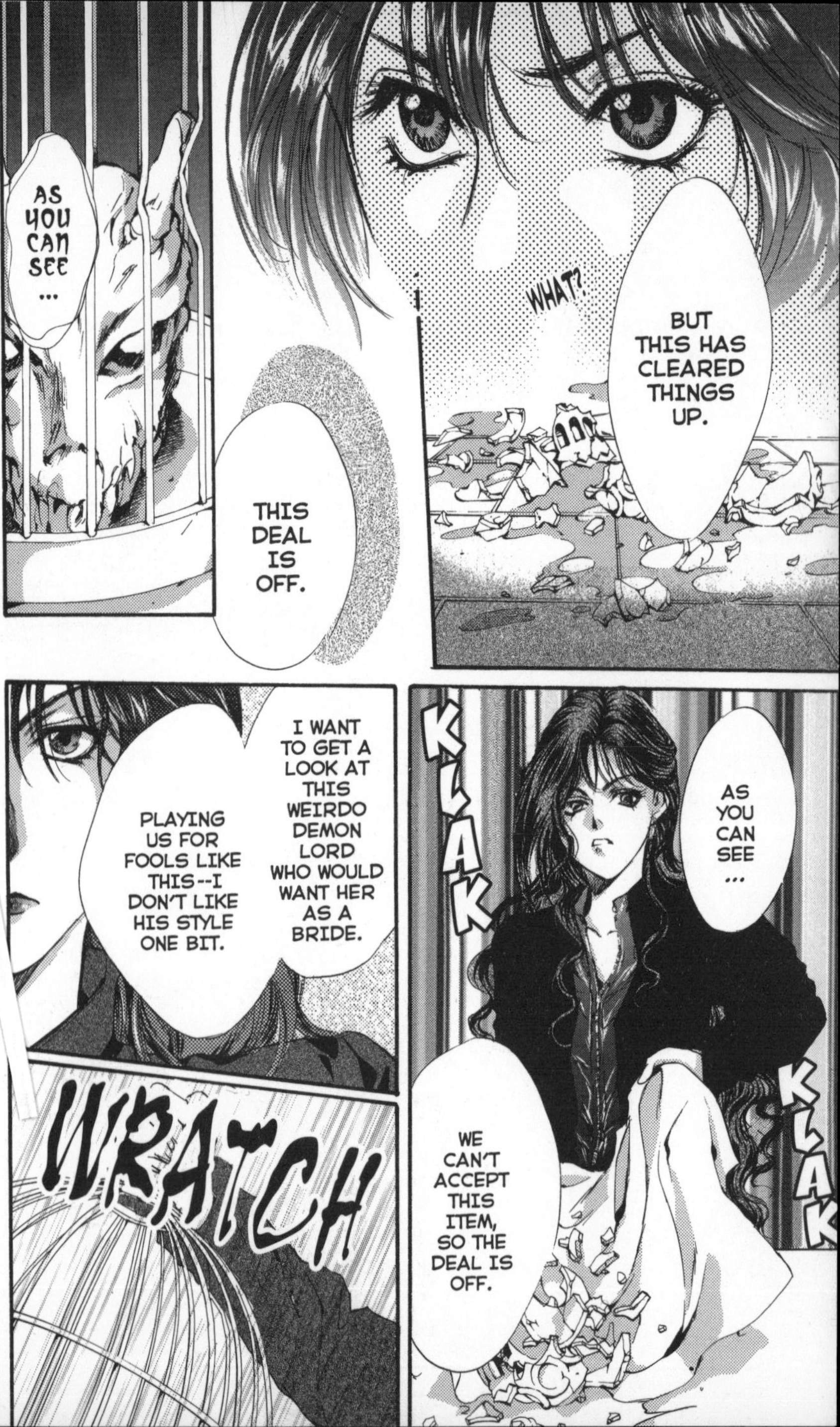
WHAT?
BUT THIS HAS CLEARED THINGS UP.
AS YOU CAN SEE ...
THIS DEAL IS OFF.
KLAK
AS YOU CAN SEE ...
KLAK
WE CAN'T ACCEPT THIS ITEM, SO THE DEAL IS OFF.
I WANT TO GET A LOOK AT THIS WEIRDO DEMON LORD WHO WOULD WANT HER AS A BRIDE.
PLAYING US FOR FOOLS LIKE THIS--I DON'T LIKE HIS STYLE ONE BIT.
WRATCH

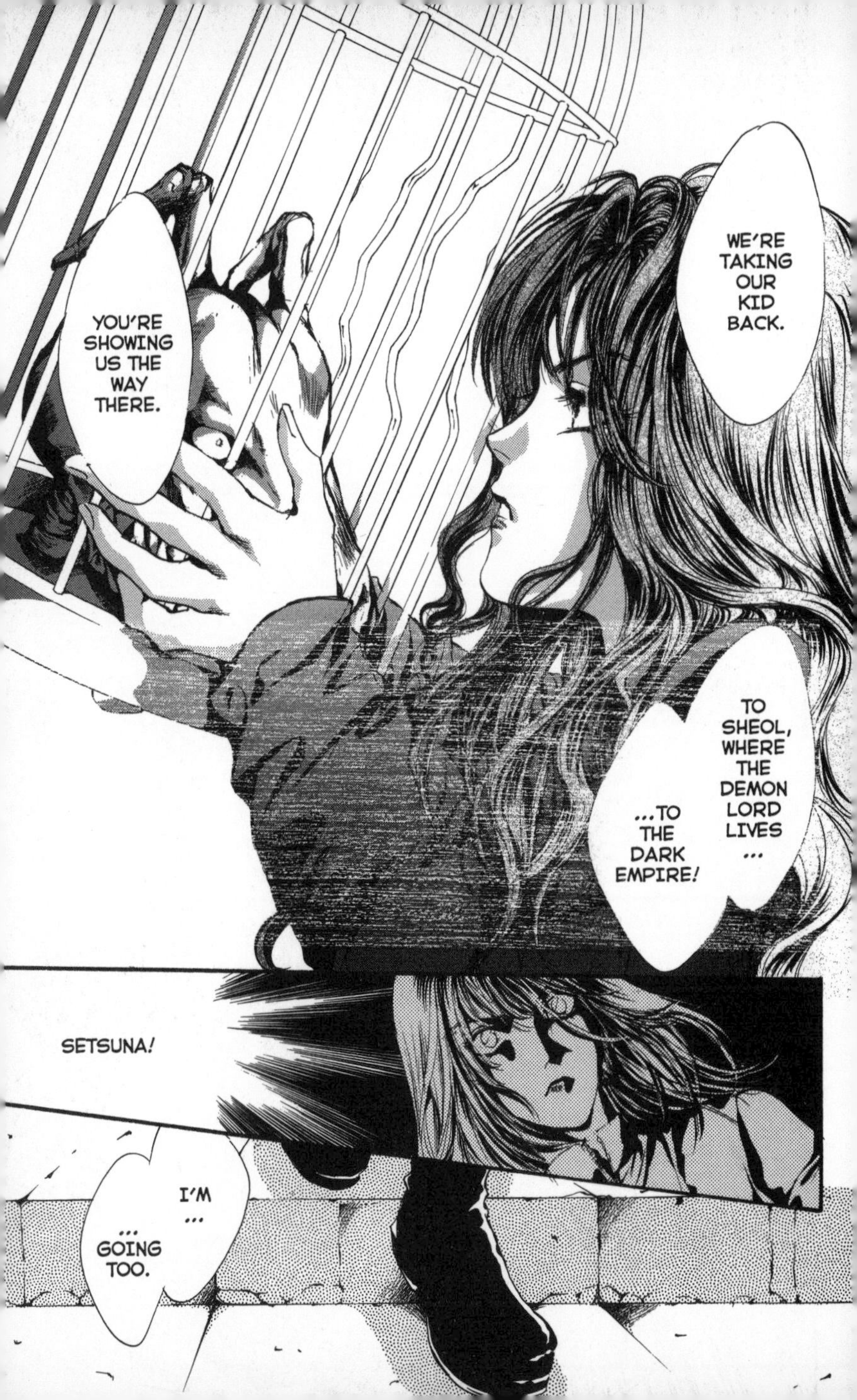
WE'RE TAKING OUR KID BACK.
YOU'RE SHOWING US THE WAY THERE.
TO SHEOL, WHERE THE DEMON LORD LIVES ...
...TO THE DARK EMPIRE!
SETSUNA!
I'M ... ... GOING TOO.

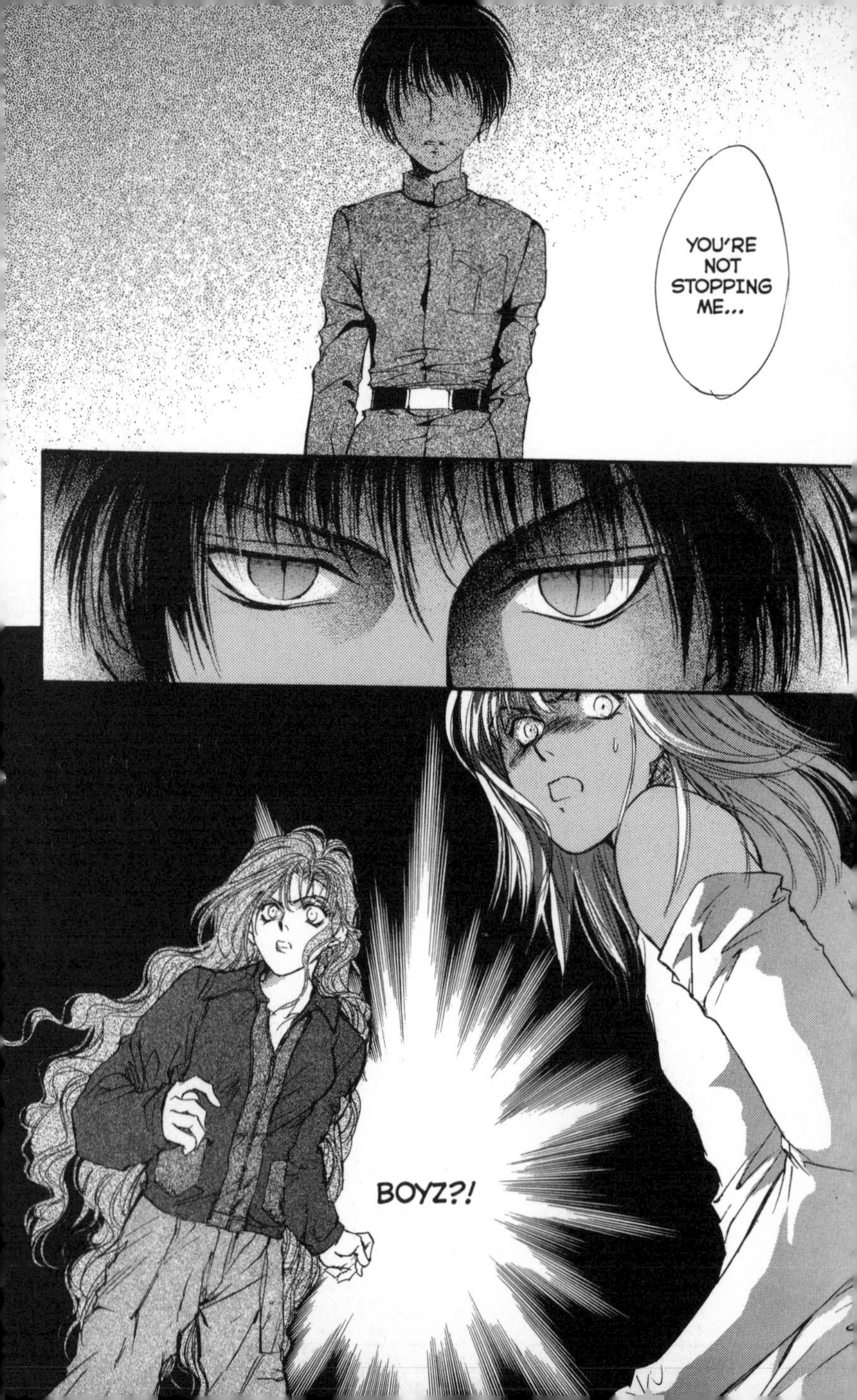
YOU'RE NOT STOPPING ME...
BOYZ?!

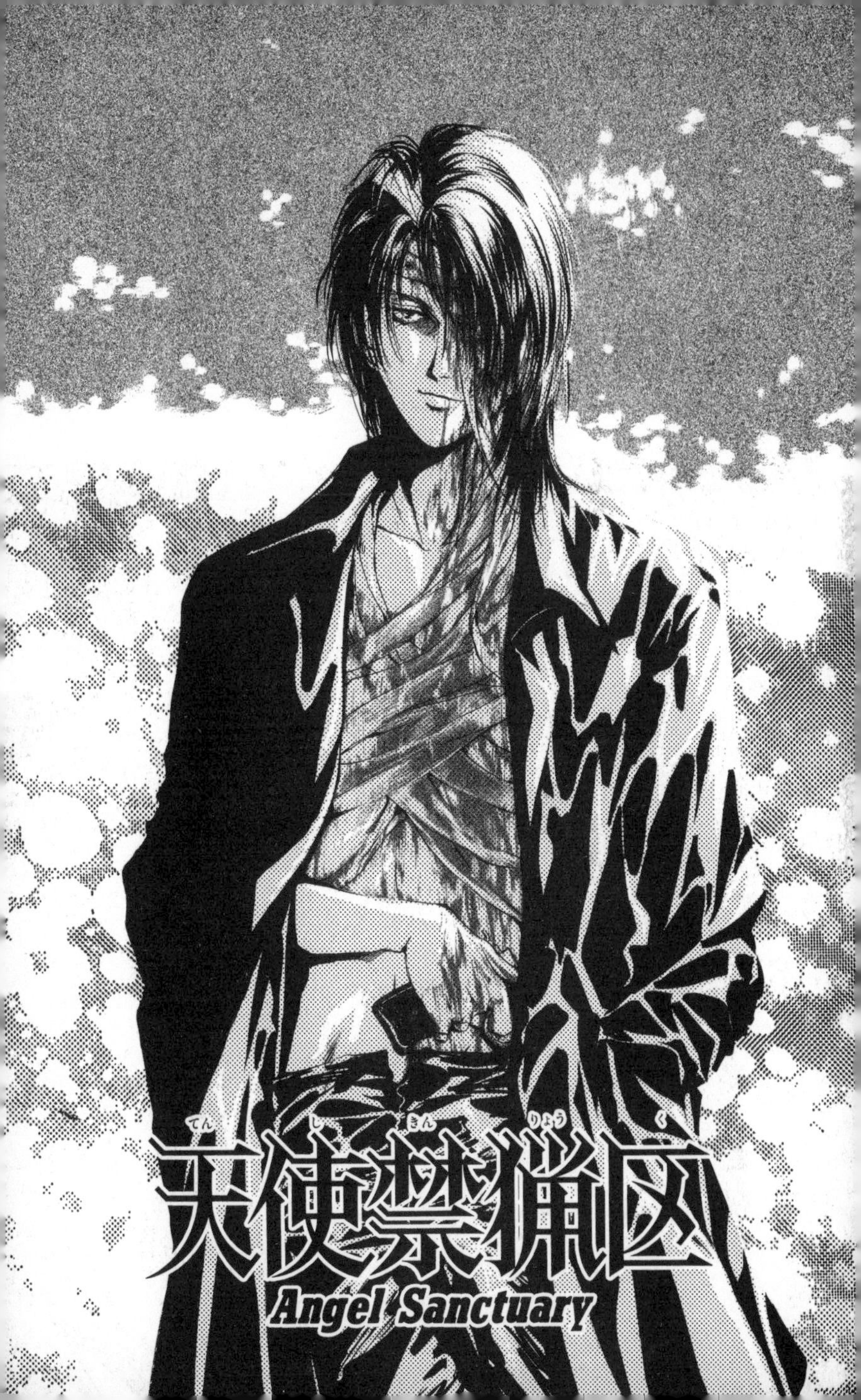

天使禁猟区
てんしきんりょうく
Angel Sanctuary

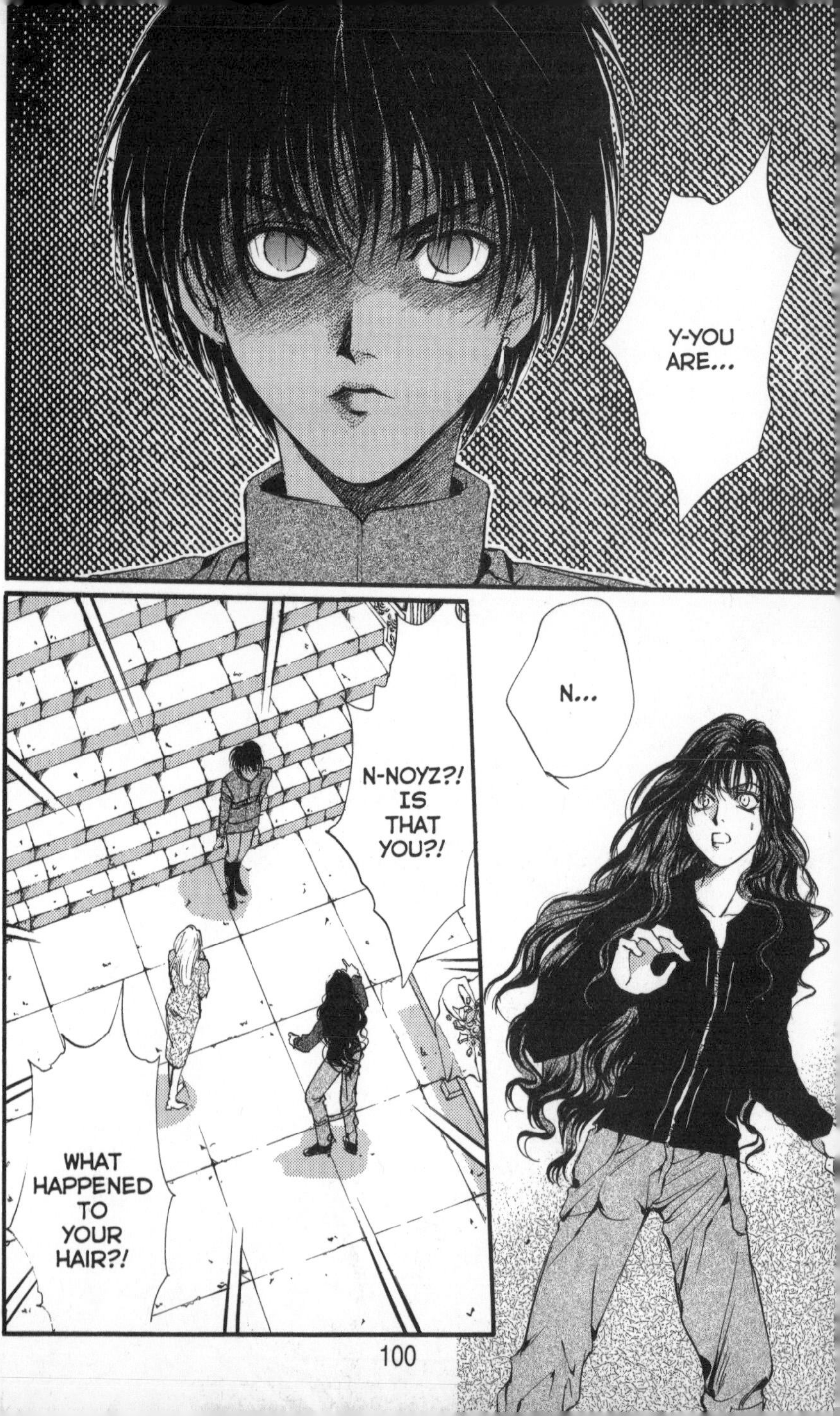
Y-YOU ARE...
N...
N-NOYZ?! IS THAT YOU?!
WHAT HAPPENED TO YOUR HAIR?!

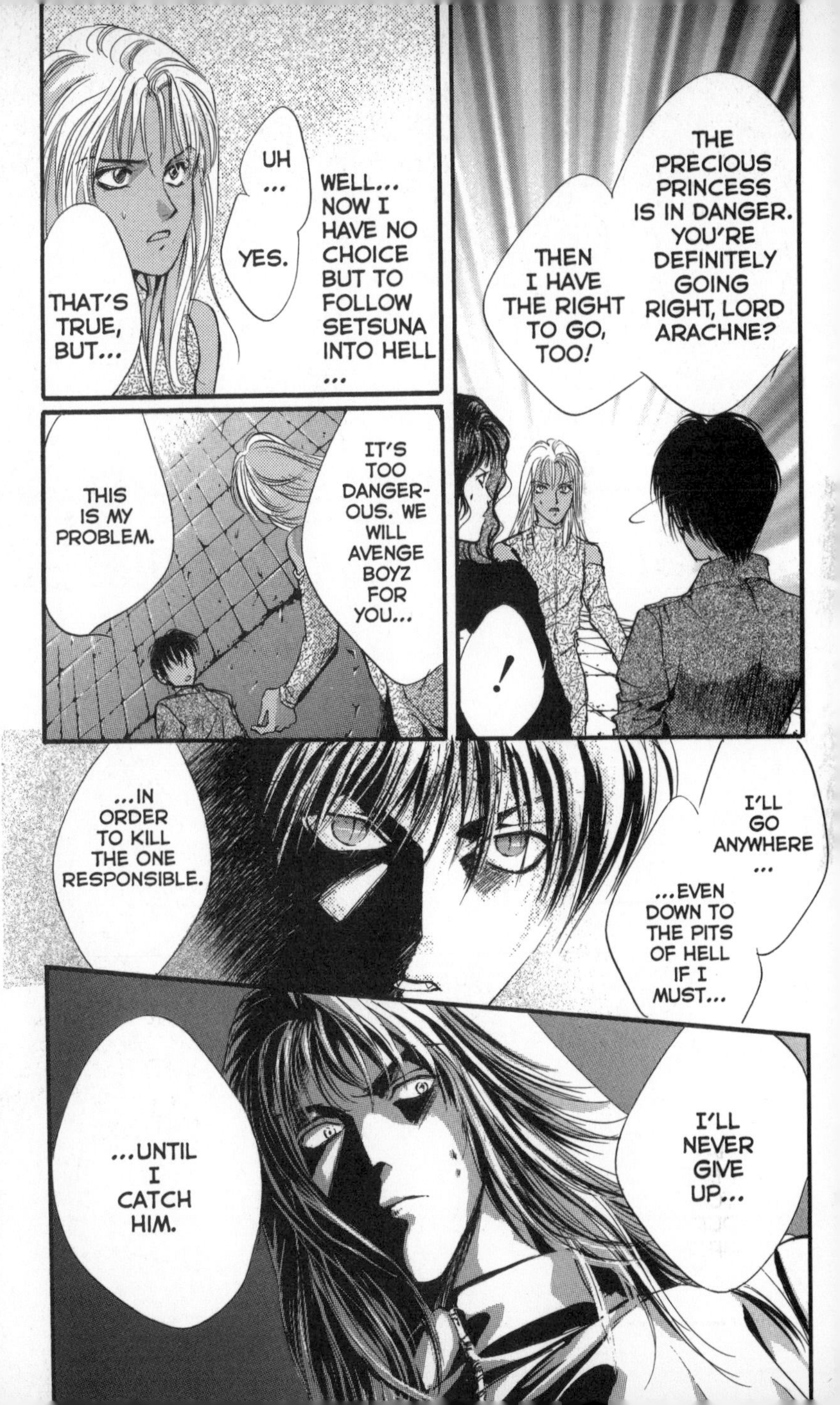
THE PRECIOUS PRINCESS IS IN DANGER. YOU'RE DEFINITELY GOING RIGHT, LORD ARACHNE?
THEN I HAVE THE RIGHT TO GO, TOO!
!
WELL... NOW I HAVE NO CHOICE BUT TO FOLLOW SETSUNA INTO HELL ...
UH ... YES.
THAT'S TRUE, BUT...
IT'S TOO DANGER-OUS. WE WILL AVENGE BOYZ FOR YOU...
THIS IS MY PROBLEM.
I'LL GO ANYWHERE ...
...EVEN DOWN TO THE PITS OF HELL IF I MUST...
...IN ORDER TO KILL THE ONE RESPONSIBLE.
I'LL NEVER GIVE UP...
...UNTIL I CATCH HIM.

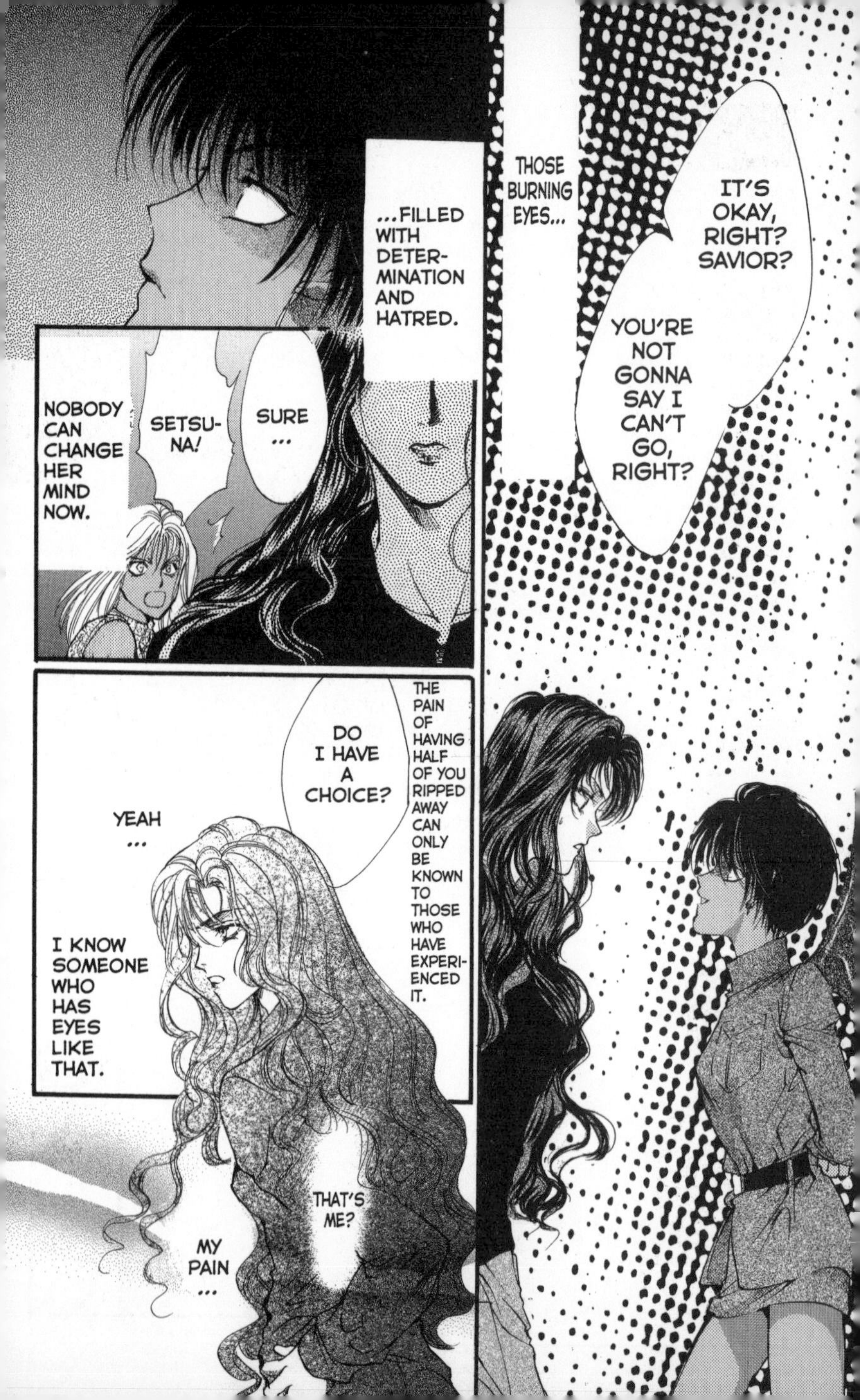
IT'S OKAY, RIGHT? SAVIOR?
YOU'RE NOT GONNA SAY I CAN'T GO, RIGHT?
THOSE BURNING EYES...
...FILLED WITH DETER-MINATION AND HATRED.
SURE ...
SETSU-NA!
NOBODY CAN CHANGE HER MIND NOW.
THE PAIN OF HAVING HALF OF YOU RIPPED AWAY CAN ONLY BE KNOWN TO THOSE WHO HAVE EXPERI-ENCED IT.
DO I HAVE A CHOICE?
YEAH ...
I KNOW SOMEONE WHO HAS EYES LIKE THAT.
THAT'S ME?
MY PAIN ...

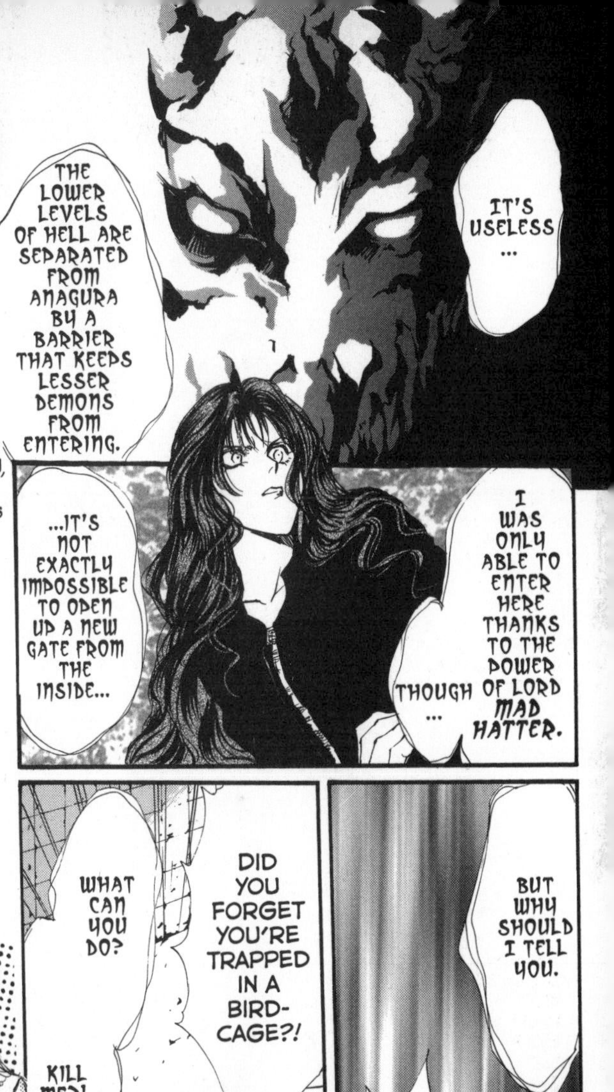
IT'S USELESS...
THE LOWER LEVELS OF HELL ARE SEPARATED FROM ANAGURA BY A BARRIER THAT KEEPS LESSER DEMONS FROM ENTERING.
I WAS ONLY ABLE TO ENTER HERE THANKS TO THE POWER OF LORD MAD HATTER.
THOUGH...
...IT'S NOT EXACTLY IMPOSSIBLE TO OPEN UP A NEW GATE FROM THE INSIDE...
BUT WHY SHOULD I TELL YOU.
WHAT?! WHY YOU...
DID YOU FORGET YOU'RE TRAPPED IN A BIRD-CAGE?!
WHAT CAN YOU DO?
KILL ME?!

I kind of liked Noyz's hair, so I didn't enjoy cutting it. Someone wrote asking about Arachne and thought that Arachne was in *love* with Kurai as a woman, but that's not the case. If that was love, then they would have been interesting, but I think it's cuter how it was. Though it's kind of too late to talk about it now... I got lots of letters saying "Arachne didn't have that mark on her chest before!" but... That's not true. I never showed that part of her body until now. There was always a bra or something covering that part. Understand?

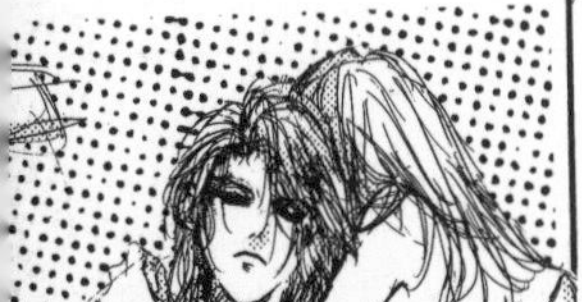

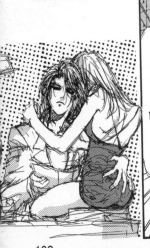

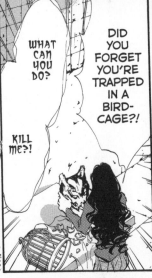

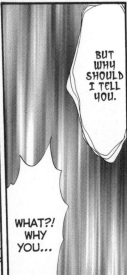

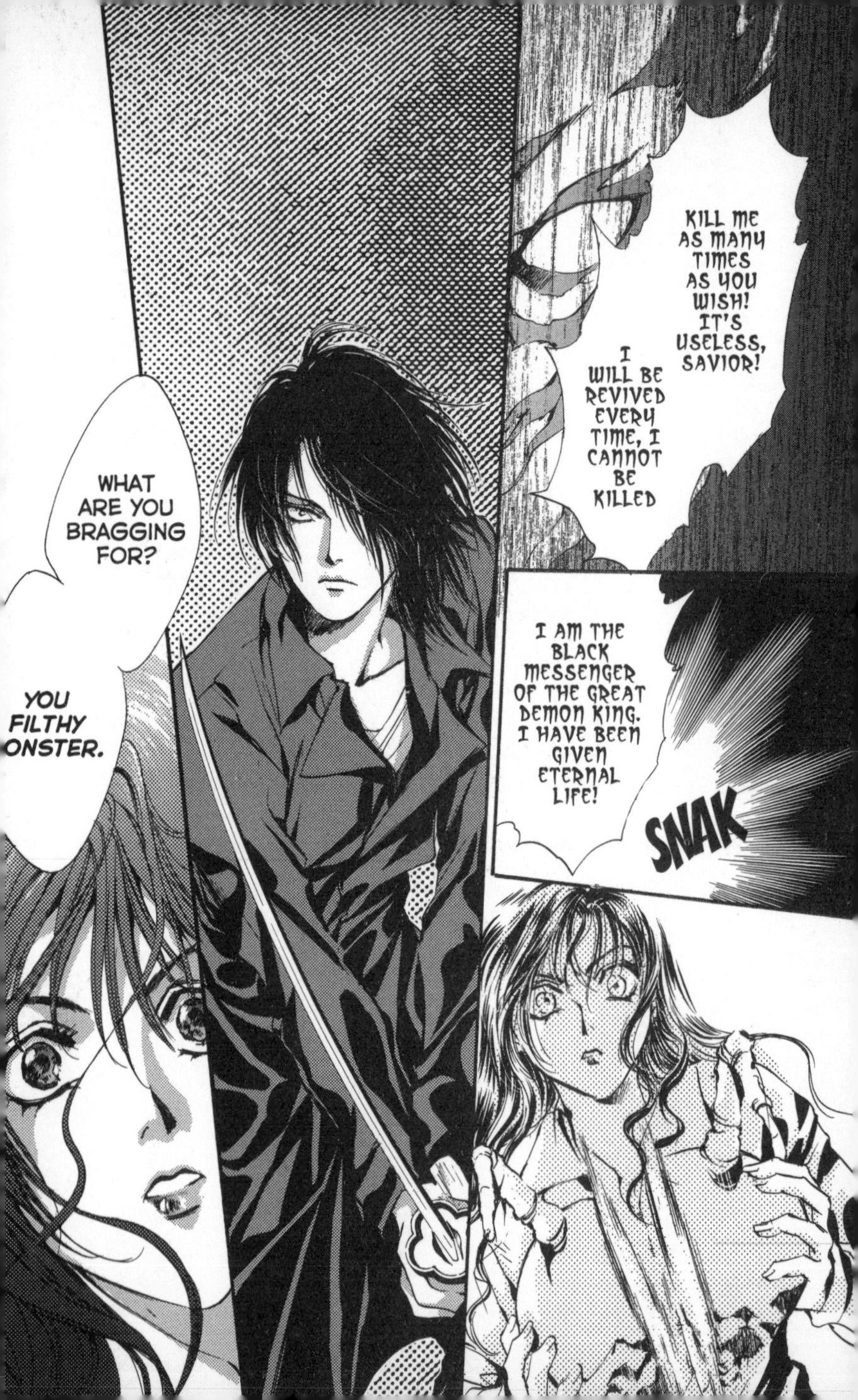
KILL ME AS MANY TIMES AS YOU WISH! IT'S USELESS, SAVIOR!
I WILL BE REVIVED EVERY TIME, I CANNOT BE KILLED
I AM THE BLACK MESSENGER OF THE GREAT DEMON KING. I HAVE BEEN GIVEN ETERNAL LIFE!
SNAK
WHAT ARE YOU BRAGGING FOR?
YOU FILTHY ONSTER.

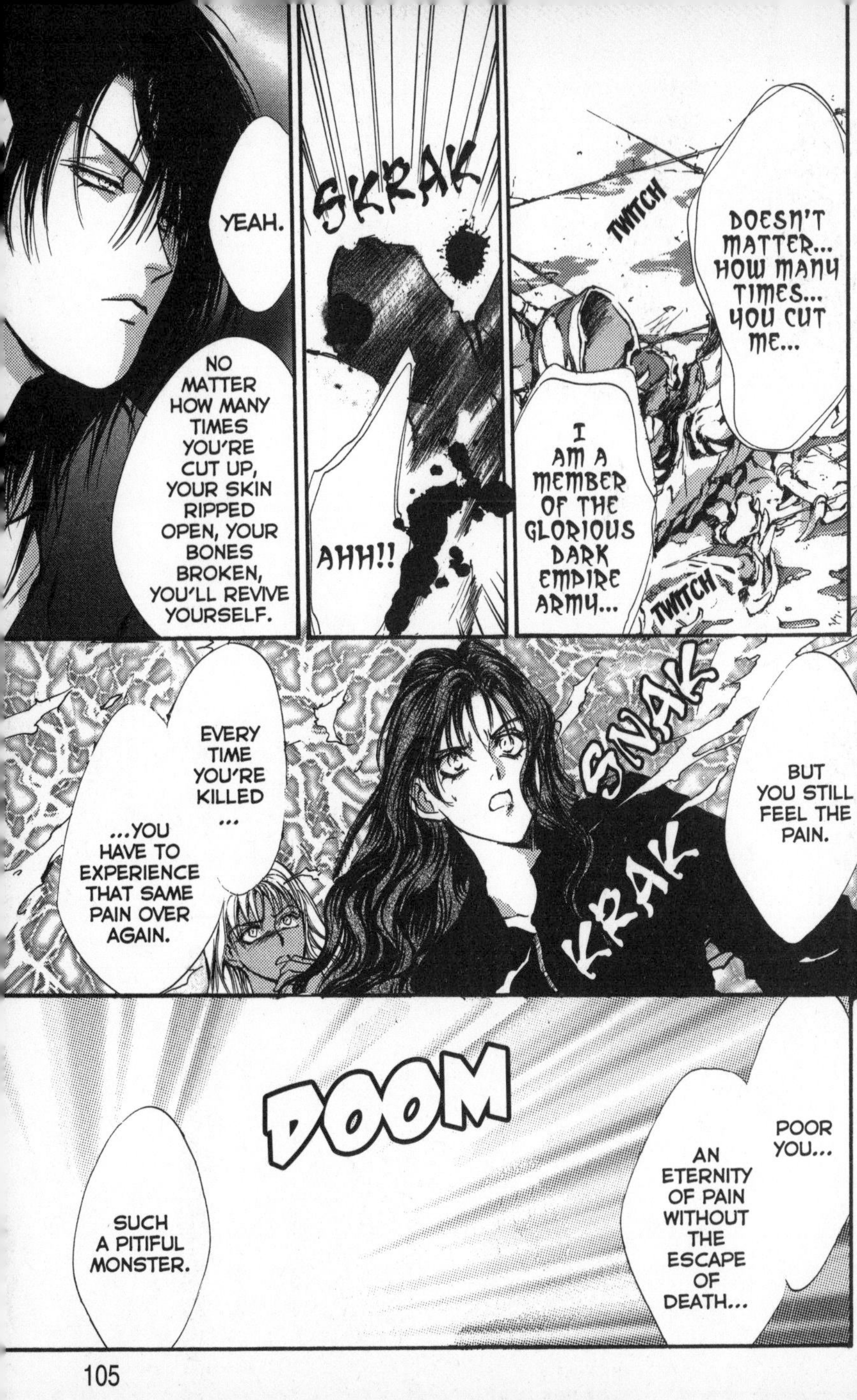

DOESN'T MATTER... HOW MANY TIMES... YOU CUT ME...
TWITCH
I AM A MEMBER OF THE GLORIOUS DARK EMPIRE ARMY...
TWITCH
SKRAK
AHH!!
YEAH.
NO MATTER HOW MANY TIMES YOU'RE CUT UP, YOUR SKIN RIPPED OPEN, YOUR BONES BROKEN, YOU'LL REVIVE YOURSELF.
BUT YOU STILL FEEL THE PAIN.
SNAK
KRAK
EVERY TIME YOU'RE KILLED ...
...YOU HAVE TO EXPERIENCE THAT SAME PAIN OVER AGAIN.
POOR YOU...
AN ETERNITY OF PAIN WITHOUT THE ESCAPE OF DEATH...
DOOM
SUCH A PITIFUL MONSTER.

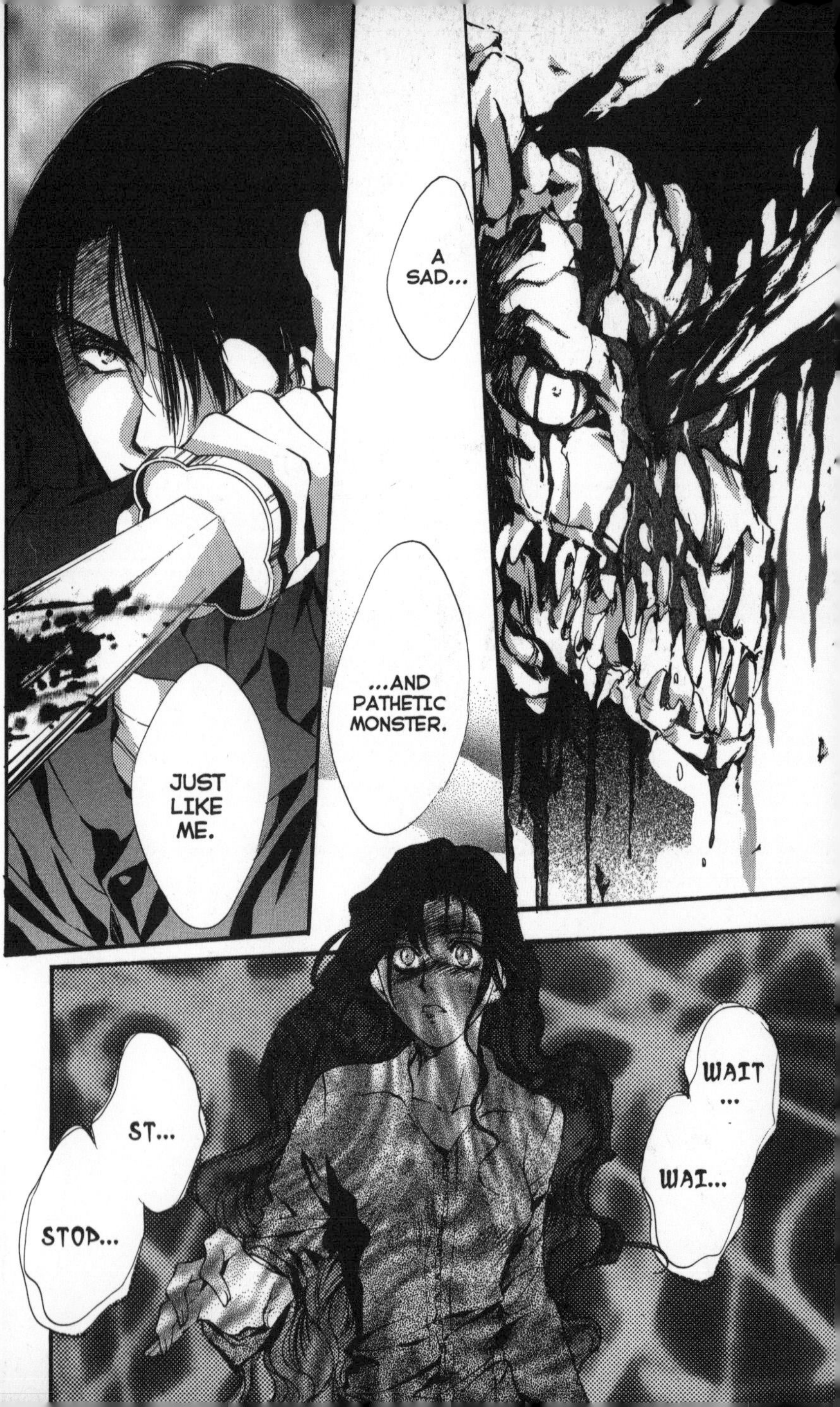
A SAD...
...AND PATHETIC MONSTER.
JUST LIKE ME.
WAIT ...
WAI...
ST...
STOP...

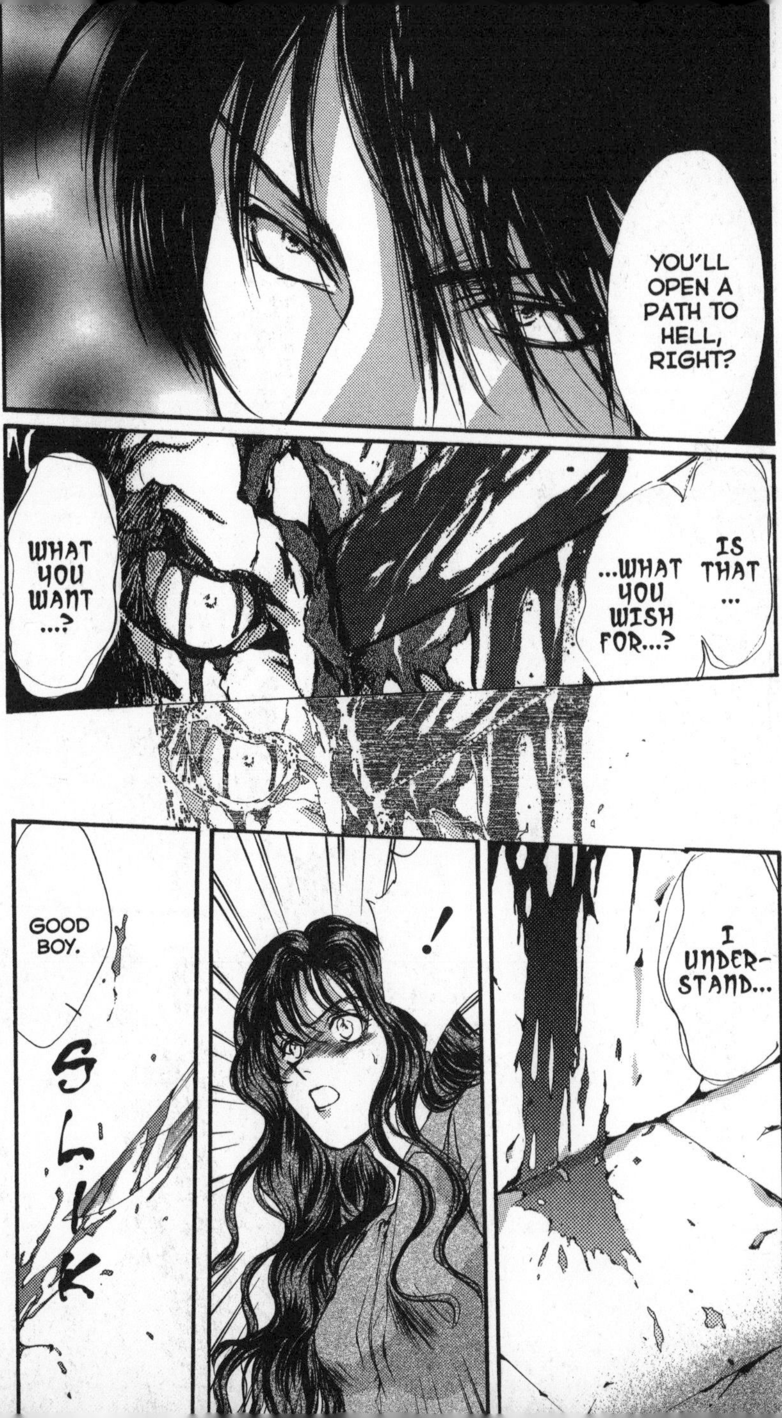
YOU'LL OPEN A PATH TO HELL, RIGHT?
IS THAT ...
...WHAT YOU WISH FOR...?
WHAT YOU WANT ...?
I UNDER-STAND...
!
GOOD BOY.
SLIK

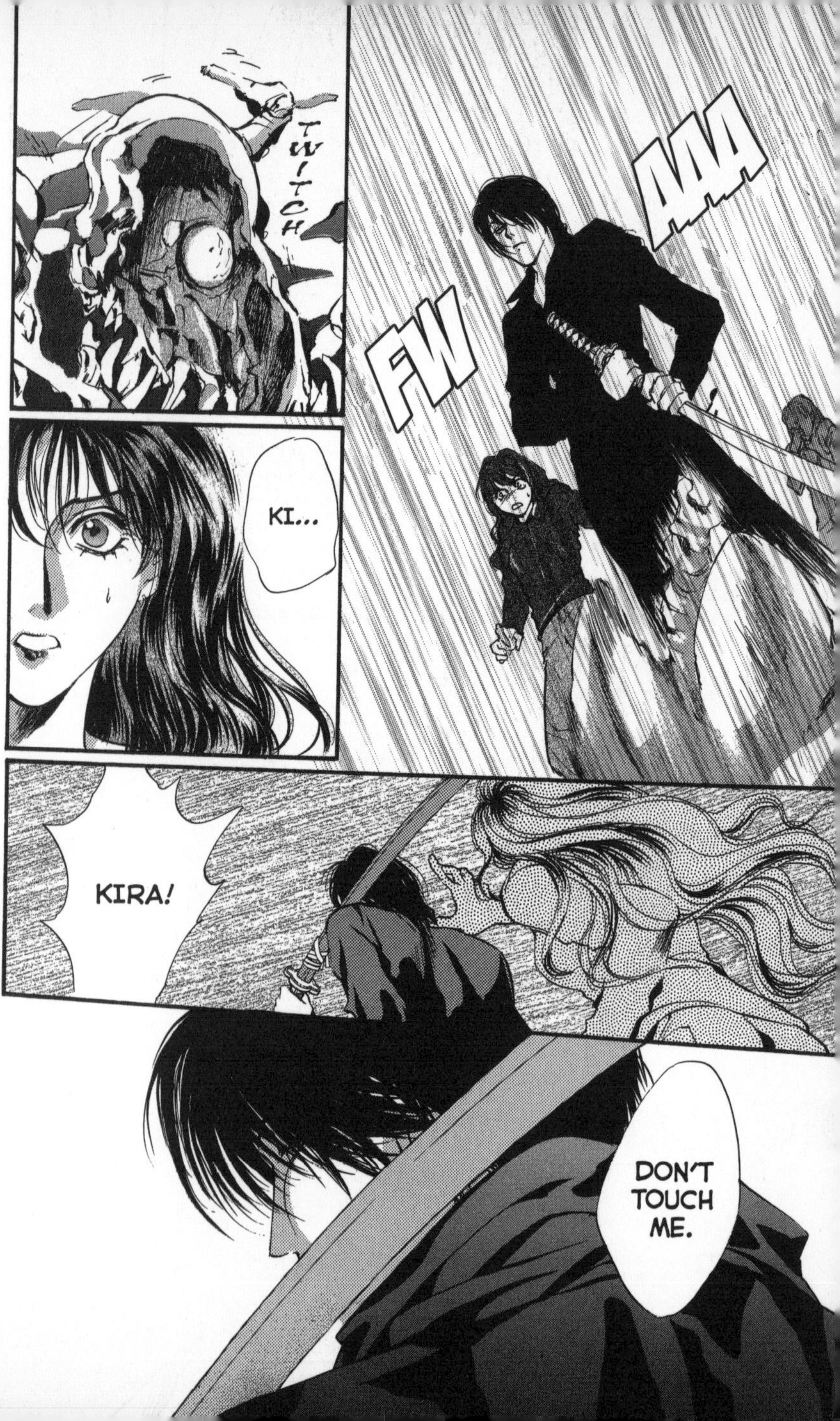
AAA
FW
TWITCH
KI...
KIRA!
DON'T TOUCH ME.

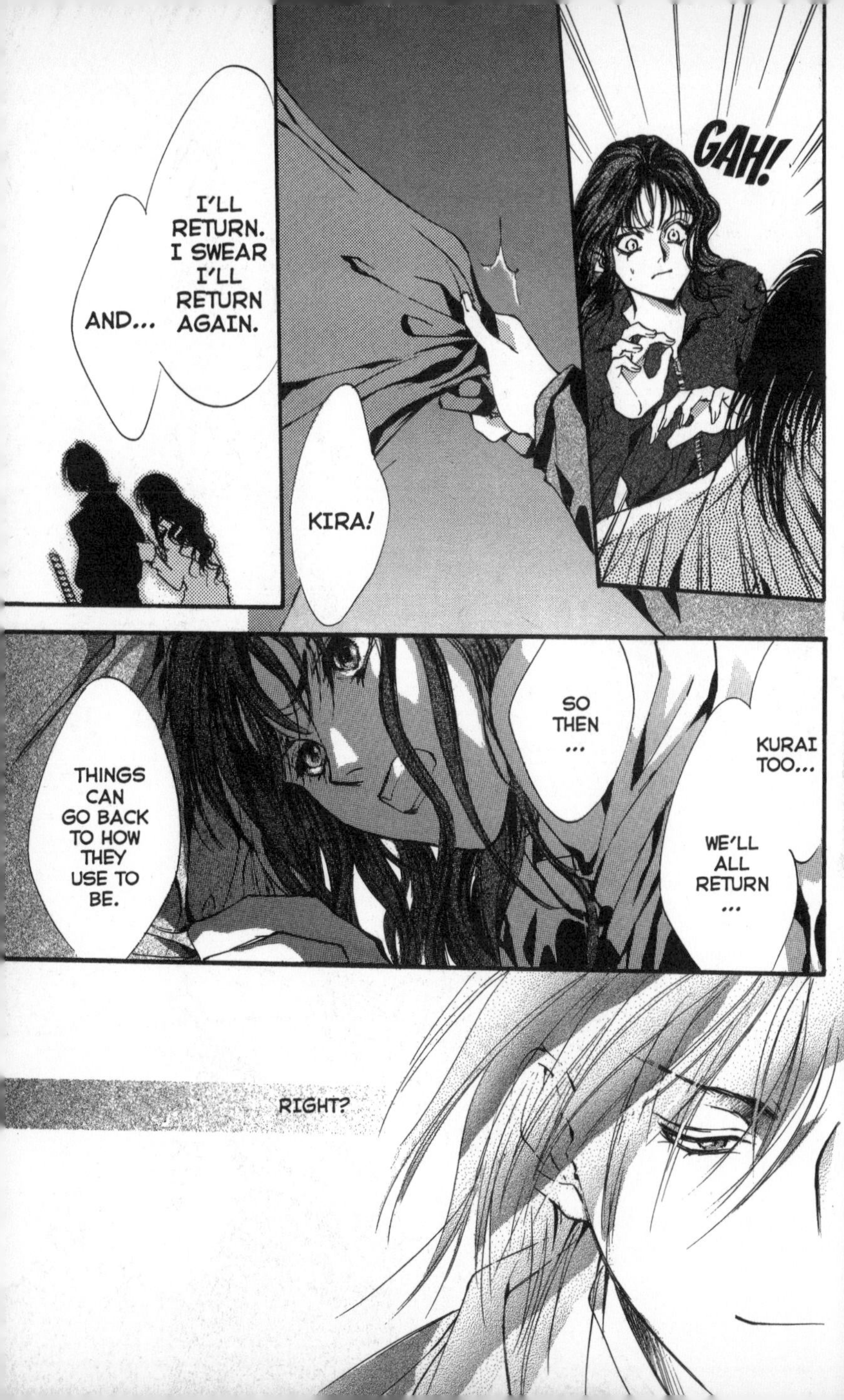
GAH!
KIRA!
I'LL RETURN. I SWEAR I'LL RETURN AGAIN.
AND...
KURAI TOO...
WE'LL ALL RETURN ...
SO THEN ...
THINGS CAN GO BACK TO HOW THEY USE TO BE.
RIGHT?

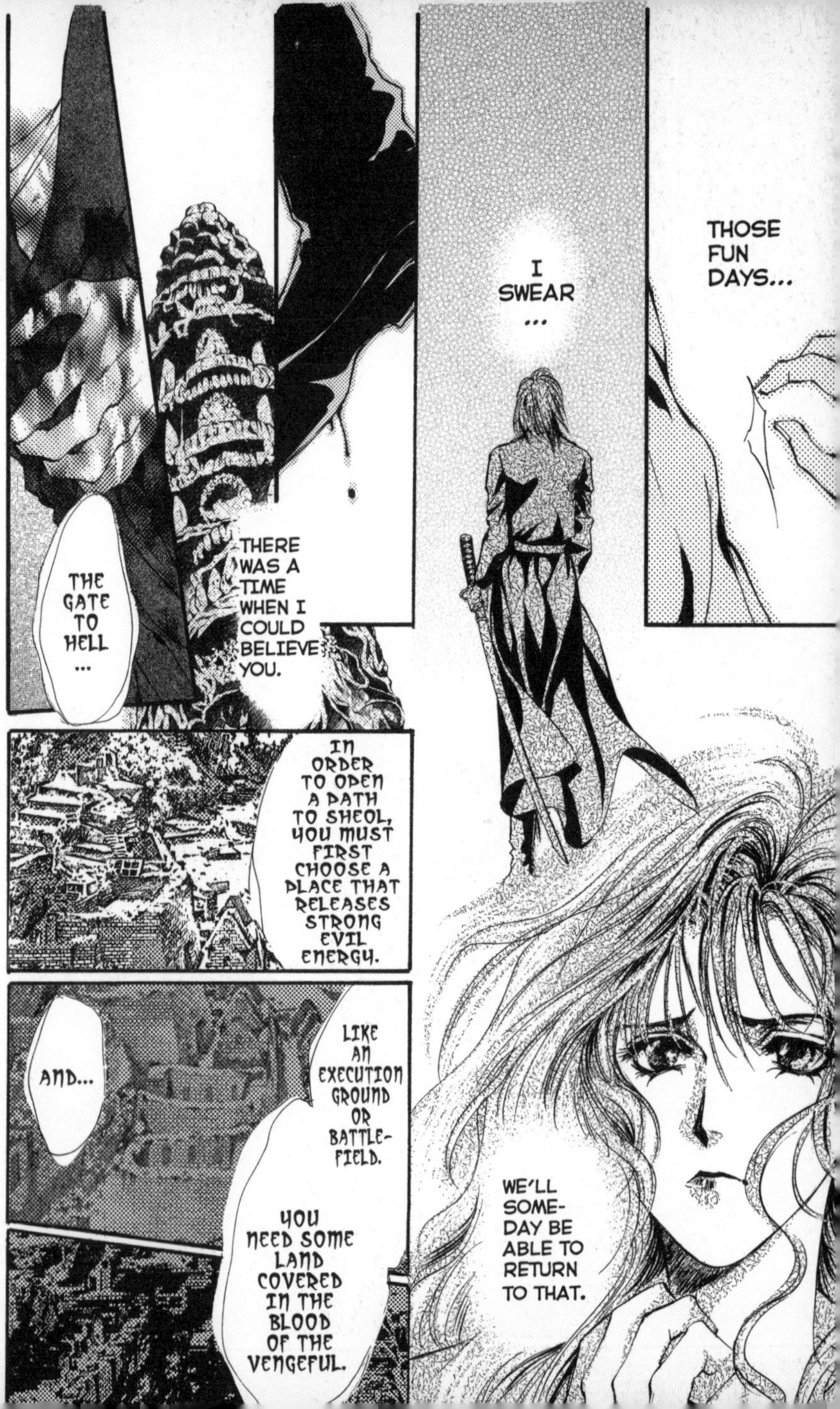
THOSE FUN DAYS...
I SWEAR ...
WE'LL SOMEDAY BE ABLE TO RETURN TO THAT.
THERE WAS A TIME WHEN I COULD BELIEVE YOU.
THE GATE TO HELL ...
IN ORDER TO OPEN A PATH TO SHEOL, YOU MUST FIRST CHOOSE A PLACE THAT RELEASES STRONG EVIL ENERGY.
LIKE AN EXECUTION GROUND OR BATTLE-FIELD.
AND...
YOU NEED SOME LAND COVERED IN THE BLOOD OF THE VENGEFUL.

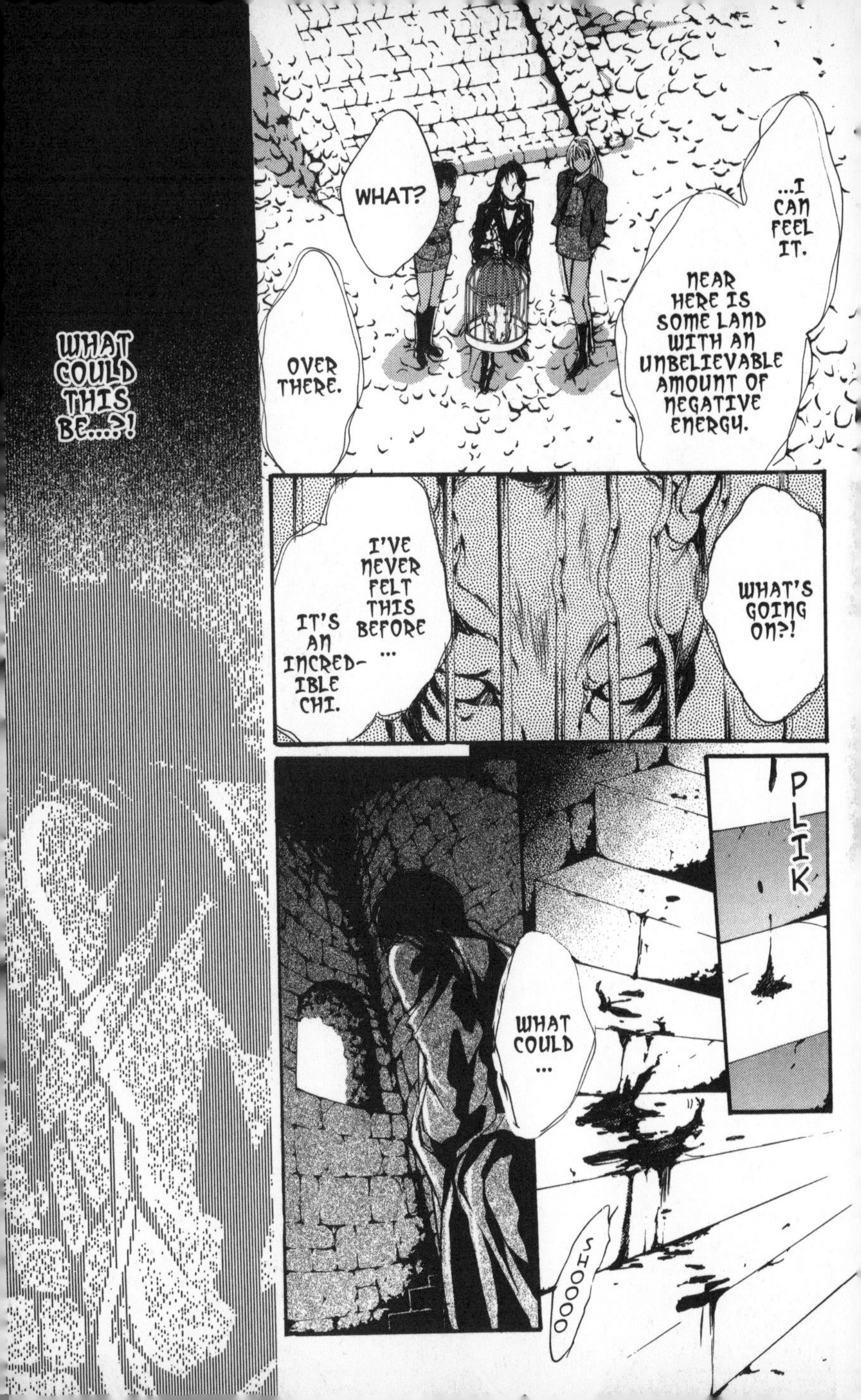
...I CAN FEEL IT.
NEAR HERE IS SOME LAND WITH AN UNBELIEVABLE AMOUNT OF NEGATIVE ENERGY.
WHAT?
OVER THERE.
WHAT'S GOING ON?!
I'VE NEVER FELT THIS BEFORE ...
IT'S AN INCRED-IBLE CHI.
PLIK
WHAT COULD ...
SHOOOOO
WHAT COULD THIS BE...?!

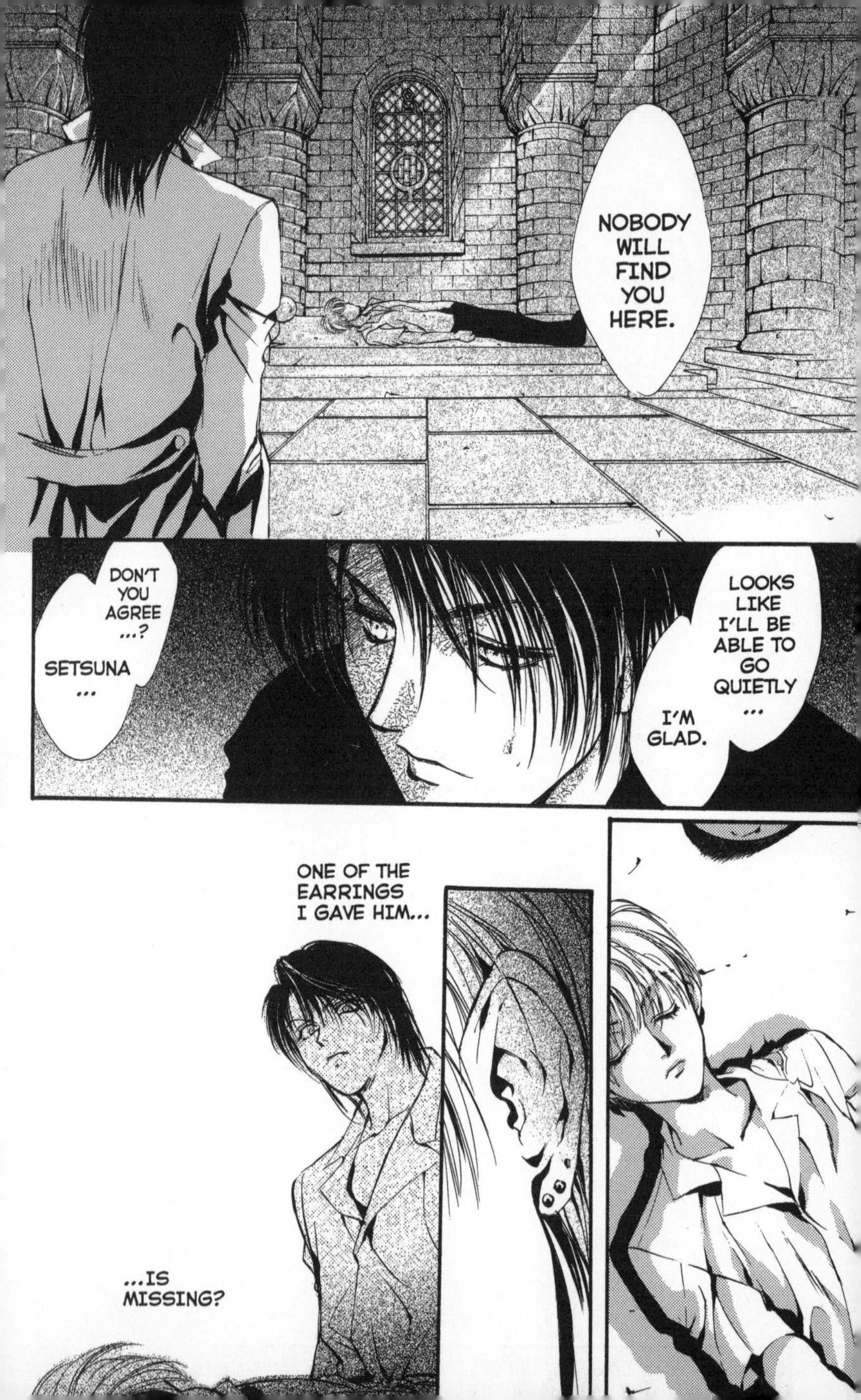
NOBODY WILL FIND YOU HERE.
LOOKS LIKE I'LL BE ABLE TO GO QUIETLY...
I'M GLAD.
DON'T YOU AGREE...?
SETSUNA...
ONE OF THE EARRINGS I GAVE HIM...
...IS MISSING?

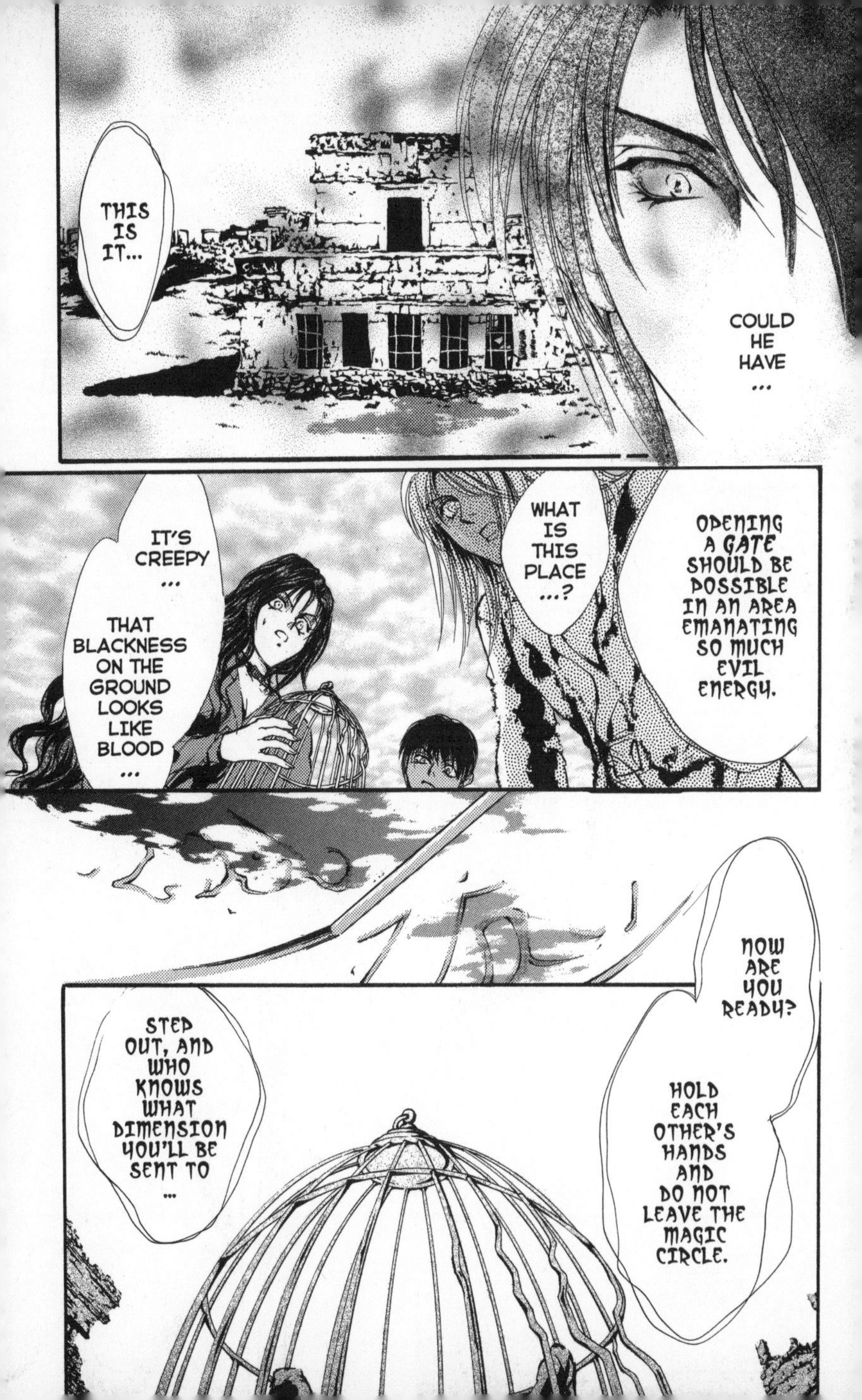
COULD HE HAVE ...
THIS IS IT...
OPENING A GATE SHOULD BE POSSIBLE IN AN AREA EMANATING SO MUCH EVIL ENERGY.
WHAT IS THIS PLACE ...?
IT'S CREEPY ...
THAT BLACKNESS ON THE GROUND LOOKS LIKE BLOOD ...
NOW ARE YOU READY?
HOLD EACH OTHER'S HANDS AND DO NOT LEAVE THE MAGIC CIRCLE.
STEP OUT, AND WHO KNOWS WHAT DIMENSION YOU'LL BE SENT TO ...

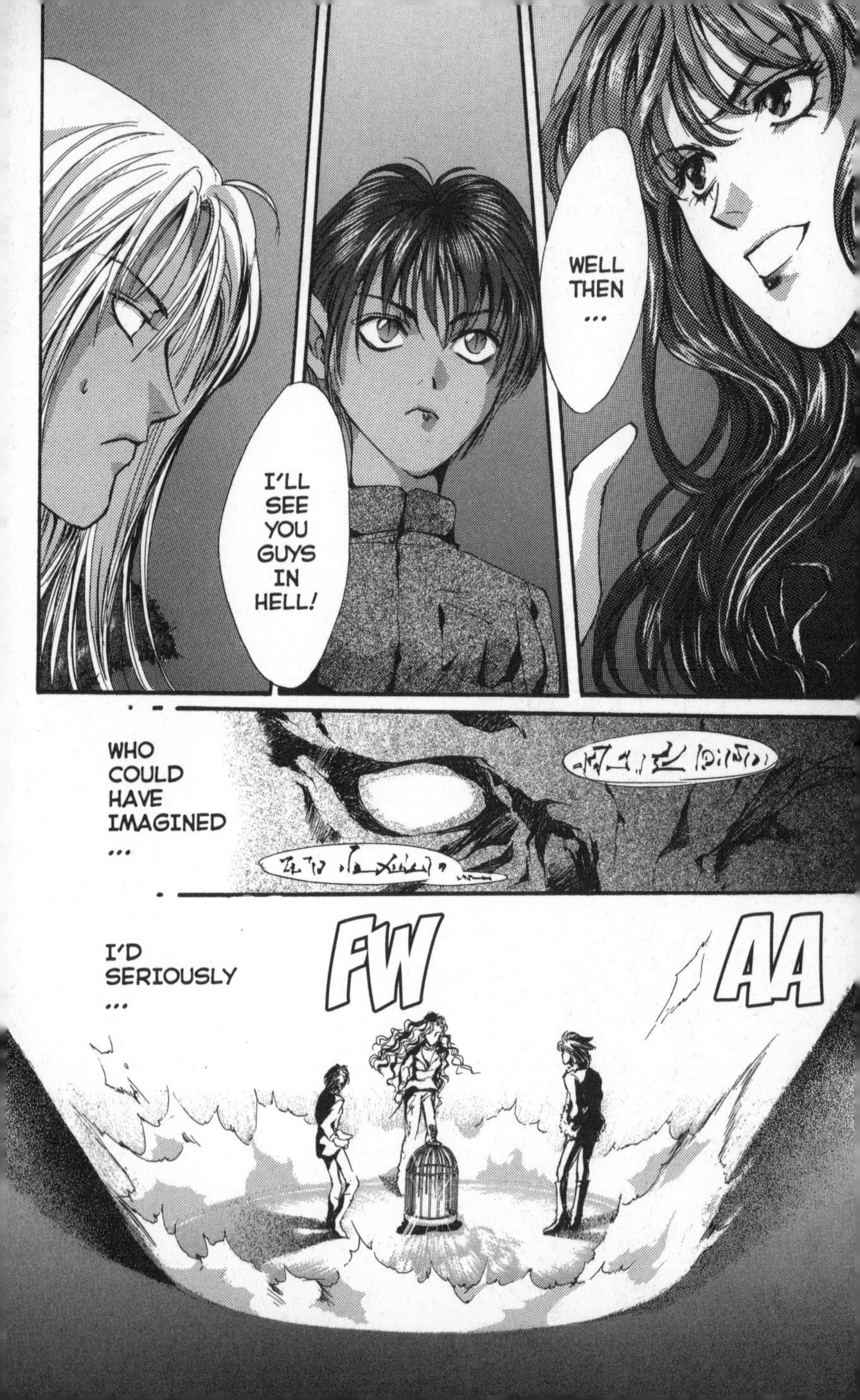
WELL THEN ...
I'LL SEE YOU GUYS IN HELL!
WHO COULD HAVE IMAGINED ...
I'D SERIOUSLY ...
FWAA

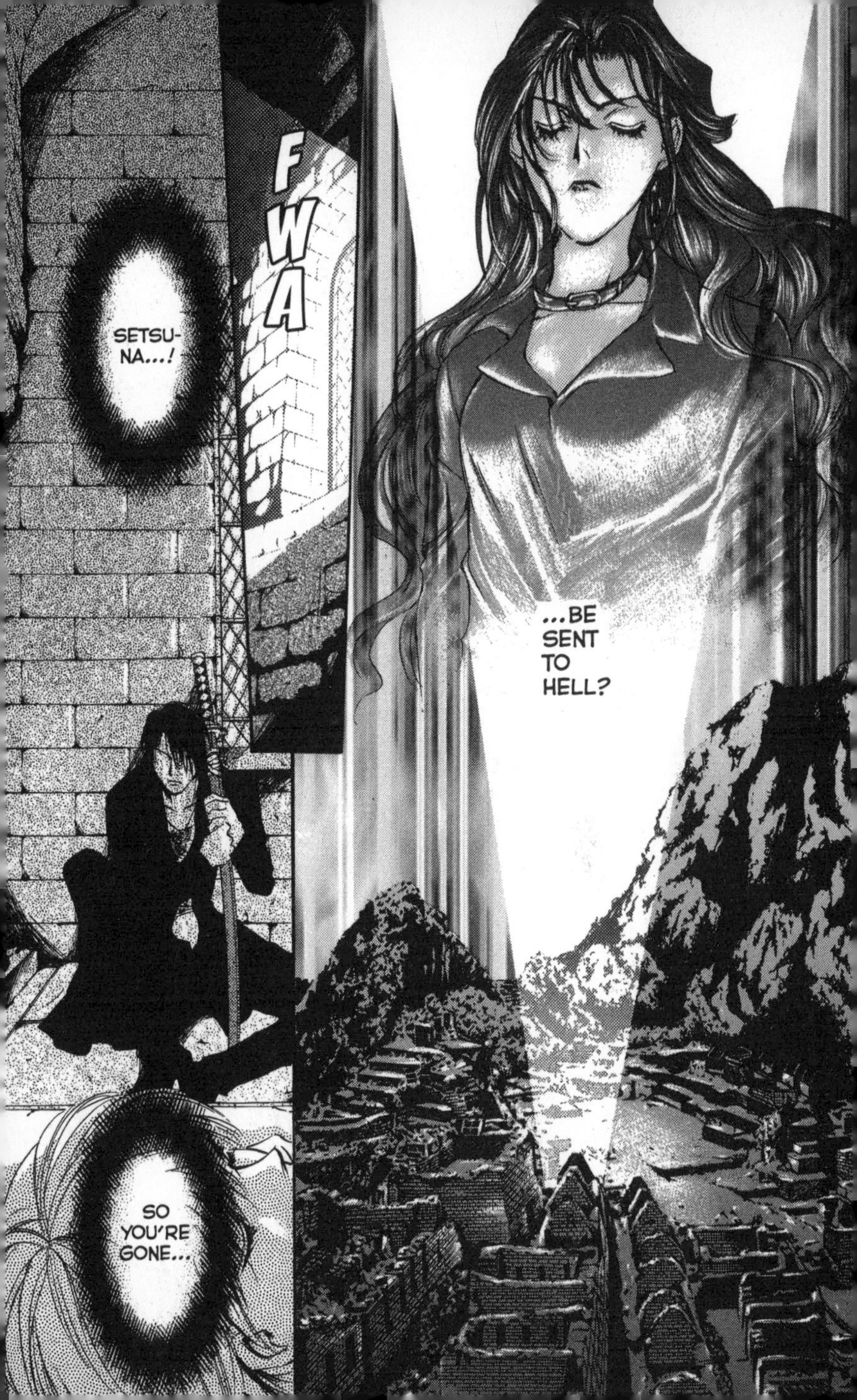
...BE SENT TO HELL?
FWA
SETSU-NA...!
SO YOU'RE GONE...

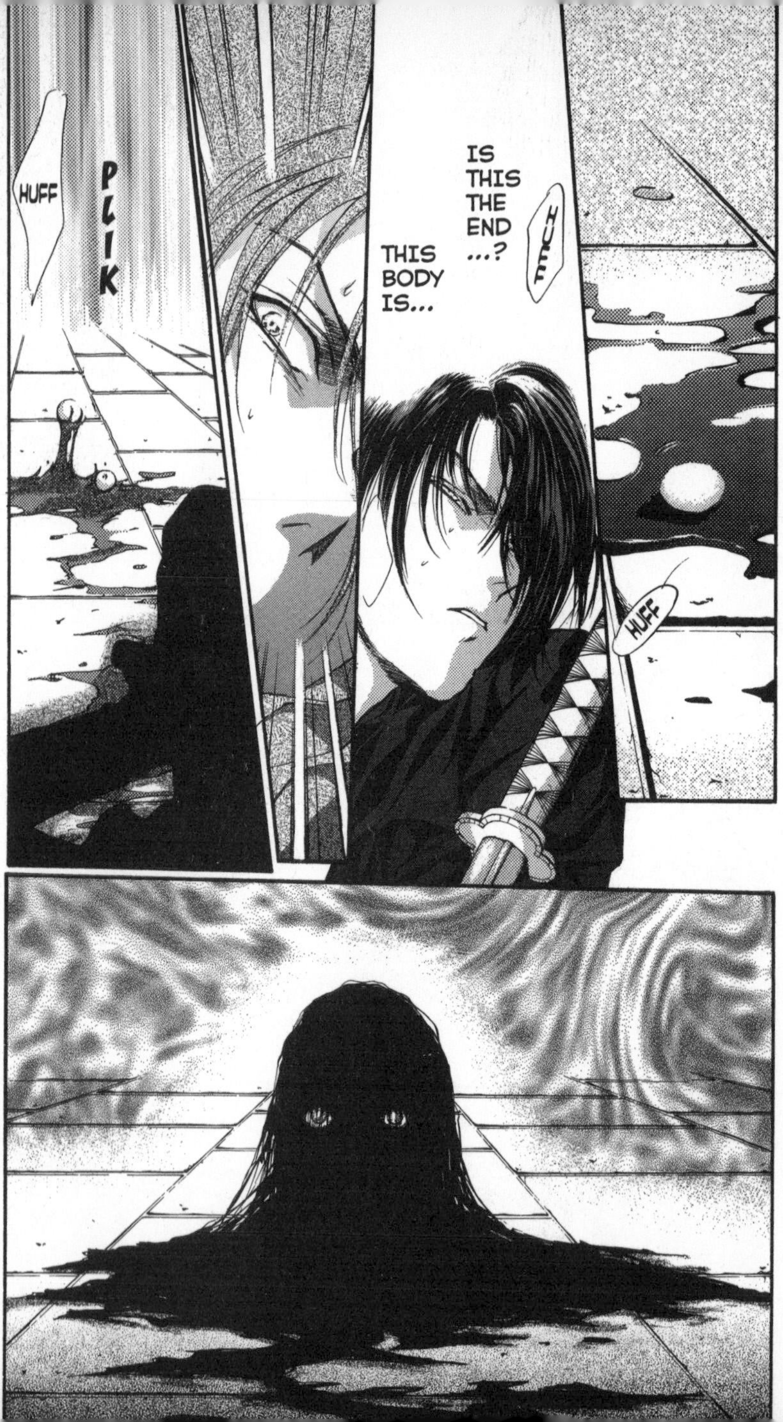
IS THIS THE END ...?
TWCH
THIS BODY IS...
HUFF
HUFF
PLIK

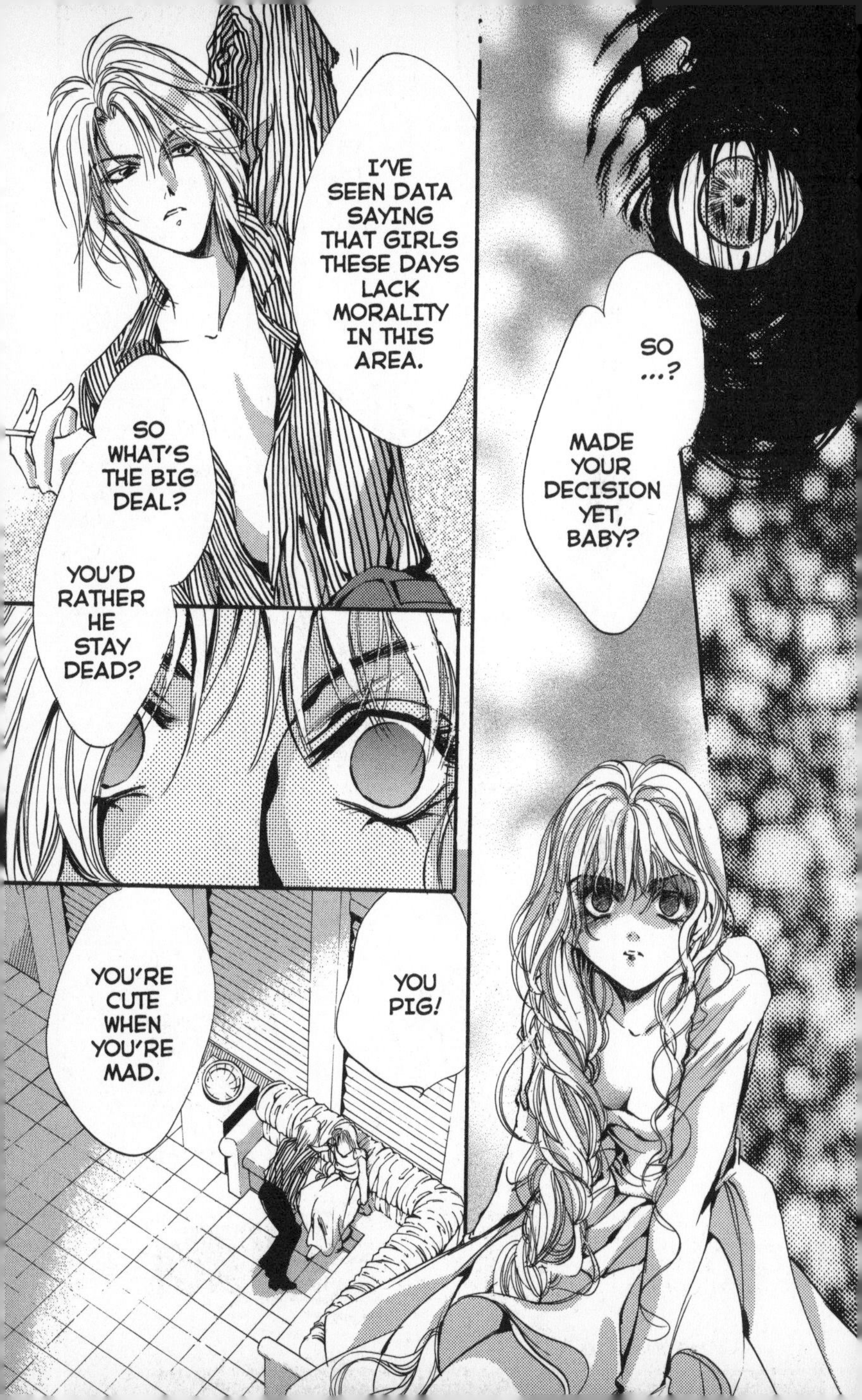
SO ...?
MADE YOUR DECISION YET, BABY?
I'VE SEEN DATA SAYING THAT GIRLS THESE DAYS LACK MORALITY IN THIS AREA.
SO WHAT'S THE BIG DEAL?
YOU'D RATHER HE STAY DEAD?
YOU PIG!
YOU'RE CUTE WHEN YOU'RE MAD.

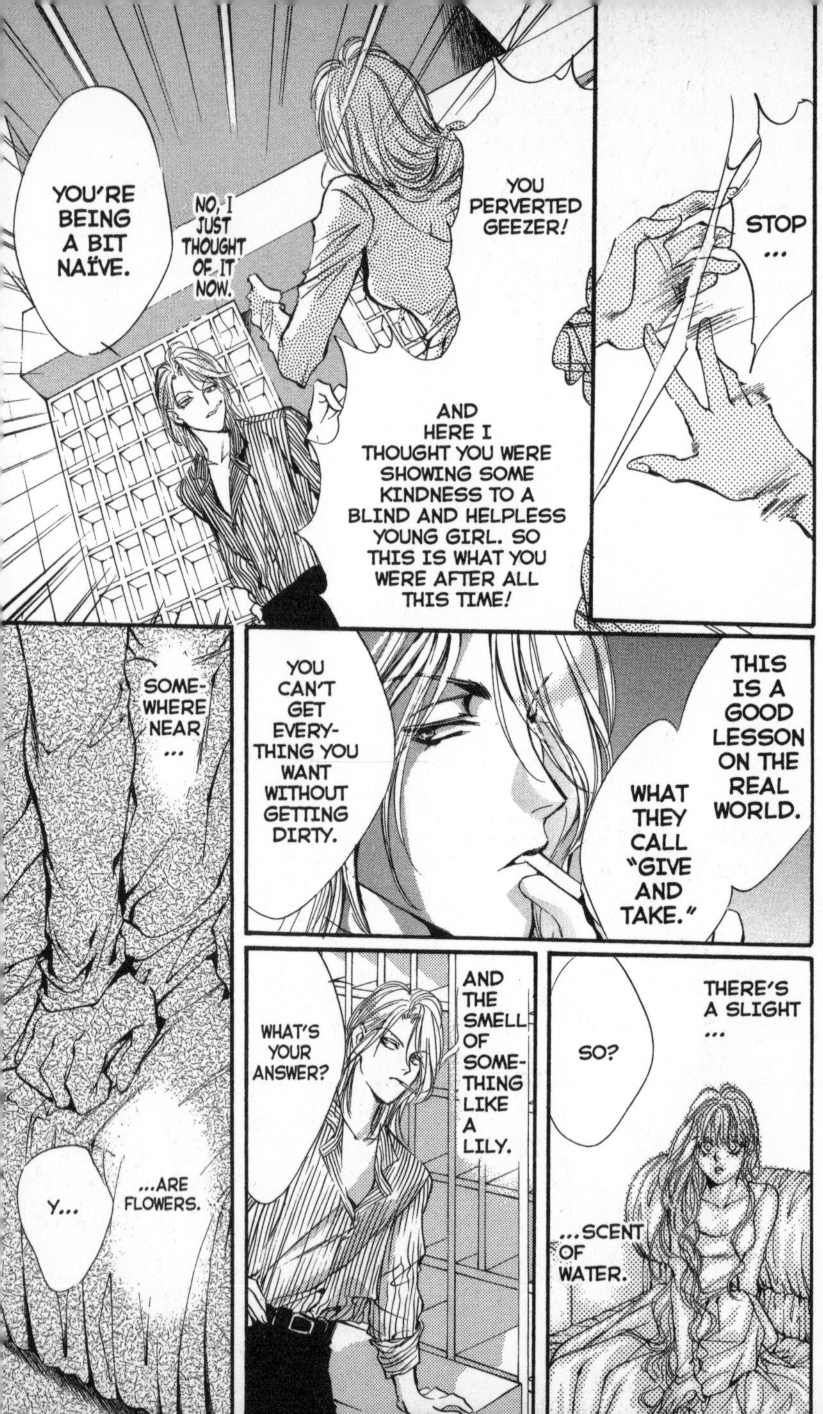
STOP ...
YOU PERVERTED GEEZER!
AND HERE I THOUGHT YOU WERE SHOWING SOME KINDNESS TO A BLIND AND HELPLESS YOUNG GIRL. SO THIS IS WHAT YOU WERE AFTER ALL THIS TIME!
NO, I JUST THOUGHT OF IT NOW.
YOU'RE BEING A BIT NAÏVE.
THIS IS A GOOD LESSON ON THE REAL WORLD.
WHAT THEY CALL "GIVE AND TAKE."
YOU CAN'T GET EVERYTHING YOU WANT WITHOUT GETTING DIRTY.
THERE'S A SLIGHT ...
...SCENT OF WATER.
SO?
AND THE SMELL OF SOMETHING LIKE A LILY.
WHAT'S YOUR ANSWER?
SOMEWHERE NEAR ...
...ARE FLOWERS.
Y...

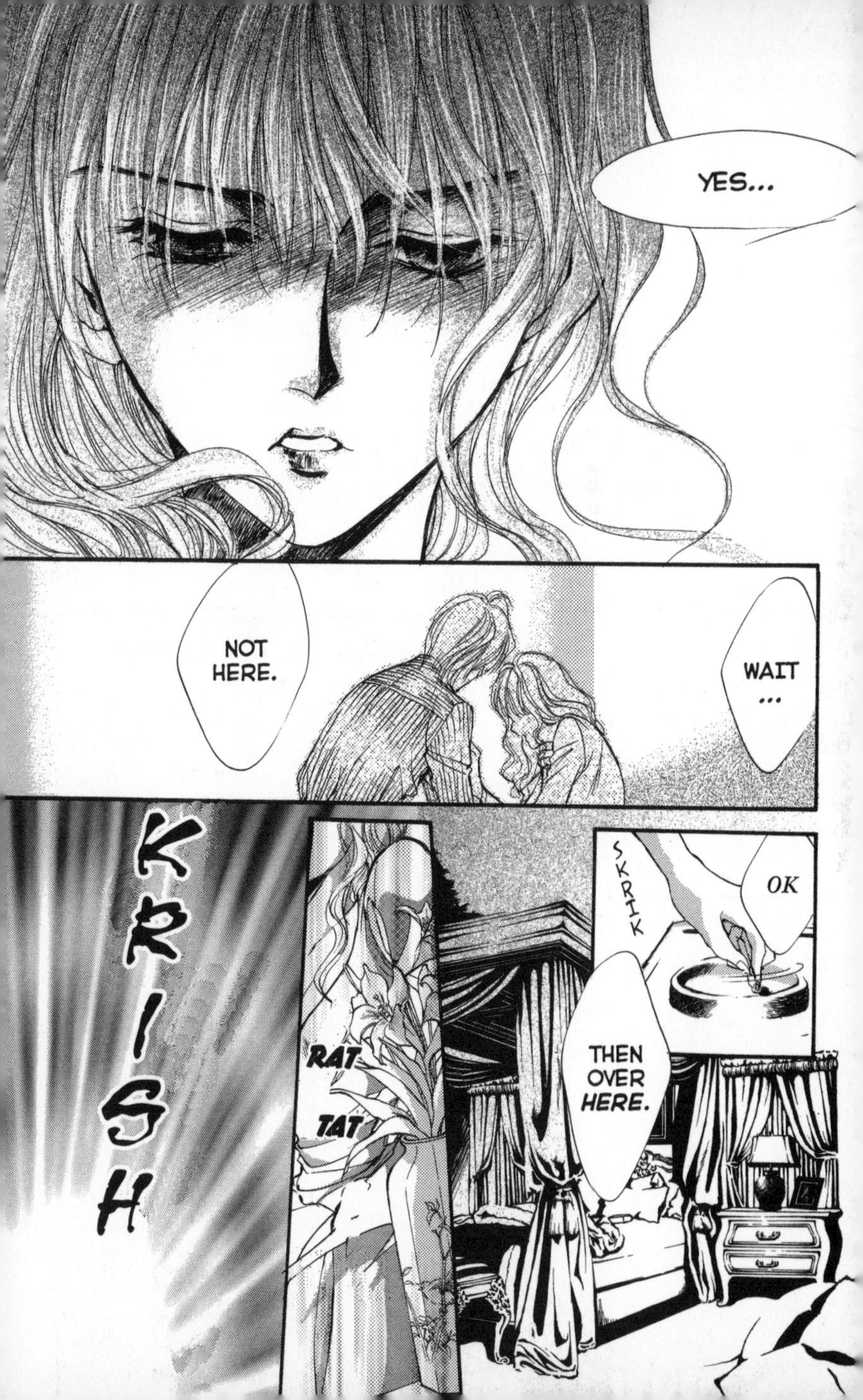
YES...
WAIT ...
NOT HERE.
OK
SKRIK
THEN OVER HERE.
RAT TAT
KRISH

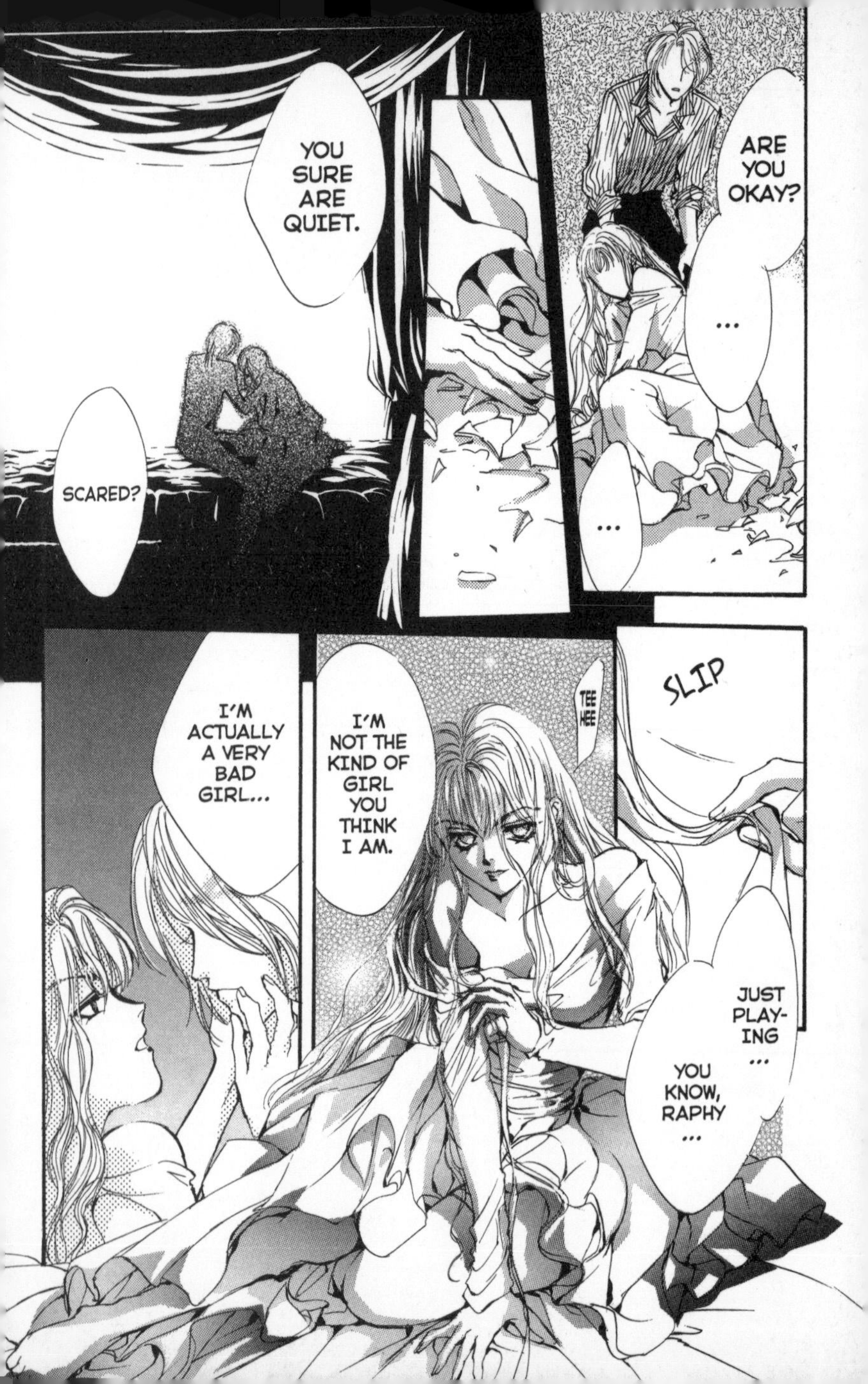
ARE YOU OKAY?
...
...
YOU SURE ARE QUIET.
SCARED?
SLIP
TEE HEE
I'M NOT THE KIND OF GIRL YOU THINK I AM.
JUST PLAYING-ING...
YOU KNOW, RAPHY...
I'M ACTUALLY A VERY BAD GIRL...

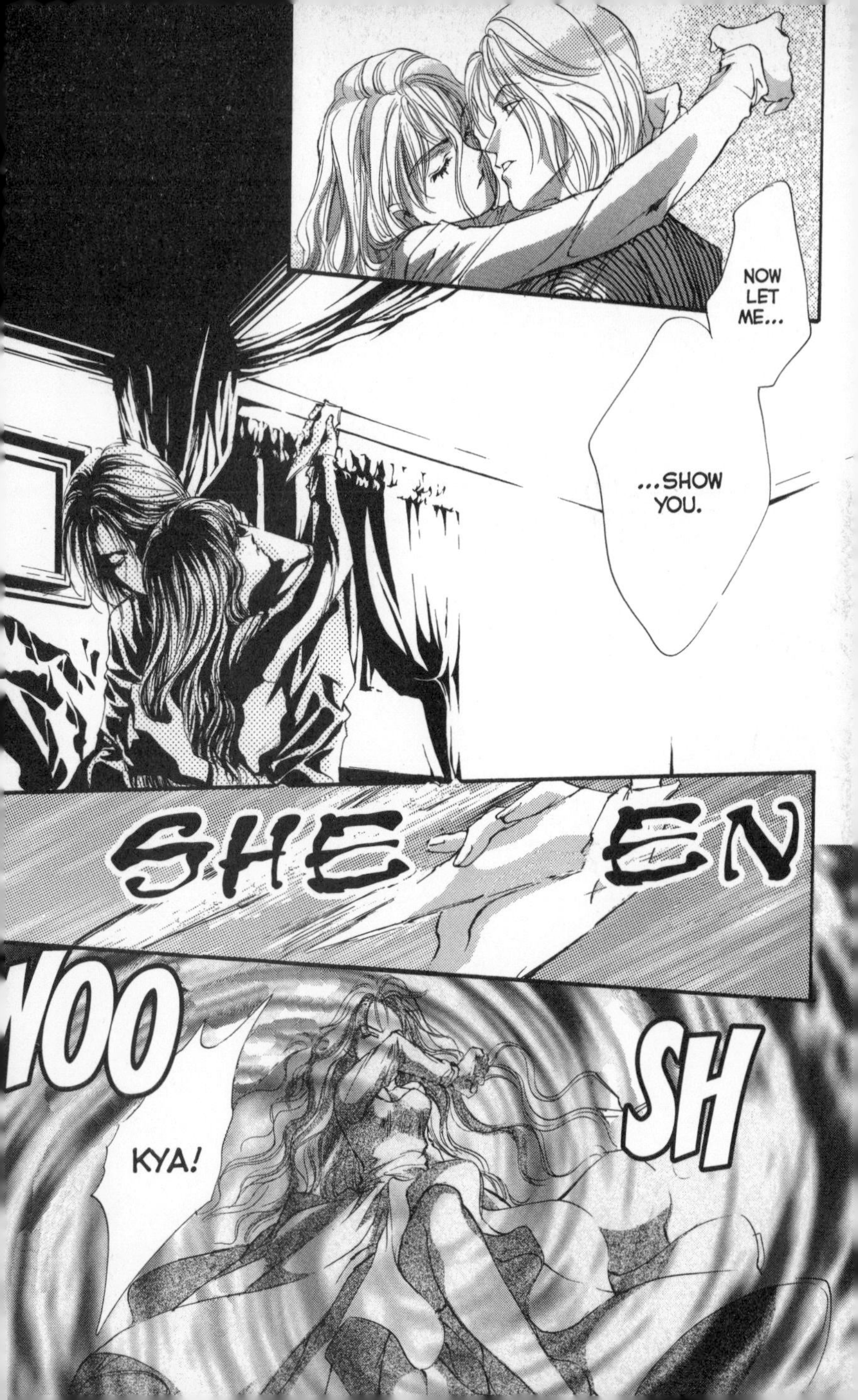
NOW LET ME...
...SHOW YOU.
SHE EN
OO SH
KYA!

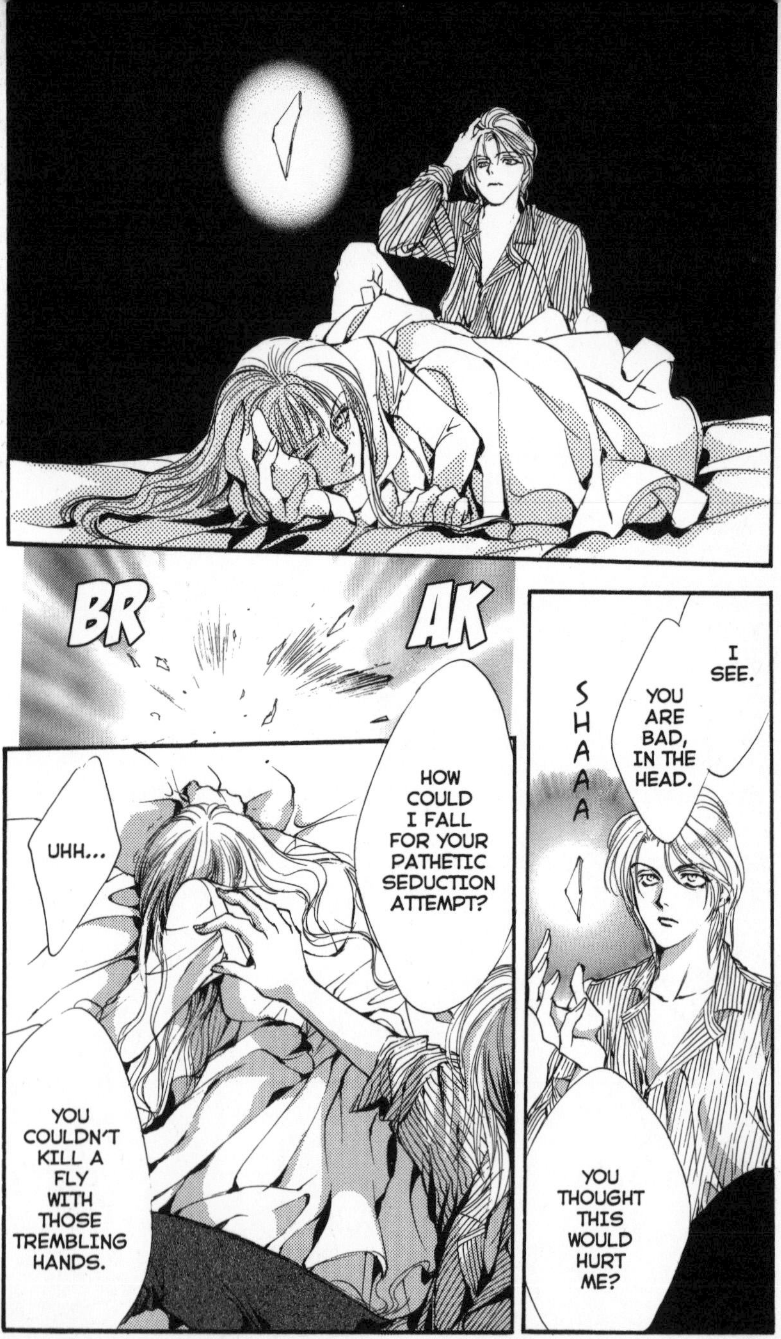

I SEE.
YOU ARE BAD, IN THE HEAD.
SHAAAA
YOU THOUGHT THIS WOULD HURT ME?
BRAK
HOW COULD I FALL FOR YOUR PATHETIC SEDUCTION ATTEMPT?
UHH...
YOU COULDN'T KILL A FLY WITH THOSE TREMBLING HANDS.

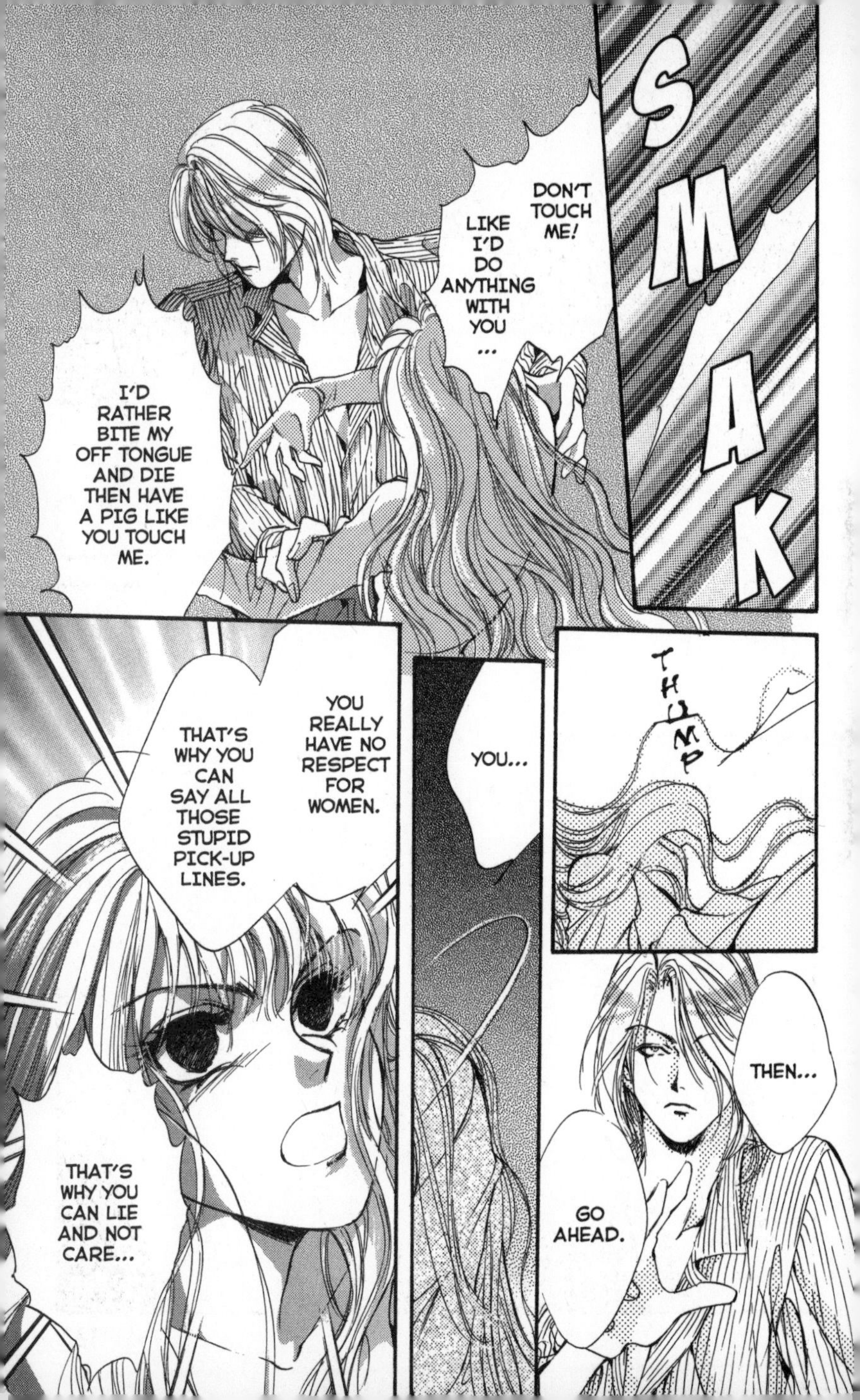
SMAK
DON'T TOUCH ME!
LIKE I'D DO ANYTHING WITH YOU...
I'D RATHER BITE MY OFF TONGUE AND DIE THEN HAVE A PIG LIKE YOU TOUCH ME.
THUMP
THEN...
GO AHEAD.
YOU...
YOU REALLY HAVE NO RESPECT FOR WOMEN.
THAT'S WHY YOU CAN SAY ALL THOSE STUPID PICK-UP LINES.
THAT'S WHY YOU CAN LIE AND NOT CARE...

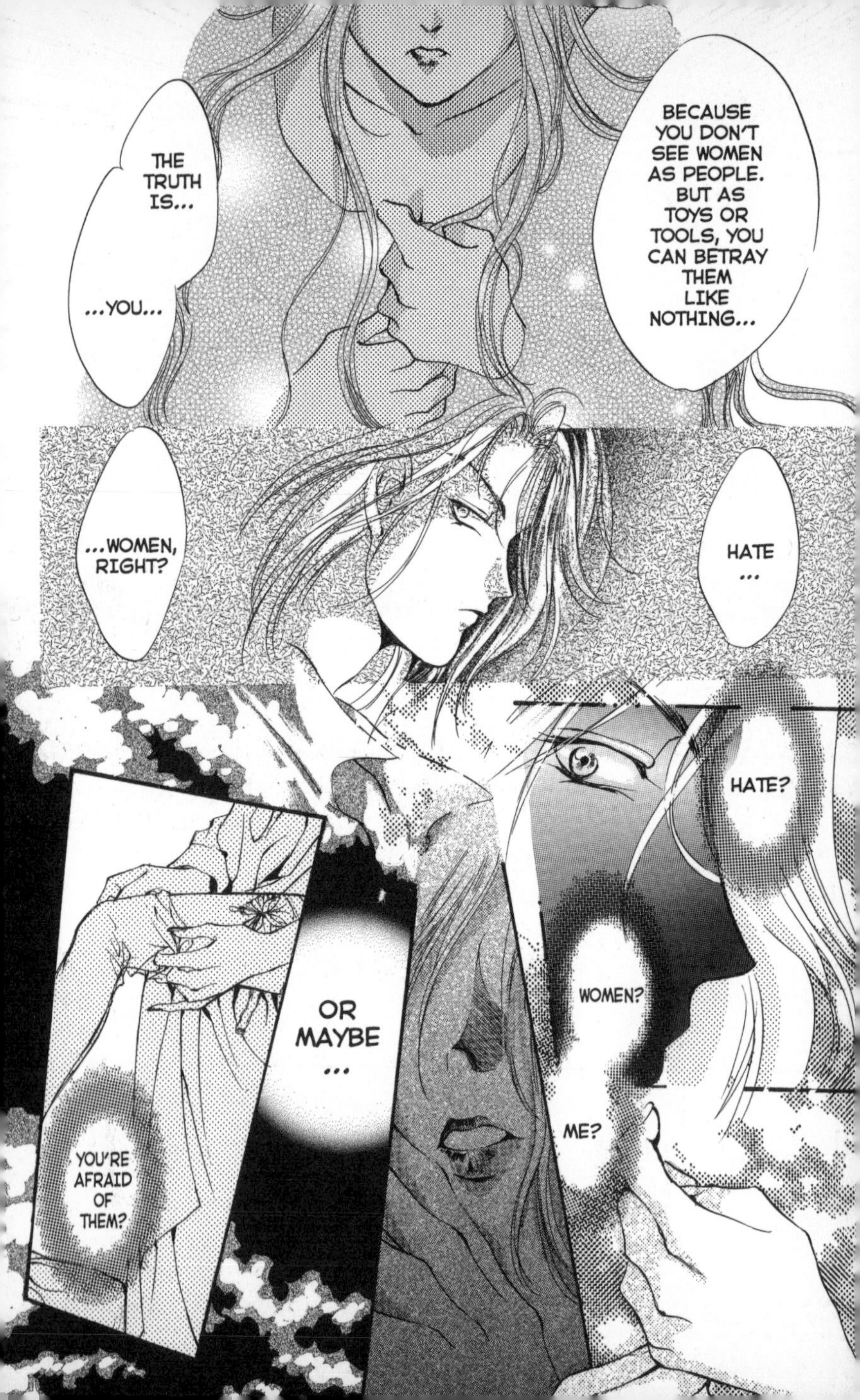
BECAUSE YOU DON'T SEE WOMEN AS PEOPLE. BUT AS TOYS OR TOOLS, YOU CAN BETRAY THEM LIKE NOTHING...
THE TRUTH IS...
...YOU...
HATE ...
...WOMEN, RIGHT?
HATE?
WOMEN?
ME?
OR MAYBE ...
YOU'RE AFRAID OF THEM?

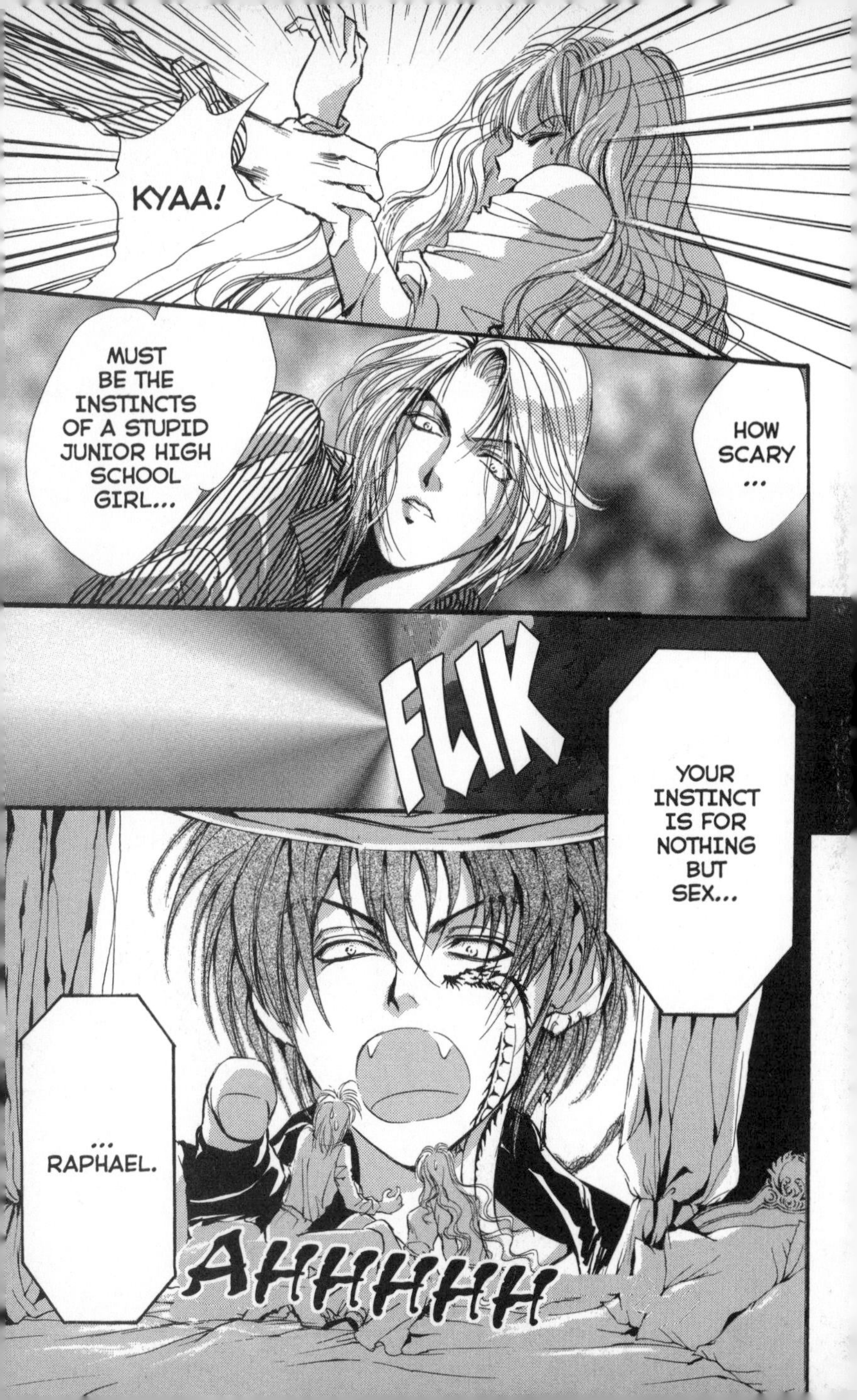
KYAA!
HOW SCARY ...
MUST BE THE INSTINCTS OF A STUPID JUNIOR HIGH SCHOOL GIRL...
FLIK
YOUR INSTINCT IS FOR NOTHING BUT SEX...
... RAPHAEL.
AHHHHHH

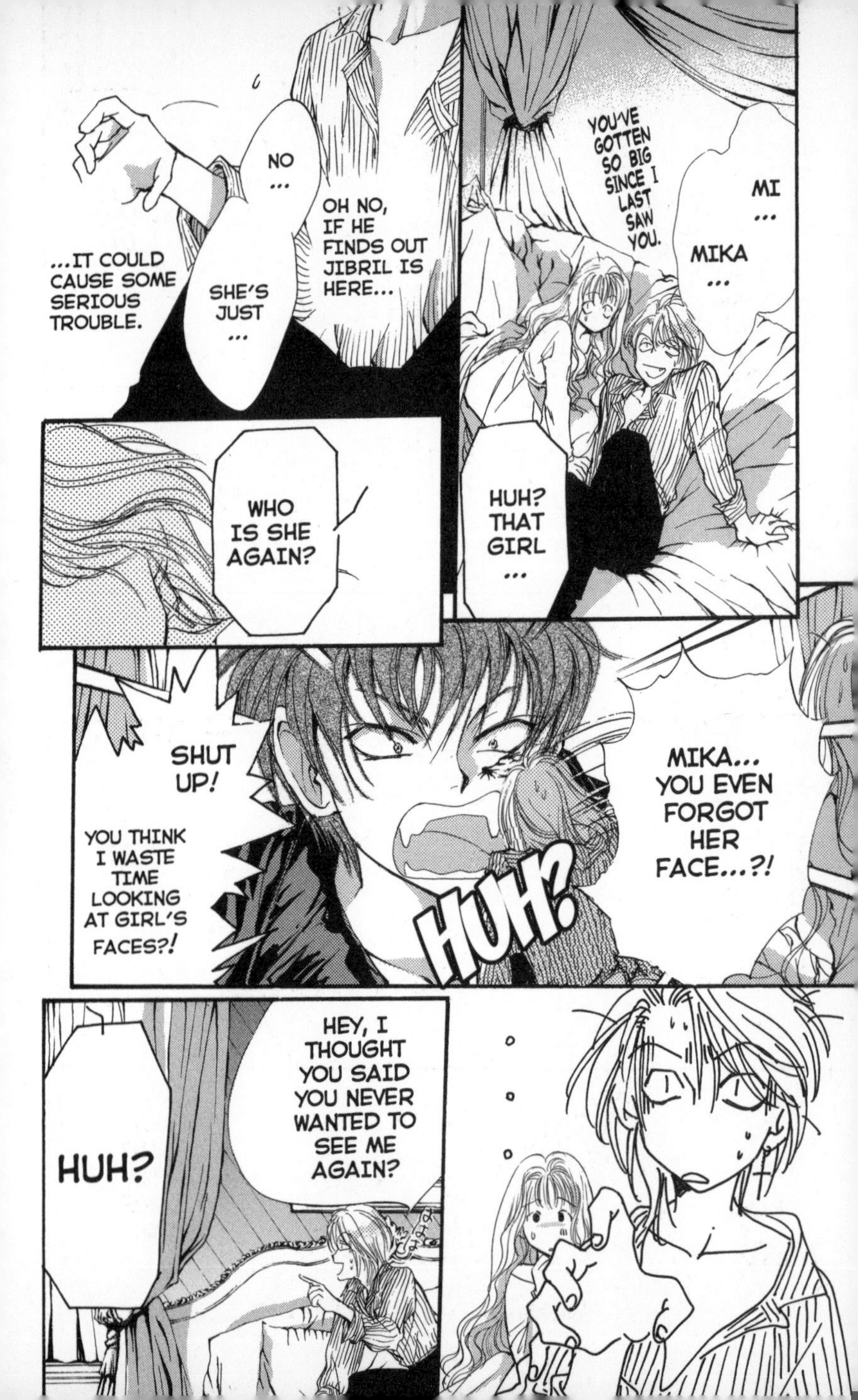
MI... MIKA...
YOU'VE GOTTEN SO BIG SINCE I LAST SAW YOU.
HUH? THAT GIRL...
NO... SHE'S JUST...
OH NO, IF HE FINDS OUT JIBRIL IS HERE...
...IT COULD CAUSE SOME SERIOUS TROUBLE.
WHO IS SHE AGAIN?
MIKA... YOU EVEN FORGOT HER FACE...?!
HUH?
SHUT UP!
YOU THINK I WASTE TIME LOOKING AT GIRL'S FACES?!
HEY, I THOUGHT YOU SAID YOU NEVER WANTED TO SEE ME AGAIN?
HUH?

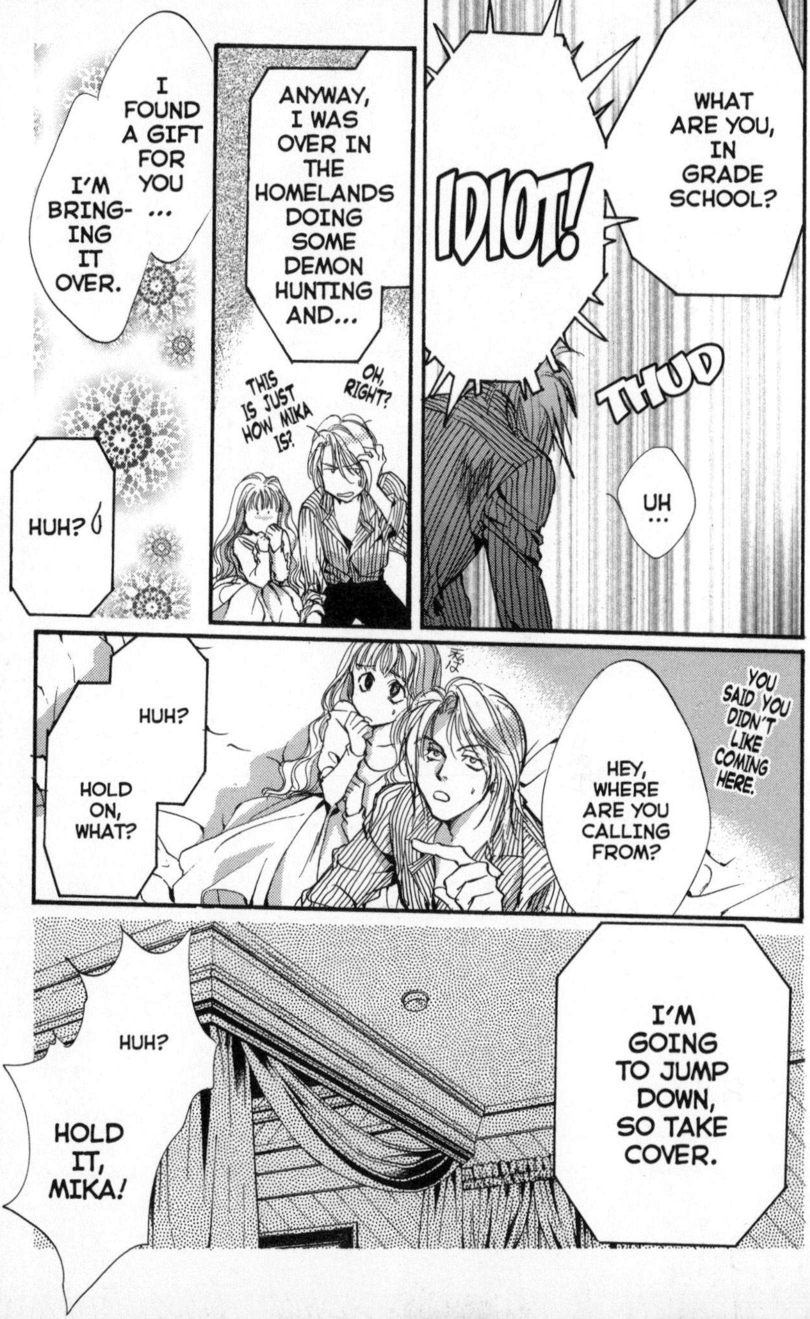
WHAT ARE YOU, IN GRADE SCHOOL?
IDIOT!
THUD
UH ...
ANYWAY, I WAS OVER IN THE HOMELANDS DOING SOME DEMON HUNTING AND...
OH, RIGHT?
THIS IS JUST HOW MIKA IS?
I FOUND A GIFT FOR YOU ...
I'M BRINGING IT OVER.
HUH?
YOU SAID YOU DIDN'T LIKE COMING HERE.
HEY, WHERE ARE YOU CALLING FROM?
HUH?
HOLD ON, WHAT?
I'M GOING TO JUMP DOWN, SO TAKE COVER.
HUH?
HOLD IT, MIKA!

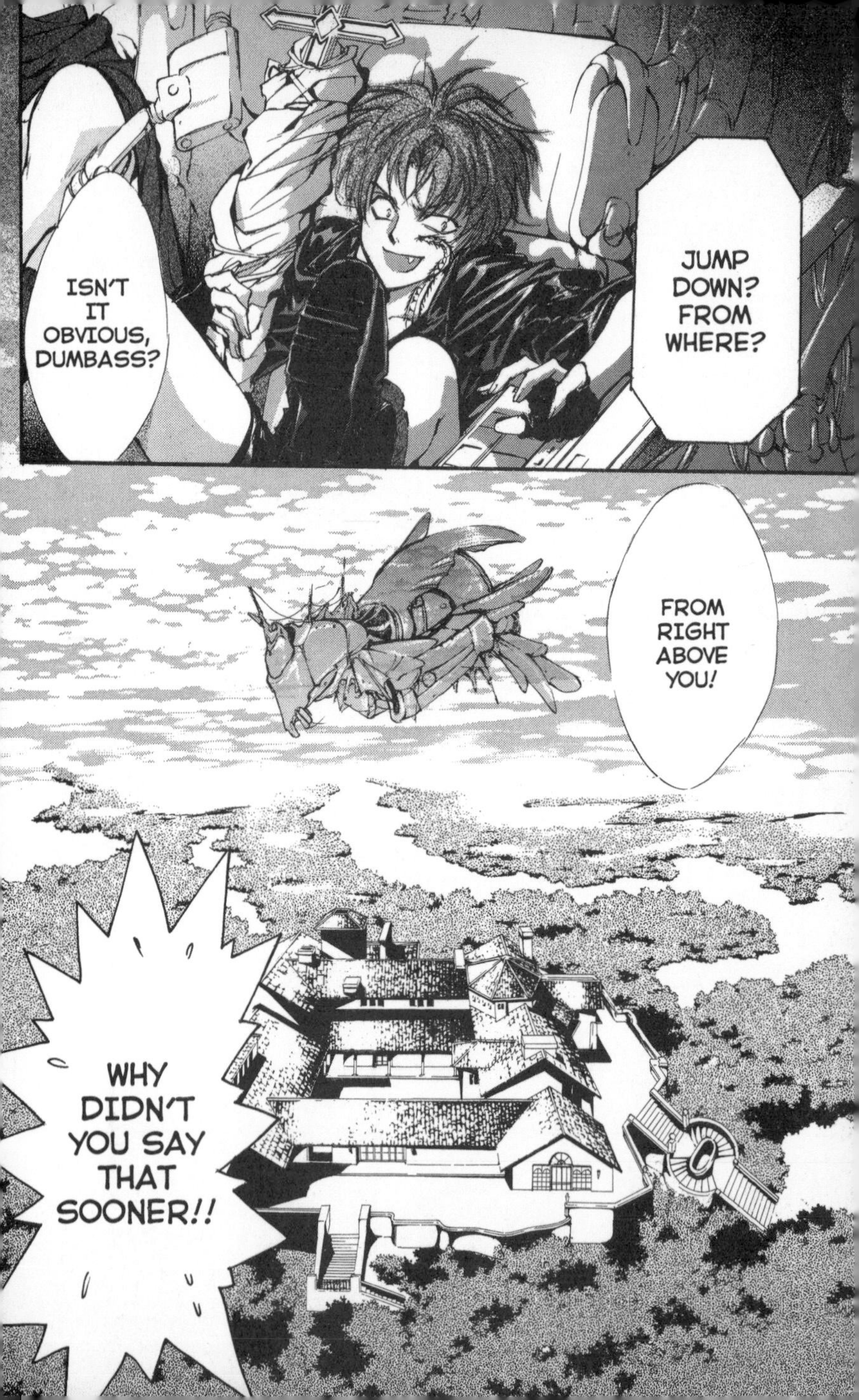
JUMP DOWN? FROM WHERE?
ISN'T IT OBVIOUS, DUMBASS?
FROM RIGHT ABOVE YOU!
WHY DIDN'T YOU SAY THAT SOONER!!

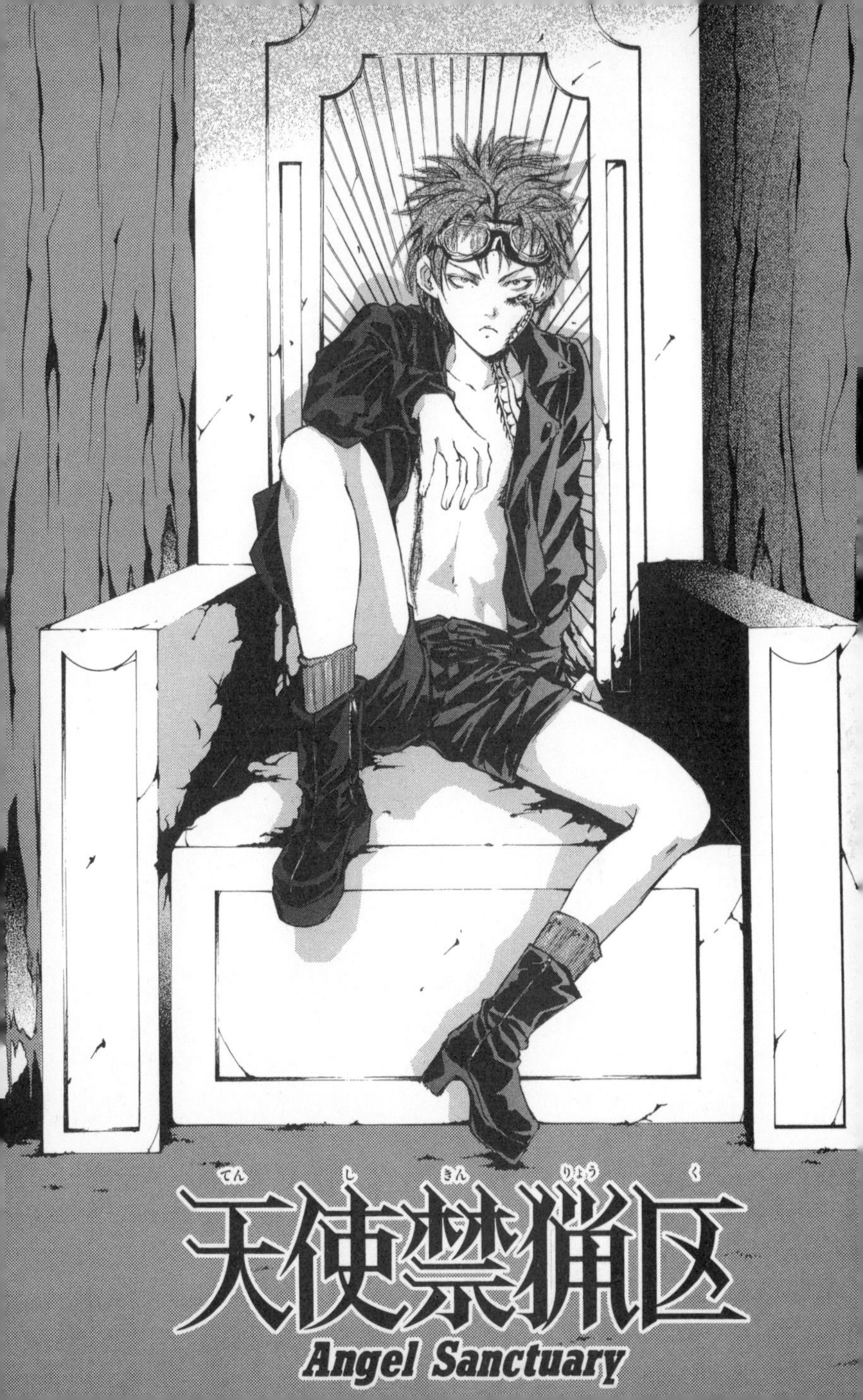
天使禁猟区
Angel Sanctuary

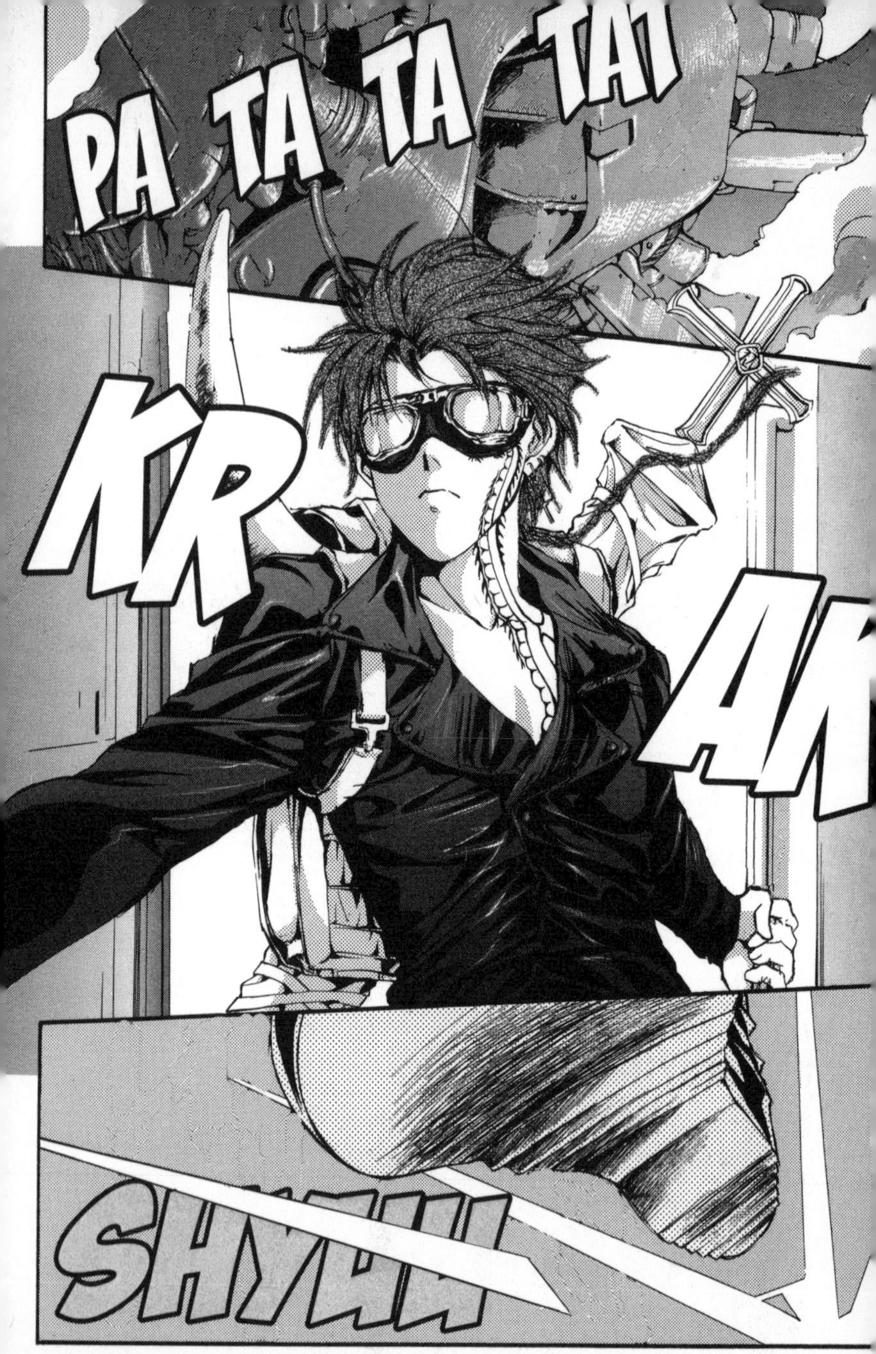
PA TA TA TA!
KRAK
SHYUU

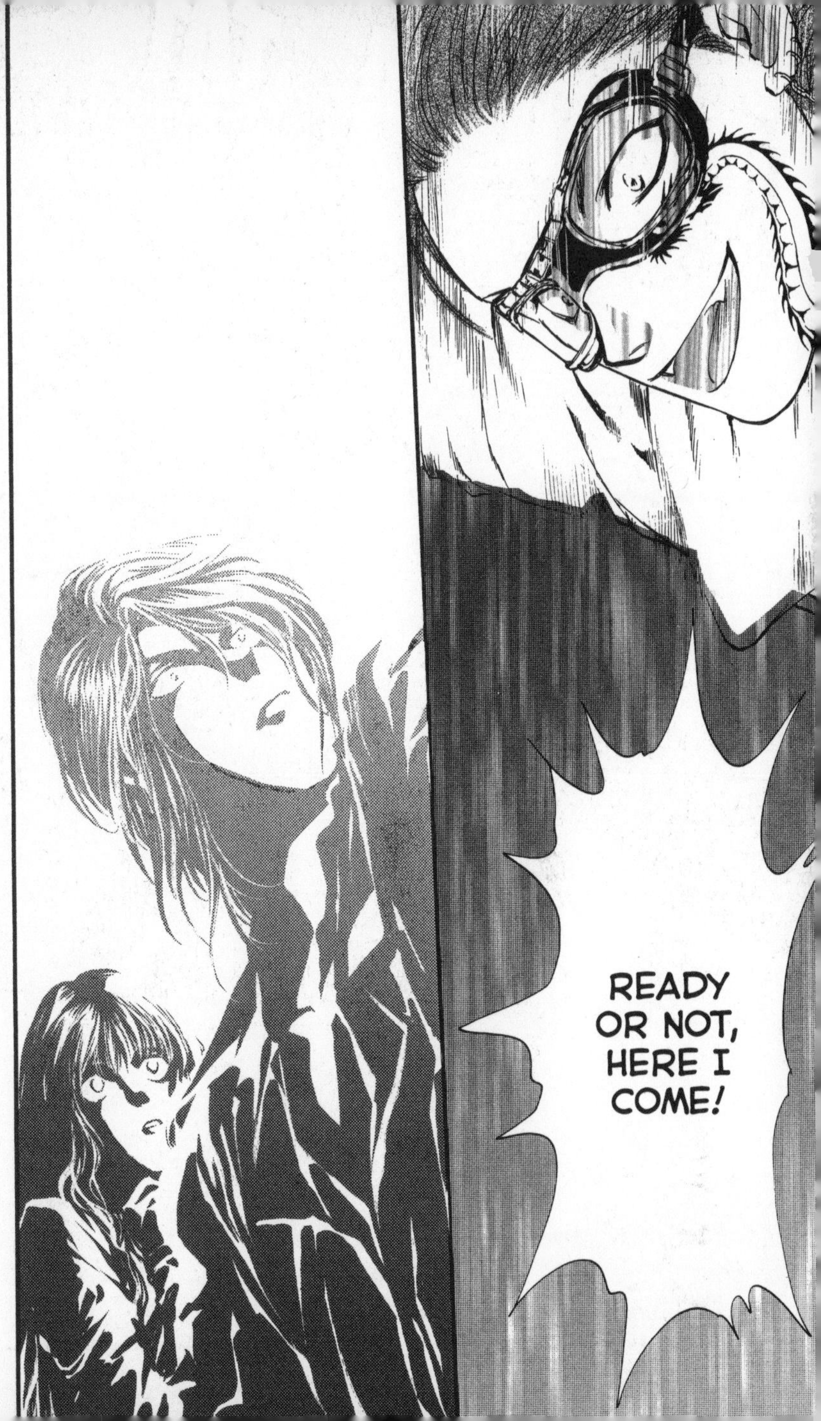
READY OR NOT, HERE I COME!

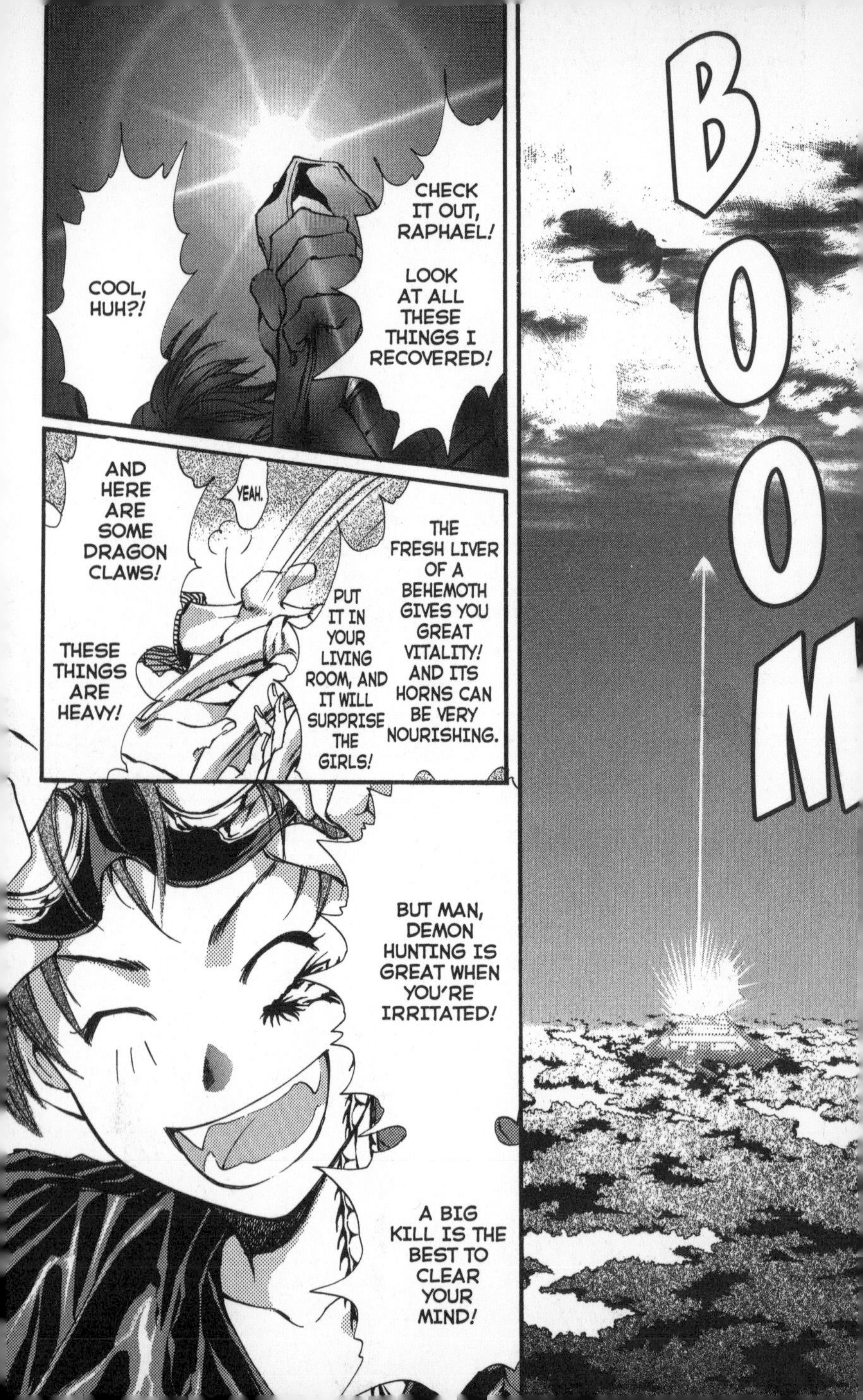
BOOM
CHECK IT OUT, RAPHAEL!
LOOK AT ALL THESE THINGS I RECOVERED!
COOL, HUH?!
THE FRESH LIVER OF A BEHEMOTH GIVES YOU GREAT VITALITY! AND ITS HORNS CAN BE VERY NOURISHING.
PUT IT IN YOUR LIVING ROOM, AND IT WILL SURPRISE THE GIRLS!
YEAH.
AND HERE ARE SOME DRAGON CLAWS!
THESE THINGS ARE HEAVY!
BUT MAN, DEMON HUNTING IS GREAT WHEN YOU'RE IRRITATED!
A BIG KILL IS THE BEST TO CLEAR YOUR MIND!

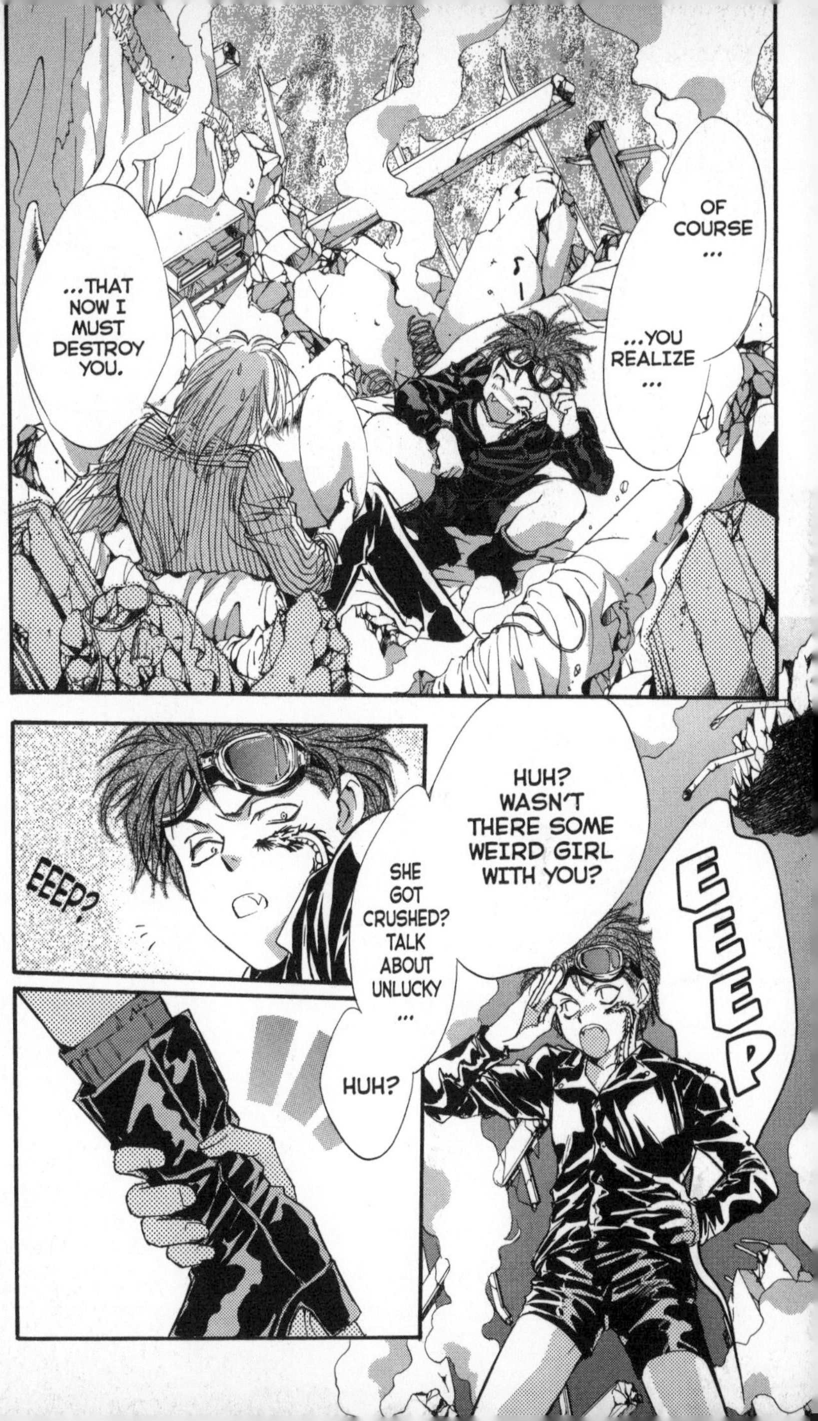
OF COURSE ...
...YOU REALIZE ...
...THAT NOW I MUST DESTROY YOU.
HUH? WASN'T THERE SOME WEIRD GIRL WITH YOU?
SHE GOT CRUSHED? TALK ABOUT UNLUCKY ...
EEEP
EEEP?
HUH?

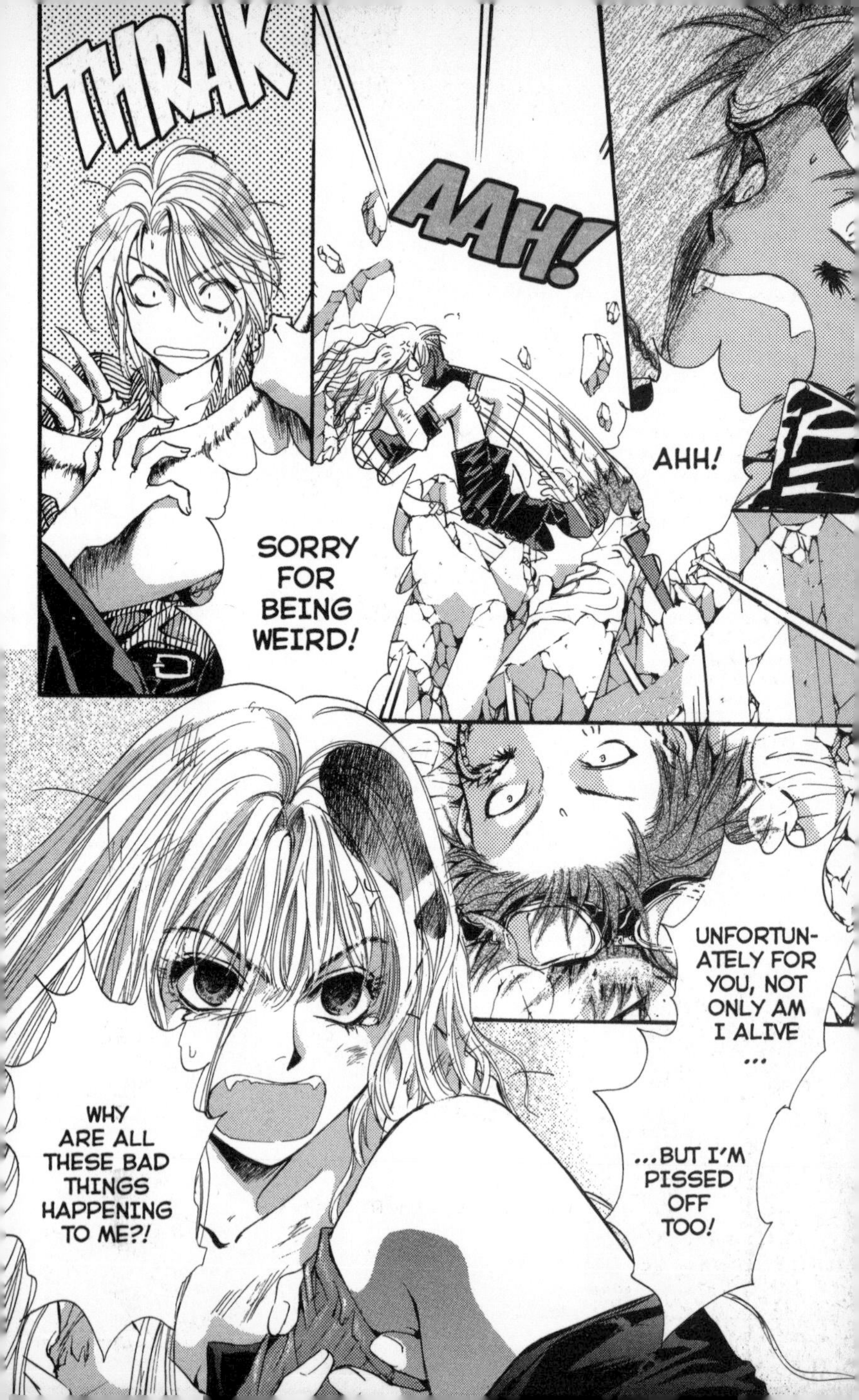
AHH!
AAH!
SORRY FOR BEING WEIRD!
THRAK
UNFORTUN-ATELY FOR YOU, NOT ONLY AM I ALIVE ...
...BUT I'M PISSED OFF TOO!
WHY ARE ALL THESE BAD THINGS HAPPENING TO ME?!

When Mika shows up, things get exciting and the story gets going. When there's things or places that I can't explain in words, I draw them instead of my assistants. One of those things appears in this chapter. I did some research into it, but if I drew it like that then it would just be too much work...So I rearranged it so it would be easier to draw. But it's still very difficult--drawing non-human things always seems hard. I always forget the details if it's too complicated, and it seems like it changes shape every time I draw it... Ahh... And the skull in the birdcage is a pain to draw too! Yes.

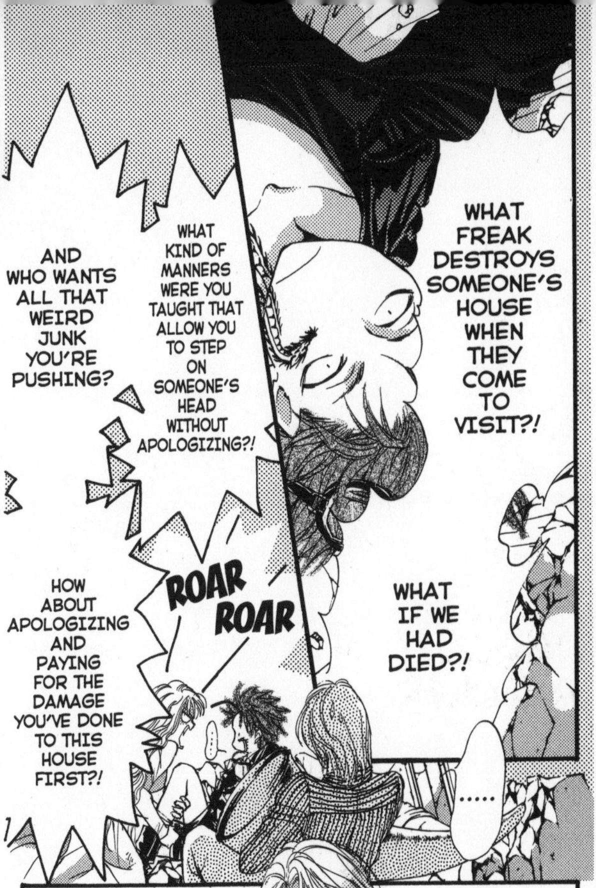
WHAT FREAK DESTROYS SOMEONE'S HOUSE WHEN THEY COME TO VISIT?!
WHAT IF WE HAD DIED?!
.....
WHAT KIND OF MANNERS WERE YOU TAUGHT THAT ALLOW YOU TO STEP ON SOMEONE'S HEAD WITHOUT APOLOGIZING?!
AND WHO WANTS ALL THAT WEIRD JUNK YOU'RE PUSHING?
ROAR ROAR
HOW ABOUT APOLOGIZING AND PAYING FOR THE DAMAGE YOU'VE DONE TO THIS HOUSE FIRST?!
...

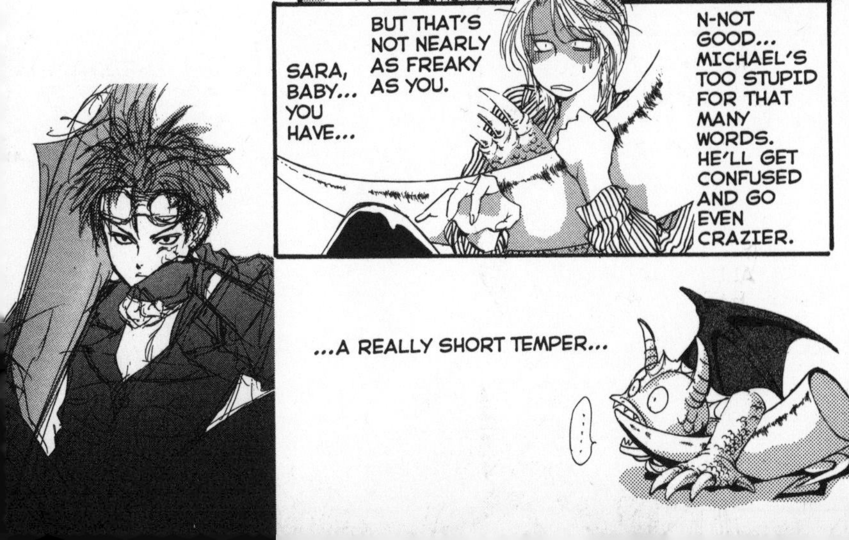
N-NOT GOOD... MICHAEL'S TOO STUPID FOR THAT MANY WORDS. HE'LL GET CONFUSED AND GO EVEN CRAZIER.
BUT THAT'S NOT NEARLY AS FREAKY AS YOU.
SARA, BABY... YOU HAVE...
...A REALLY SHORT TEMPER...
...

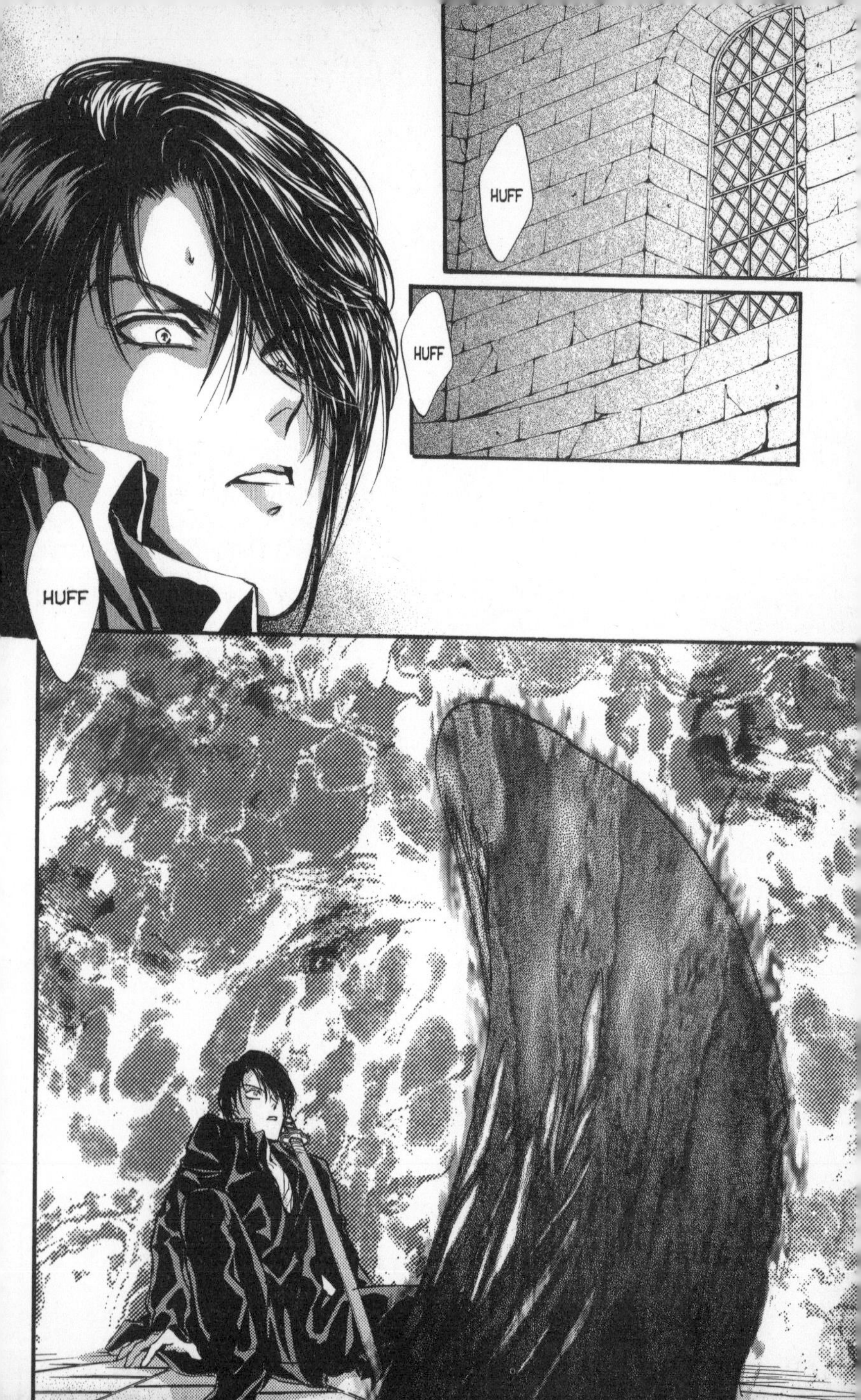
HUFF
HUFF
HUFF

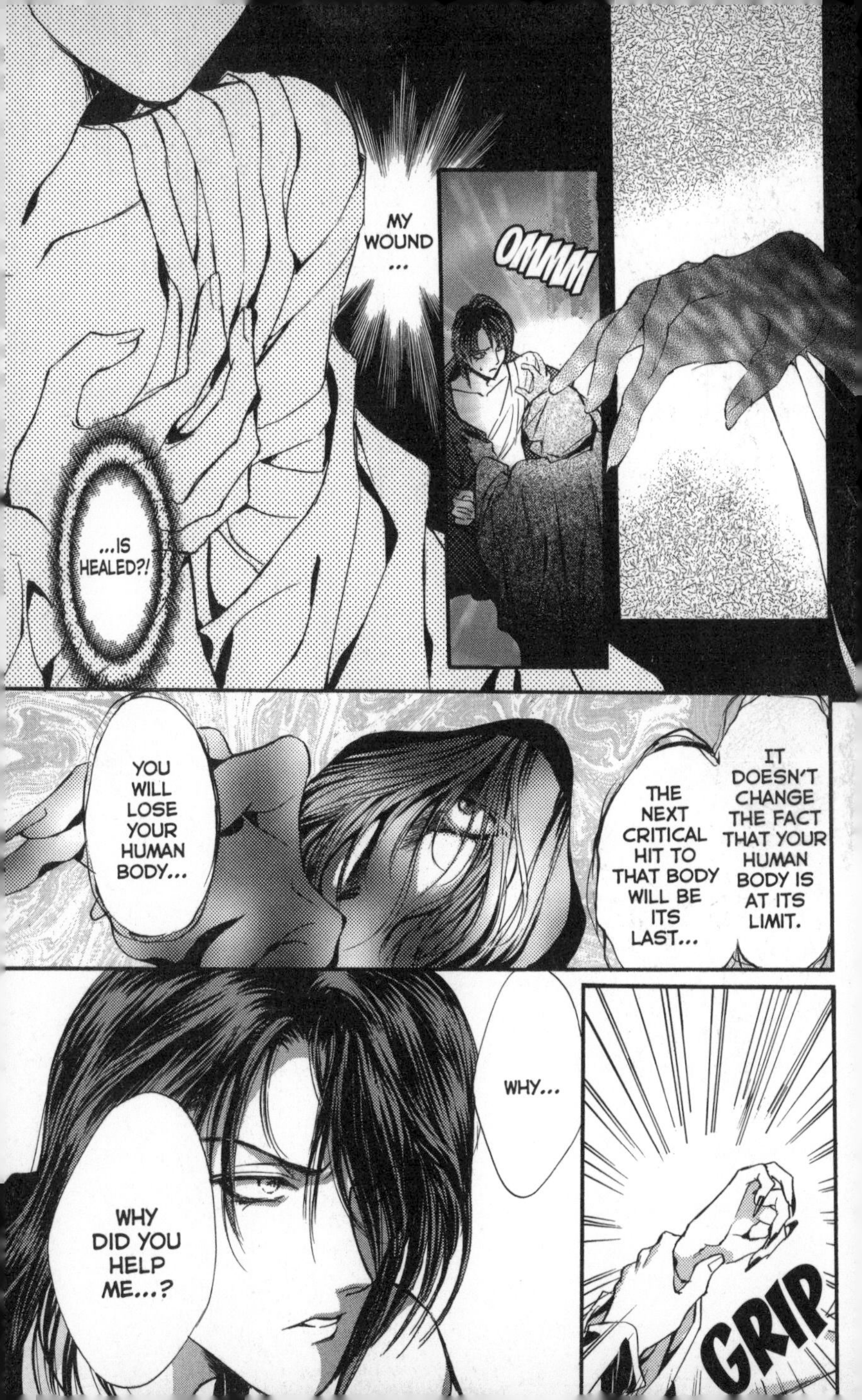
OMMM
MY WOUND ...
...IS HEALED?!
IT DOESN'T CHANGE THE FACT THAT YOUR HUMAN BODY IS AT ITS LIMIT.
THE NEXT CRITICAL HIT TO THAT BODY WILL BE ITS LAST...
YOU WILL LOSE YOUR HUMAN BODY...
GRIP
WHY...
WHY DID YOU HELP ME...?

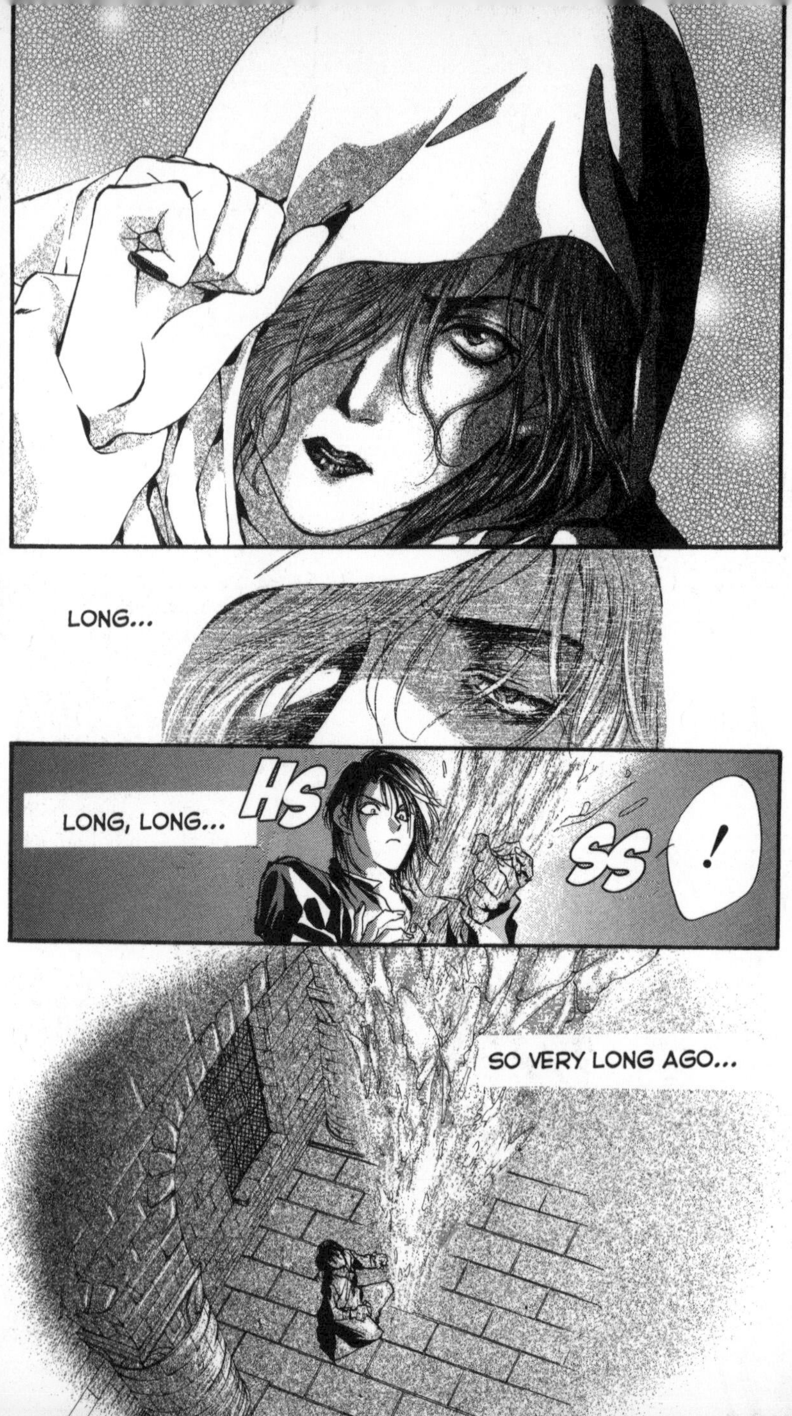
LONG...
!
SS
HS
LONG, LONG...
SO VERY LONG AGO...

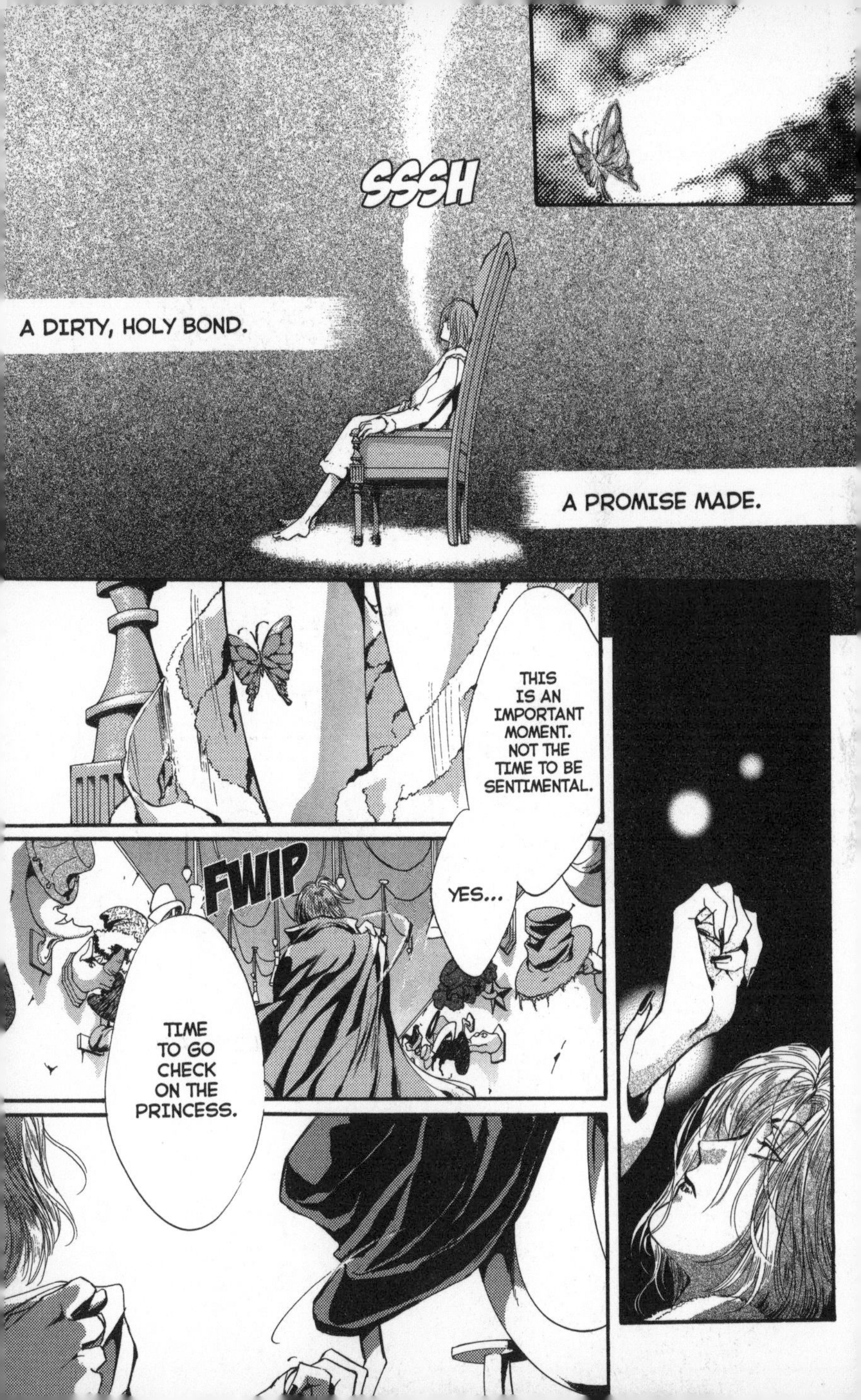
SSSH
A DIRTY, HOLY BOND.
A PROMISE MADE.
THIS IS AN IMPORTANT MOMENT. NOT THE TIME TO BE SENTIMENTAL.
YES...
FWIP
TIME TO GO CHECK ON THE PRINCESS.

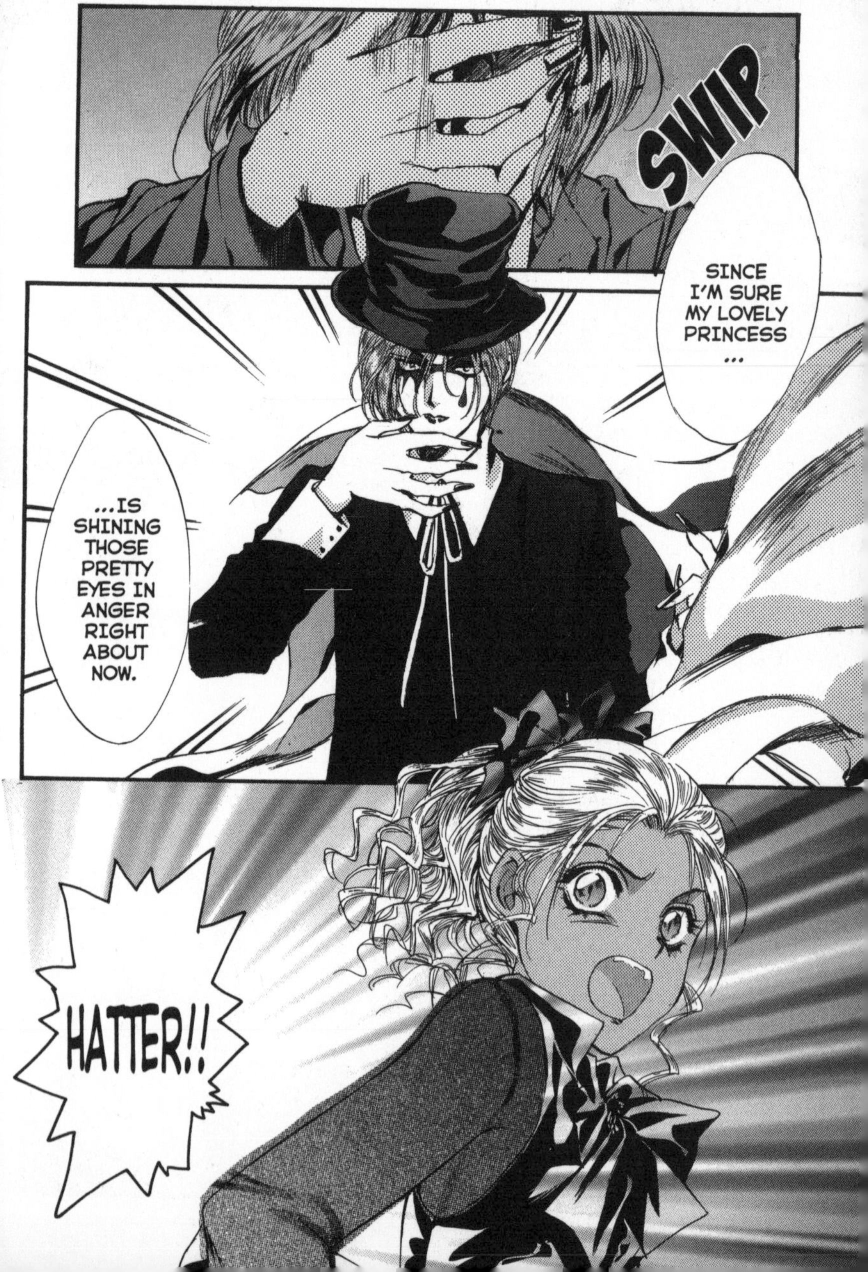
SWIP
SINCE I'M SURE MY LOVELY PRINCESS ...
...IS SHINING THOSE PRETTY EYES IN ANGER RIGHT ABOUT NOW.
HATTER!!

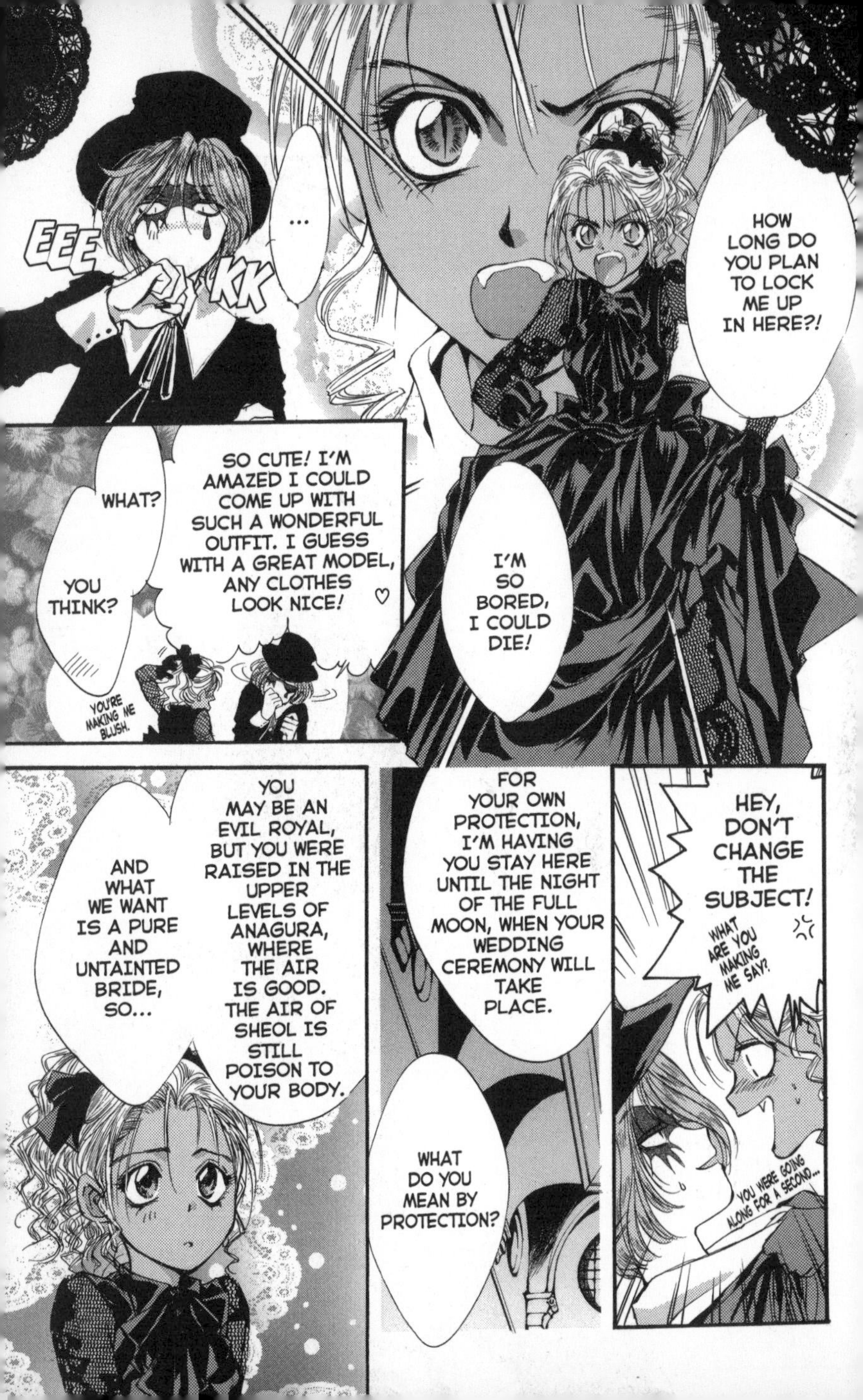
HOW LONG DO YOU PLAN TO LOCK ME UP IN HERE?!
I'M SO BORED, I COULD DIE!
...
EEEKK
SO CUTE! I'M AMAZED I COULD COME UP WITH SUCH A WONDERFUL OUTFIT. I GUESS WITH A GREAT MODEL, ANY CLOTHES LOOK NICE! ♡
WHAT?
YOU THINK?
YOU'RE MAKING ME BLUSH.
HEY, DON'T CHANGE THE SUBJECT!
WHAT ARE YOU MAKING ME SAY?
YOU WERE GOING ALONG FOR A SECOND...
FOR YOUR OWN PROTECTION, I'M HAVING YOU STAY HERE UNTIL THE NIGHT OF THE FULL MOON, WHEN YOUR WEDDING CEREMONY WILL TAKE PLACE.
WHAT DO YOU MEAN BY PROTECTION?
YOU MAY BE AN EVIL ROYAL, BUT YOU WERE RAISED IN THE UPPER LEVELS OF ANAGURA, WHERE THE AIR IS GOOD. THE AIR OF SHEOL IS STILL POISON TO YOUR BODY.
AND WHAT WE WANT IS A PURE AND UNTAINTED BRIDE, SO...

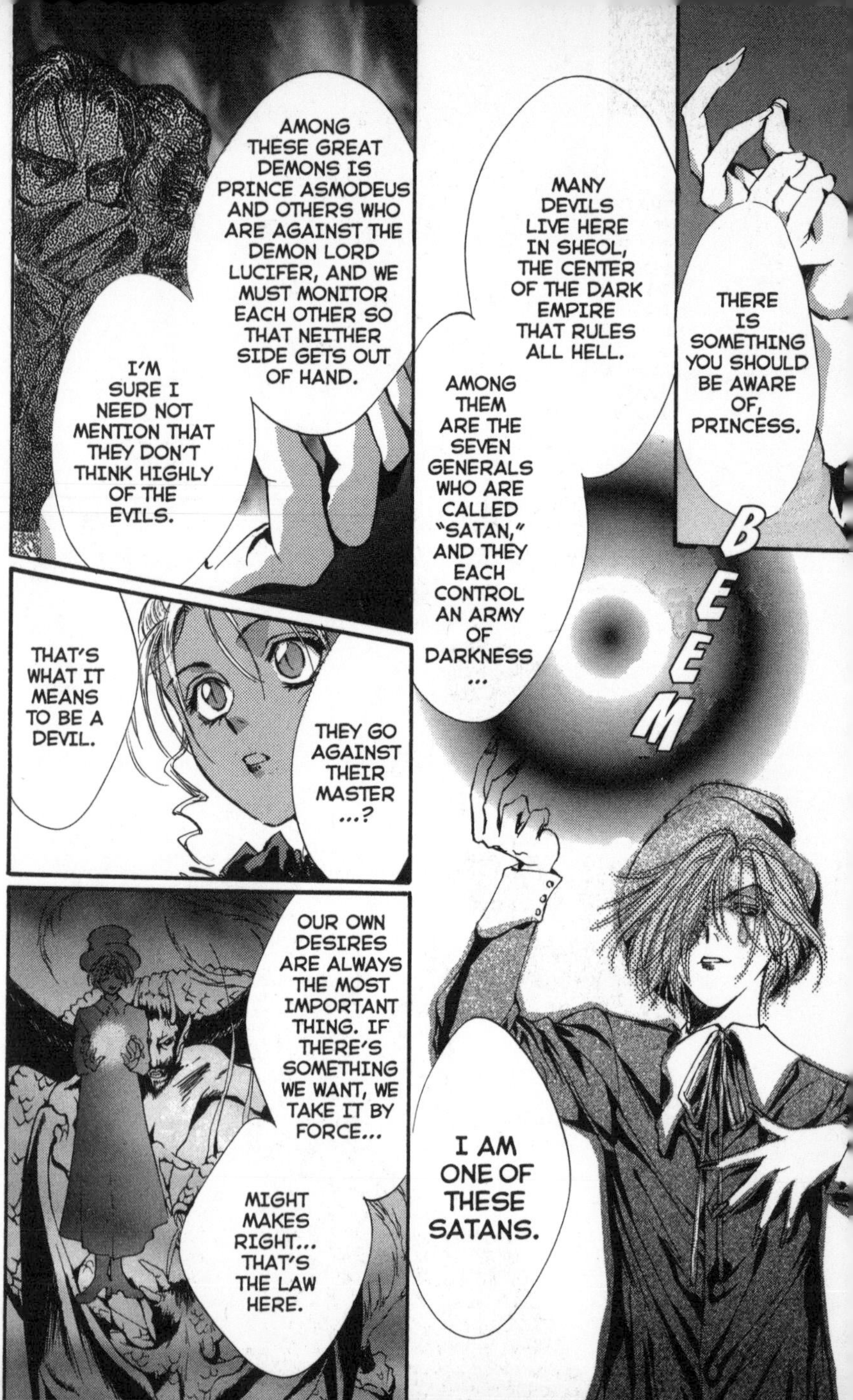
THERE IS SOMETHING YOU SHOULD BE AWARE OF, PRINCESS.
MANY DEVILS LIVE HERE IN SHEOL, THE CENTER OF THE DARK EMPIRE THAT RULES ALL HELL.
AMONG THEM ARE THE SEVEN GENERALS WHO ARE CALLED "SATAN," AND THEY EACH CONTROL AN ARMY OF DARKNESS ...
BEEEM
I AM ONE OF THESE SATANS.
AMONG THESE GREAT DEMONS IS PRINCE ASMODEUS AND OTHERS WHO ARE AGAINST THE DEMON LORD LUCIFER, AND WE MUST MONITOR EACH OTHER SO THAT NEITHER SIDE GETS OUT OF HAND.
I'M SURE I NEED NOT MENTION THAT THEY DON'T THINK HIGHLY OF THE EVILS.
THEY GO AGAINST THEIR MASTER ...?
THAT'S WHAT IT MEANS TO BE A DEVIL.
OUR OWN DESIRES ARE ALWAYS THE MOST IMPORTANT THING. IF THERE'S SOMETHING WE WANT, WE TAKE IT BY FORCE...
MIGHT MAKES RIGHT... THAT'S THE LAW HERE.

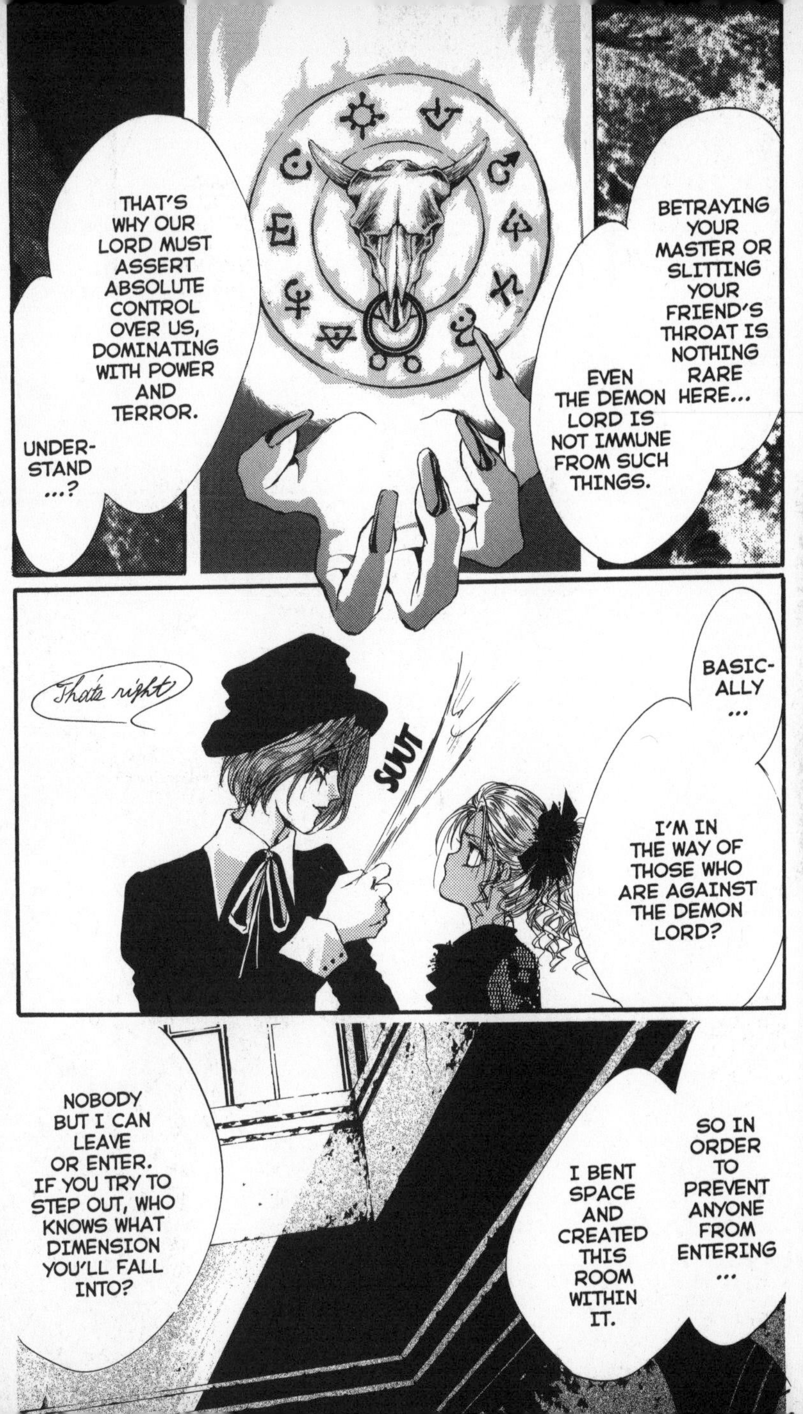
BETRAYING YOUR MASTER OR SLITTING YOUR FRIEND'S THROAT IS NOTHING RARE HERE...
EVEN THE DEMON LORD IS NOT IMMUNE FROM SUCH THINGS.
THAT'S WHY OUR LORD MUST ASSERT ABSOLUTE CONTROL OVER US, DOMINATING WITH POWER AND TERROR.
UNDER-STAND ...?
BASIC-ALLY ...
I'M IN THE WAY OF THOSE WHO ARE AGAINST THE DEMON LORD?
SUUT
That's right
SO IN ORDER TO PREVENT ANYONE FROM ENTERING ...
I BENT SPACE AND CREATED THIS ROOM WITHIN IT.
NOBODY BUT I CAN LEAVE OR ENTER. IF YOU TRY TO STEP OUT, WHO KNOWS WHAT DIMENSION YOU'LL FALL INTO?

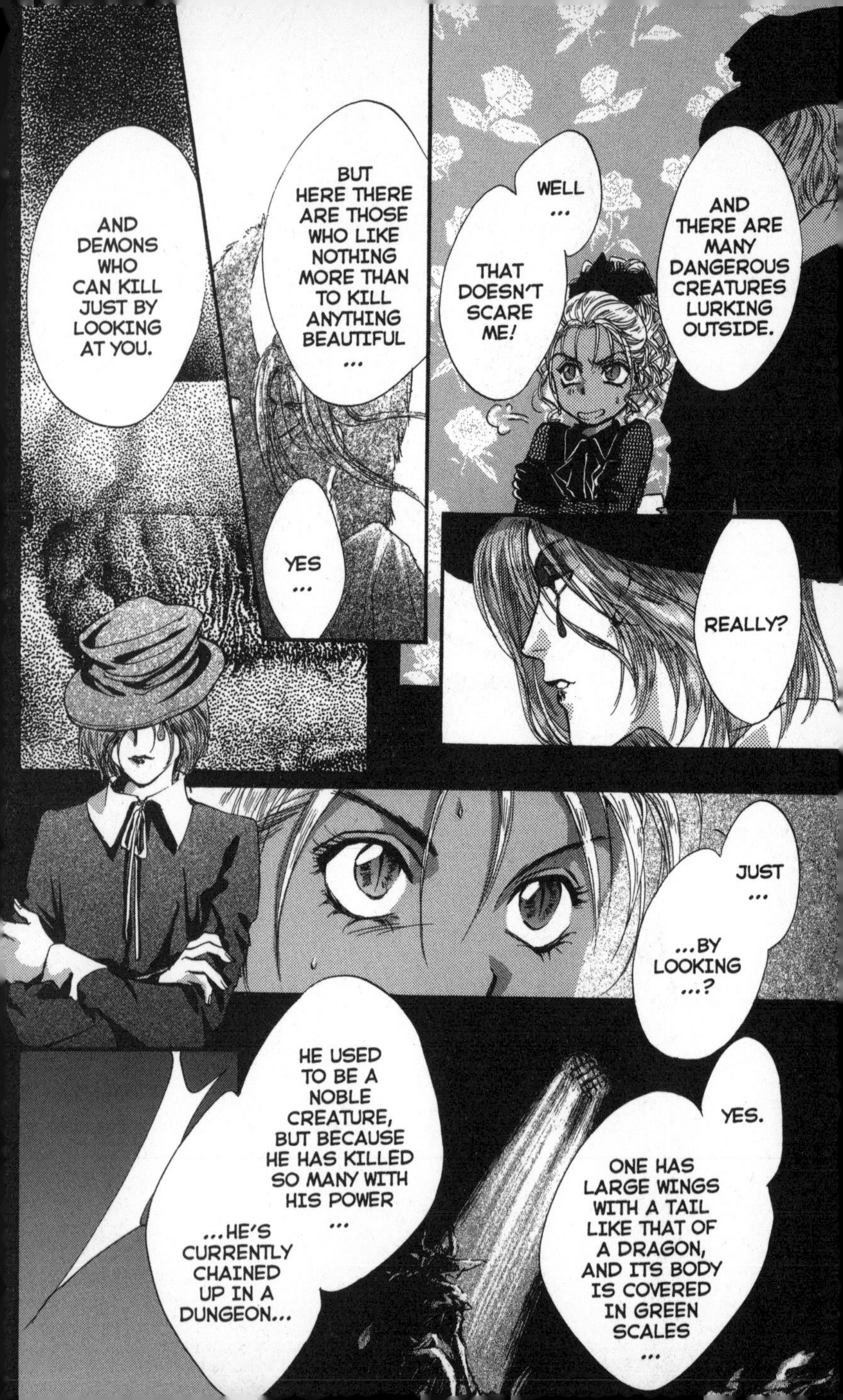
AND THERE ARE MANY DANGEROUS CREATURES LURKING OUTSIDE.
WELL ...
THAT DOESN'T SCARE ME!
REALLY?
BUT HERE THERE ARE THOSE WHO LIKE NOTHING MORE THAN TO KILL ANYTHING BEAUTIFUL ...
YES ...
AND DEMONS WHO CAN KILL JUST BY LOOKING AT YOU.
JUST ...
...BY LOOKING ...?
YES.
ONE HAS LARGE WINGS WITH A TAIL LIKE THAT OF A DRAGON, AND ITS BODY IS COVERED IN GREEN SCALES ...
HE USED TO BE A NOBLE CREATURE, BUT BECAUSE HE HAS KILLED SO MANY WITH HIS POWER ...
...HE'S CURRENTLY CHAINED UP IN A DUNGEON...

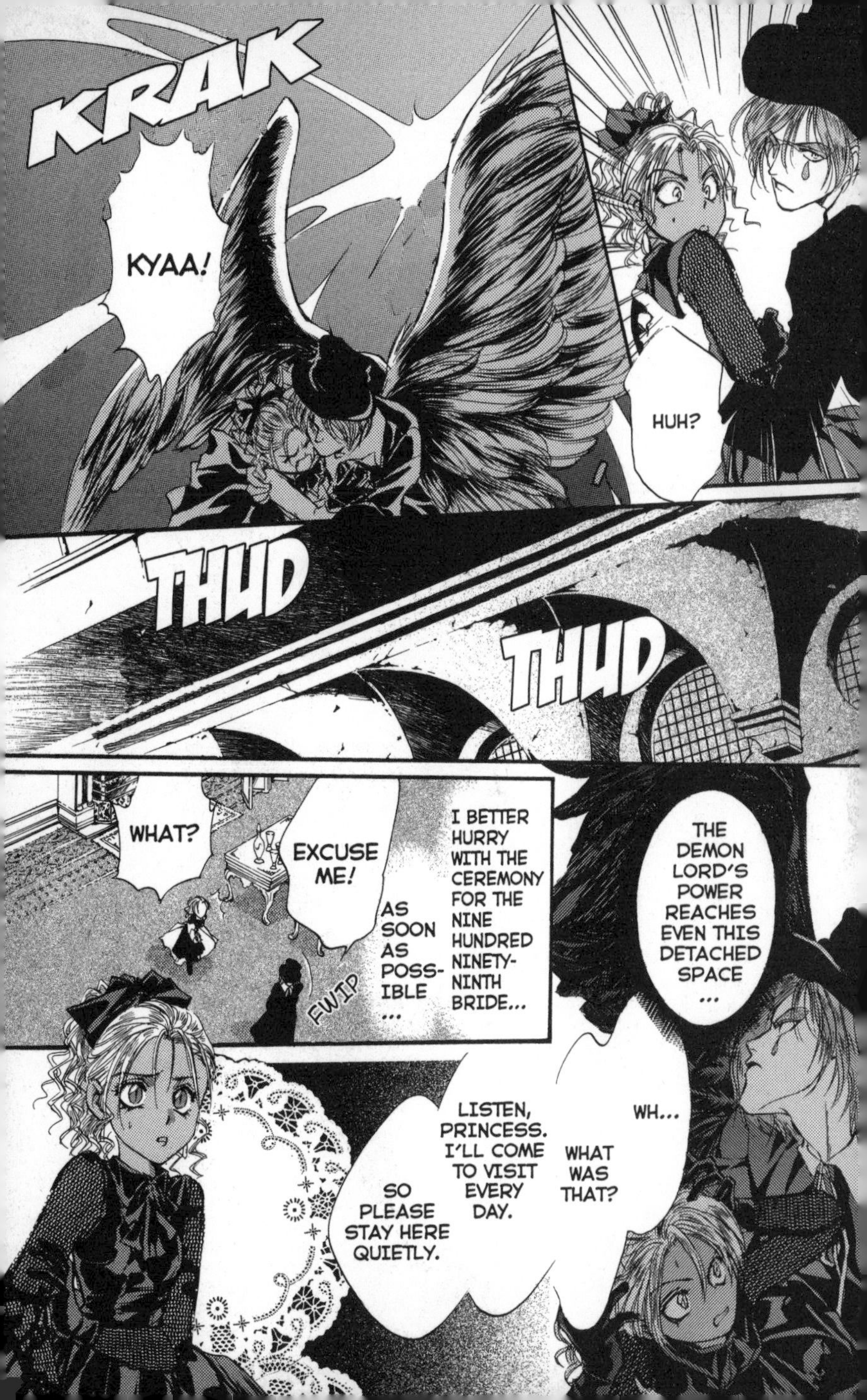
HUH?
KRAK
KYAA!
THUD
THUD
THE DEMON LORD'S POWER REACHES EVEN THIS DETACHED SPACE ...
I BETTER HURRY WITH THE CEREMONY FOR THE NINE HUNDRED NINETY-NINTH BRIDE...
AS SOON AS POSS-IBLE ...
EXCUSE ME!
WHAT?
FWIP
WH...
WHAT WAS THAT?
LISTEN, PRINCESS. I'LL COME TO VISIT EVERY DAY.
SO PLEASE STAY HERE QUIETLY.

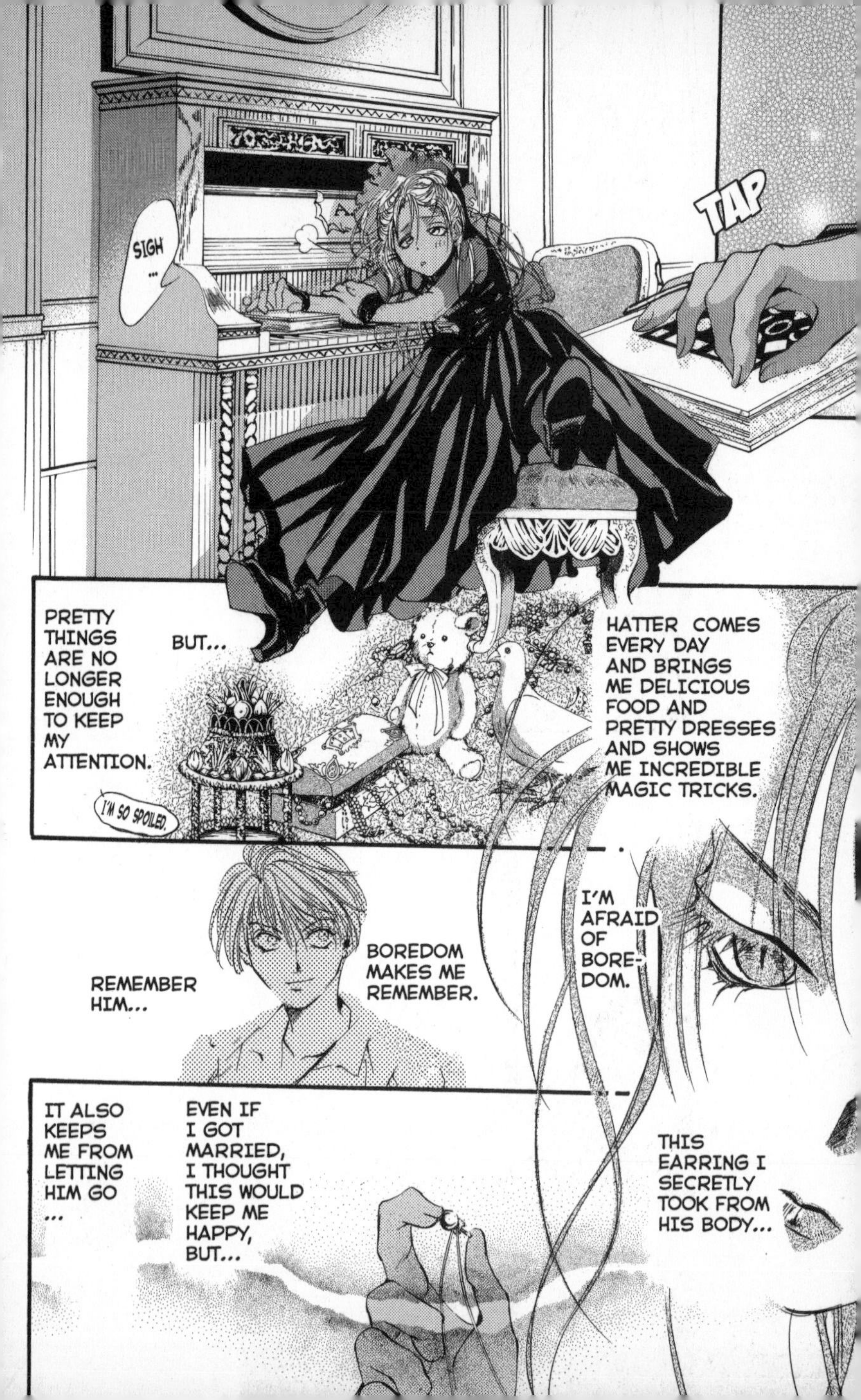

TAP
SIGH ...
HATTER COMES EVERY DAY AND BRINGS ME DELICIOUS FOOD AND PRETTY DRESSES AND SHOWS ME INCREDIBLE MAGIC TRICKS.
BUT...
PRETTY THINGS ARE NO LONGER ENOUGH TO KEEP MY ATTENTION.
I'M SO SPOILED.
I'M AFRAID OF BORE-DOM.
BOREDOM MAKES ME REMEMBER.
REMEMBER HIM...
THIS EARRING I SECRETLY TOOK FROM HIS BODY...
EVEN IF I GOT MARRIED, I THOUGHT THIS WOULD KEEP ME HAPPY, BUT...
IT ALSO KEEPS ME FROM LETTING HIM GO ...

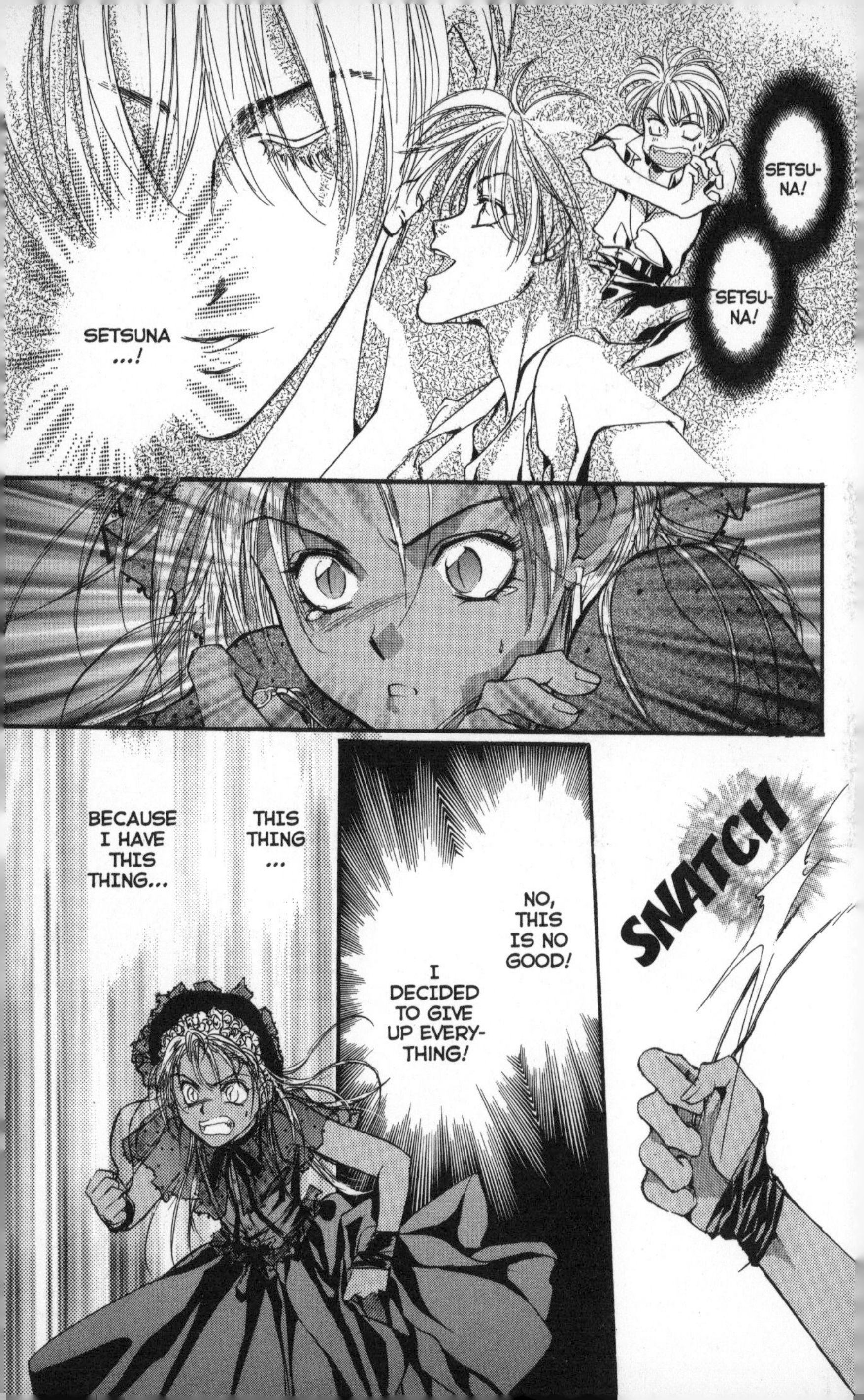
SETSU-NA!
SETSU-NA!
SETSUNA...!
SNATCH
NO, THIS IS NO GOOD!
I DECIDED TO GIVE UP EVERY-THING!
THIS THING...
BECAUSE I HAVE THIS THING...

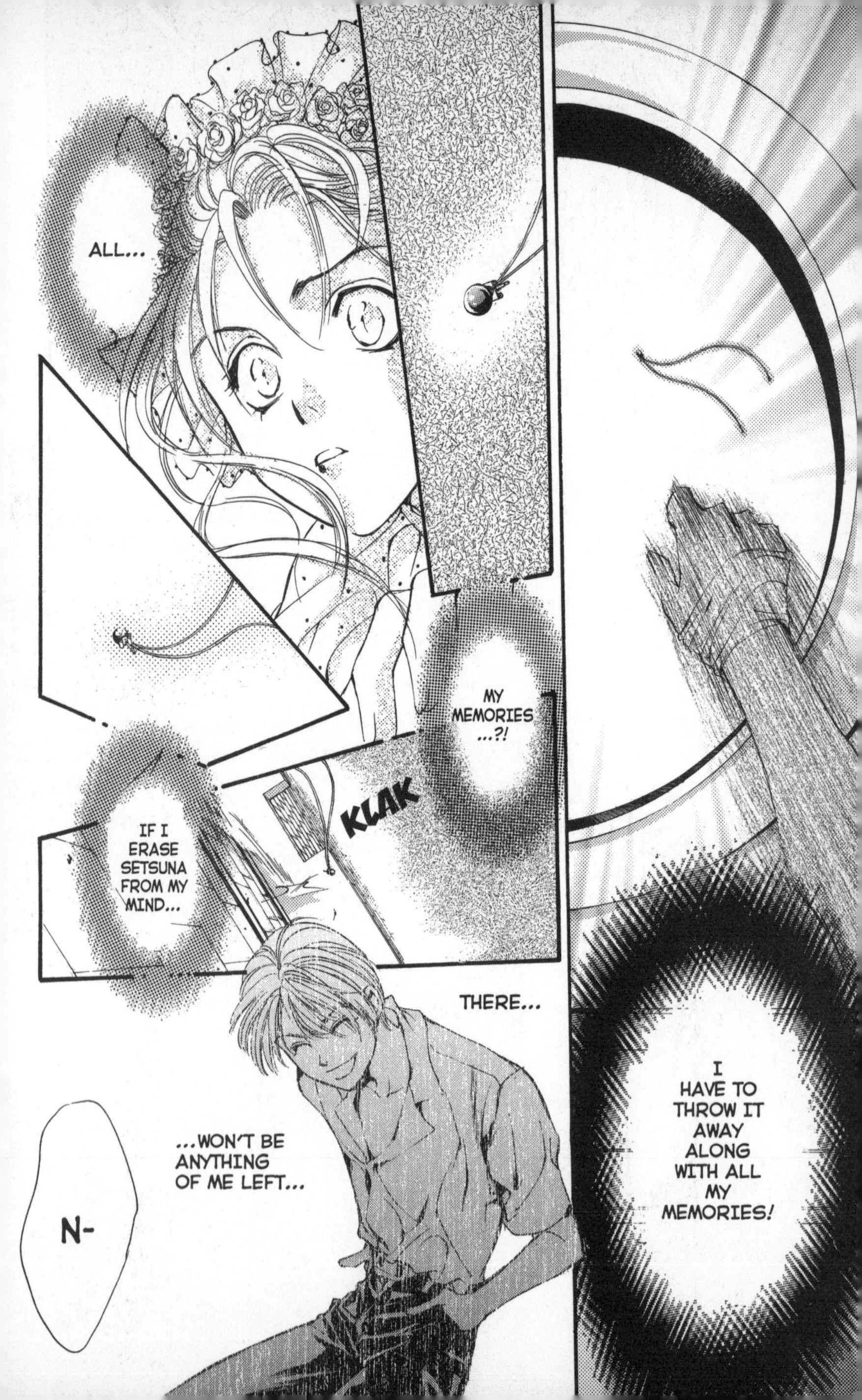
I HAVE TO THROW IT AWAY ALONG WITH ALL MY MEMORIES!
ALL...
MY MEMORIES ...?!
KLAK
IF I ERASE SETSUNA FROM MY MIND...
THERE...
...WON'T BE ANYTHING OF ME LEFT...
N-

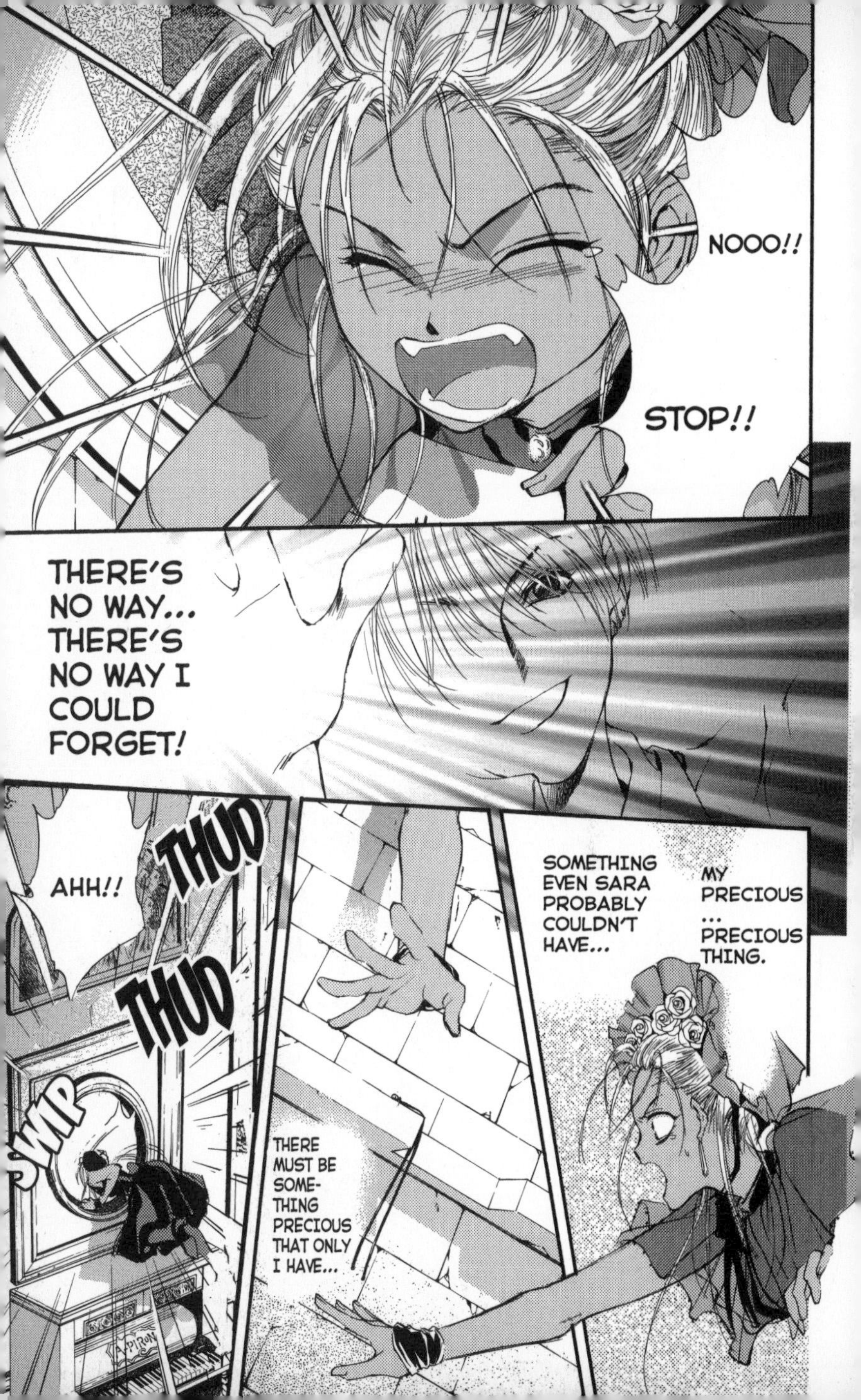
NOOO!!
STOP!!
THERE'S NO WAY... THERE'S NO WAY I COULD FORGET!
MY PRECIOUS ... PRECIOUS THING.
SOMETHING EVEN SARA PROBABLY COULDN'T HAVE...
THERE MUST BE SOME-THING PRECIOUS THAT ONLY I HAVE...
THUD
AHH!!
THUD
SWIP

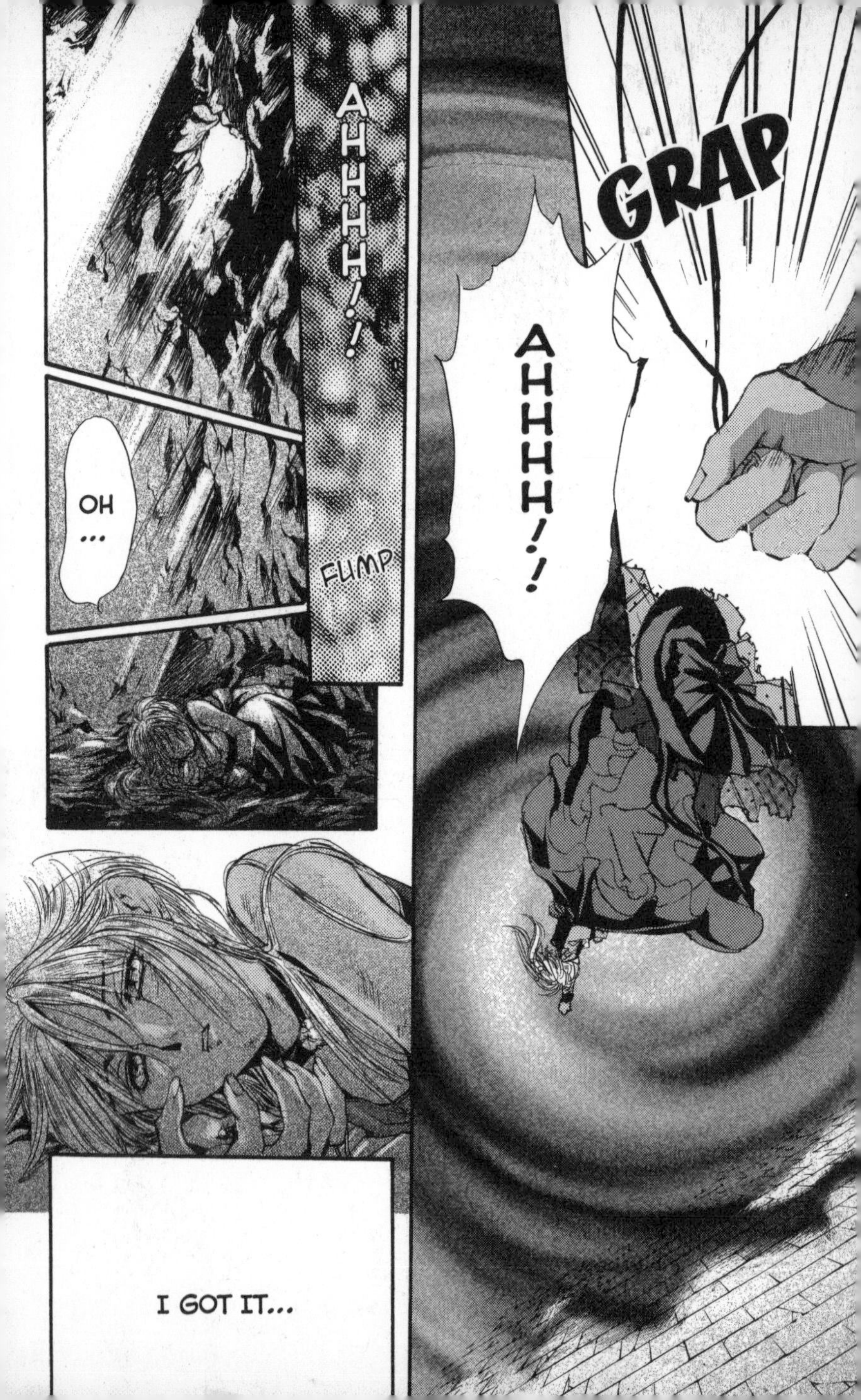
GRAP
AHHHHH!!
AHHHHH!!
OH ...
FUMP
I GOT IT...

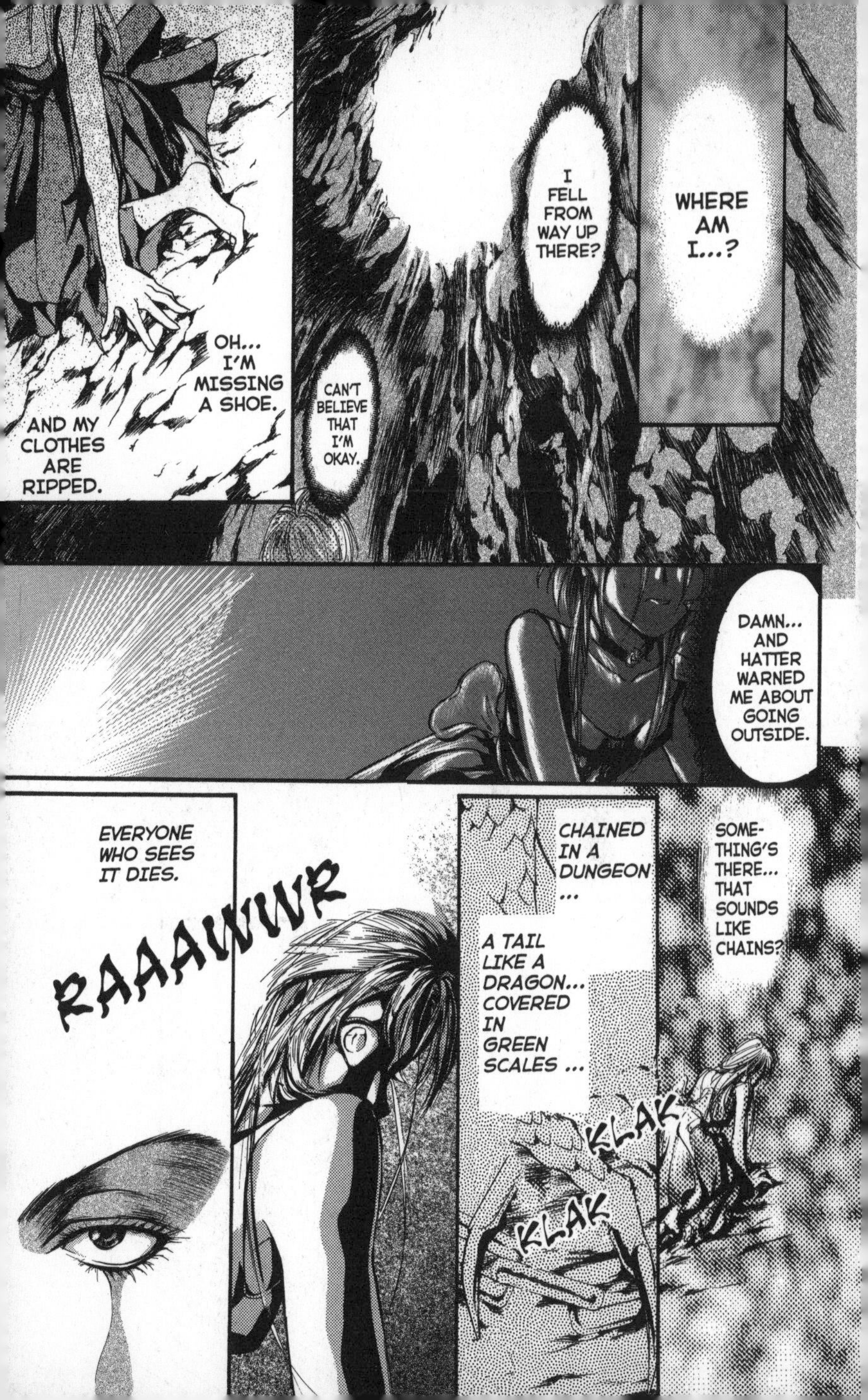
WHERE AM I...?
I FELL FROM WAY UP THERE?
CAN'T BELIEVE THAT I'M OKAY.
OH... I'M MISSING A SHOE.
AND MY CLOTHES ARE RIPPED.
DAMN... AND HATTER WARNED ME ABOUT GOING OUTSIDE.
SOME-THING'S THERE... THAT SOUNDS LIKE CHAINS?
KLAK
KLAK
CHAINED IN A DUNGEON ...
A TAIL LIKE A DRAGON... COVERED IN GREEN SCALES ...
RAAAWWR
EVERYONE WHO SEES IT DIES.

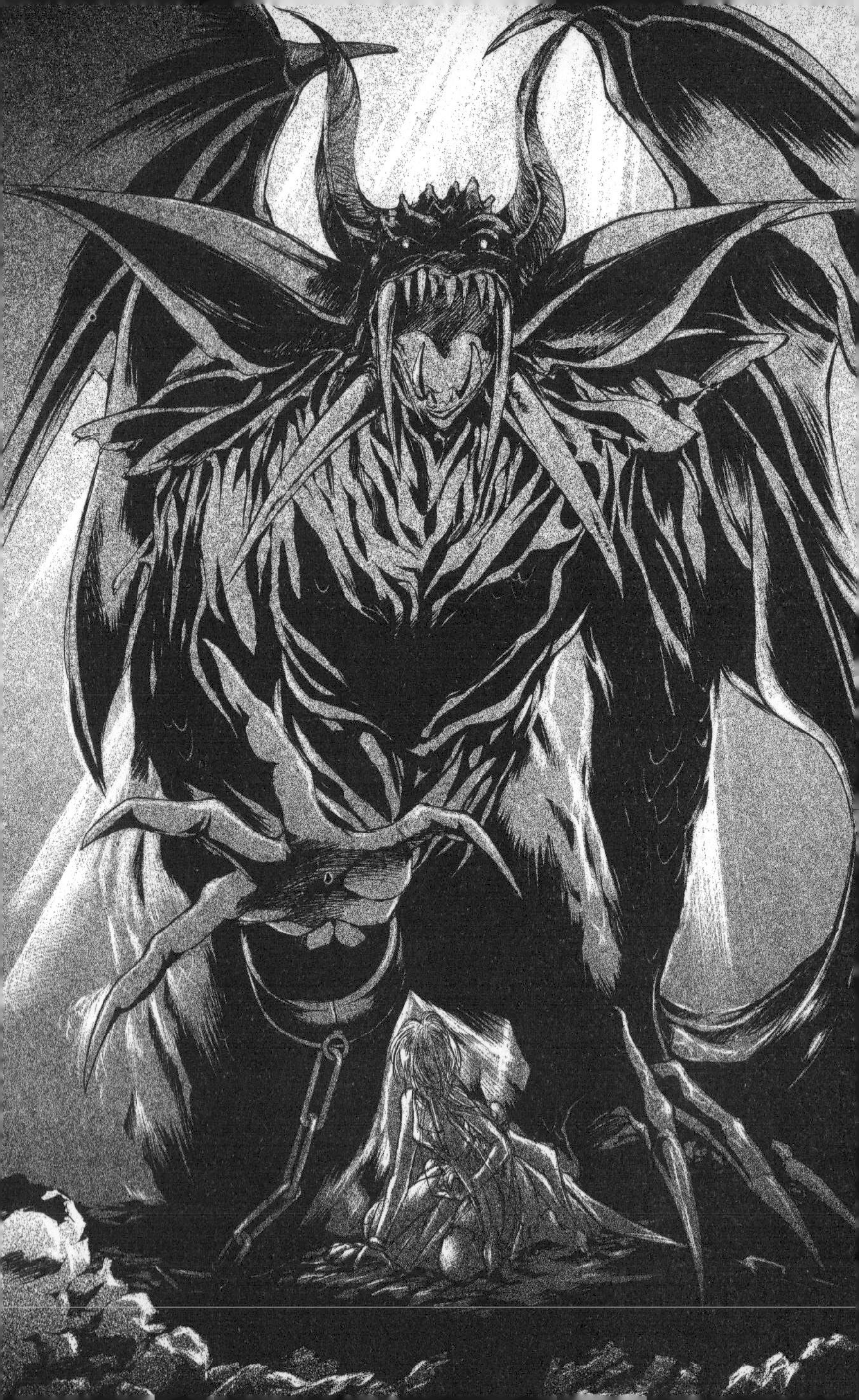

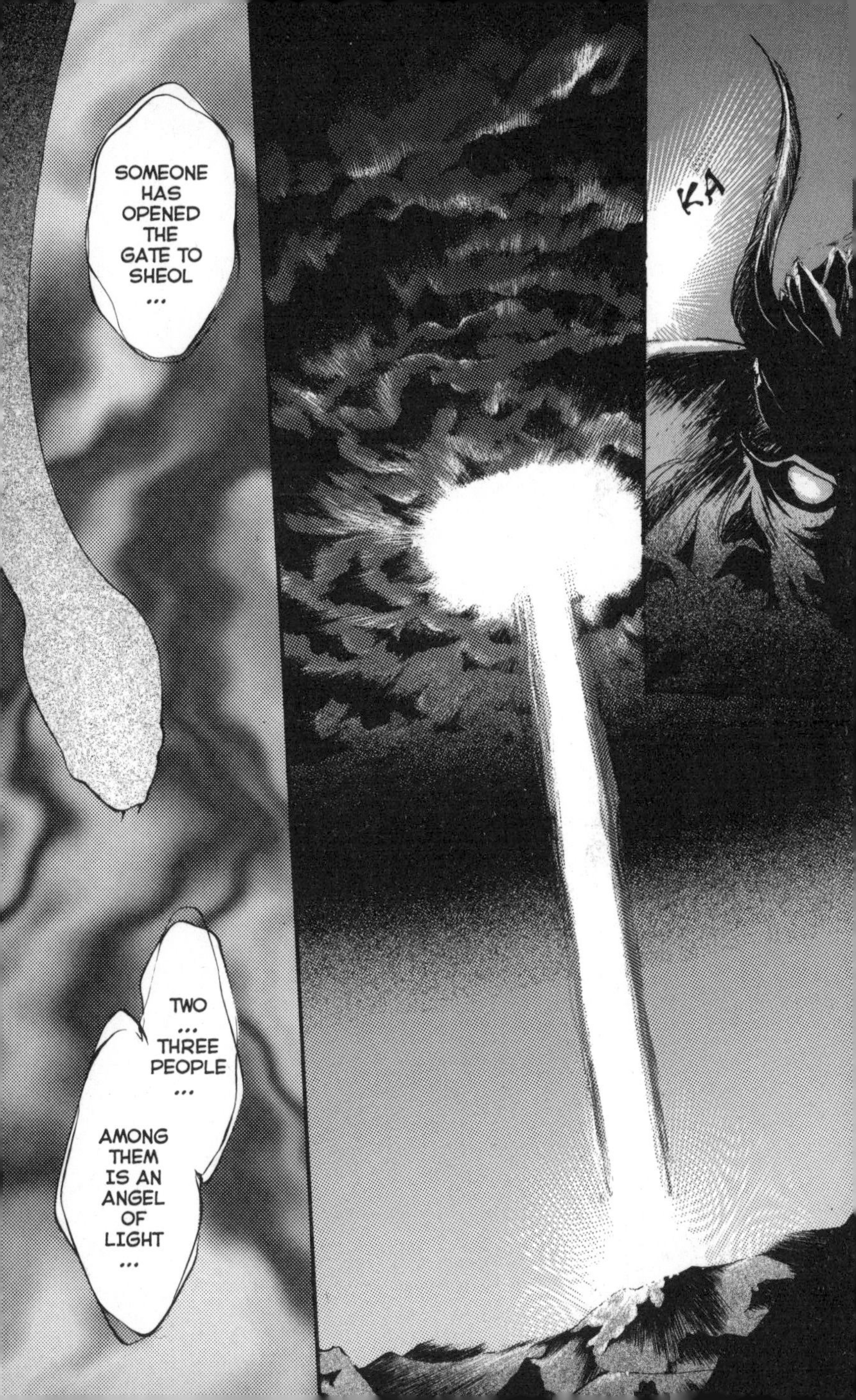
KA
SOMEONE HAS OPENED THE GATE TO SHEOL ...
TWO ... THREE PEOPLE ...
AMONG THEM IS AN ANGEL OF LIGHT ...

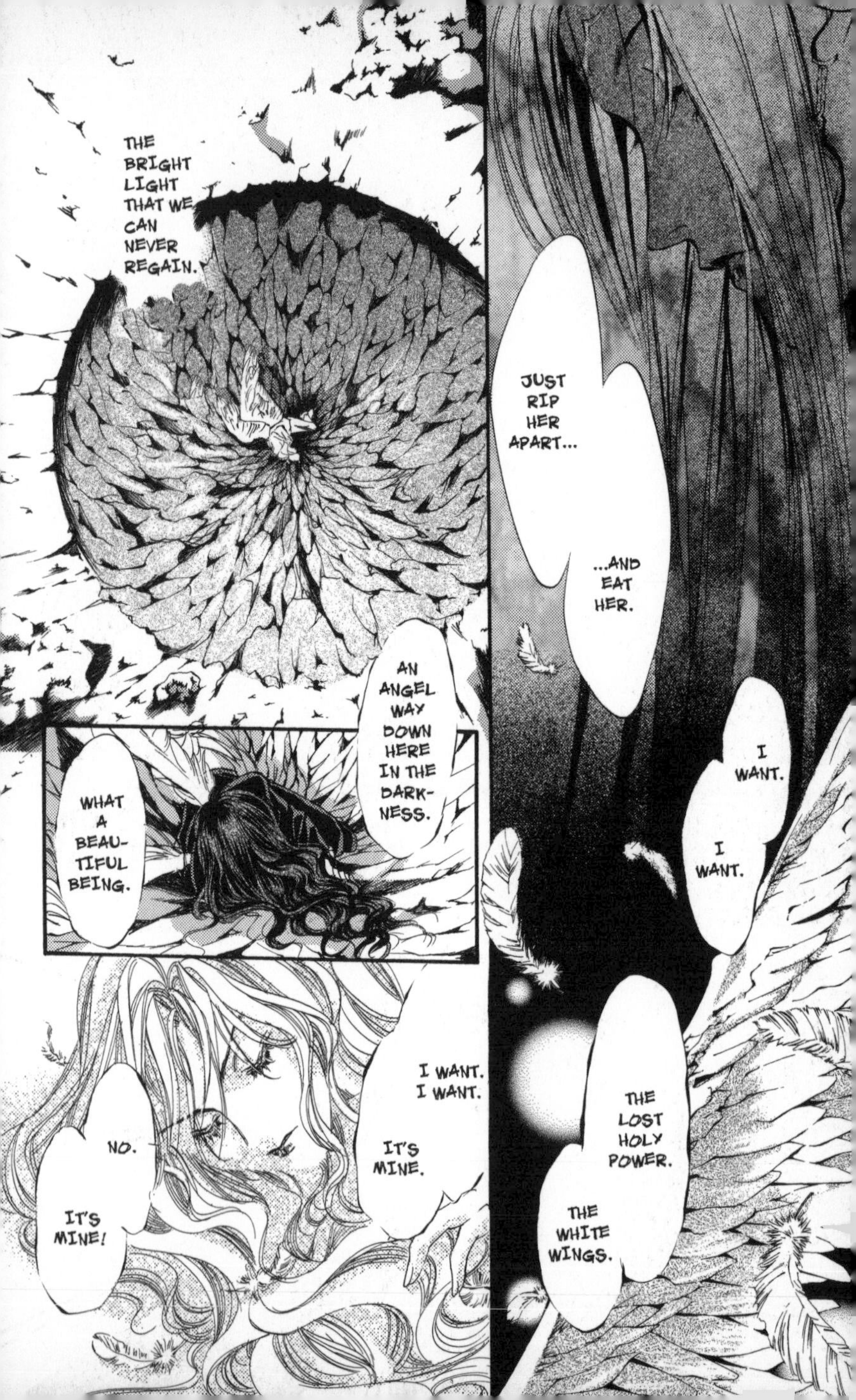
JUST RIP HER APART...
...AND EAT HER.
I WANT.
I WANT.
THE LOST HOLY POWER.
THE WHITE WINGS.
THE BRIGHT LIGHT THAT WE CAN NEVER REGAIN.
AN ANGEL WAY DOWN HERE IN THE DARKNESS.
WHAT A BEAUTIFUL BEING.
I WANT. I WANT.
IT'S MINE.
NO.
IT'S MINE!

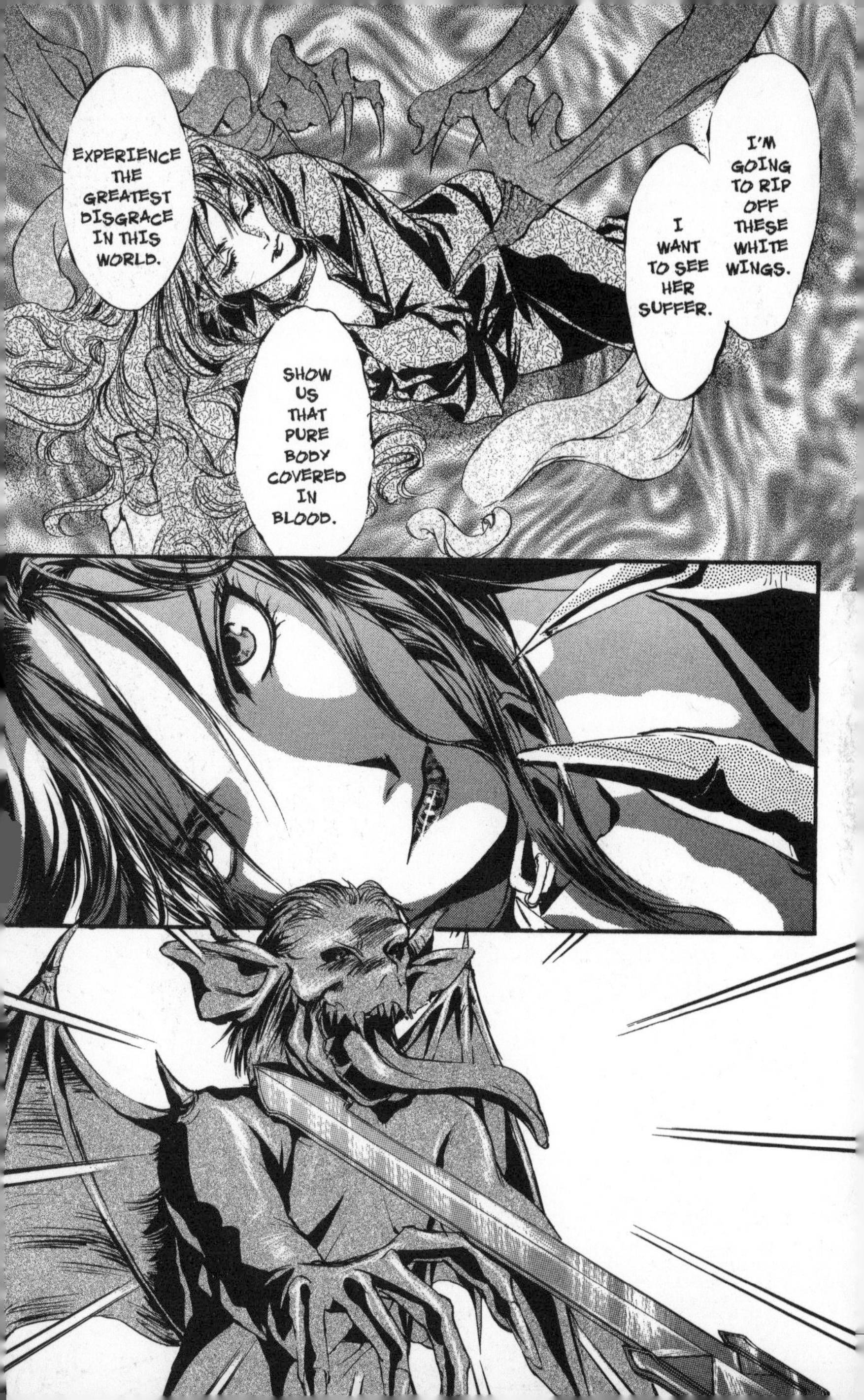
I'M GOING TO RIP OFF THESE WHITE WINGS.
I WANT TO SEE HER SUFFER.
EXPERIENCE THE GREATEST DISGRACE IN THIS WORLD.
SHOW US THAT PURE BODY COVERED IN BLOOD.

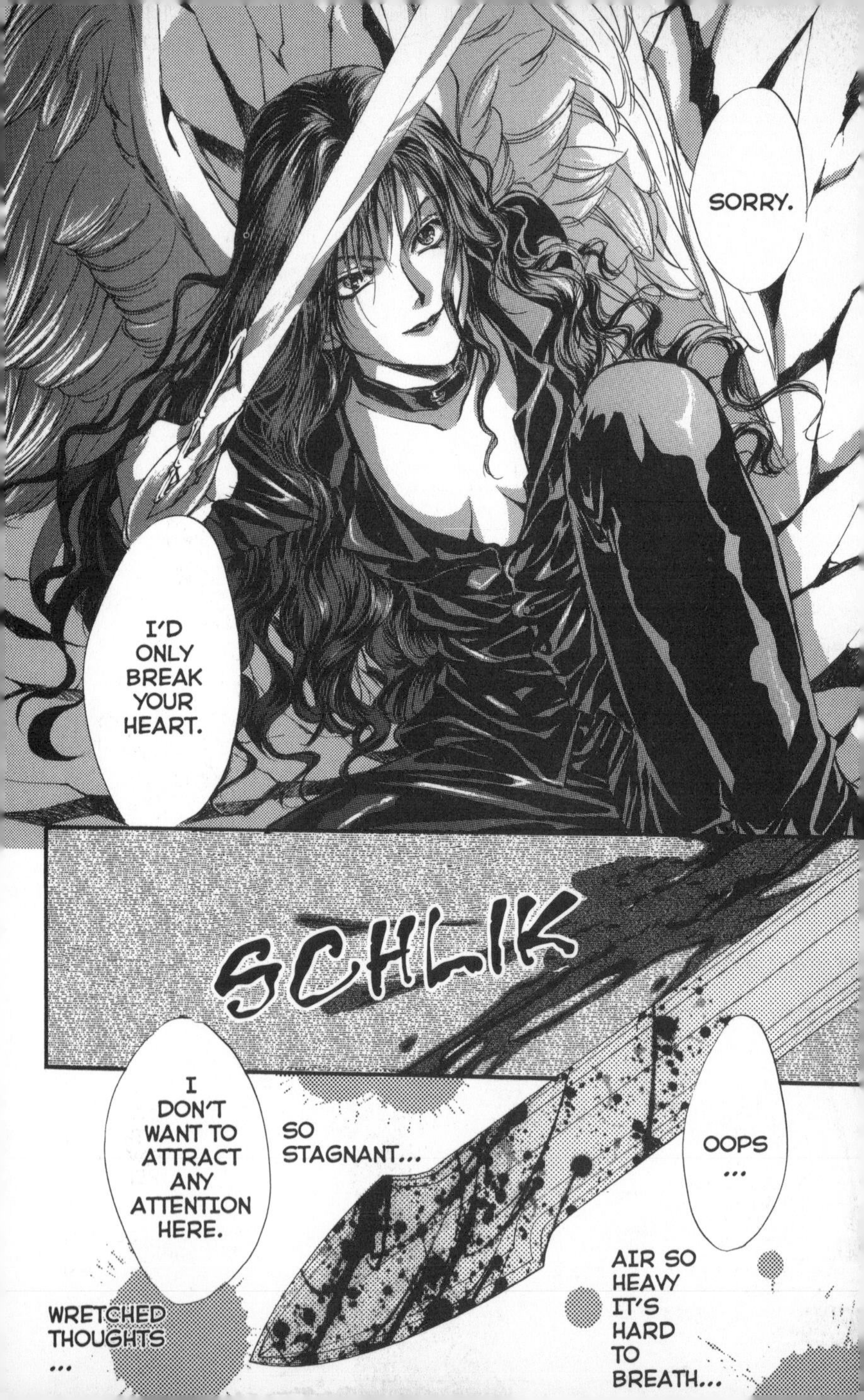
SORRY.
I'D ONLY BREAK YOUR HEART.
SCHLIK
OOPS ...
I DON'T WANT TO ATTRACT ANY ATTENTION HERE.
SO STAGNANT...
AIR SO HEAVY IT'S HARD TO BREATH...
WRETCHED THOUGHTS ...

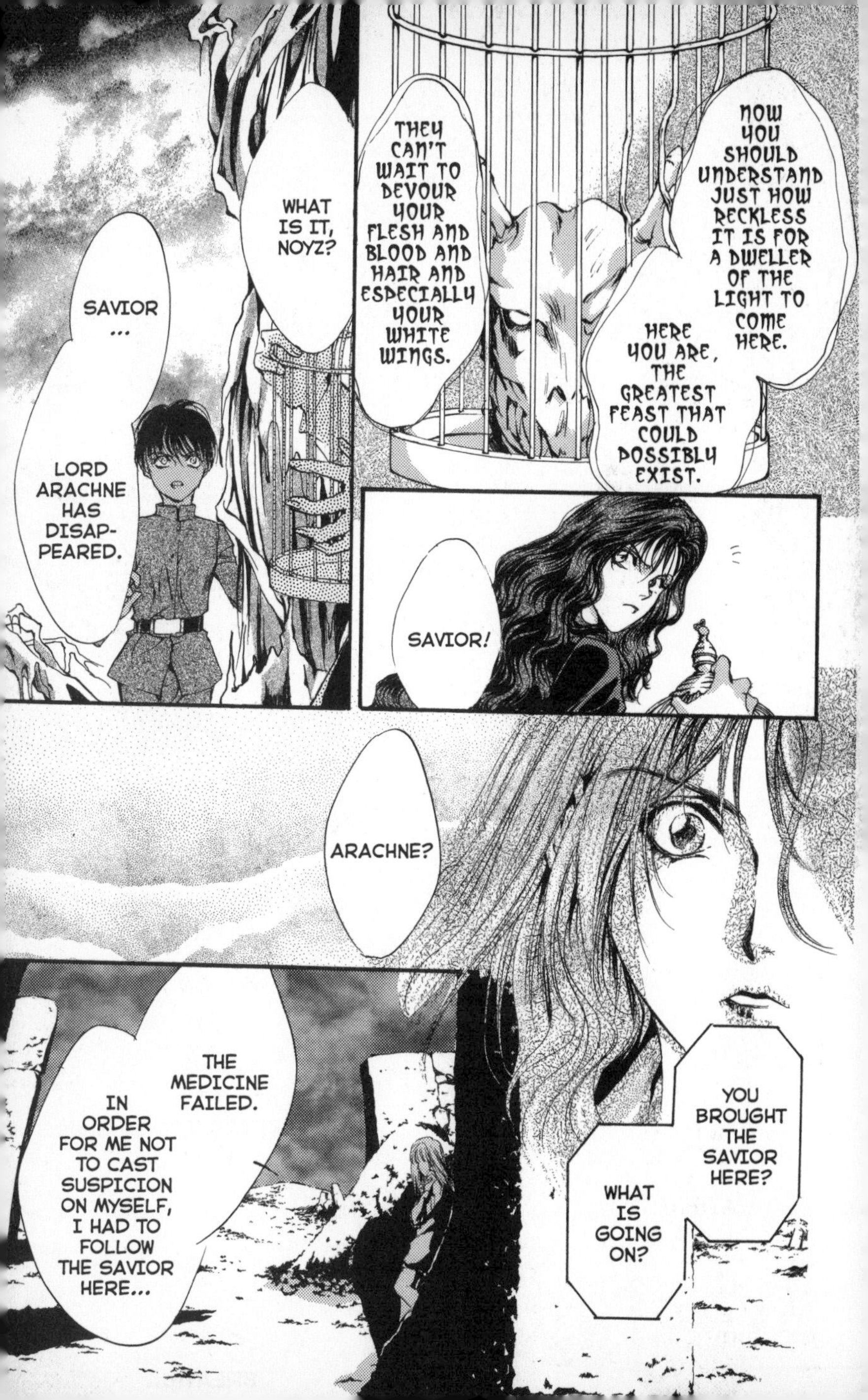
NOW YOU SHOULD UNDERSTAND JUST HOW RECKLESS IT IS FOR A DWELLER OF THE LIGHT TO COME HERE.
HERE YOU ARE, THE GREATEST FEAST THAT COULD POSSIBLY EXIST.
THEY CAN'T WAIT TO DEVOUR YOUR FLESH AND BLOOD AND HAIR AND ESPECIALLY YOUR WHITE WINGS.
SAVIOR!
WHAT IS IT, NOYZ?
SAVIOR ...
LORD ARACHNE HAS DISAP-PEARED.
ARACHNE?
YOU BROUGHT THE SAVIOR HERE?
WHAT IS GOING ON?
THE MEDICINE FAILED.
IN ORDER FOR ME NOT TO CAST SUSPICION ON MYSELF, I HAD TO FOLLOW THE SAVIOR HERE...

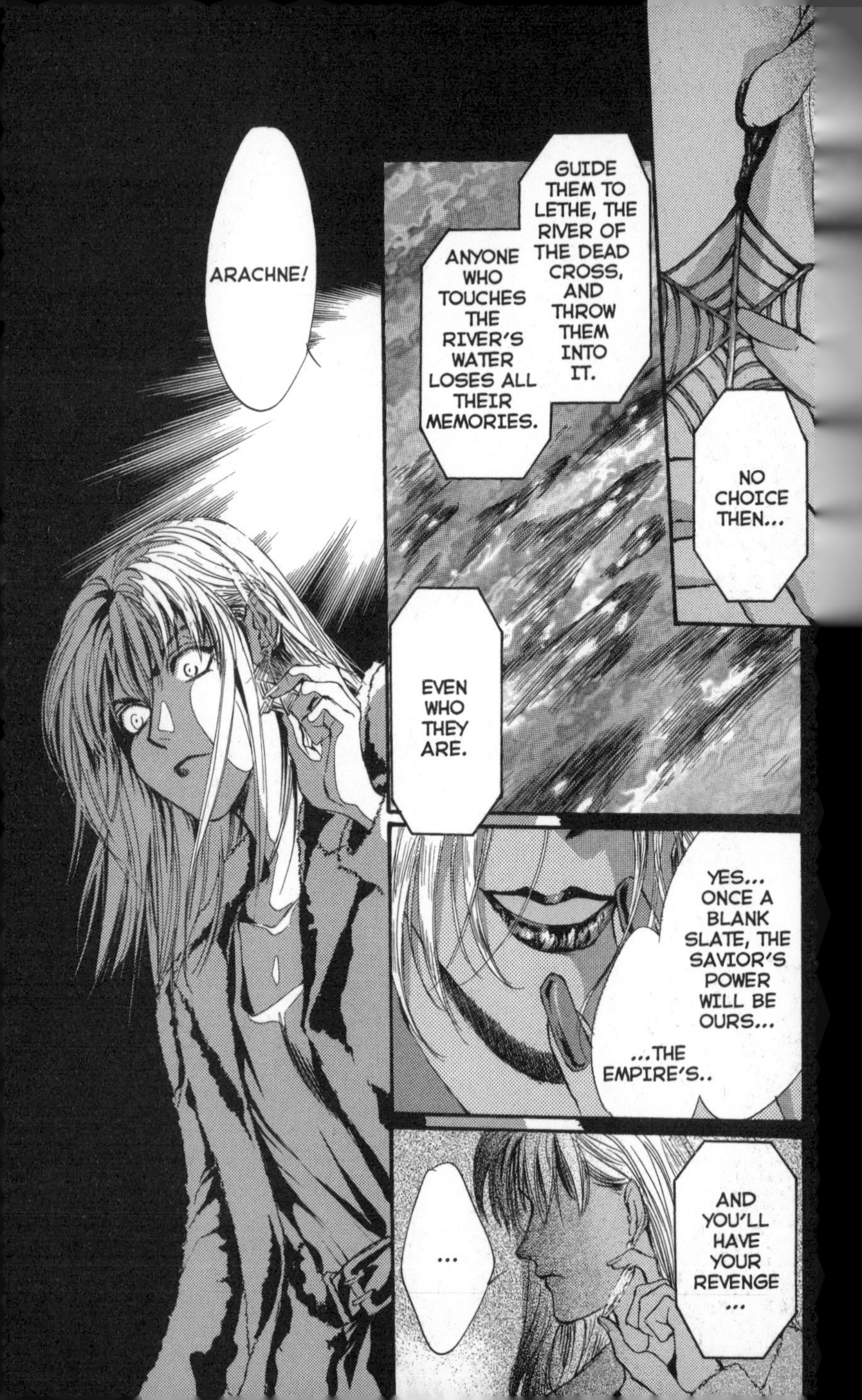
NO CHOICE THEN...
GUIDE THEM TO LETHE, THE RIVER OF THE DEAD CROSS, AND THROW THEM INTO IT.
ANYONE WHO TOUCHES THE RIVER'S WATER LOSES ALL THEIR MEMORIES.
EVEN WHO THEY ARE.
YES... ONCE A BLANK SLATE, THE SAVIOR'S POWER WILL BE OURS...
...THE EMPIRE'S..
AND YOU'LL HAVE YOUR REVENGE ...
...
ARACHNE!

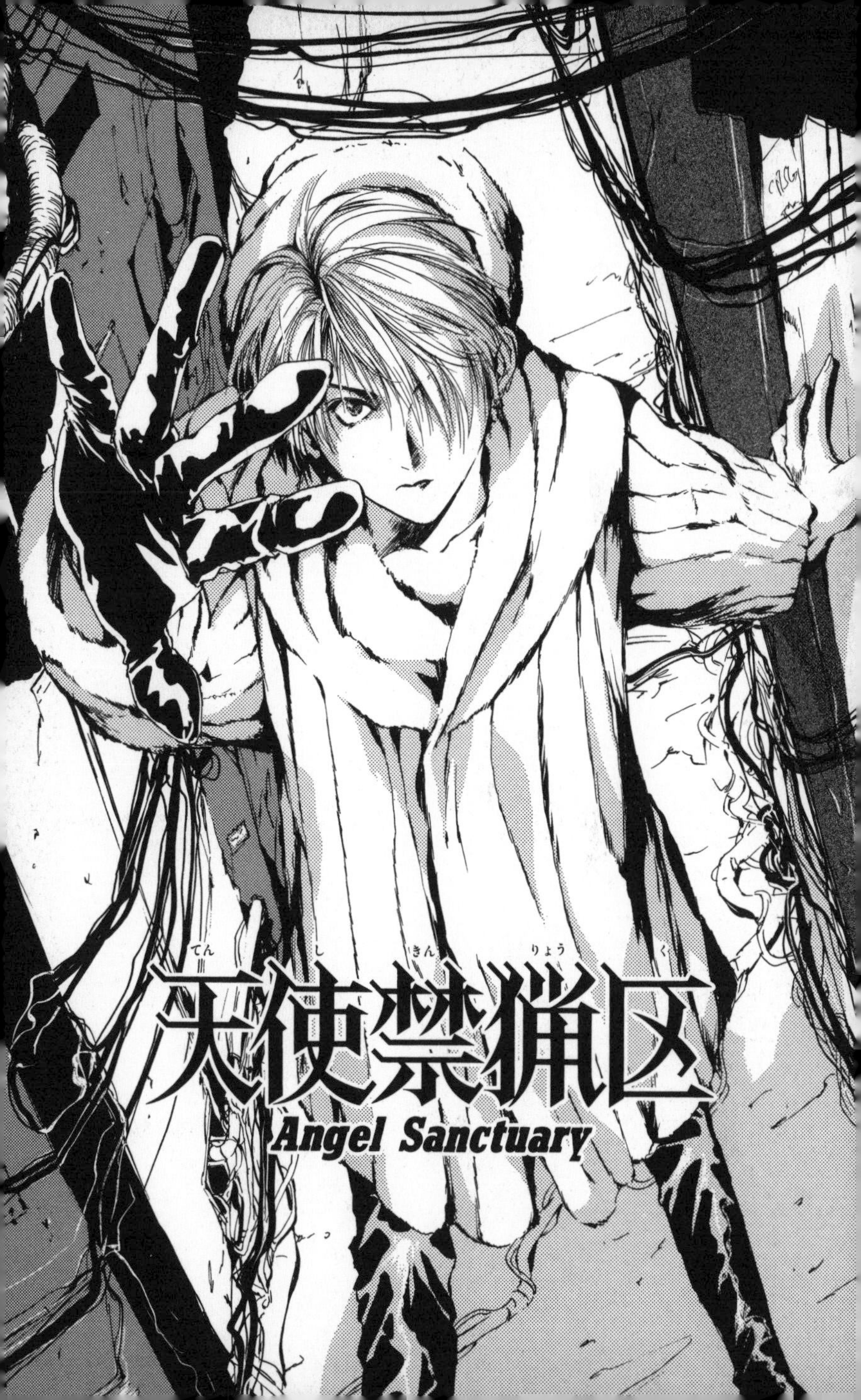

天使禁猟区
Angel Sanctuary

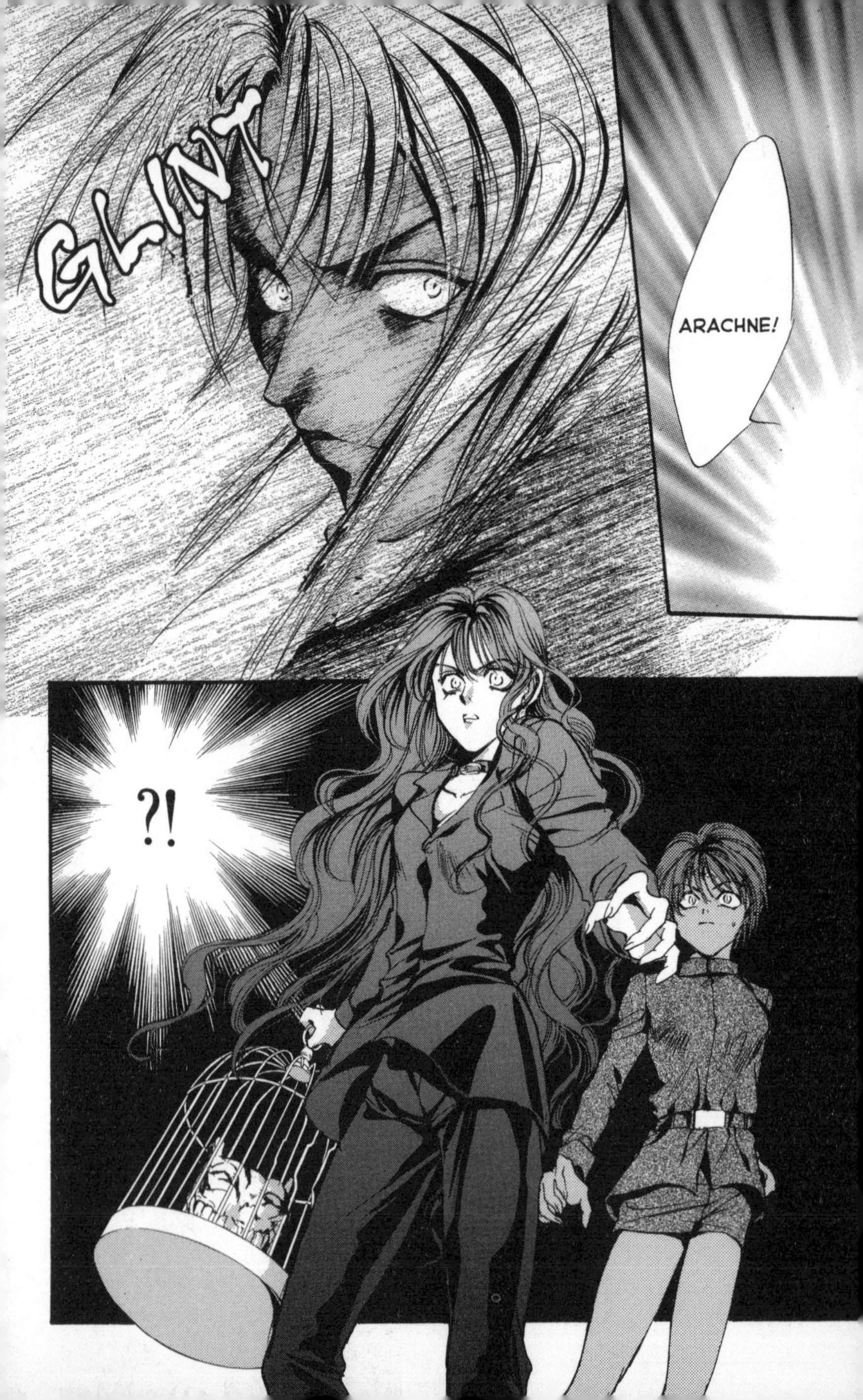
ARACHNE!
GLINT
?!

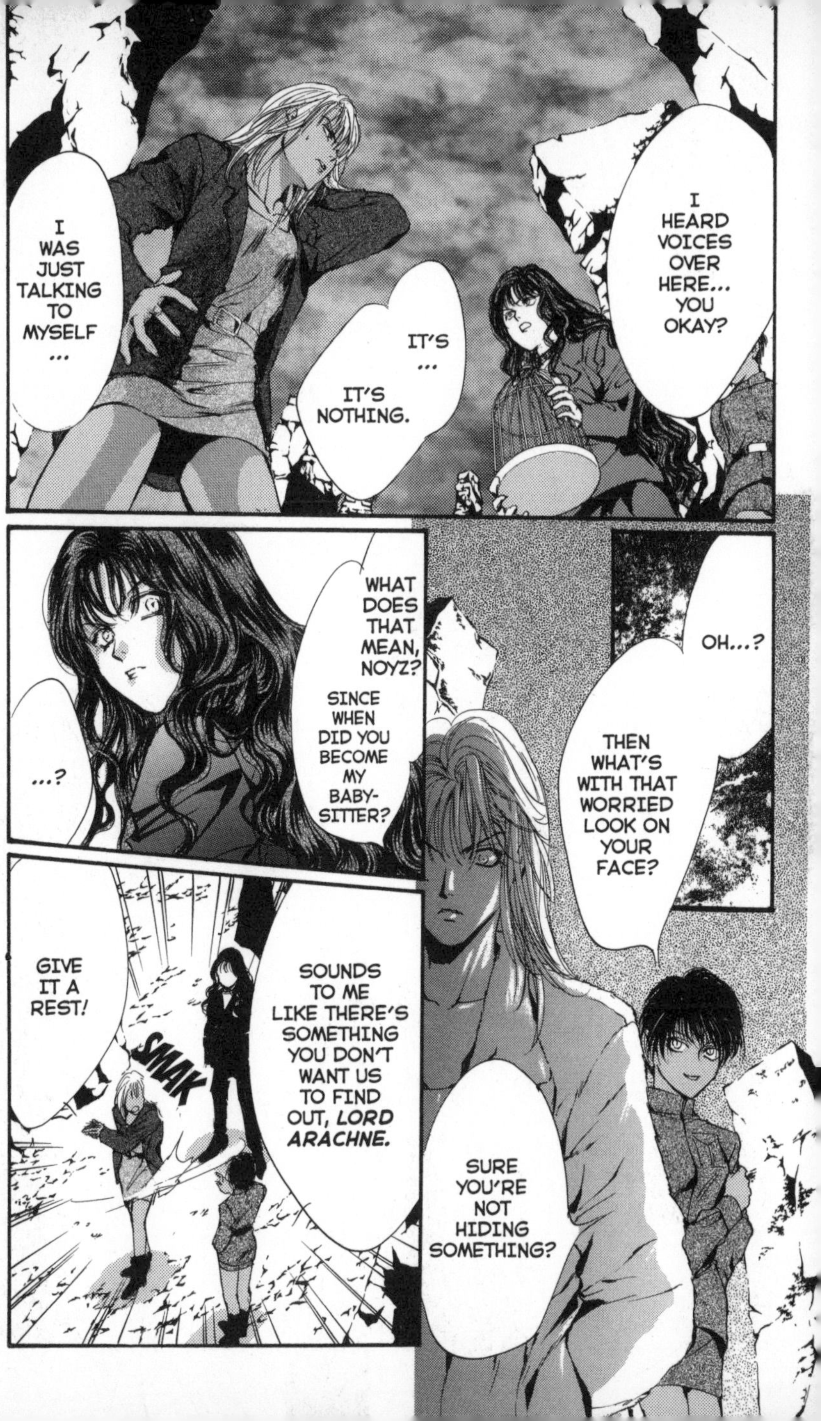
I HEARD VOICES OVER HERE... YOU OKAY?
IT'S ... IT'S NOTHING.
I WAS JUST TALKING TO MYSELF ...
OH...?
THEN WHAT'S WITH THAT WORRIED LOOK ON YOUR FACE?
SURE YOU'RE NOT HIDING SOMETHING?
WHAT DOES THAT MEAN, NOYZ?
SINCE WHEN DID YOU BECOME MY BABY-SITTER?
...?
SOUNDS TO ME LIKE THERE'S SOMETHING YOU DON'T WANT US TO FIND OUT, *LORD ARACHNE.*
SMAK
GIVE IT A REST!

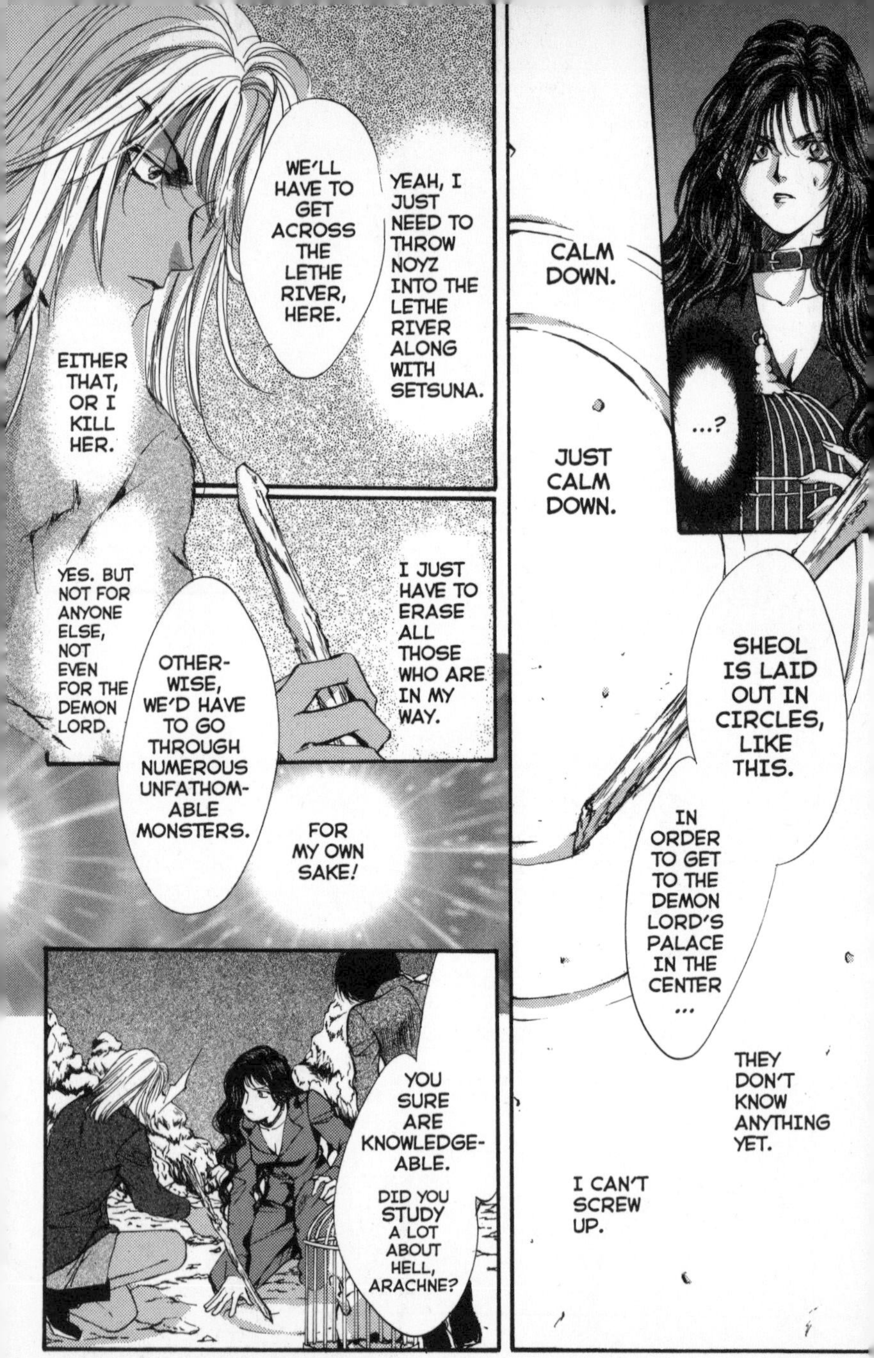
CALM DOWN.
...?
JUST CALM DOWN.
SHEOL IS LAID OUT IN CIRCLES, LIKE THIS.
IN ORDER TO GET TO THE DEMON LORD'S PALACE IN THE CENTER...
THEY DON'T KNOW ANYTHING YET.
I CAN'T SCREW UP.
WE'LL HAVE TO GET ACROSS THE LETHE RIVER, HERE.
YEAH, I JUST NEED TO THROW NOYZ INTO THE LETHE RIVER ALONG WITH SETSUNA.
EITHER THAT, OR I KILL HER.
OTHER-WISE, WE'D HAVE TO GO THROUGH NUMEROUS UNFATHOM-ABLE MONSTERS.
I JUST HAVE TO ERASE ALL THOSE WHO ARE IN MY WAY.
YES. BUT NOT FOR ANYONE ELSE, NOT EVEN FOR THE DEMON LORD.
FOR MY OWN SAKE!
YOU SURE ARE KNOWLEDGE-ABLE.
DID YOU STUDY A LOT ABOUT HELL, ARACHNE?

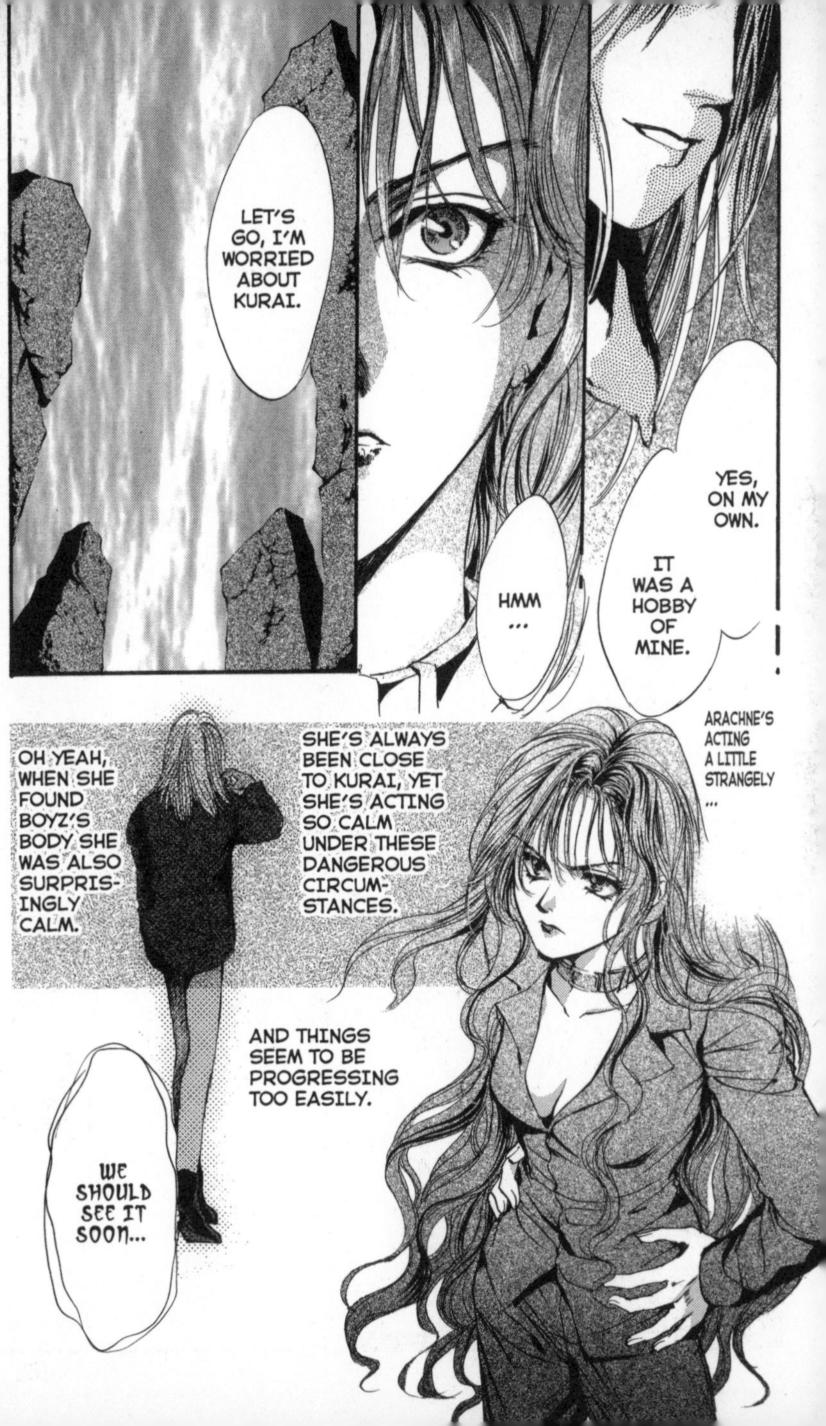
YES, ON MY OWN.
IT WAS A HOBBY OF MINE.
HMM ...
LET'S GO, I'M WORRIED ABOUT KURAI.
ARACHNE'S ACTING A LITTLE STRANGELY ...
SHE'S ALWAYS BEEN CLOSE TO KURAI, YET SHE'S ACTING SO CALM UNDER THESE DANGEROUS CIRCUM-STANCES.
OH YEAH, WHEN SHE FOUND BOYZ'S BODY SHE WAS ALSO SURPRIS-INGLY CALM.
AND THINGS SEEM TO BE PROGRESSING TOO EASILY.
WE SHOULD SEE IT SOON...

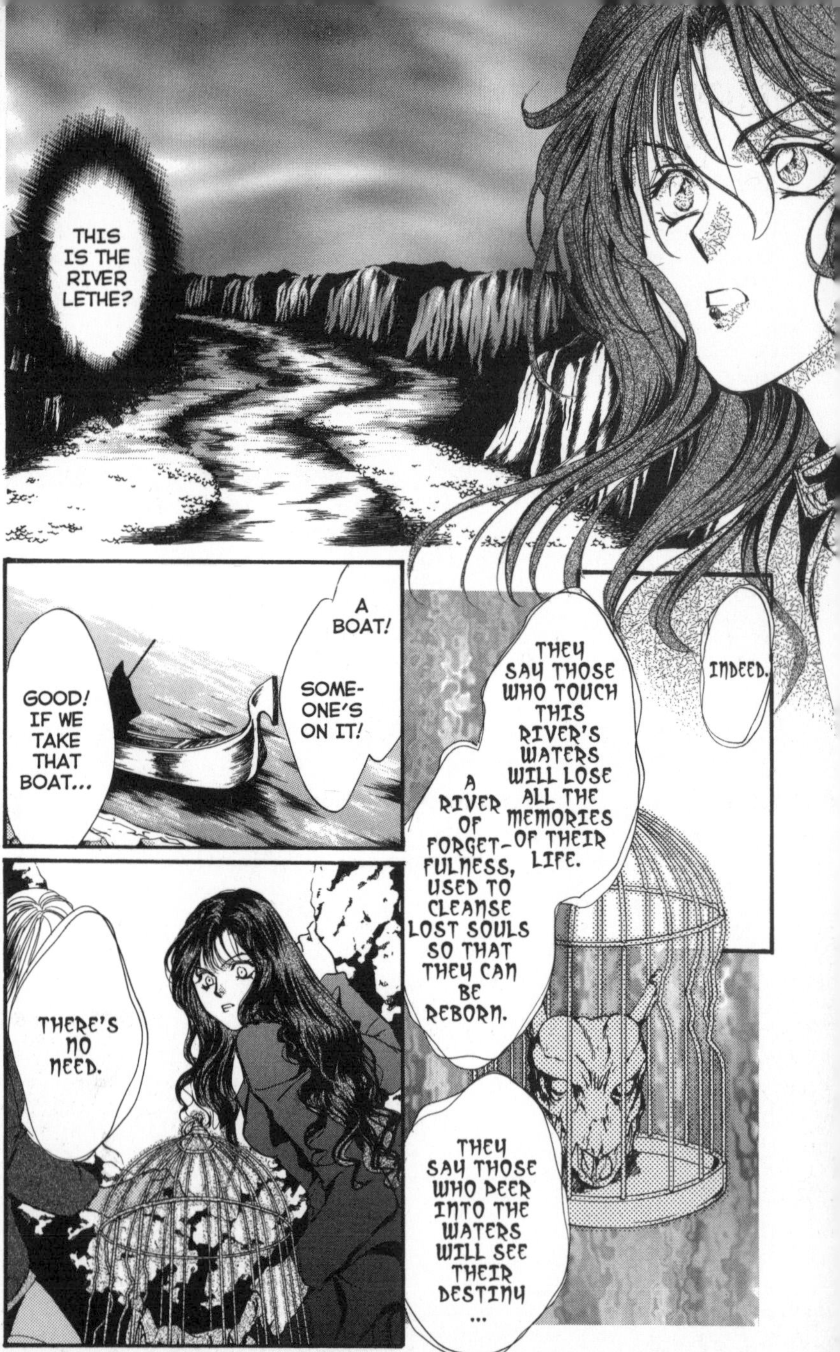
THIS IS THE RIVER LETHE?
INDEED.
THEY SAY THOSE WHO TOUCH THIS RIVER'S WATERS WILL LOSE ALL THE MEMORIES OF THEIR LIFE.
A RIVER OF FORGET-FULNESS, USED TO CLEANSE LOST SOULS SO THAT THEY CAN BE REBORN.
A BOAT!
SOME-ONE'S ON IT!
GOOD! IF WE TAKE THAT BOAT...
THEY SAY THOSE WHO PEER INTO THE WATERS WILL SEE THEIR DESTINY ...
THERE'S NO NEED.

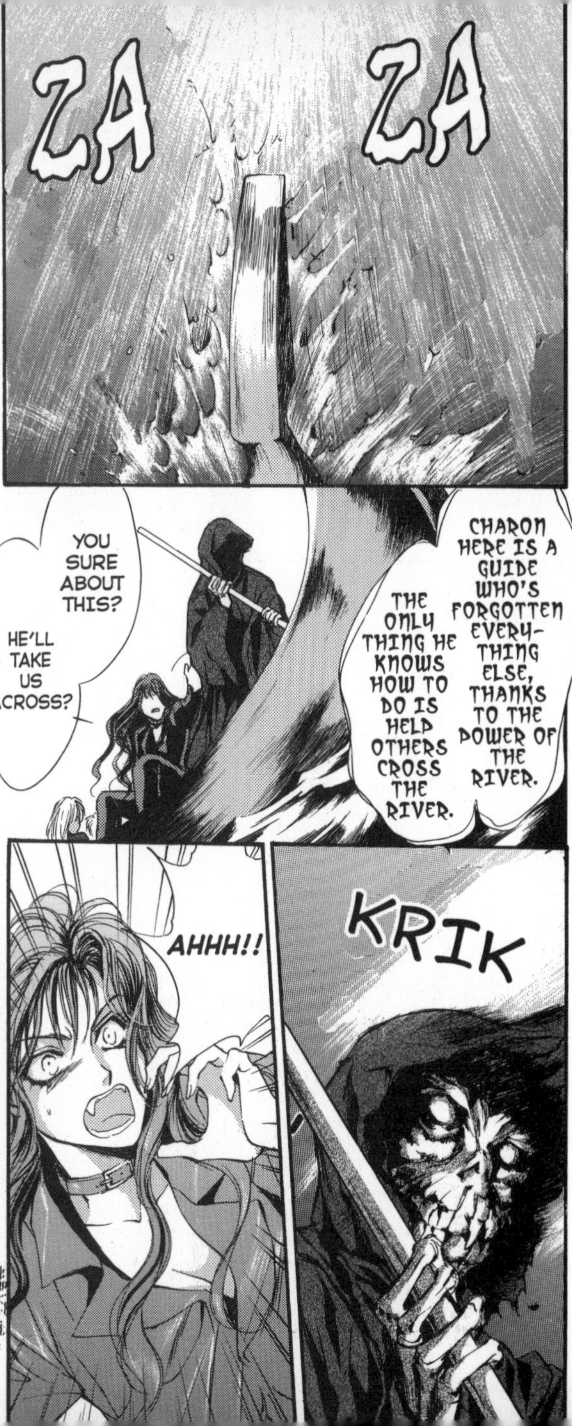
ZA
ZA
CHARON HERE IS A GUIDE WHO'S FORGOTTEN EVERYTHING ELSE, THANKS TO THE POWER OF THE RIVER.
THE ONLY THING HE KNOWS HOW TO DO IS HELP OTHERS CROSS THE RIVER.
YOU SURE ABOUT THIS?
HE'LL TAKE US ACROSS?
KRIK
AHHH!!

After I wrote about cosplayers in book eight, I got tons of pictures from those people! (One was a Kirie. And a Jibril one, too.) Sorry that I've been too busy to respond, but I really enjoyed them. All the girls were so cute! And Kira and Setsuna were really cool. I was really surprised with all the detail, even the cross rods! Though Nanatsusaya... I felt bad that I had changed the shape of it. Hatter and Kato were really nice, too. And that hottie Rosiel was like a queen--I wish I could see more. Someone please do Astaroth--his hair is red/brown and his clothes are black. Anyway, thank you very much! Keep it up.

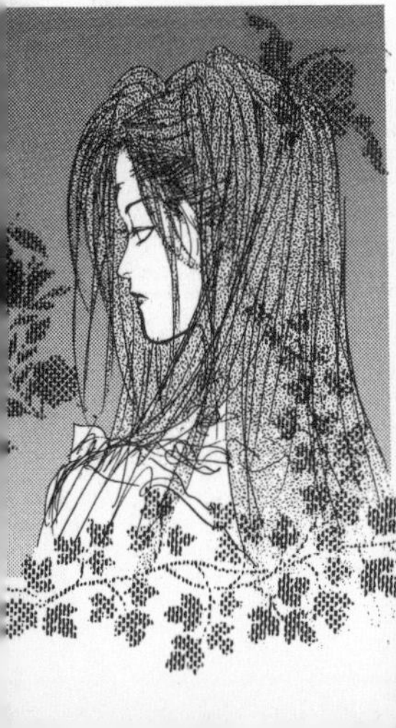

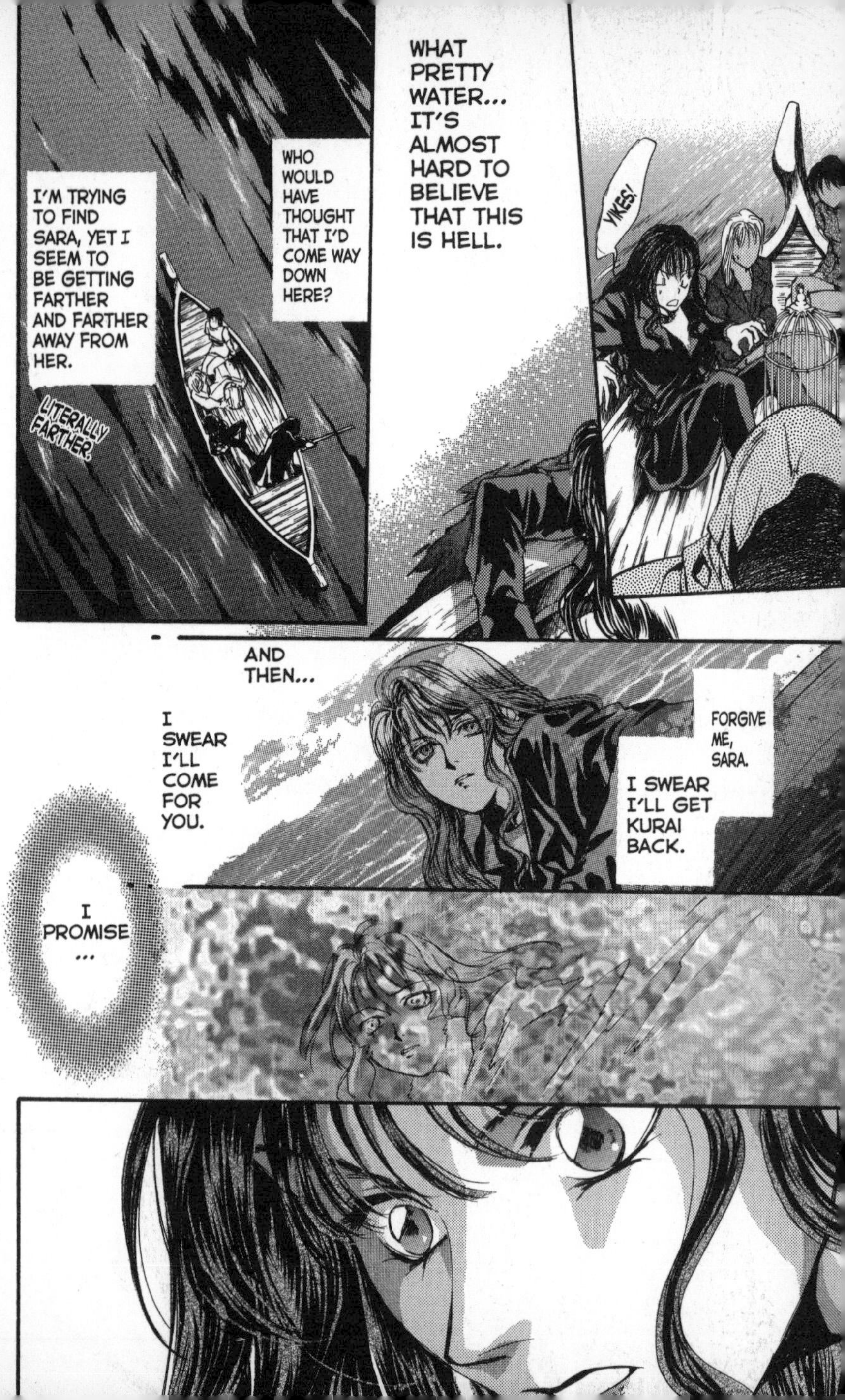
YIKES!
WHAT PRETTY WATER... IT'S ALMOST HARD TO BELIEVE THAT THIS IS HELL.
WHO WOULD HAVE THOUGHT THAT I'D COME WAY DOWN HERE?
I'M TRYING TO FIND SARA, YET I SEEM TO BE GETTING FARTHER AND FARTHER AWAY FROM HER.
LITERALLY FARTHER.
AND THEN...
FORGIVE ME, SARA.
I SWEAR I'LL GET KURAI BACK.
I SWEAR I'LL COME FOR YOU.
I PROMISE...

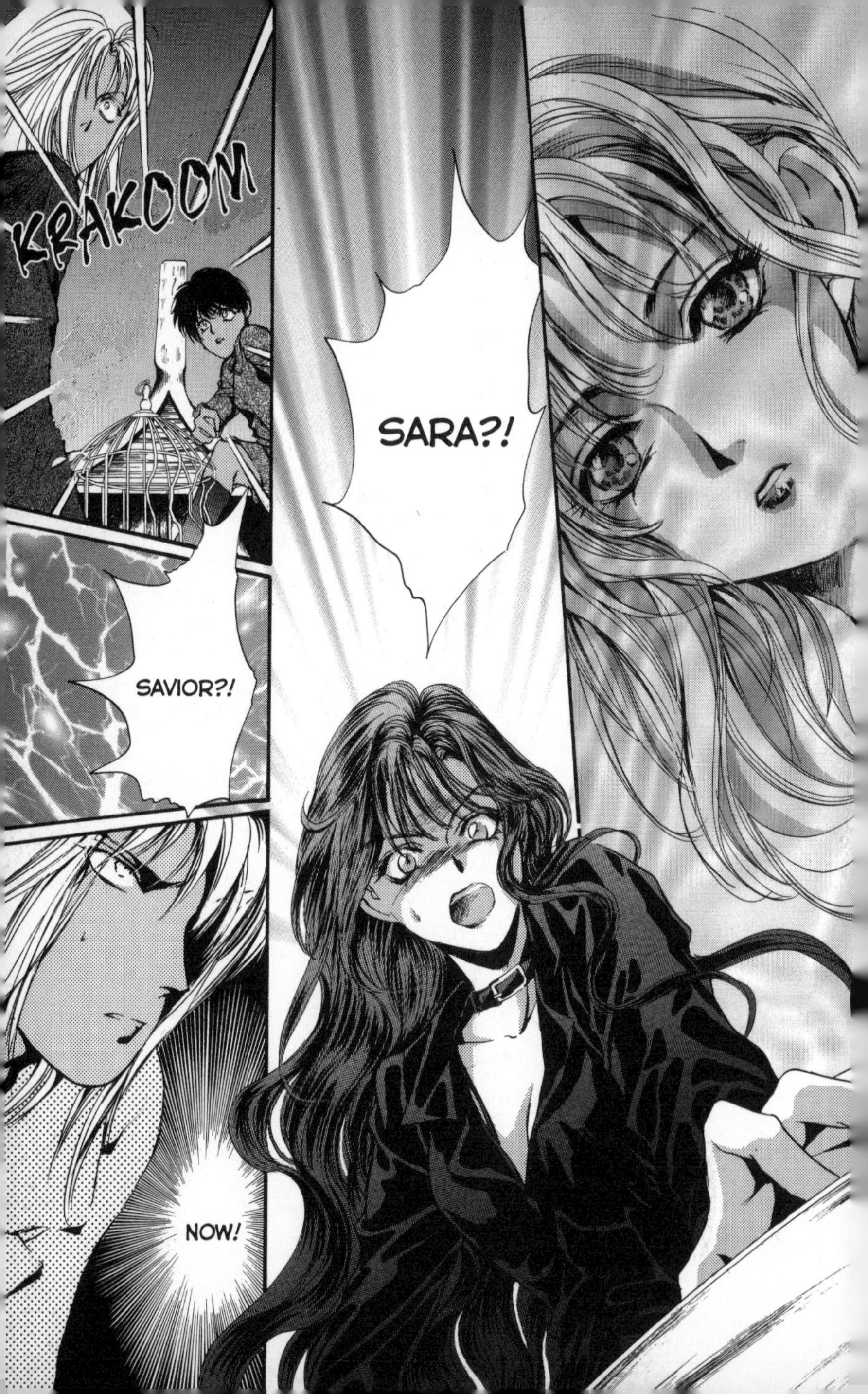
SARA?!
KRAKOOM
SAVIOR?!
NOW!

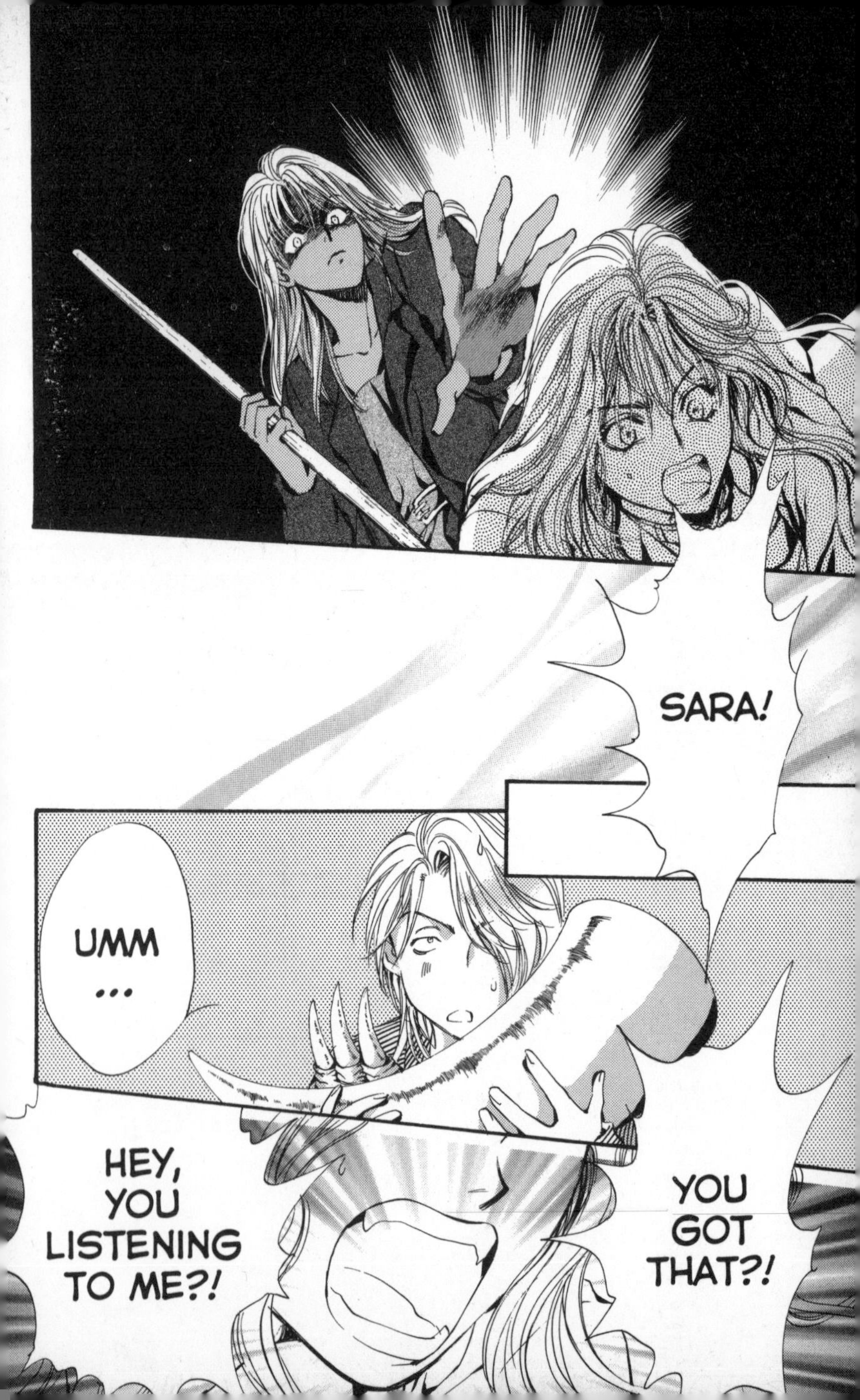
SARA!
UMM ...
YOU GOT THAT?!
HEY, YOU LISTENING TO ME?!

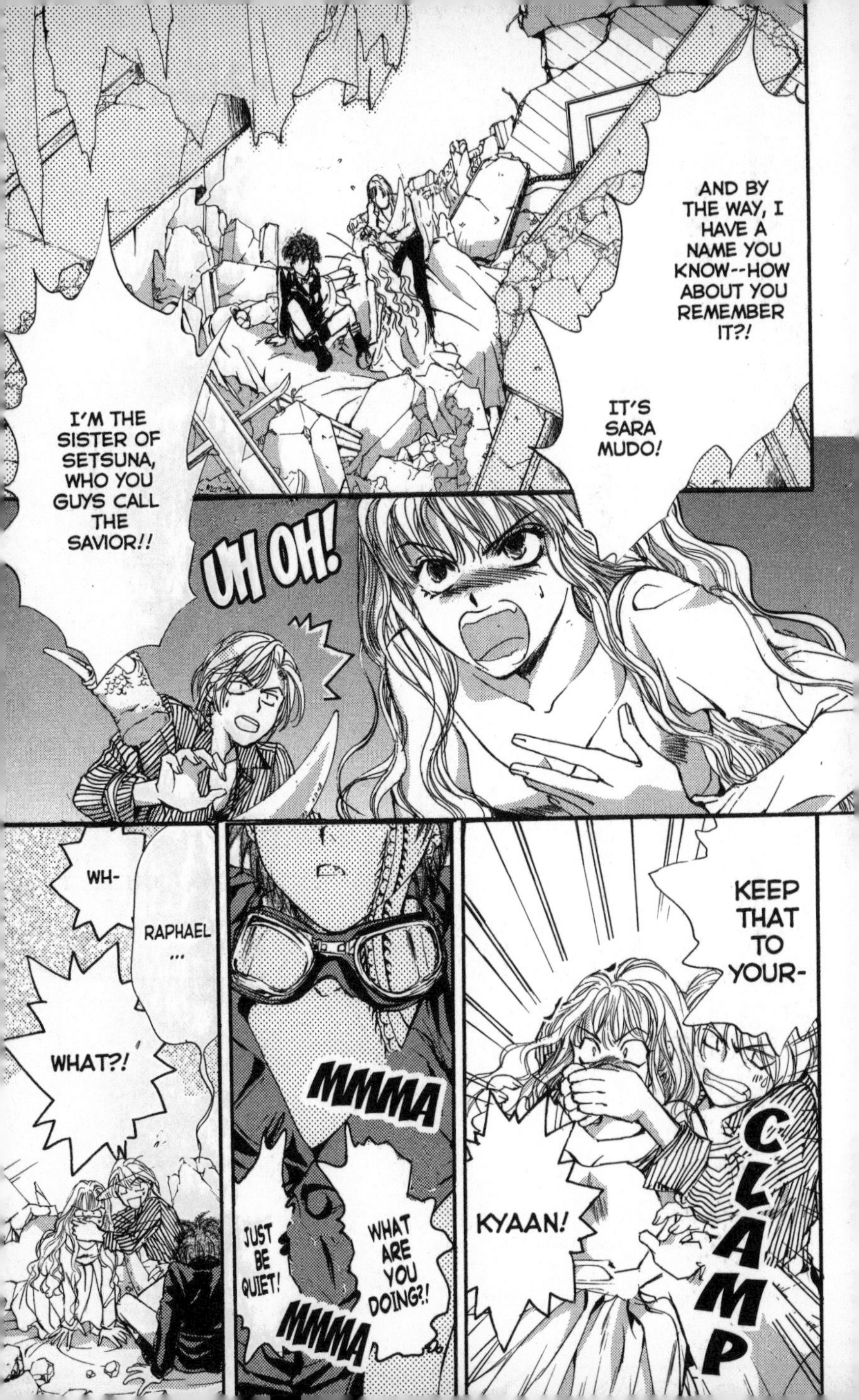
AND BY THE WAY, I HAVE A NAME YOU KNOW--HOW ABOUT YOU REMEMBER IT?!
IT'S SARA MUDO!
I'M THE SISTER OF SETSUNA, WHO YOU GUYS CALL THE SAVIOR!!
UH OH!
KEEP THAT TO YOUR-
KYAAN!
CLAMP
MMMA
WHAT ARE YOU DOING?!
JUST BE QUIET!
MMMA
WH-
RAPHAEL ...
WHAT?!

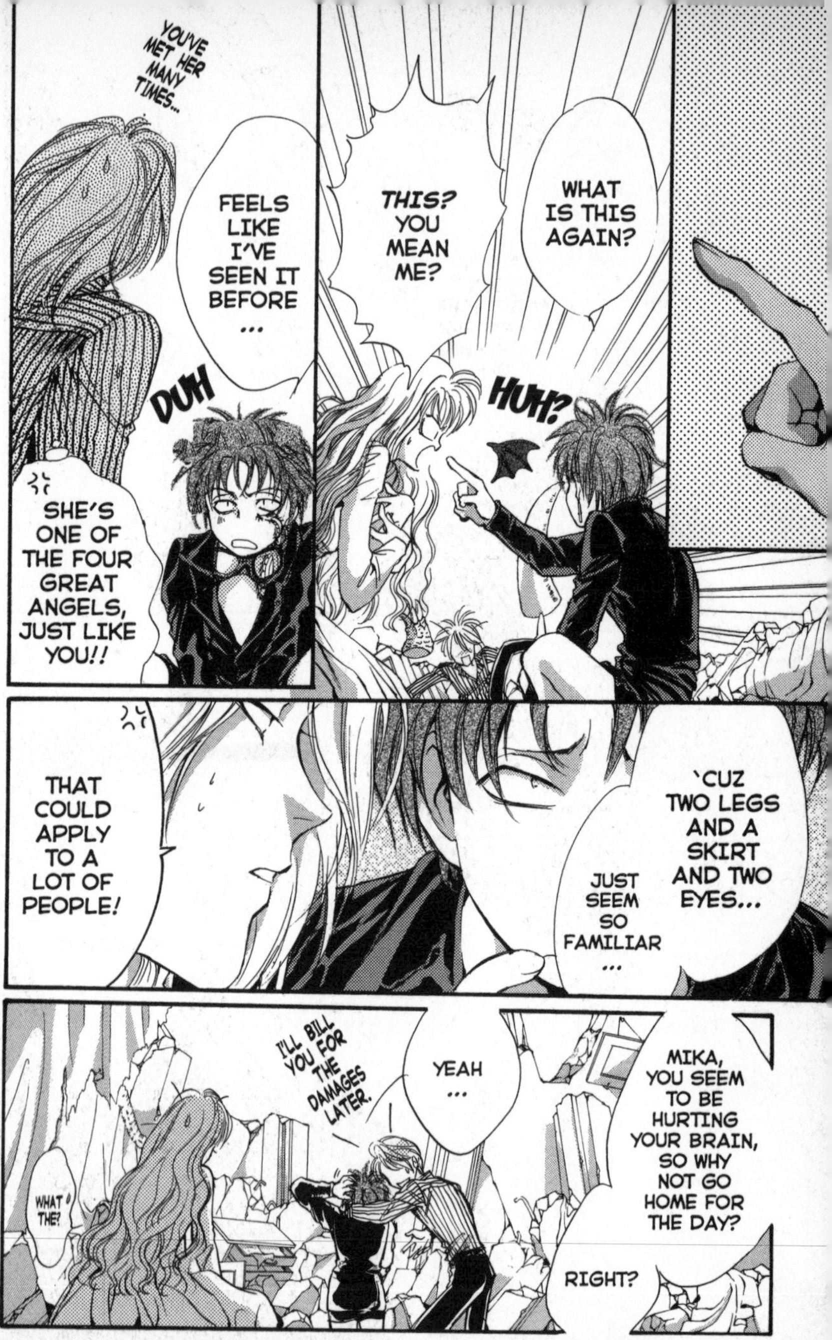
WHAT IS THIS AGAIN?
THIS? YOU MEAN ME?
HUH?
FEELS LIKE I'VE SEEN IT BEFORE ...
YOU'VE MET HER MANY TIMES...
DUH
SHE'S ONE OF THE FOUR GREAT ANGELS, JUST LIKE YOU!!
`CUZ TWO LEGS AND A SKIRT AND TWO EYES...
JUST SEEM SO FAMILIAR ...
THAT COULD APPLY TO A LOT OF PEOPLE!
MIKA, YOU SEEM TO BE HURTING YOUR BRAIN, SO WHY NOT GO HOME FOR THE DAY?
RIGHT?
YEAH ...
I'LL BILL YOU FOR THE DAMAGES LATER.
WHAT THE?

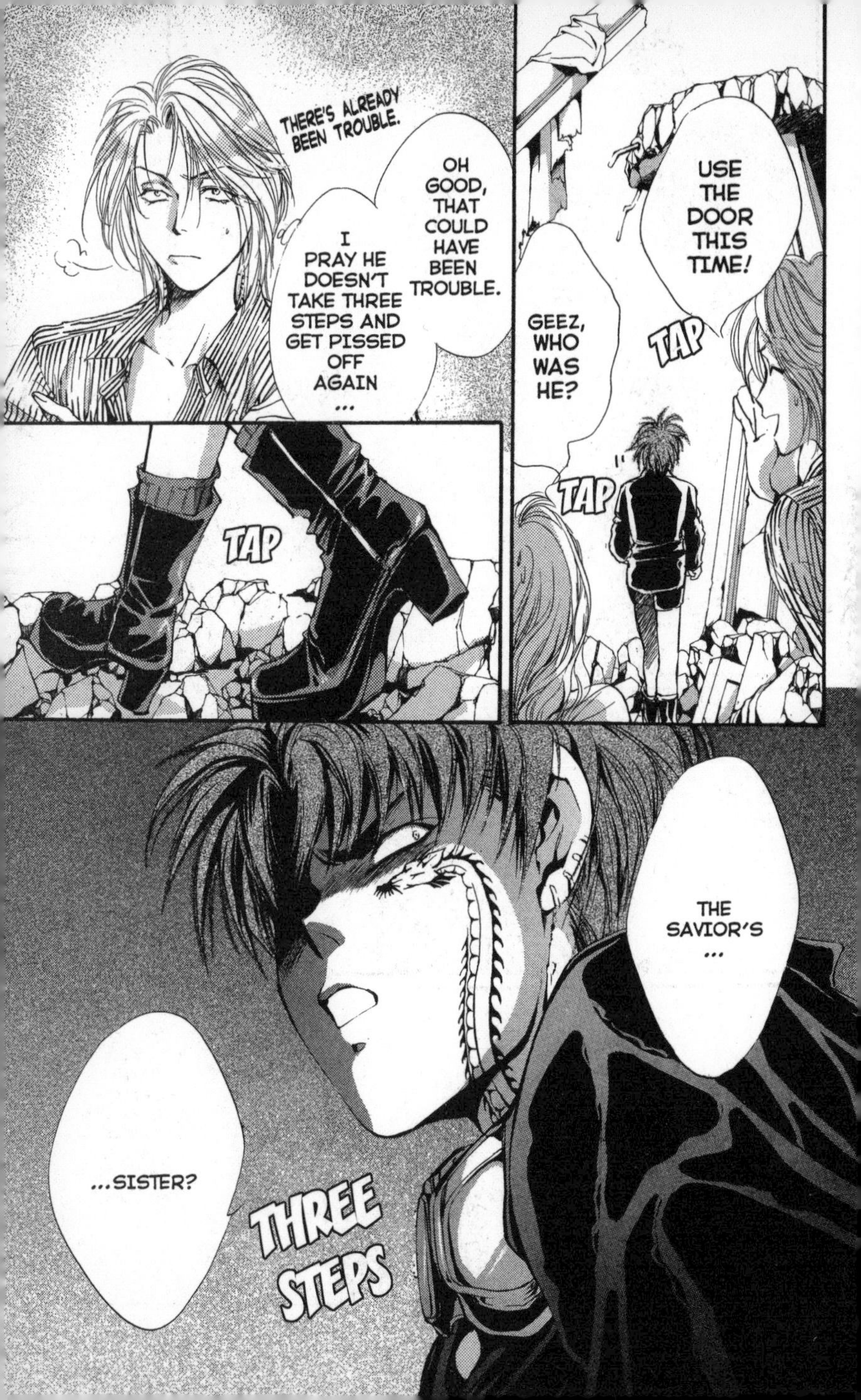
USE THE DOOR THIS TIME!
TAP
GEEZ, WHO WAS HE?
TAP
OH GOOD, THAT COULD HAVE BEEN TROUBLE.
I PRAY HE DOESN'T TAKE THREE STEPS AND GET PISSED OFF AGAIN ...
THERE'S ALREADY BEEN TROUBLE.
TAP
THE SAVIOR'S ...
...SISTER?
THREE STEPS

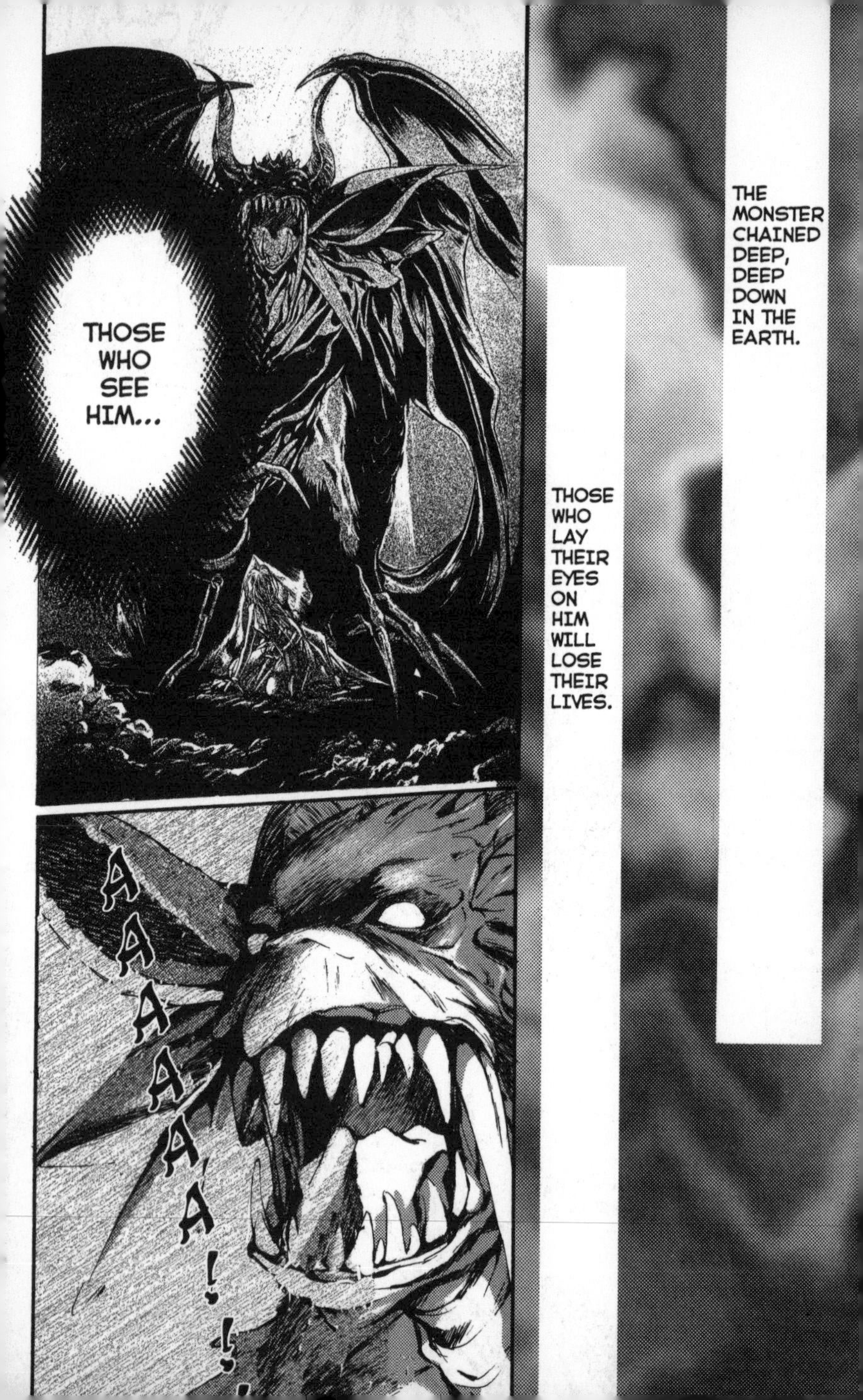
THE MONSTER CHAINED DEEP, DEEP DOWN IN THE EARTH.
THOSE WHO LAY THEIR EYES ON HIM WILL LOSE THEIR LIVES.
THOSE WHO SEE HIM...
AAAAAAA!!

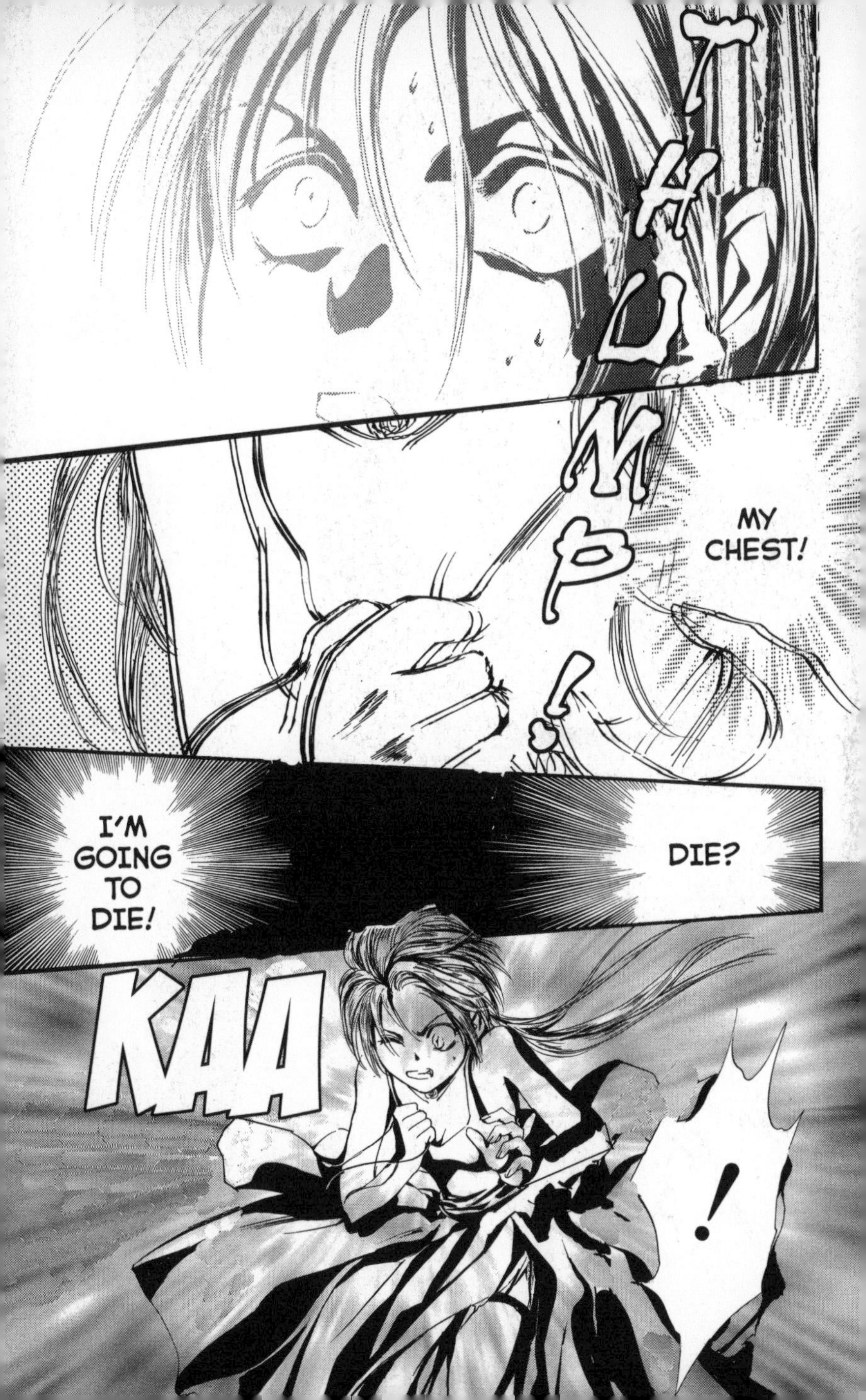
THUMP!
MY CHEST!
DIE?
I'M GOING TO DIE!
!
KAA

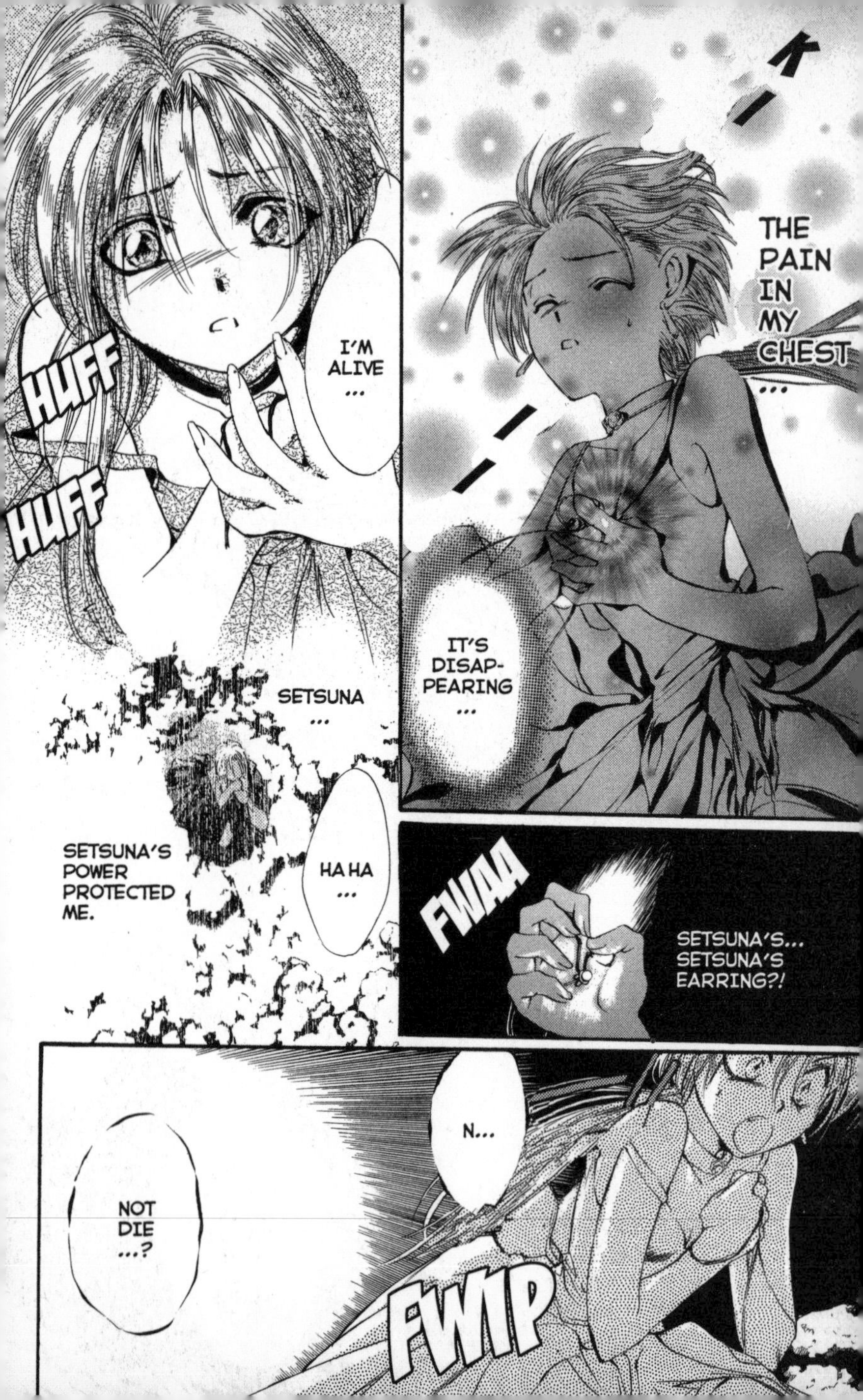
K—I—
THE PAIN IN MY CHEST ...
IT'S DISAP-PEARING ...
FWAA
SETSUNA'S... SETSUNA'S EARRING?!
I'M ALIVE ...
HUFF
HUFF
SETSUNA ...
HA HA ...
SETSUNA'S POWER PROTECTED ME.
N...
NOT DIE ...?
FWIP

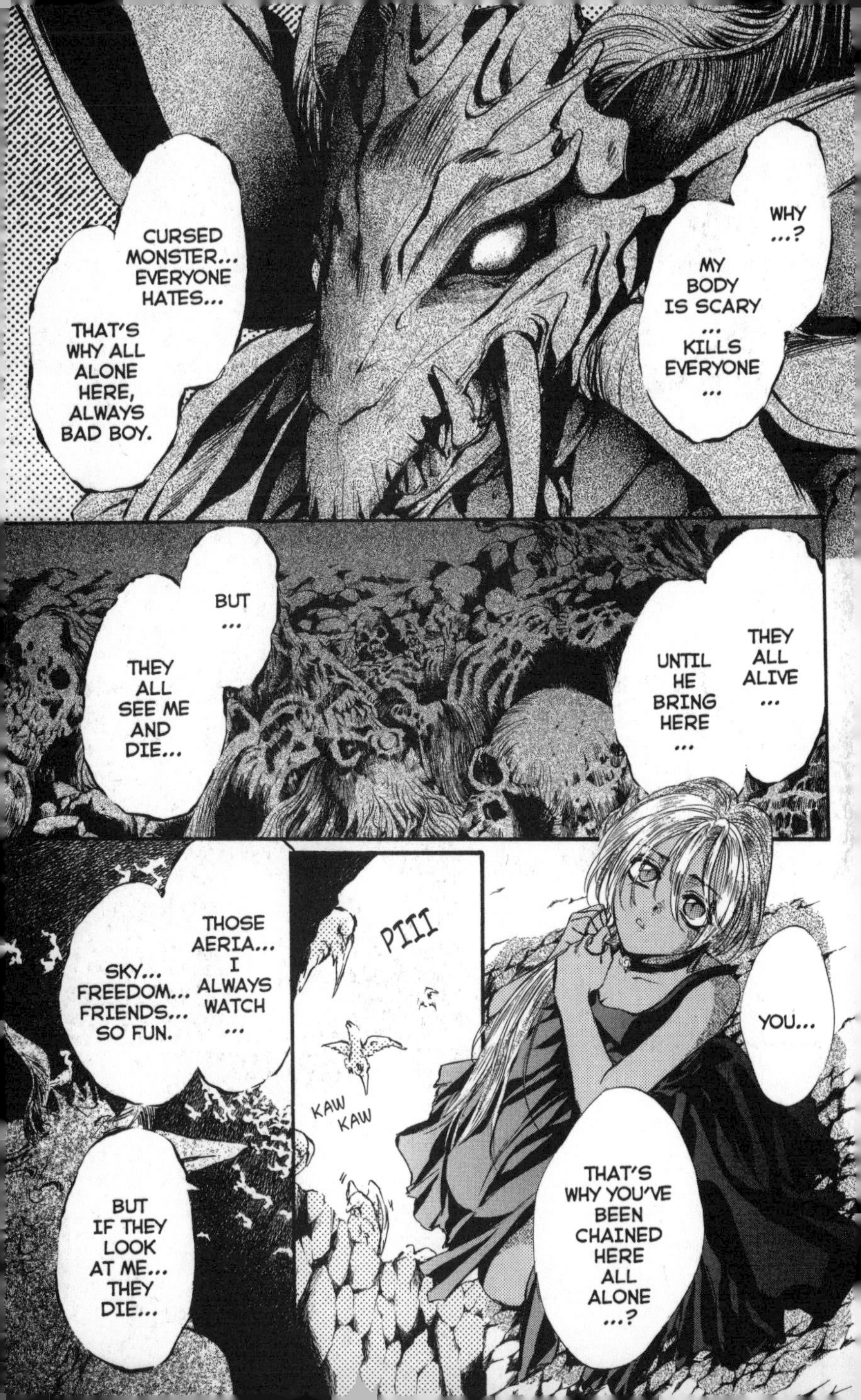
WHY ...?
MY BODY IS SCARY ... KILLS EVERYONE ...
CURSED MONSTER... EVERYONE HATES...
THAT'S WHY ALL ALONE HERE, ALWAYS BAD BOY.
THEY ALL ALIVE ...
UNTIL HE BRING HERE ...
BUT ...
THEY ALL SEE ME AND DIE...
YOU...
THAT'S WHY YOU'VE BEEN CHAINED HERE ALL ALONE ...?
PIII
KAW KAW
THOSE AERIA... I ALWAYS WATCH ...
SKY... FREEDOM... FRIENDS... SO FUN.
BUT IF THEY LOOK AT ME... THEY DIE...

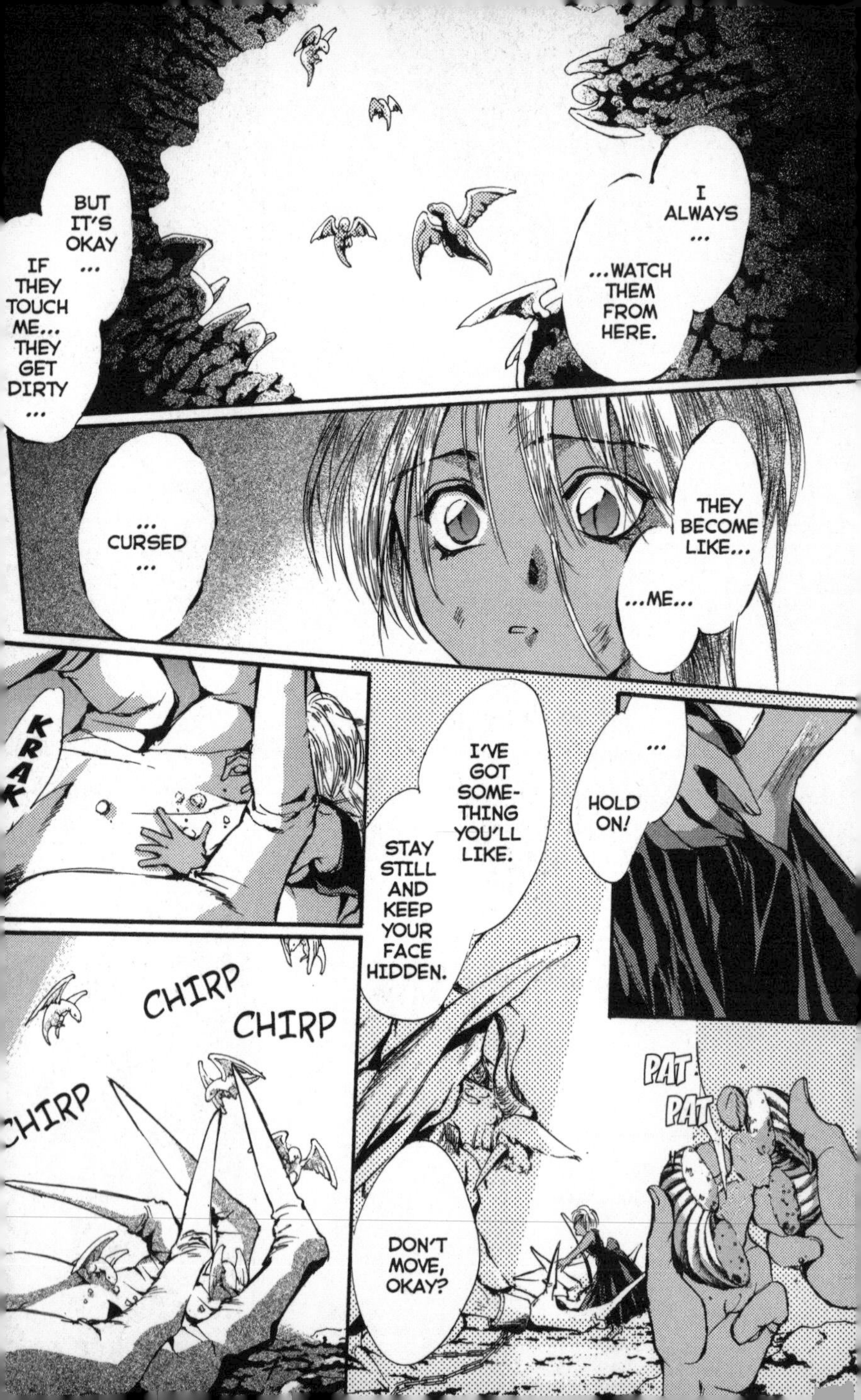
I ALWAYS ...
...WATCH THEM FROM HERE.
BUT IT'S OKAY ...
IF THEY TOUCH ME... THEY GET DIRTY ...
THEY BECOME LIKE...
...ME...
... CURSED ...
... HOLD ON!
I'VE GOT SOME-THING YOU'LL LIKE.
STAY STILL AND KEEP YOUR FACE HIDDEN.
KRAK
PAT PAT
DON'T MOVE, OKAY?
CHIRP
CHIRP
CHIRP

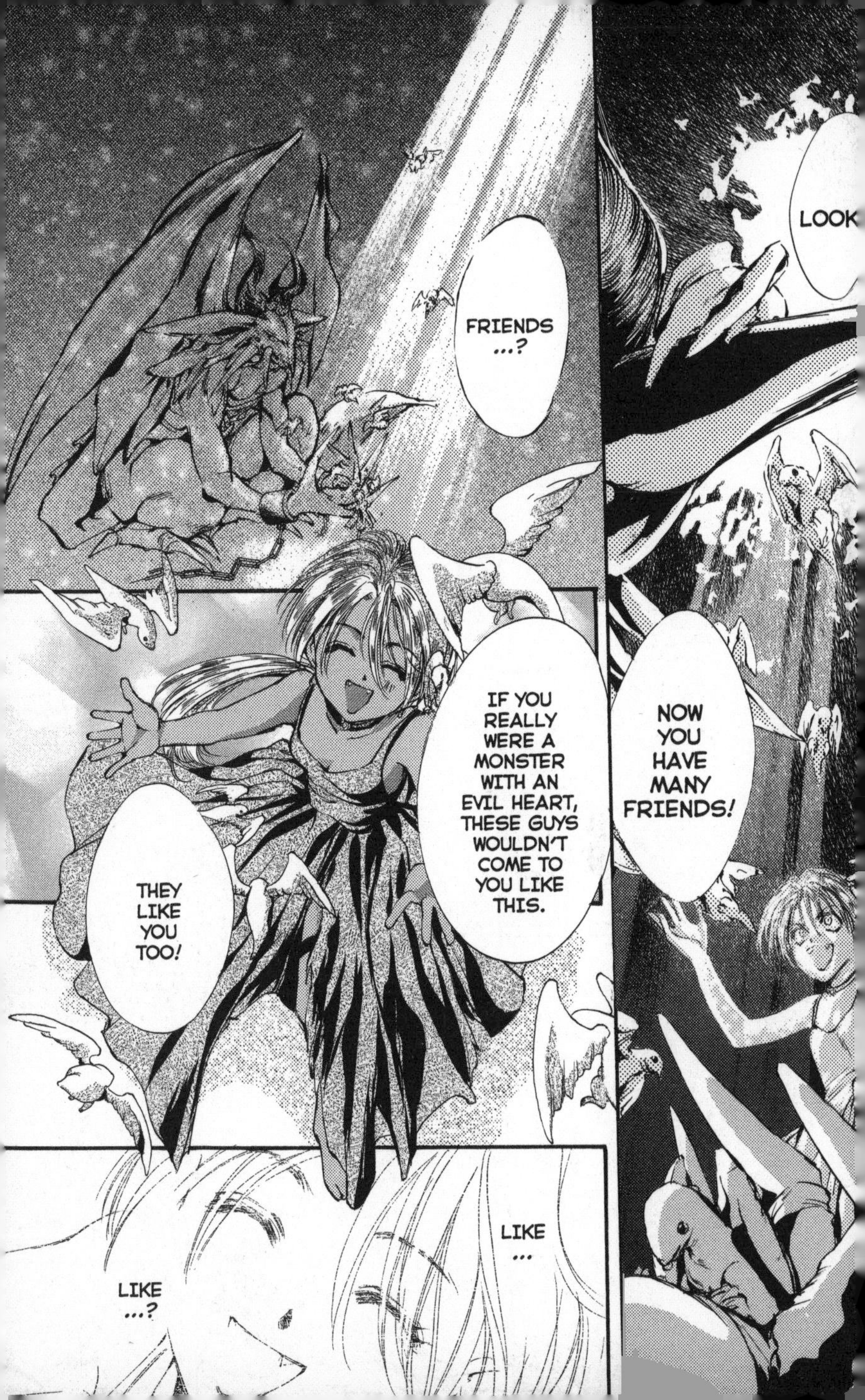
LOOK
NOW YOU HAVE MANY FRIENDS!
FRIENDS ...?
IF YOU REALLY WERE A MONSTER WITH AN EVIL HEART, THESE GUYS WOULDN'T COME TO YOU LIKE THIS.
THEY LIKE YOU TOO!
LIKE ...
LIKE ...?

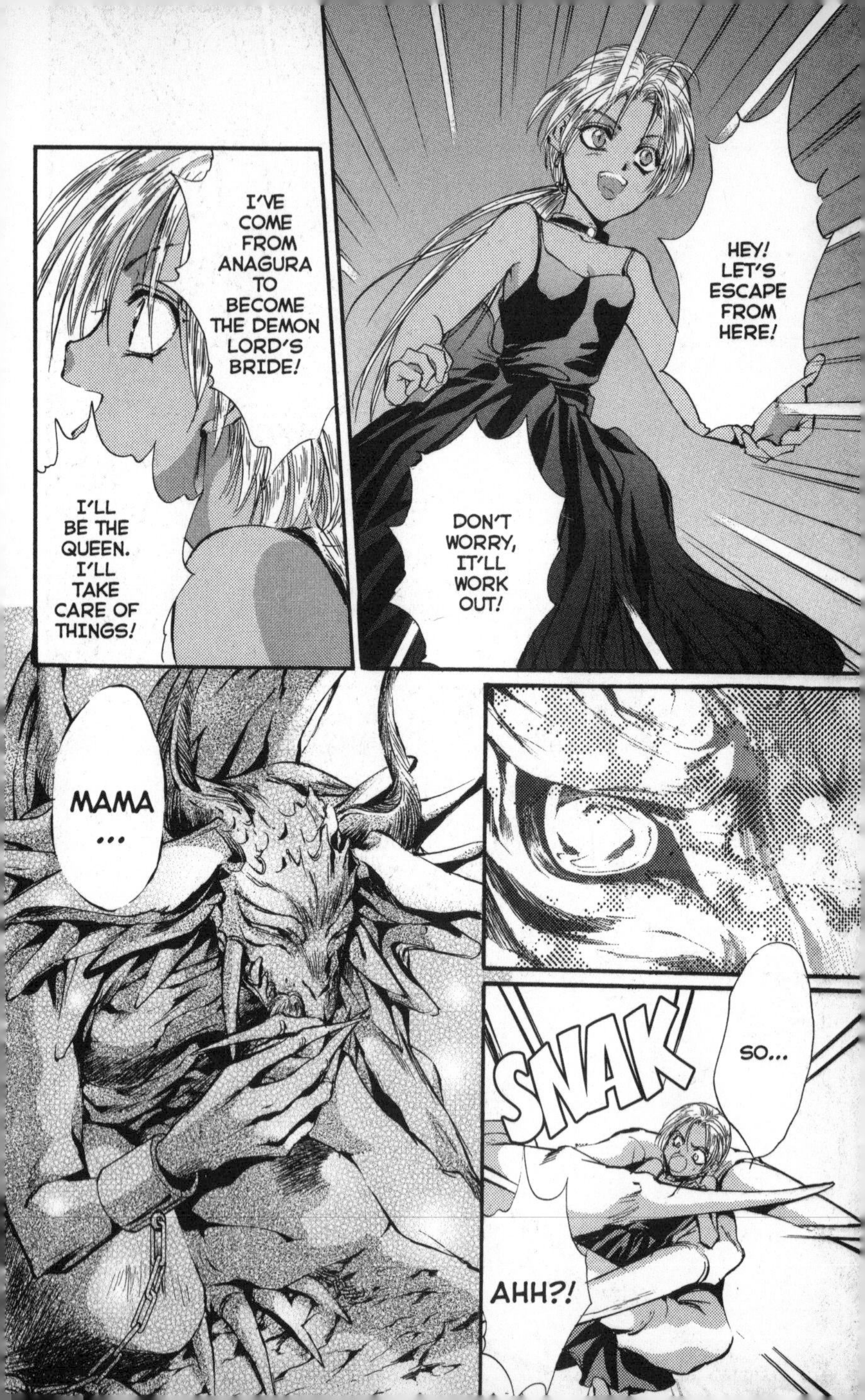
HEY! LET'S ESCAPE FROM HERE!
DON'T WORRY, IT'LL WORK OUT!
I'VE COME FROM ANAGURA TO BECOME THE DEMON LORD'S BRIDE!
I'LL BE THE QUEEN. I'LL TAKE CARE OF THINGS!
SO...
SNAK
AHH?!
MAMA ...

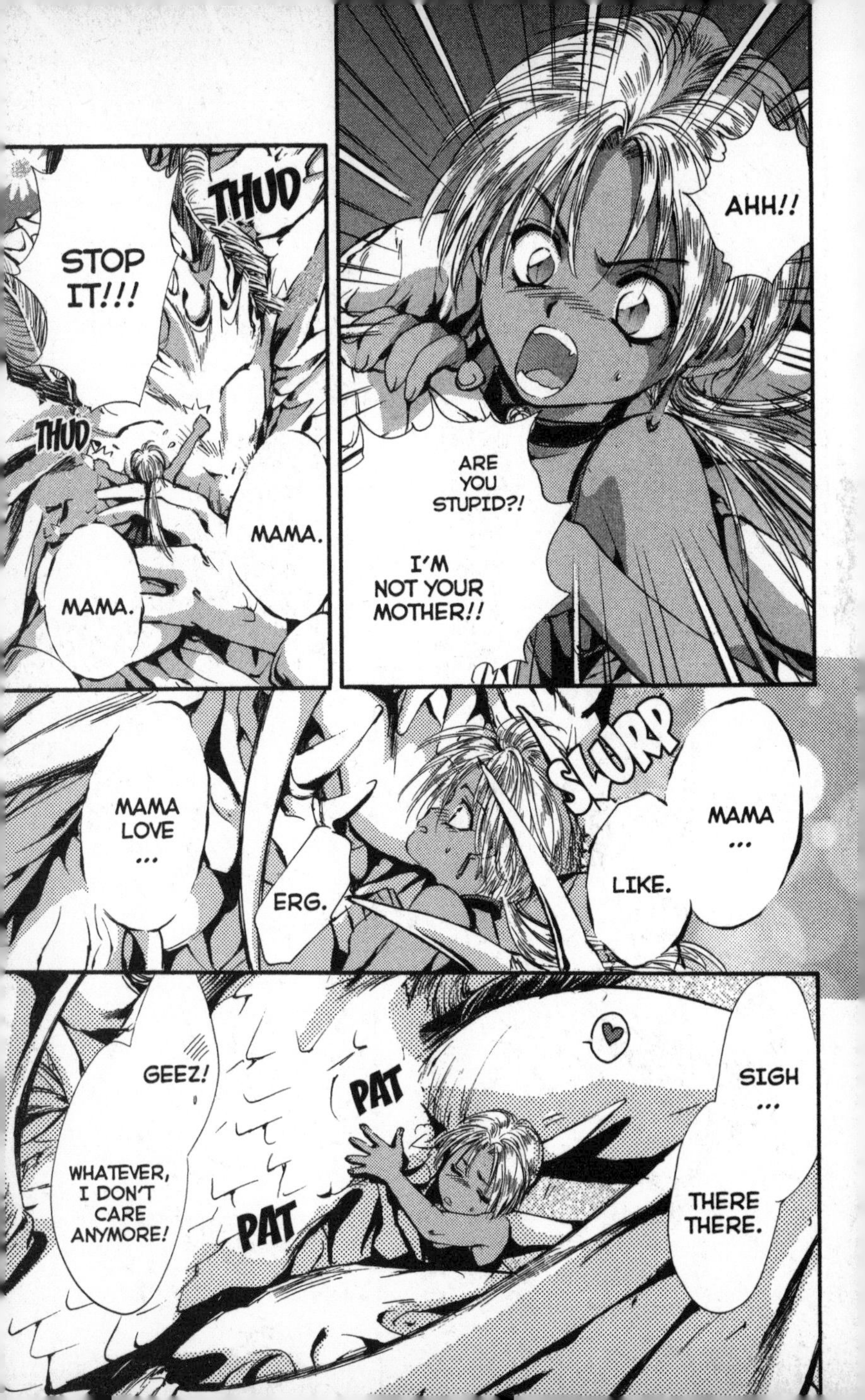
AHH!!
ARE YOU STUPID?!
I'M NOT YOUR MOTHER!!
THUD
STOP IT!!!
MAMA.
THUD
MAMA.
SLURP
MAMA ... LIKE.
ERG.
MAMA LOVE ...
SIGH ... THERE THERE.
PAT
PAT
GEEZ!
WHATEVER, I DON'T CARE ANYMORE!

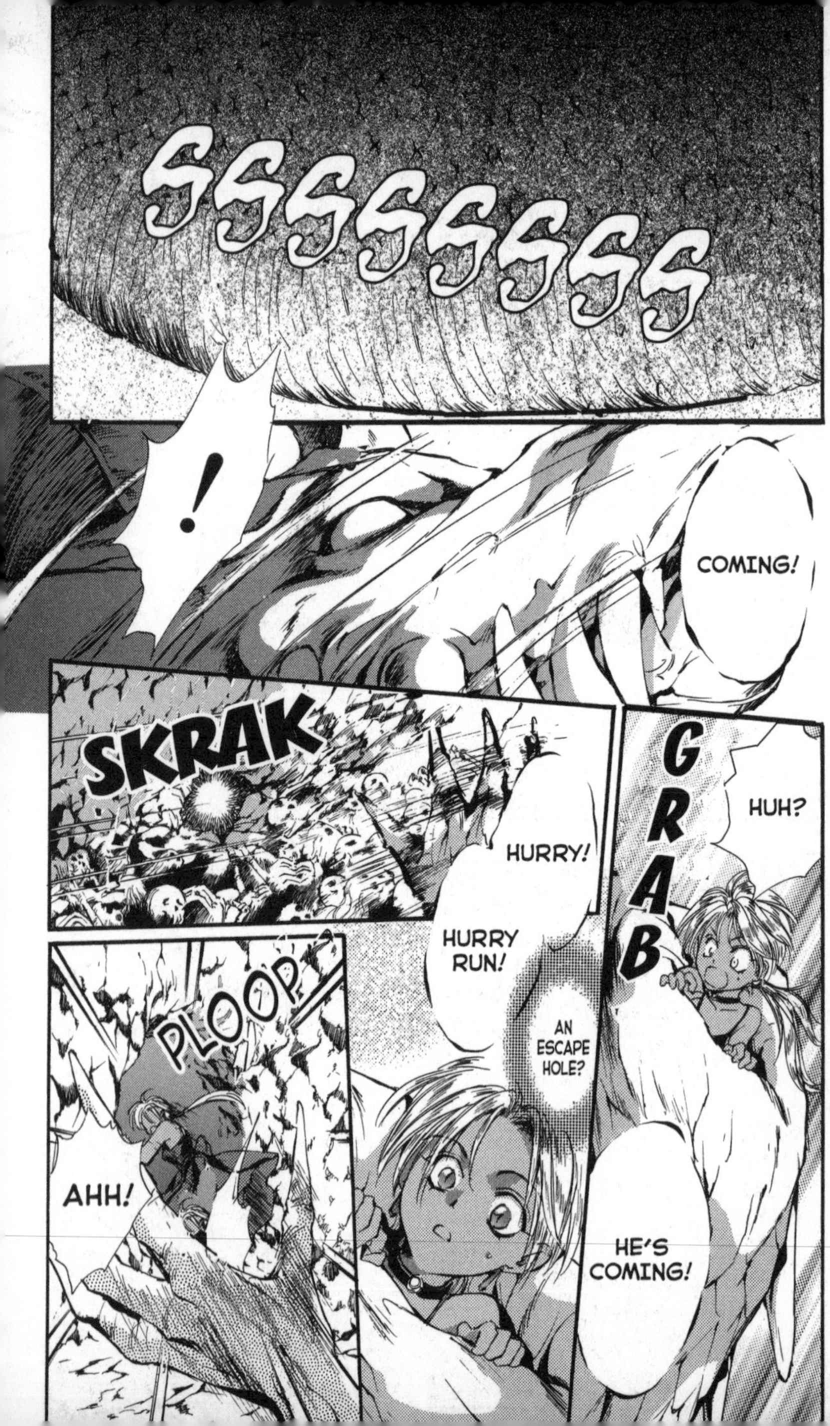
SSSSSSSSS
!
COMING!
GRAB
HUH?
SKRAK
HURRY!
HURRY RUN!
AN ESCAPE HOLE?
HE'S COMING!
PLOOP
AHH!

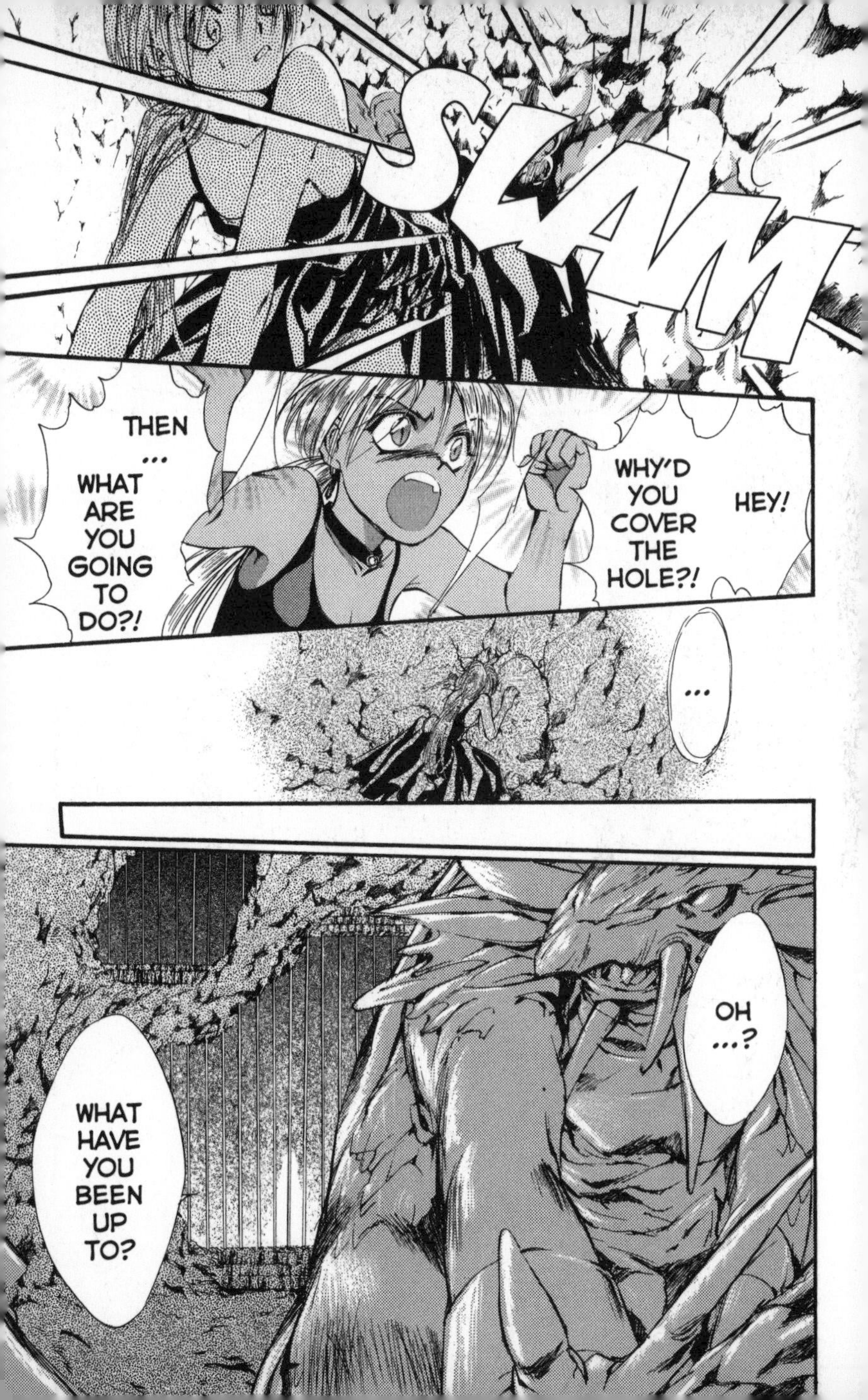
SLAM
HEY!
WHY'D YOU COVER THE HOLE?!
THEN ... WHAT ARE YOU GOING TO DO?!
...
OH ...?
WHAT HAVE YOU BEEN UP TO?

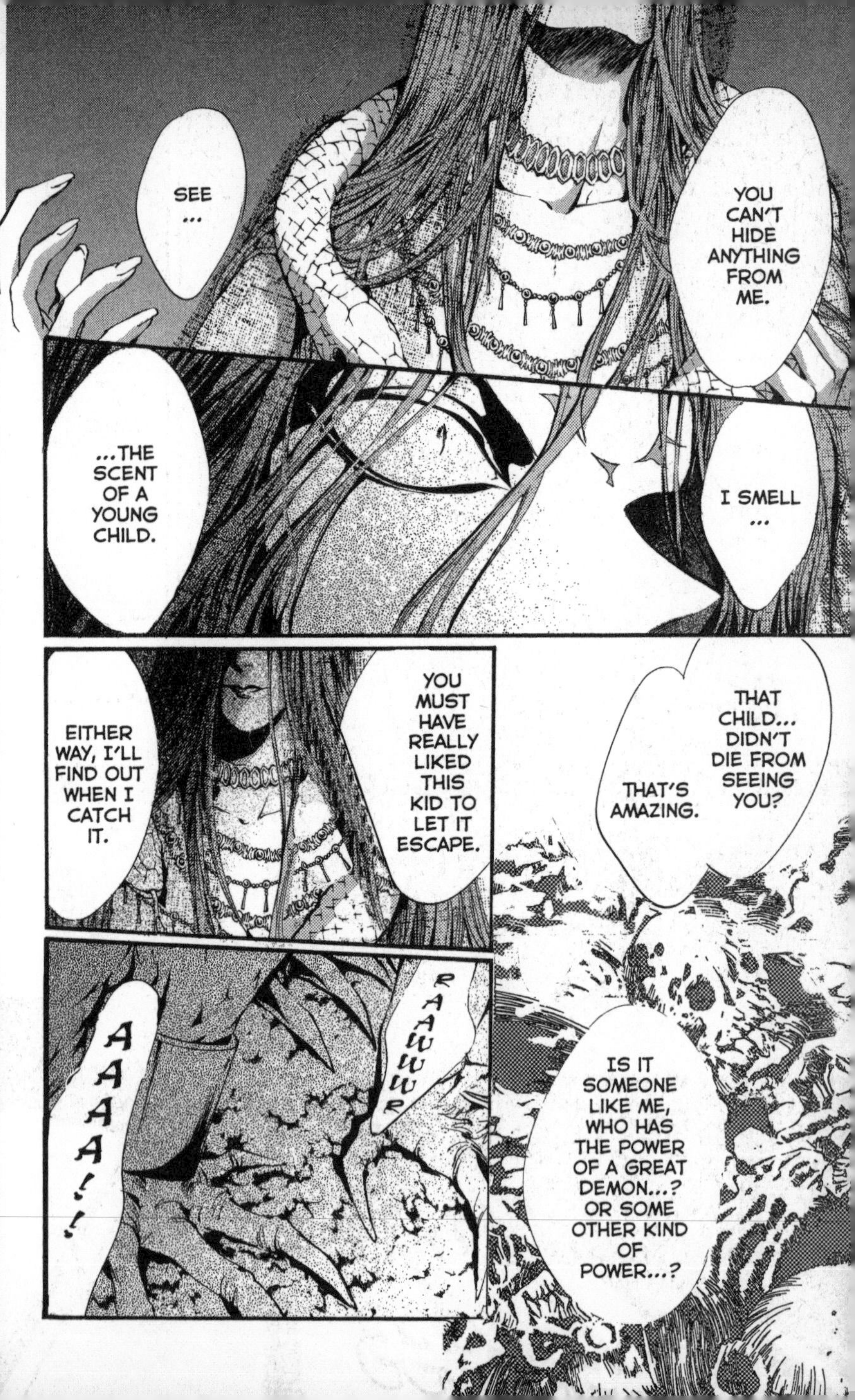
YOU CAN'T HIDE ANYTHING FROM ME.
SEE...
I SMELL...
...THE SCENT OF A YOUNG CHILD.
THAT CHILD... DIDN'T DIE FROM SEEING YOU?
THAT'S AMAZING.
IS IT SOMEONE LIKE ME, WHO HAS THE POWER OF A GREAT DEMON...? OR SOME OTHER KIND OF POWER...?
YOU MUST HAVE REALLY LIKED THIS KID TO LET IT ESCAPE.
EITHER WAY, I'LL FIND OUT WHEN I CATCH IT.
RAAWWWR
AAAAA!!!

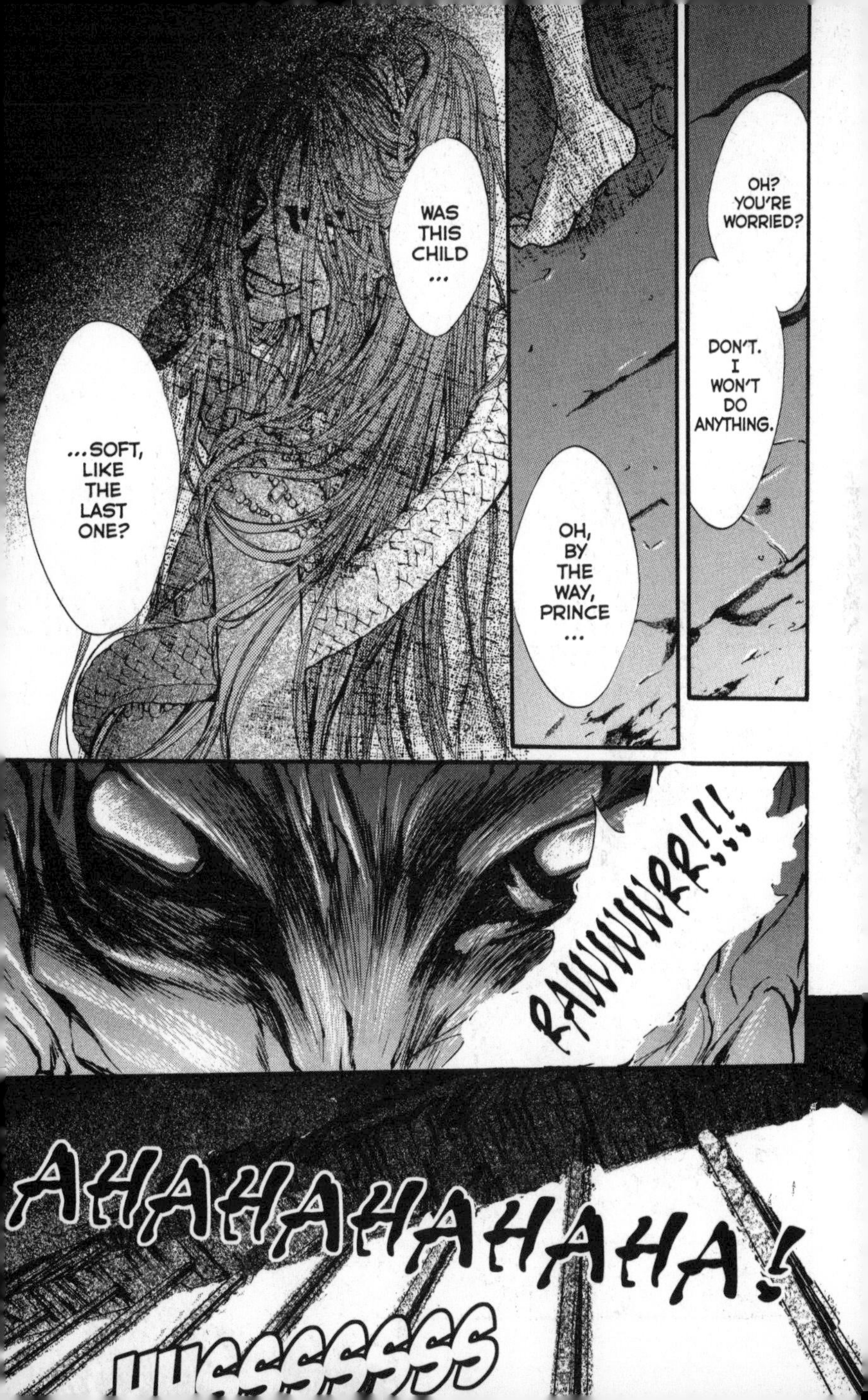
OH? YOU'RE WORRIED?
DON'T. I WON'T DO ANYTHING.
OH, BY THE WAY, PRINCE ...
WAS THIS CHILD ...
...SOFT, LIKE THE LAST ONE?
RAWWWRR!!!
AHAHAHAHAHAHA!

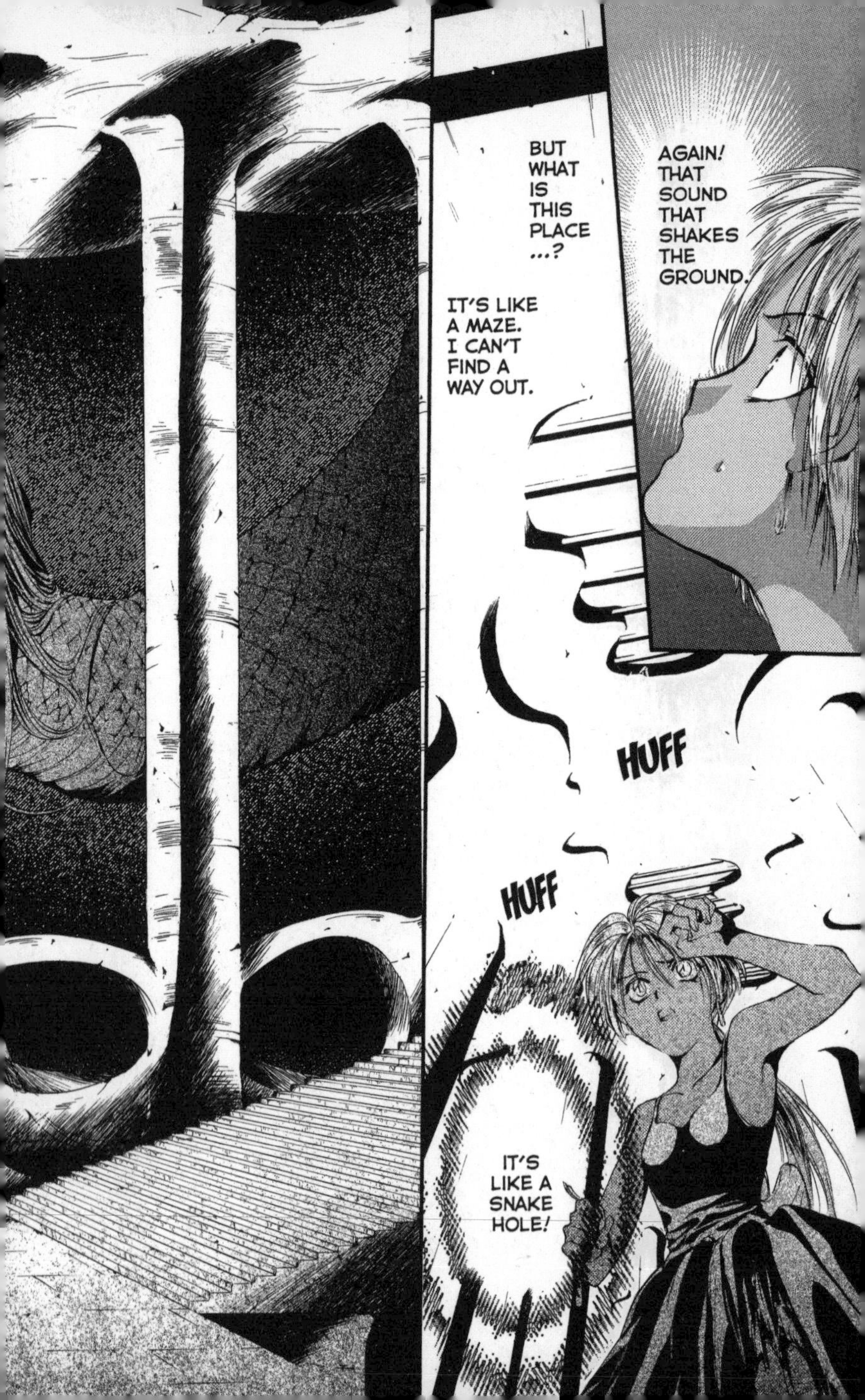
AGAIN! THAT SOUND THAT SHAKES THE GROUND.
BUT WHAT IS THIS PLACE ...?
IT'S LIKE A MAZE. I CAN'T FIND A WAY OUT.
HUFF
HUFF
IT'S LIKE A SNAKE HOLE!

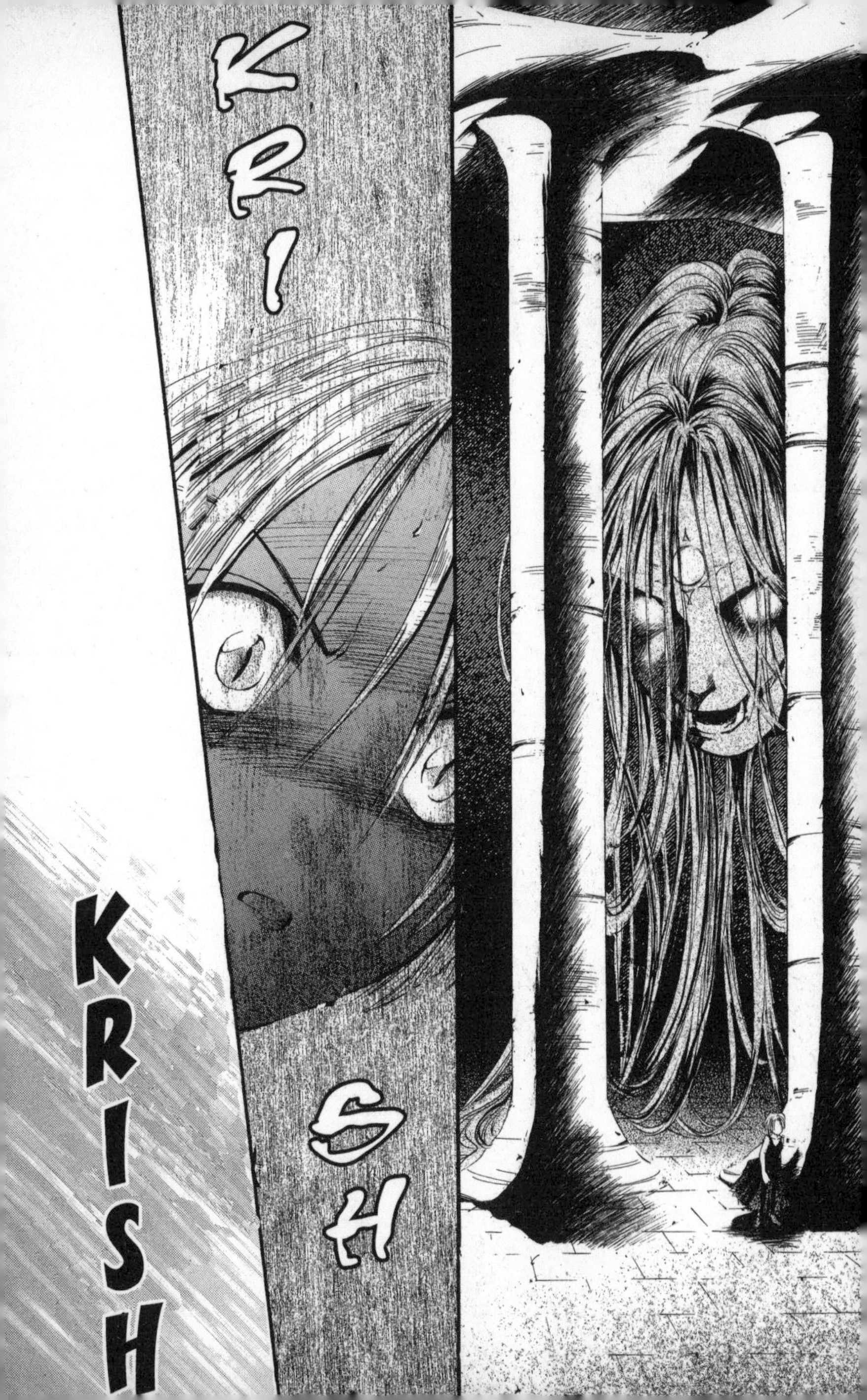
KRISH
KRISH

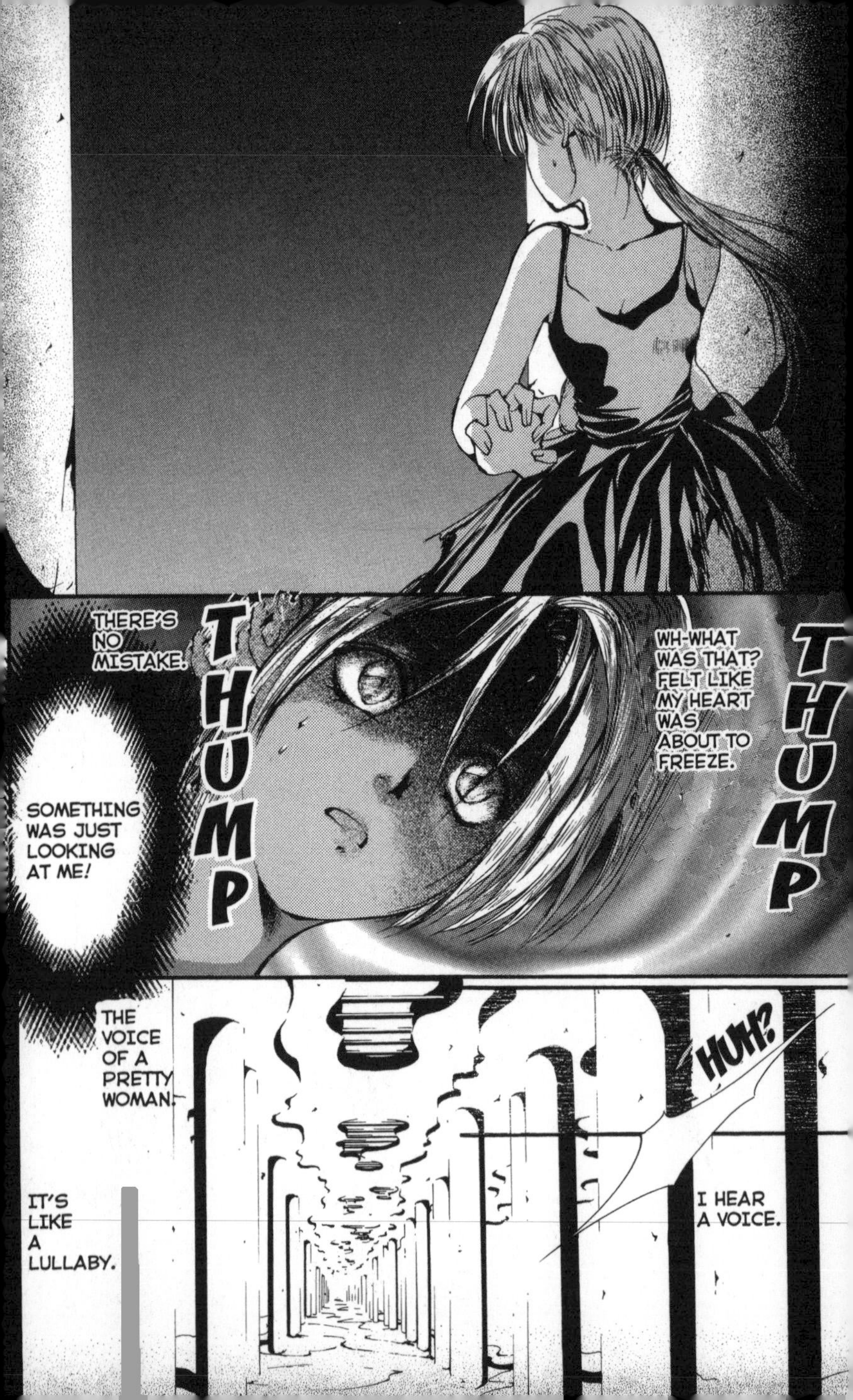
THUMP
WH-WHAT WAS THAT? FELT LIKE MY HEART WAS ABOUT TO FREEZE.
THUMP
THERE'S NO MISTAKE.
SOMETHING WAS JUST LOOKING AT ME!
HUH?
I HEAR A VOICE.
THE VOICE OF A PRETTY WOMAN.
IT'S LIKE A LULLABY.

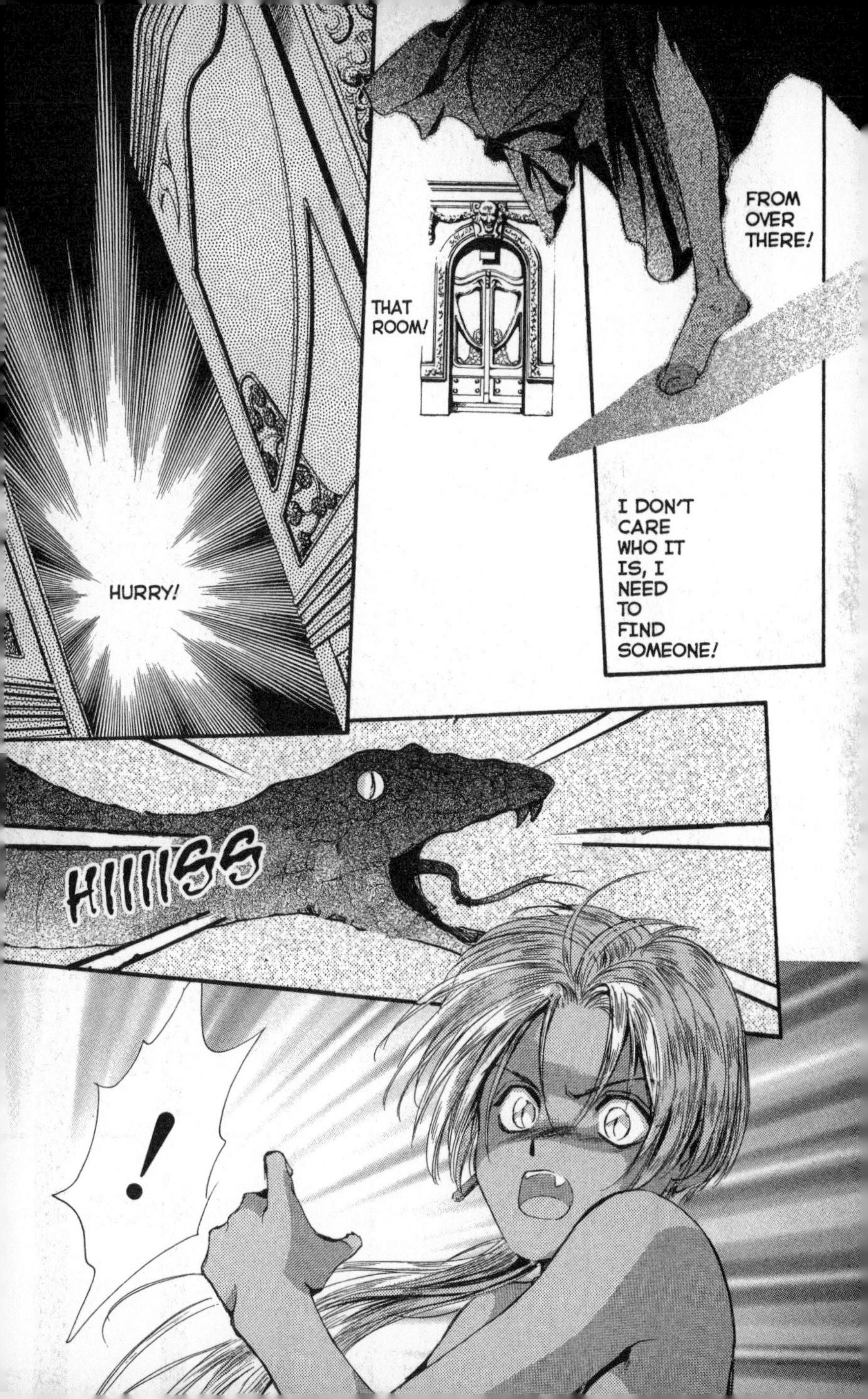
FROM OVER THERE!
THAT ROOM!
I DON'T CARE WHO IT IS, I NEED TO FIND SOMEONE!
HURRY!
HIIISS
!

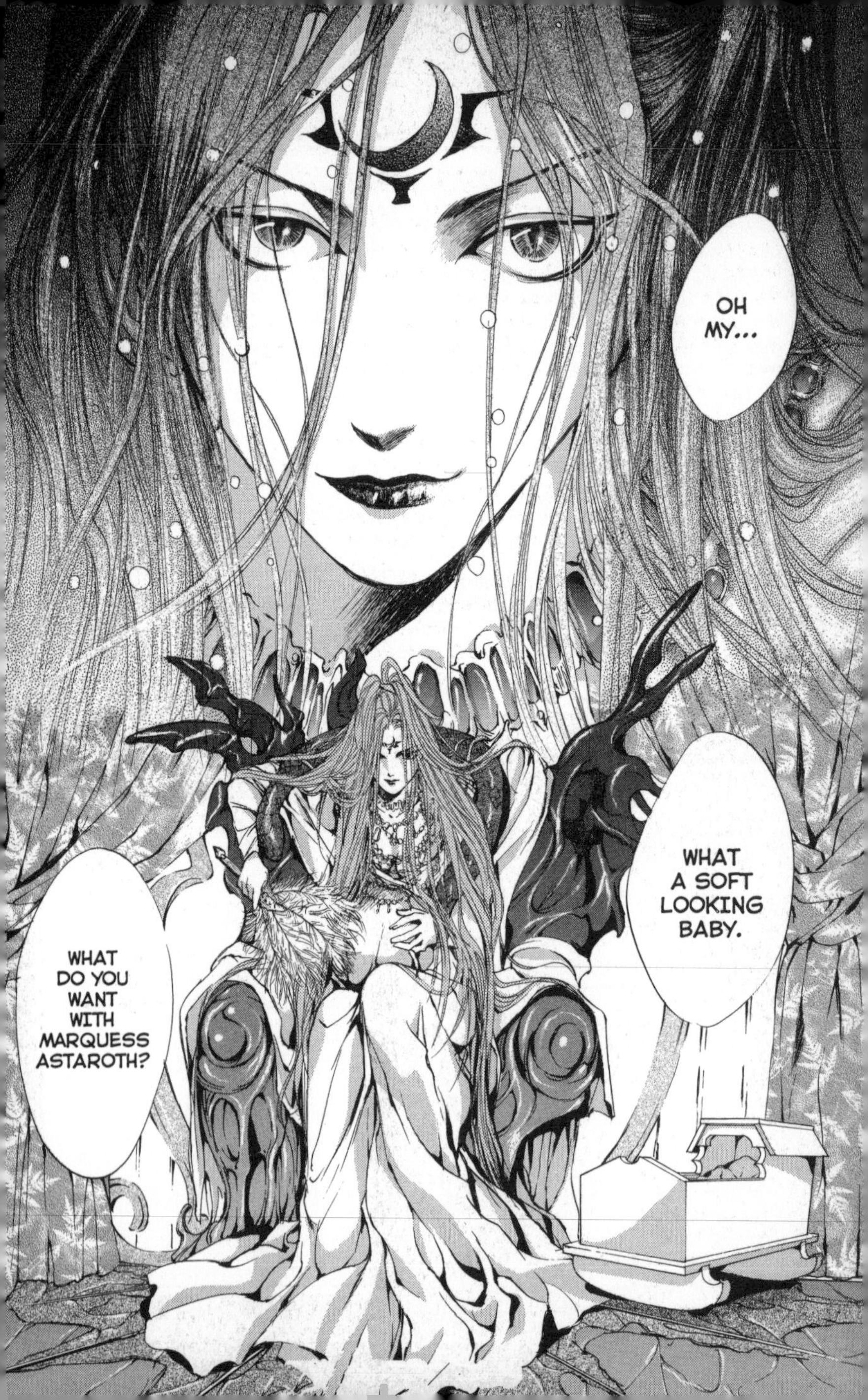
OH MY...
WHAT A SOFT LOOKING BABY.
WHAT DO YOU WANT WITH MARQUESS ASTAROTH?

ANGEL LIES, DEVIL FLATTERY AND MUSIC AND MANGA

It was sudden, but the other day I had the chance to meet two musicians. I was invited by someone from P-magazine and was told "I'm interviewing Yoshikawa-san from Guniw Tools who you like so much, so how about you come along?" I was actually really busy at the time, but I knew I'd regret it if I didn't go, so I went (sorry to my assistants who I left behind--I won't do it again). I hadn't slept much that day, so I was in really bad condition, seriously. But with FuruFuru right in front of me, I got super nervous and totally awake. Wow, it's really him! I had seen him in a live performance not too long ago, but he seemed so far away then. And Mr. FuruFuru came off so much funnier and nice than in the interviews I've read. We talked about many things, and he's very interesting. His hair had all the color taken out and was so pretty! The air around him seemed different. I was lacking sleep and on a natural high and kept saying a bunch of stupid stuff... it seems. And after that I returned to the pain that is my workplace.

But soon another miracle happened. This time I was invited to an interview with Mr. Hakuei from "Penicillin." It was for his first role in a movie. So while the interviewer asked question about the movie I watched quietly from the side. Man, he's so tall and thin, seriously cool! Seems like C and O were in the other room, what about G? I was really busy too, and didn't get the chance to talk to him though. I only had time to request a song for their next concert. I was so nervous I couldn't even look him in the face... I'll have to send them both some copies of my manga. Hope they don't look at it and say "why?" I'm so happy I got the opportunity to meet them!

I'll be going to their next concerts for sure! And thank you to S-san from P magazine!

This is Hatter.

There's a demon named FuruFuru too, though it's spelled FurFur.

?

Setsuna'

NEXT ACCESS

?

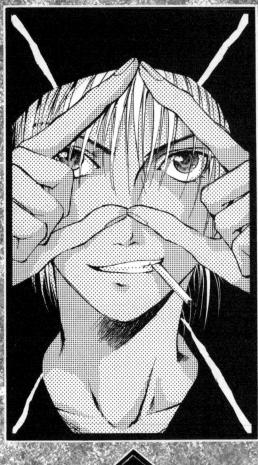

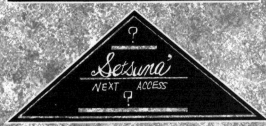

…TO BE CONTINUED

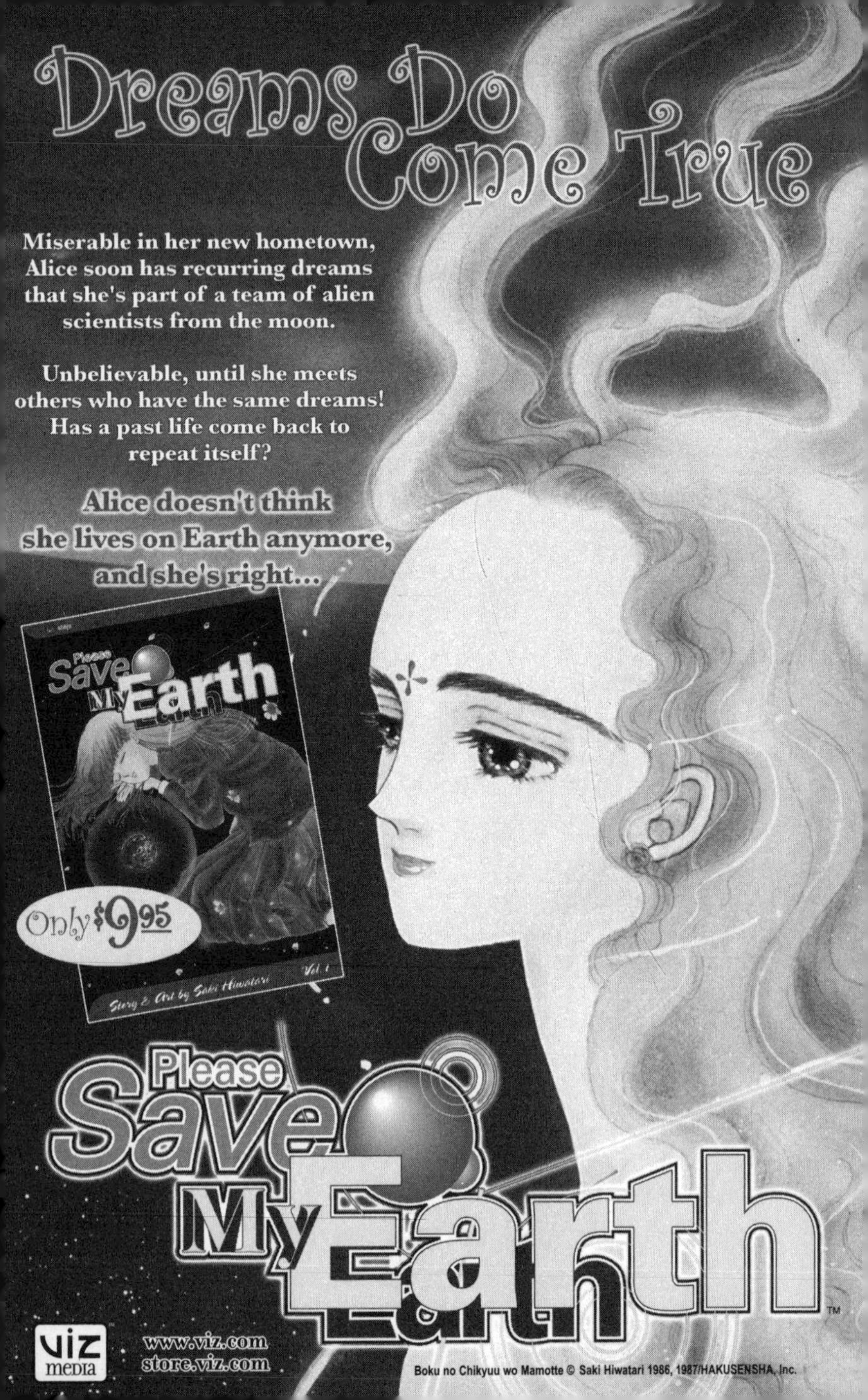
Dreams Do Come True
Miserable in her new hometown, Alice soon has recurring dreams that she's part of a team of alien scientists from the moon.
Unbelievable, until she meets others who have the same dreams! Has a past life come back to repeat itself?
Alice doesn't think she lives on Earth anymore, and she's right...
Please Save My Earth
Story & Art by Saki Hiwatari
Vol. 1
Only $9.95
Please Save My Earth™
viz media
www.viz.com
store.viz.com
Boku no Chikyuu wo Mamotte © Saki Hiwatari 1986, 1987/HAKUSENSHA, Inc.

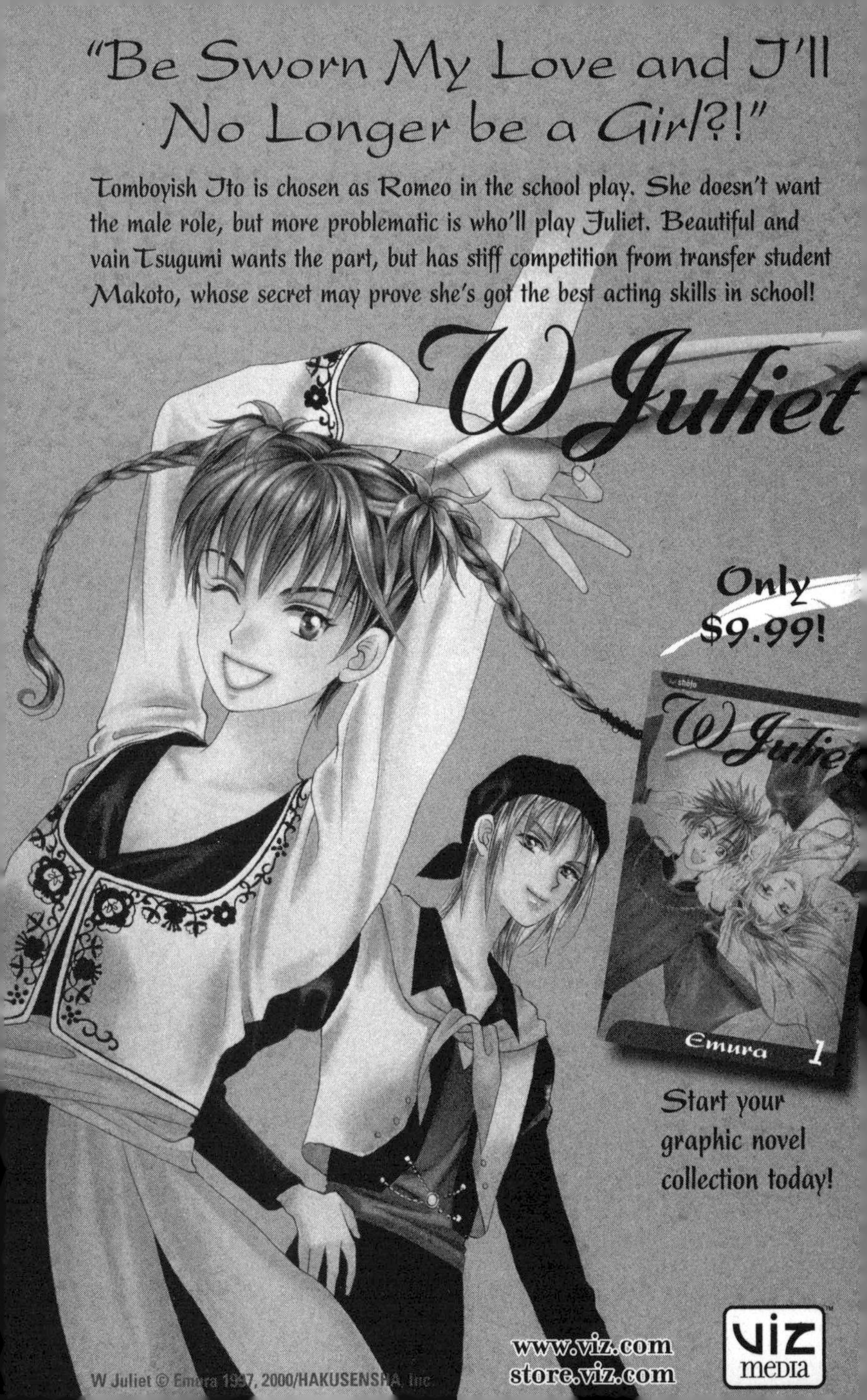
"Be Sworn My Love and I'll No Longer be a Girl?!"
Tomboyish Ito is chosen as Romeo in the school play. She doesn't want the male role, but more problematic is who'll play Juliet. Beautiful and vain Tsugumi wants the part, but has stiff competition from transfer student Makoto, whose secret may prove she's got the best acting skills in school!
W Juliet
Only $9.99!
W Juliet
Emura 1
Start your graphic novel collection today!
www.viz.com
store.viz.com
VIZ MEDIA
W Juliet © Emura 1997, 2000/HAKUSENSHA, Inc.

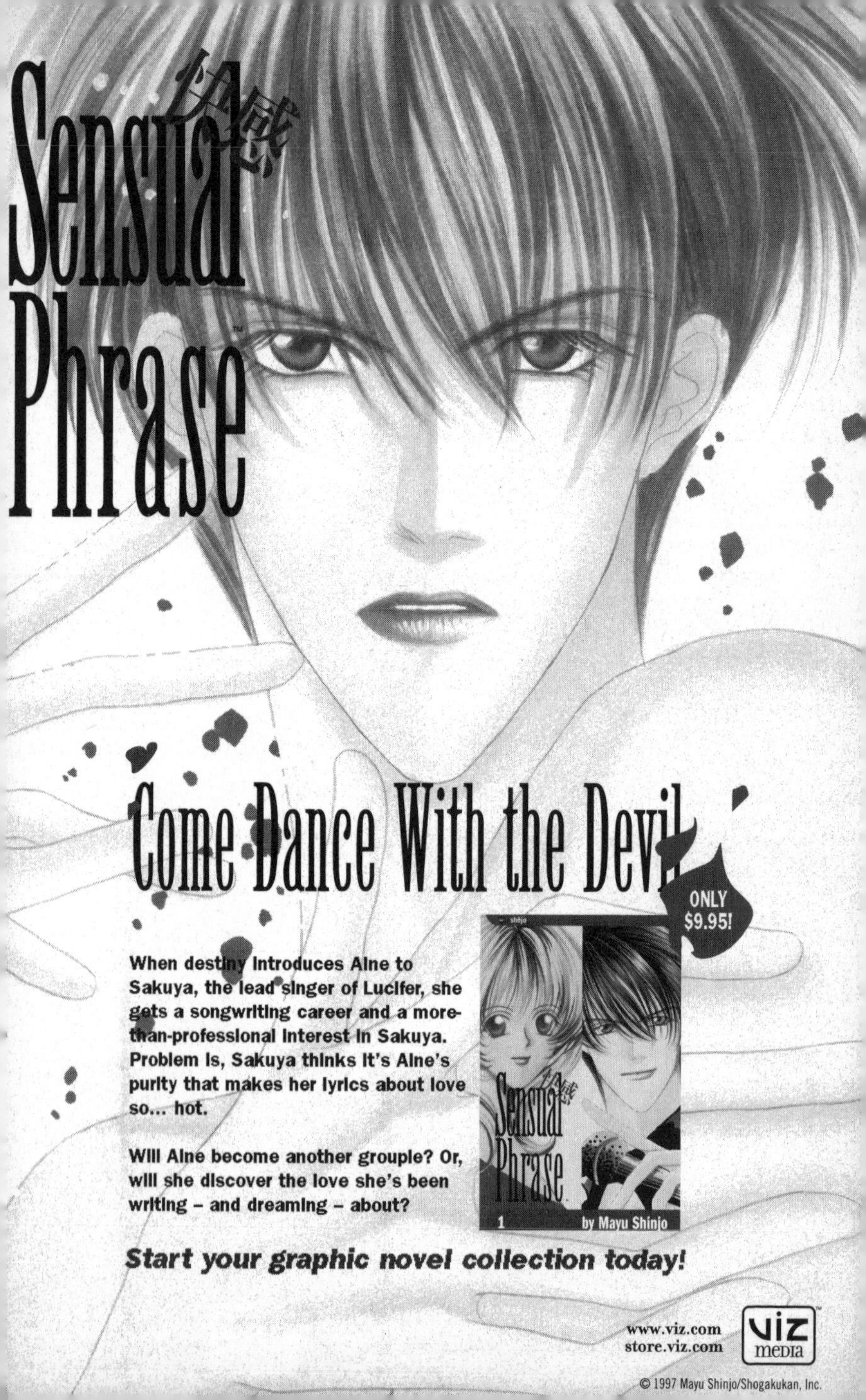
快感
Sensual Phrase™
Come Dance With the Devil
ONLY $9.95!
When destiny introduces Aine to Sakuya, the lead singer of Lucifer, she gets a songwriting career and a more-than-professional interest in Sakuya. Problem is, Sakuya thinks it's Aine's purity that makes her lyrics about love so... hot.
Will Aine become another groupie? Or, will she discover the love she's been writing – and dreaming – about?
shōjo
Sensual Phrase
1
by Mayu Shinjo
Start your graphic novel collection today!
www.viz.com
store.viz.com
VIZ MEDIA
© 1997 Mayu Shinjo/Shogakukan, Inc.

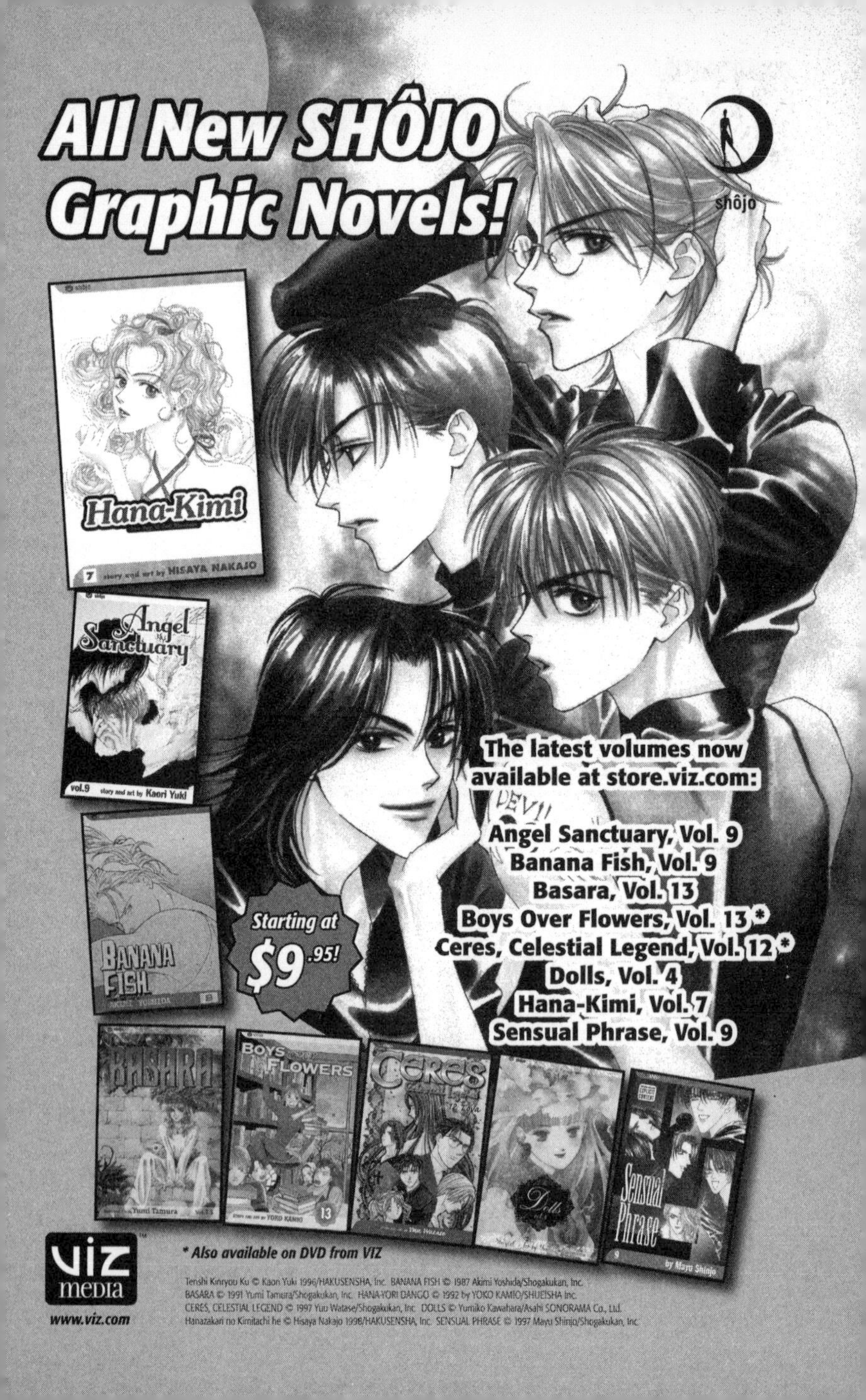
All New SHÔJO Graphic Novels!
shôjo
Hana-Kimi
7 story and art by HISAYA NAKAJO
Angel Sanctuary
vol.9 story and art by Kaori Yuki
BANANA FISH
Starting at $9.95!
The latest volumes now available at store.viz.com:
Angel Sanctuary, Vol. 9
Banana Fish, Vol. 9
Basara, Vol. 13
Boys Over Flowers, Vol. 13 *
Ceres, Celestial Legend, Vol. 12 *
Dolls, Vol. 4
Hana-Kimi, Vol. 7
Sensual Phrase, Vol. 9
BASARA
Yumi Tamura
BOYS FLOWERS
YOKO KAMIO
13
Ceres
Dolls
Sensual Phrase
by Mayu Shinjo
* Also available on DVD from VIZ
VIZ media
www.viz.com
Tenshi Kinryou Ku © Kaori Yuki 1996/HAKUSENSHA, Inc. BANANA FISH © 1987 Akimi Yoshida/Shogakukan, Inc.
BASARA © 1991 Yumi Tamura/Shogakukan, Inc. HANA-YORI DANGO © 1992 by YOKO KAMIO/SHUEISHA Inc.
CERES, CELESTIAL LEGEND © 1997 Yuu Watase/Shogakukan, Inc. DOLLS © Yumiko Kawahara/Asahi SONORAMA Co., Ltd.
Hanazakari no Kimitachi he © Hisaya Nakajo 1998/HAKUSENSHA, Inc. SENSUAL PHRASE © 1997 Mayu Shinjo/Shogakukan, Inc.

LOVE SHOJO? LET US KNOW!

☐ Please do NOT send me information about VIZ Media products, news and events, special offers, or other information.

☐ Please do NOT send me information from VIZ' trusted business partners.

Name: _____

Address: _____

City: _____ State: _____ Zip: _____

E-mail: _____

☐ Male ☐ Female Date of Birth (mm/dd/yyyy): ___ / ___ / ___ (Under 13? Parental consent required)

What race/ethnicity do you consider yourself? (check all that apply)

☐ White/Caucasian ☐ Black/African American ☐ Hispanic/Latino

☐ Asian/Pacific Islander ☐ Native American/Alaskan Native ☐ Other: _____

What VIZ shojo title(s) did you purchase? (indicate title(s) purchased)

_____

What other shojo titles from other publishers do you own? _____

_____

Reason for purchase: (check all that apply)

☐ Special offer ☐ Favorite title / author / artist / genre

☐ Gift ☐ Recommendation ☐ Collection

☐ Read excerpt in VIZ manga sampler ☐ Other _____

Where did you make your purchase? (please check one)

☐ Comic store ☐ Bookstore ☐ Mass/Grocery Store

☐ Newsstand ☐ Video/Video Game Store

☐ Online (site: _____) ☐ Other _____

How many shojo titles have you purchased in the last year? How many were VIZ shojo titles?
(please check one from each column)

SHOJO MANGA	VIZ SHOJO MANGA
☐ None	☐ None
☐ 1 – 4	☐ 1 – 4
☐ 5 – 10	☐ 5 – 10
☐ 11+	☐ 11+

What do you like most about shojo graphic novels? **(check all that apply)**

☐ Romance ☐ Drama / conflict ☐ Fantasy

☐ Comedy ☐ Real-life storylines ☐ Relatable characters

☐ Other ________________________________

Do you purchase every volume of your favorite shojo series?

☐ Yes! Gotta have 'em as my own

☐ No. Please explain: ______________________________

Who are your favorite shojo authors / artists? ______________________________

____

What shojo titles would like you translated and sold in English? ____________________

____

THANK YOU! Please send the completed form to:

NJW Research
ATTN: VIZ Media Shojo Survey
42 Catharine Street
Poughkeepsie, NY 12601

Your privacy is very important to us. All information provided will be used for internal purposes only and will not be sold or otherwise divulged.